# THEIR ROCK

## IS NOT LIKE

# OUR ROCK

Daniel Strange is one of the brightest and most articulate contemporary theologians in the Reformational tradition, and in *Their Rock Is Not Like Our Rock* he provides a theology of religions which at once is theologically sound, analytically rigorous and lucidly written. Highly recommended.
*Bruce Riley Ashford, Provost and Dean of Faculty, Southeastern Baptist Theological Seminary*

Dan Strange has written what will become both an important textbook in the theology of religions and one of the most incisive and original contributions to the recent debate. His biblical Reformed tradition is employed to rigorously address complex questions about religious pluralism and his answers are uncompromising, challenging and deeply christological. His prose is a delight and this book is accessible to both trained theologians and the novice. Miss it at your peril.
*Gavin D'Costa, Professor of Catholic Theology, University of Bristol*

Deeply learned, theologically solid, well-informed in anthropology, this riveting study will guide the reader into the best ways to evaluate the religions of the world. Standing on the shoulders of Hendrik Kraemer and J. H. Bavinck, Dr Strange illuminates both the spiritual longings of people in different religions and their need for the gospel of Jesus Christ.
*William Edgar, Professor of Apologetics, Westminster Theological Seminary*

What might a robust, strongly Reformed theology of religions look like? . . . Daniel Strange offers an important and provocative perspective that sees non-Christian religions as idolatrous responses to God which are 'subversively fulfilled' in the gospel of Jesus Christ.
*Harold Netland, Professor of Philosophy of Religion and Intercultural Studies and Director of PhD Intercultural Studies, Trinity Evangelical Divinity School*

Dan sets before us the Scriptures, viewed as a trustworthy record of God's self-revelation, that portray a decline in human understanding from creation rather than an evolutionary development towards monotheism. . . . This is a book that should be on the reading list of anyone concerned to see the nations become disciples of the Lord Jesus.
*Ray Porter, Chair of Global Connections (Evangelical Mission Association)*

Dr Strange takes his readers down paths rarely explored in the study of world religions. . . . He embraces the reality that neither he, nor anyone else, can evaluate any human religion as a disengaged bystander. After explaining his own commitments as a follower of Christ, Dr Strange explores how Christians can engage other religions while remaining faithful to their own beliefs. His presentation is scholarly, but easily understood. It is theoretical, but thoroughly practical. You won't be disappointed.
*Richard Pratt, President of Third Millennium Ministries (thirdmill.org)*

Thoughtful, nuanced and biblically faithful evaluations on the role of other religions are unfortunately rare. Strange fills an important gap by offering us a bold but humble perspective on other religions, repristinating the thought of J. H. Bavinck and Hendrik Kraemer for a new day. . . . Even those who are not Reformed or entirely convinced will be challenged and provoked and helped by Strange's contribution. . . . This crucially important book should be read by missionaries, professors, pastors, and all those who teach the word of God and who long to see God's name praised among the nations.
*Thomas R. Schreiner, James Buchanan Harrison Professor of New Testament Interpretation, Southern Baptist Theological Seminary*

# THEIR ROCK

## IS NOT LIKE

# OUR ROCK

## A THEOLOGY OF RELIGIONS

## DANIEL STRANGE

ZONDERVAN

*Their Rock Is Not Like Our Rock*
Copyright © 2014 by Daniel Strange

First published in 2014 by Apollos (an imprint of Inter-Varsity Press) in the United Kingdom under the title *For Their Rock Is Not As Our Rock* (ISBN 1-78359-100-5)

This title is also available as a Zondervan ebook.
Visit www.zondervan.com/ebooks.

Requests for information should be addressed to:
Zondervan, 3900 *Sparks Drive SE, Grand Rapids, Michigan 49546*

ISBN 978-0-310-52077-1

Any Internet addresses (websites, blogs, etc.) and telephone numbers in this book are offered as a resource. They are not intended in any way to be or imply an endorsement by Zondervan, nor does Zondervan vouch for the content of these sites and numbers for the life of this book.

*Cover design: Tammy Johnson*

*Printed in the United States of America*

14 15 16 17 18 19 20 /DCI/ 22 21 20 19 18 17 16 15 14 13 12 11 10 9 8 7 6 5 4 3 2 1

*In the spirit and*
*on the shoulders of*
*J. H. Bavinck*

'For their rock is not as our Rock . . .'

(Deuteronomy 32:31a ESV)

This apprehension of the essential 'otherness' of the world of divine realities revealed in Jesus Christ from the atmosphere of religion as we know it in the history of the race cannot be grasped merely by way of investigation and reasoning. Only an attentive study of the Bible can open the eyes to the fact that Christ, 'the power of God' and 'the wisdom of God', stands in contradiction to the power and wisdom of man. Perhaps in some respects it is proper to speak of contradictive or *subversive fulfillment*.

(Hendrik Kraemer)

I may say that for 40 years, as at the University of Oxford I carried out my duties as professor of Sanskrit, I devoted as much time to the study of the holy books of the East as any other human being in the world. And I ventured to tell this gathering what I have found to be the basic note, the one single chord, of all these holy books – be it the Veda of the Brahmans, the Purana of Siwa and Vishnu, the Qur'an of the Muslims, the Sendavesta of the Parsis etc. – the one basic note or chord that runs through all of them is salvation by works. They all teach that salvation must be bought and that your own works and merits must be the purchase price. Our own Bible, *our* sacred book from the East, is from start to finish a protest against this doctrine. True, good works are also required from this holy book from the East, and that even more emphatically than in any other holy book from the East, but the works referred to are the outflow of a grateful heart. They are only the thank offerings, only the fruits of our faith. They are never the ransom of the true disciples of Christ. Let us not close our eyes to whatever is noble and true and pleasing in these holy books. But let us teach Hindus, Buddhists and Muslims that there is but one book from the East that can be their comfort in that solemn hour when they must pass, entirely alone, into the invisible world. It is that holy book which contains the message – a message which is surely true and worthy of full acceptance, and concerns all humans, men, women and children – that Christ Jesus came into the world to save sinners.

(Max Müller, from a speech delivered before
the British and Foreign Bible Society.
Cited in *Der Beweis des Glaubens*, April 1901)

# CONTENTS

9

# ACKNOWLEDGMENTS

There are a number of people to whom I would like to express gratitude and whose contributions to this project are greatly appreciated.

To all the Oak Hill College postgraduate students who have taken part in my MTh *Theology of World Religions* course over the last four years. Like it or not, they have had the contents of this book thrust upon them in class and have offered invaluable comments and critique. The book would be poorer without their input. I would especially like to thank the following students whose assessed work for me in this module has made a genuine contribution to some of the book's contents and who have unwittingly acted as research assistants(!): Chris Flint, Luke Foster, Steffen Jenkins, Jon Putt and Nathan Weston.

To Bill Edgar, Ray Porter, Jonty Rhodes and Garry Williams, who all kindly read earlier drafts of the manuscript and offered helpful comments and suggestions.

To Evelyn Cornell, who provided invaluable assistance in getting the bibliographic apparatus into shape.

To the anonymous external reader for IVP who offered substantial comments and queries on an earlier draft.

To Phil Duce, my editor at IVP, who has been patient when deadlines have been missed and who has offered advice whenever it has been sought.

Finally to my wonderful family: the kids – Noah, Isaac, Micah, Hetty, Keturah, Ezra and Gideon – and my wife, Elly. She above all has been such an encouragement and spur in bringing this to completion, and has endured my often-illegitimate (read 'sinful') frustrations when I have railed against 'life' getting in the way of my working on this project.

*Daniel Strange*

# AUTOBIOGRAPHICAL PROLOGUE

For some, starting a work like this with a shallow autobiography might appear somewhat pretentious and indulgent, especially for a thirty-something-year-old. For others, it will certainly be seen as 'unacademic', such personal and private musings being judged to belong in more 'popular' writing. However, such a beginning is entirely appropriate given that I am keen to 'practice what I preach'. First, a biblical epistemological insight that postmodern philosophy has rightly used in its critique of modernism is that though we may cry 'neutrality' and brute 'objectivity', we all come from 'somewhere', with tradition-specific presuppositions and ultimate commitments. It may help the reader to know where my 'somewhere' is, given not only that my theology of religions is coming from a particular theological tradition, but also that I shall be stressing the importance of 'person-variable'[1] engagement and interaction with those of other religions. The author is a person too! Secondly, our worldviews through which we interpret reality are not less than propositional but are often articulated narratively: who we are, where we have come from, where we are going. I hope that by retelling something of my story you may start, even only for argument's sake, to inhabit my theological world. Thirdly, it is my intention in this book to model a larger

---

1. I have borrowed this term from George Mavrodes, *Belief in God* (New York: Random House, 1970), pp. 7–8.

theological agenda that seeks to reintegrate various aspects of the Christian world that have become ghettoized, often with disastrous results for all parties. On the one hand is the often rarefied atmosphere of 'academic' theology as against the practical everyday 'nitty-gritty' ministry of the local church. On the other hand is the compartmentalization of theological disciplines: most pertinently here, systematic theology and missiology. Even though the tenor of the book is more 'academic' in style and written by someone with a background in systematic theology, I hope the following section will demonstrate the inextricable links between theory and praxis, dogmatics and missiology, and a sympathy and desire to work cross-disciplinarily. Enough justification . . .

My theological interest in the nature and meaning of other religions has been born out of a longstanding inquisitiveness. I put my faith in the Lord Jesus Christ at the age of sixteen but brought with me lots of questions arising from my own family background. Although my white English mother is a Christian, my late Indo-Guyanese father was not. Indeed, my grandmother, who is still alive at the time of writing, is a Hindu believer. In the early 1960s my dad was the first of ten brothers and sisters to leave Demerrara, Guyana,[2] where he joined the British army and eventually found himself in London,[3] where he met my mother who had moved down from the county of Yorkshire to pursue a career in teaching. Not unusually for those times, my grandfather on my mother's side did not attend the wedding. I suppose I would describe my dad as an agnostic and 'secular' Hindu with some syncretistic tendencies! He never really wanted to speak about his Guyanese background and upbringing; indeed, when he arrived in Britain he changed his name from 'Persaud' to 'Strange', the reason for which has never been made clear to me.[4] He had no problems with our going to church, and even came when I was preaching, singing along to the hymns. In the infrequent conversations we used to have about belief, he took a fairly pluralistic line, although sometimes spoke about 'his' god as opposed to my God. Occasionally, though, usually around momentous events, one discerned something of the cultural 'Hindu' residue. When I was six or seven, Dad took us for our only trip to Guyana to see the family (after that time, and certainly by the early 1990s, nearly all the family had emigrated to New York and Toronto). The only memories I have of that holiday are the taste of raw sugar cane, my granddad terrorizing us with cockroaches among the rice sacks, and our 'partic-

---

2. The only English-speaking country in South America.

3. Guyana would gain independence in 1966.

4. There is an apocryphal story, never verified, that it is somehow related to the Peter Sellers film *Dr. Strangelove*, recently released at that time.

ipation' in the Hindu spring celebration of Pagwa (known also as Holi), where we were positively encouraged to throw brightly coloured powder and water over each other for a whole day. Suffice it to say, given our age, encouragement was not needed. Back in England and looking back, I vividly remember sitar music in the house, calypso-style bedtime songs my dad had had sung to him as a child,[5] egg-and-potato curry and his encouraging us on Saturday mornings to watch serializations of the *Bhagavadgītā* on television. I also remember trappings of another religious culture, as he taught us all judo (he was an instructor), and his love of watching reruns of the 1970s television series and cult classic *Kung-Fu*, starring the late David Carradine.

When my gran was seventy, my dad and I went to Toronto to celebrate her birthday. My gran had asked my dad to participate in a Hindu ceremony with the local pandit. Although my dad was only the second-eldest son, I presume he had been asked because my oldest uncle is a Christadelphian. I was happy to observe the proceedings, although another of my uncles, an Elim minister, refused to come in, and sat on the stairs outside. In the room, and surrounded by family and friends, I was amazed that without any book or script my dad, on cue, sang out all the songs and chants. Finally, and more recently, as cancer ate away at his body, my dad's tongue was loosened somewhat when nearly all his family came over to see him and say their goodbyes. I overheard many conversations accompanied with laughter, as they reminisced about the 'good times' of growing up in Guyana. Suddenly, gaps about my dad's life were being filled in, but these perhaps added to the ambiguity; for not only did I discover that he was idolized by his brothers and sisters, having a somewhat brave and adventurous reputation in the village, but that he had gone to a convent school and apparently once sneaked off to a Billy Graham rally unbeknown to his mum and dad.[6]

Academically, such a personal history generated various questions of a theology of religions nature and eventually led to my studying Theology and Religious Studies at Bristol University, where I had the opportunity to study under, and interact with, various tutors of other faiths,[7] and come into contact with a

---

5. Remembering that Guyana is often ethnically and culturally (or should I say 'cricketly') associated with the West Indies.

6. The year was probably 1962, when Graham visited South America in two separate trips.

7. Including my Buddhist lecturer Professor Paul Williams, who converted to Roman Catholicism about five years after I left Bristol. See Paul Williams, *The Unexpected Way: On Converting from Buddhism to Catholicism* (London: Continuum, 2002).

number of important scholars, including Ursula King, John Hick and Ninian Smart. In an extremely 'pluralistic' and academic university department I was unashamedly (but looking back, maybe not that winsomely) confessional and 'evangelistically' evangelical. Such a combination inevitably gave rise to some 'tumbleweed moments', those times when with excruciating embarrassment you stop all conversation and silence an entire room with something you have said or done. Two such incidents, which bookended my time there as an undergraduate, stick in my mind, not only because they were embarrassing, but because they were so informative.

First, and during my first week as an undergraduate, I had been invited to the professor's house for drinks, and 'bright eyed and bushy tailed' I had been eager to impress. After what seemed like an age, the professor got round to speaking to me. 'I understand you had a gap year,' said the professor. 'What did you get up to?' Having waited for this opportunity all evening, I replied eagerly, 'I was a missionary in Italy, telling other people about the good news of Jesus.' There now followed silence together with an X-ray-like unblinking stare from the professor. Finally, she muttered (no, that's too soft, 'spat out') words but in a stage whisper so all could hear, 'Missionaries? I didn't think they had any of those anymore. I trust you won't be doing any of that in my department!' So began a not so beautiful relationship in my theological education.

Secondly, and towards the end of my time as an undergraduate, all the students in the department were invited to a nearby church for an interfaith 'service' where a very well-known pluralist theologian was giving a 'sermon'. After the event, I plucked up the courage to ask this theologian some questions. Knowing that he had had some kind of evangelical awakening earlier in his life, I asked him what he thought now of his evangelical 'phase' of belief. His reply was something along the lines of its being an important stage to go through, but one that one must grow out of. I probably should have called it quits there, but for some reason decided to ask just one more question: 'So what do you think of those theologians who stay evangelical?' This time, no X-ray stare, but merely a matter-of-fact 'Well, I think they are retarded.' I didn't come back with anything this time.

While I was at Bristol, the courses that made the greatest impact upon me personally, and whetted my appetite for further questioning and research, were the modern theology and theology of religions modules brilliantly and graciously taught by Gavin D'Costa. It was Gavin who now encouraged me to undertake doctoral studies with him on evangelical approaches to the question of the fate of the unevangelized (my grandmother on my mother's side had once asked me a question about what happens to people who never have a chance to hear about Jesus), looking specifically at the inclusivism of Clark Pinnock, a scholar I was able to meet personally and interview on a number of occasions during my research.[8] Around the time I was commencing my research at Bristol, a fellow evangelical student who was finishing his doctoral work on John Hick[9] kindly gave me copy of Don Carson's recently published *The Gagging of God: Christianity Confronts Pluralism.*[10] This work was a great encouragement to me as an evangelical Christian in a theology and religious studies department like mine, and I was particularly inspired by the book's cross-disciplinary scope and breadth.

Five years of theological student ministry and now eight years of teaching and training at Oak Hill Theological College in North London, as well as leadership in local church ministry, have further fuelled my passion and sense of urgency in reflecting upon the nature and status of other religions in the light of the gospel of Jesus Christ.

8. Daniel Strange, *The Possibility of Salvation Among the Unevangelised: An Analysis of Inclusivism in Recent Evangelical Theology* (Carlisle: Paternoster, 2001).

9. Christopher Sinkinson, *The Universe of Faiths: A Critical Study of John Hick's Religious Pluralism* (Carlisle: Paternoster, 2001).

10. D. A. Carson, *The Gagging of God: Christianity Confronts Pluralism* (Leicester: Apollos, 1996).

# ABBREVIATIONS

| | |
|---|---|
| AB | Anchor Bible |
| AOTC | Apollos Old Testament Commentary |
| *BBR* | *Bulletin for Biblical Research* |
| BECNT | Baker Exegetical Commentary on the New Testament |
| *Bib* | *Biblica* |
| *BSac* | *Bibliotheca sacra* |
| BST | The Bible Speaks Today |
| CCC | Crossway Classic Commentaries |
| CFTL | Clark's Foreign Theological Library |
| *ChrCent* | *Christian Century* |
| *CTJ* | *Calvin Theological Journal* |
| *CurTM* | *Currents in Theology and Mission* |
| EPSC | Evangelical Press Study Commentary |
| *ERT* | *Evangelical Review of Theology* |
| ESV | English Standard Version |
| *EvQ* | *Evangelical Quarterly* |
| FAT | Forschungen zum Alten Testament |
| *FUQ* | *Free University Quarterly* |
| *GTJ* | *Grace Theological Journal* |
| *HeyJ* | *Heythrop Journal* |
| ICC | International Critical Commentary |

| | |
|---|---|
| *IJST* | *International Journal of Systematic Theology* |
| *IRM* | *International Review of Missions* |
| *JBL* | *Journal of Biblical Literature* |
| *JETS* | *Journal of the Evangelical Theological Society* |
| JPSTC | Jewish Publication Society Torah Commentary |
| *JRPC* | *Journal of Religion and Popular Culture* |
| JSOTSup | Journal for the Study of the Old Testament, Supplement Series |
| LCC | Library of Christian Classics |
| LXX | Septuagint |
| n.d. | no date given |
| n.p. | no page number given |
| NAC | New American Commentary |
| NIBCOT | New International Biblical Commentary on the Old Testament |
| NICNT | New International Commentary on the New Testament |
| NICOT | New International Commentary on the Old Testament |
| NRSV | New Revised Standard Version |
| NS | new series |
| NT | New Testament |
| OBT | Overtures to Biblical Theology |
| OT | Old Testament |
| OTT | Old Testament Theology |
| *RTR* | *Reformed Theological Review* |
| SBTS | Sources for Biblical and Theological Study |
| *SCB* | *Science and Christian Belief* |
| *SEAJT* | *South East Asia Journal of Theology* |
| *SFM* | *St Francis Magazine* |
| SIA | Studia Instituti Anthropos |
| *Them* | *Themelios* |
| tr. | translated/translated by |
| *TrinJ* | *Trinity Journal* |
| WBC | Word Biblical Commentary |
| *WTJ* | *Westminster Theological Journal* |
| WUNT | Wissenschaftliche Untersuchungen zum Neuen Testament |
| *ZAW* | *Zeitschrift für die alttestamentliche Wissenschaft* |

# 1. THE TASK BEFORE US: CHRISTIANS IN A WORLD OF THE RELIGIOUS OTHER

## Introduction

We live in a strange world, a world which presents us with tremendous contrasts. The high and the low, the great and the small, the sublime and the ridiculous, the beautiful and the ugly, the tragic and the comic, the good and the evil, the truth and the lie, all these are heaped in unfathomable interrelationship. The gravity and the vanity of life seize on us in turn. Man weeping is constantly giving way to man laughing. The whole world stands in the sign of humour, which has been well described as a laugh in a tear. The deepest cause of this present world is this: because of the sin of man, God is continually manifesting his wrath and yet, by reason of His own good pleasure, is always revealing His grace also . . . Curse and blessing are so singularly interdependent that the one sometimes seems to become the other. Work in the sweat of the brow is curse and blessing at once. Both point to the cross which at one and the same time is the highest judgement and the richest grace. And that is why the cross is the mid-point of history and the reconciliation of all antitheses.

(Herman Bavinck)[1]

---

1. Herman Bavinck, *Our Reasonable Faith* (Grand Rapids: Baker Book House, 1956), pp. 44–45.

The post 9/11, 7/7, multi-ethnic and multicultural Britain in which I live is indeed often very strange, leaving many evangelical Christians bewitched, bothered and bewildered by the tremendous contrasts presented to them. Starting with the positives, certain aspects of plurality are not to be feared but rather celebrated as a blessing from the triune God whose very being is characterized by diversity in unity and unity in diversity. Ecclesiologically, many like me will have been edifyingly challenged and enriched from being part of local multi-ethnic church families which at their best demonstrate the rich diversity of gospel expression as opposed to what could be a bland mono-ethnic uniformity. However, at the public level confusion often abounds as we try to make our way in a society that imagines and then creates cultural artefacts such as 'winterval',[2] and 'mega-mosques'. Such confusion is increasingly mixed with terror, be it a terror attack in Woolwich, London,[3] together with the almost inevitable reprisals over the following days,[4] or those simply terrified by such events and who just cannot believe such things can be happening in our green and pleasant land. At an international level conflict and casualties continue in Afghanistan, and as I write, the Middle East situation is as volatile as ever, with Syria and Egypt taking their turn in the spotlight. Our media networks not only look *on* with incredulity and frustration but often look *down* with disdain, calling for 'solutions', 'peace', 'tolerance' and 'security'.

In a fevered climate such as this, for us as evangelical Christians to continue to defend and proclaim the uniqueness and exclusivity of Jesus Christ as *the* way, *the* truth and *the* life, as the *only* name under heaven by which we must be saved, and as *the* 'reconciliation of all antitheses' often appears to those both inside and outside the church as exacerbating misunderstanding, marginalization and oppression. Both intellectually and morally such claims – sounding naive, offensive, arrogant and imperialistic – are an apologetic embarrassment in communicating Christian truth to its late-modern cultured despisers. For in liberal Western culture generally there continues to be a deep implausibility structure

---

2. Birmingham City Council's short-lived attempt in the 1990s to rename Christmas to make it acceptable to non-Christians.

3. The brutal attack and murder in broad daylight and in front of many witnesses of British soldier Lee Rigby in May 2013 in what has been described as an Islamic terrorist attack.

4. E.g. the burning down of the Al-Rahma Islamic Centre in North London (a centre I drive past each week on my way home from church) in June 2013 in what has been described as a 'hate crime'.

regarding such claims, with 'defeaters' being legion.[5] Despite strong sociological support that testifies worldwide to the withering of secularization and the flourishing of sacralization,[6] the catch-all term of 'religion' into which we are often unceremoniously dumped continues to be seen by many (at the level of both popular conversation and academic discourse) not as the solution, but as the problem.[7] Far from being a blessing, *we* are seen as an instantiation of the curse.

What may be worse still, though, is that we have become an irrelevance. For many we are simply religious relics, an uncomfortable memory of a more primitive religiosity now reinterpreted as the times of ignorance and infancy when Christians did not know any better because they did not know other religions any better. To put it another way, in the world we are told we all want, which lauds inclusive plurality, equality, tolerance and peace, and in the story that we tell ourselves about who we are, where we have come from and where we are going, a perceived 'exclusive' Christianity is at best given the role of the villain – worse, given the role of the pantomime villain (because militant Islam has taken the part of the real villain) or, even worse still, is not even deemed worthy to have a part in the story, even a bit part. The legacy of the gospel's impact on Western culture has been airbrushed out.

As evangelical believers, who continue to affirm the 'scandal of particularity', how do we respond in such a hostile context? While we may not succumb to the siren of pluralism, there remain some unhelpful responses that do us little good. The first could be called 'timid acquiescence'. While we believe in the exclusivity of Jesus Christ, when faced with criticism of such views we either downplay exclusivity completely or affirm it, but rather apologetically and with not a little embarrassment. The second could be called 'bold arrogance'. Here there is a tendency when questioned simply to trot out verses like Acts 4:12 and John 14:6 with little explanation or apologetic defence (because we don't have one), or to give the impression of 'self-righteousness', implying we have achieved total enlightenment on these issues and that there are simple and easy answers when it comes to this topic. We use a machete to bludgeon when what is needed is a scalpel to subvert. While these approaches may be doctrinally orthodox, none are winsome or persuasive. Perhaps a better approach, and one in keeping

5. A 'defeater belief' is a philosophical term to say that if Belief A is true, Belief B *cannot* be true.

6. See, perhaps most famously, Peter Berger (ed.), *The Desecularization of the World: Resurgent Religion and World Politics* (Grand Rapids: Eerdmans, 1999).

7. Note e.g. the rise of the 'new atheism' associated with writers such as Richard Dawkins, Christopher Hitchens and Philip Pullman.

with the tenor of much apologetic teaching in the New Testament, is one that both defends and proclaims Christian exclusivity with what might be called a 'bold humility', a stance that seeks first to understand the world of religion and religions through a biblical worldview before then applying unique and satisfying gospel truth to a world of pseudo-gospels that promise much but can never ultimately deliver. We are to give a reason for the hope that we have, but to do so with gentleness and respect (1 Pet. 3:15). In other words, *fortiter in re, suaviter in modo* (boldy in action, gently in manner).

## 1. Describing the tasks of an evangelical theology of religions

In a recent article addressed to evangelical pastors I outlined a three-point 'to do' list that might begin to move us into this stance:[8]

- Develop and deploy a biblically rich and nuanced theology of religions.
- Discern and denounce the arrogance and intolerance of pluralism.
- Demonstrate and display, in both word and deed, the unique power of the gospel to change lives and communities.

Concerning the second and third points, there have been some encouraging signs in recent years that evangelicals are becoming more confident and starting to shift, as in a sport, from defence to offence. In the Reformed tradition one prominent example of someone at the forefront of this move is the teaching, preaching and leadership of Tim Keller, pastor of Redeemer Presbyterian Church, New York.[9]

First, and concerning the unmasking of pluralism, Keller, crucially at a popular level, disseminates and communicates the work of Christian philosophers such as Alvin Plantinga.[10] Plantinga deals not with the *truth* of exclusivism but rather the *propriety* or *rightness* of exclusivism against claims that such a position 'is irrational, or egotistical and unjustified, or intellectually

---

8. Daniel Strange, 'Defending the Indefensible: The Exclusivity of Christ in an Intolerable World', *Tabletalk* 25 (summer 2009), n.p.
9. Go to http://timothykeller.com (accessed 11 Sept. 2013).
10. Alvin Plantinga, 'A Defense of Religious Exclusivism', in Thomas D. Senor (ed.), *The Rationality of Belief and the Plurality of Faith* (London: Cornell University Press, 1995), pp. 191–215; Gavin D'Costa, *The Meeting of Religions and the Trinity* (Maryknoll: Orbis, 2000).

arrogant, or elitist, or a manifestation of harmful pride, or even oppressive and imperialistic'.[11] He groups such charges into two categories: moral objections (that exclusivism is arbitrary and arrogant) and epistemic objections (that exclusivism is irrational and unjustified). In both cases Plantinga shows that these common objections to exclusivism are not *necessary* objections, and even if they are valid, they *equally* apply to other positions with the result that so-called 'non-exclusive' positions become guilty of self-referential incoherence.

Using this insight, Keller demonstrates that far from demonstrating epistemic humility, pluralism is epistemologically arrogant in its claims. Newbigin's commentary on the infamous 'pluralist' illustration based on the ancient fable of the blind man and elephant is also cited:[12]

> In the famous story of the blind man and the elephant, so often quoted in the interest of religious agnosticism, the real point of the story is constantly overlooked. The story is told from the point of view of the king and his courtiers, who are not blind but can see that the blind men are unable to grasp the full reality of the elephant and are only able to get a hold of part of the truth. The story is constantly told in order to neutralise the affirmation of the great religions, to suggest that they learn more humility and recognise that none of them can have more than one aspect of the truth. But of course, the real point of the story is exactly the opposite. If the king were also blind there would be no story. The story is told by the king, and it is the immensely arrogant claim of one who sees the full truth which all the world's religions are only groping after. It embodies the claim to know the full reality which relativizes all the claims of the religions.[13]

The practical application here is that Keller is able to equip Christians to respond to a number of objections non-Christians often raise regarding the exclusive claims of Christ:

- You say 'no one has the right to have the whole truth', but your view assumes you have the whole truth, an absolute vantage point to look down and interpret all religions. Tell me, where did you get this insight from exactly? Where does your superior knowledge come from?
- You say 'no one should try to convert them to their religion', but you want me to convert to your story with its own understanding of god and reality. On what basis?

---

11. Plantinga, 'Defense of Religious Exclusivism', p. 8.
12. John Hick, *God and the Universe of Faiths* (Oxford: Oneworld, 1973), p. 140.
13. Lesslie Newbigin, *The Gospel in a Pluralistic Society* (London: SPCK, 1989), pp. 9–10.

- You say that 'Christian belief is too culturally conditioned to be "truth" and that if you were born in Morocco, you wouldn't even be a Christian but a Muslim', but the same is true for you. If you were born in Morocco, you wouldn't be a religious pluralist. Do you think you are wrong because you've come from a particular culture? It's just not fair to say, 'All claims about religions are historically conditioned except the one I'm making just now.'[14]

The result is a 'levelling of the playing field', showing that pluralism (and other worldviews) are in some ways exclusive and have their own interpretation of a god (or gods) and reality, which they seek to convince others of and 'convert' them to.

Secondly, and with the above point established, Keller now asks which exclusive set of beliefs actually delivers the world we all want: delivers lasting peace, delivers tolerance, delivers loving relationships and peaceful behaviour. His answer is that it is only the unique and exclusive good news of historic, orthodox Christianity that has the power to change lives, communities and cultures. Concentrating on 1 John 4:1–12, Keller argues that it is precisely the *unique* aspects of the Christian gospel that will provide the lasting reconciliation people long for and chase after in their unbelief – and all these focus on Jesus Christ.[15] First, he mentions the *origin* of Jesus' salvation: unlike the human founders of many of the world religions, Jesus Christ has come 'from God' (v. 2). Jesus is God incarnate. Secondly, he mentions the *purpose* of Jesus' salvation: unlike many other religions that seek liberation or escape from creation and the physical world, Jesus has 'come in the flesh' (v. 2). Christianity says that in the incarnation God received a body, and in the resurrection we see that salvation is not about escaping creation but redeeming and transforming creation: 'this world'. Christianity gives hope for 'this' world. Thirdly, he mentions the *method* of grace: unlike other religions in which you have to perform in certain ways to be saved, love God, love neighbor, and so on, the gospel says the opposite: 'This is love: not that we loved God but that he loved us and sent his Son as an atoning sacrifice for our sins' (v. 10). Jesus is not mainly a teacher, but a Saviour.

---

14. Timothy J. Keller, *The Reason for God: Belief in an Age of Scepticism* (London: Hodder & Stoughton, 1998), pp. 7–18.
15. See Tim Keller, *Exclusivity: How Can There Be Just One Religion?* (audio talk, 2006), available online at http://www.bethinking.org/other-religions/intermediate/exclusivity-how-can-there-be-just-one-true-religion.htm (accessed 9 Oct. 2012). See also Keller, *The Reason for God*, pp. 3–21.

Why are these unique distinctives so important? Keller argues that these doctrinal distinctives are the foundation for truly loving behaviour. Without these foundations, a concept such as 'love' loses its meaning and quickly becomes self-righteousness and intolerance. How so? Keller argues that in the method of grace, Christians know they are not saved because of their performance, so they are to be humble, not self-righteous; in the purpose of Jesus' salvation, Christians know they are to serve others in their communities, because the resurrection shows us that God's creation matters, 'this world' matters; finally, in the origin of Jesus' salvation, Christians know that a self-sacrificing God must lead to self-sacrificing followers, not self-righteous followers. It turns out that so-called 'exclusive' Christianity is actually the most 'inclusive', 'loving' and 'peaceful' view of the world.

The ministries of Keller and others like him (e.g. Don Carson[16]) have been able to give confidence to a younger generation of evangelicals to be both biblically faithful and culturally relevant: to go on the offensive against cherished pluralism but without being unnecessarily offensive.[17]

## 2. Delineating the task of this study

In the Western context and atmosphere that I have already outlined, the front-line work of Keller and others has been desperately needed, for what we have here are faithful, relevant and, importantly, 'winsome' contextualizations of gospel truth for our 'strange' times. It is interesting to reflect here on both the 'success' and 'originality' of someone like Keller. There is no doubt that he is a very gifted communicator and strategist, but theologically he is not innovative and 'radical' in that he self-consciously remains totally within the tradition of Dutch Reformed theology and missiology, sitting on the shoulders of his teacher Harvie Conn, who himself was influenced heavily by the apologetics and systematic theology of Cornelius Van Til and the missiology of J. H. Bavinck. What Keller has done, though, like Newbigin before him, is to reflect missiologically

---

16. See the recent D. A. Carson, *The Intolerance of Tolerance* (Nottingham: Inter-Varsity Press, 2012).

17. I would count myself as one of this younger generation and have benefited from those such as Keller and Carson. For signs of this influence see my responses to the pluralist Paul Knitter in Gavin D'Costa, Paul Knitter and Daniel Strange, *Only One Way? Three Christian Responses to the Uniqueness of Christ in a Religiously Pluralist World* (London: SCM, 2011), pp. 167–173, 221–228.

upon our Western culture and apply missiological tools to areas that have not been considered to be 'mission' fields.

Starting from the same confessional foundations, and with the same formative theological and missiological influences, this book is an attempt to complement and consolidate the work of Keller and others like him by expounding and developing the theology of religions upon which such practical theology or missiology is based. In other words, my subject matter concerns the first point of my 'to do' list: to develop and deploy a biblically rich and nuanced theology of religions. It is my contention that, as a tradition, evangelical theology of religions has been stunted in its growth, often lagging well behind other tradition-specific 'theologies of religions' in their depth and sophistication.[18] Again, one of the reasons for this has been a justified defensive stance that has constantly had to defend the exclusivity and uniqueness of Christ against the criticisms of pluralism and (to a lesser extent) inclusivism. However, the result has been, albeit with some notable exceptions, a major preoccupation with questions of soteriology at the expense of other questions concerning the nature, meaning and purpose of religions in the economy of God's providence and purpose.

Alarmingly, not only are evangelicals behind other Christian traditions, but also behind other religions. As Leithart notes:

> Islam's account of history has a place for Jesus and Christianity. To be sure, the Jesus of Islam is not the Jesus of the New Testament: He is not the divine Son incarnate, He is not crucified and raised (cf. Sura 4.157), and He is not reigning at the Father's right hand. Still, the prophet Jesus has a place in Muslim 'redemptive history,' and this poses the challenge to Christians: Has Christian theology been able to locate Islam within *its* history . . . Can Christians make theological sense of the persistence of Islam? Can we fit them [i.e. Muslims] into our story?[19]

Questions such as these demand detailed investigation, for it is not enough to

---

18. Slightly tongue in cheek and perhaps a little unfairly, one could say that when it comes to tradition-specific resources, while Roman Catholics have been able to consult and cite *Vatican II* and other encyclicals for their theology of religions, evangelicals have often ended up falling back on the theological weight and precision of C. S. Lewis's *The Chronicles of Narnia*.

19. P. J. Leithart, *Mirror of Christendom* (Mars Hill audio resource essay, 2005), available online at https://marshillaudio.org/downloads/Mirror-of-Christendom.pdf (accessed 4 Oct. 2013), p. 3.

say what other religions are not: we must know what they are, for this affects our missiology and praxis. Such investigations are ambitious, but, as will be seen in subsequent chapters, while the modern academic study of religions has disregarded such questions, these questions have been present throughout the history of Christian theological reflection and particularly around discussions within Reformed theology during the sixteenth and seventeenth centuries.

Before outlining the contours of subsequent chapters, it will be helpful to comment on the basis and boundaries of this work.

First, this is a book for evangelical Christians, written by an evangelical Christian. While I have previously engaged directly and in dialogue with scholars whose theologies of religions are from very different Christian traditions,[20] this work is an intra-evangelical attempt at theological construction. Therefore, for those reading who are not evangelical, or not even Christian, I shall not be spending a great amount of time describing and justifying fundamental presuppositions of evangelical belief. These must be looked for elsewhere.[21] More specifically, and given the diversity within evangelical theology, this is particularly a book for Reformed Christians, written by a Reformed Christian. The theological grammar out of which I shall be articulating my theology of religions is that of Reformed theology, for this is the confessional tradition I believe to be closest to God's revelation in Scripture. Again, for those evangelical Christians who are not Reformed, I do not intend to describe or justify in great detail certain Reformed doctrinal loci that Reformed believers take for granted.[22] However, because biblical authority is professed by all evangelicals, I hope there is a common authoritative source by which my theology of religions can be engaged with and critiqued.

Secondly, in this work I do not intend to describe or analyse the overall discipline known as the theology of religions (including the much discussed issue of

---

20. See most recently D'Costa, Knitter and Strange, *Only One Way?* Gavin D'Costa can be labelled 'mainstream Catholic', and Paul Knitter 'progressive liberationist'.

21. For starters see D. A. Carson, *Evangelicalism: What Is It and Is It Worth Keeping?* (Wheaton: Crossway, 2009).

22. For contemporary introductory texts see William Edgar, *Truth in All Its Glory: Commending the Reformed Faith* (Phillipsburg: P & R, 2004); John M. Frame, *Salvation Belongs to the Lord: An Introduction to Systematic Theology* (Phillipsburg: P & R, 2006). For a more detailed contemporary Reformed systematic theology see Michael S. Horton, *The Christian Faith: A Systematic Theology for Pilgrims on the Way* (Grand Rapids: Zondervan, 2011).

typology), nor shall I describe or analyse the history and current state of evangelical theology of religions. Such work has been ably done elsewhere.[23]

Thirdly, and still regarding sources, I am happy to declare up front the somewhat 'derived' nature of my theology of religions.[24] In general I wish to demonstrate that there is a Reformed historical pedigree reaching back to the time of the Reformation regarding many of the conclusions I reach concerning the nature of the religious Other. In particular I note my indebtedness to the Dutch Reformed theological and missiological tradition, and in particular the work of J. H. Bavinck (1895–1964), Hendrik Kraemer (1888–1965) and Cornelius Van Til (1895–1987).[25] Inexcusably, both Bavinck and Kraemer have become forgotten figures in recent years, but their writing is, to my mind, the most theologically rich, missiologically erudite and pastorally sensitive work in the tradition. If my work does nothing more than republicize and champion Kraemer and even more particularly J. H. Bavinck to a new generation of Christians, then I shall have achieved much.

Fourthly, and as indicated above, my *primary* focus in this study will not revolve around questions of soteriology, although these questions are never far

---

23. On the former see Gavin D'Costa, *Christianity and World Religions: Disputed Questions in the Theology of Religions* (Chichester: Wiley-Blackwell, 2009); Alan Race and Paul Hedges (eds.), *Christian Approaches to Other Faiths*, SCM Core Text (London: SCM, 2008). On the latter see Daniel Strange, 'Exclusivisms: "Indeed Their Rock Is Not Like Our Rock"', in Race and Hedges, *Christian Approaches to Other Faiths*, pp. 36–62; Veli-Matti Kärkkäinen, 'Evangelical Theology and the Relgions', in Timothy Larsen and Daniel J. Treier (eds.), *The Cambridge Companion to Evangelical Theology* (Cambridge: Cambridge University Press, 2007), pp. 199–212; *An Introduction to the Theology of Religions: Biblical, Historical and Contemporary Perspectives* (Downers Grove: InterVarsity Press, 2003), pp. 144–150; Harold Netland, 'Christian Mission Among Other Faiths: The Evangelical Tradition', in Lalsangkima Pachuau and Knud Jørgensen (eds.), *Witnessing to Christ in a Pluralistic Age: Christian Mission Among Other Faiths* (London: Regnum, 2011), pp. 45–56.

24. Both in terms of my argument and also in my decision to give more extensive direct quotations than might be normal in a monograph like this.

25. Studies of the theological importance of these figures can be found in Paul Visser, *Heart for the Gospel, Heart for the World: The Life and Thought of a Reformed Pioneer Missiologist, Johan Herman Bavinck (1895–1964)* (Eugene: Wipf & Stock, 2003); Tim S. Perry, *Radical Difference: A Defence of Hendrik Kraemer's Theology of Religions* (Waterloo, Ont.: Wilfrid Laurier University Press, 2001); John M. Frame, *Cornelius Van Til: An Analysis of His Thought* (Phillipsburg: P & R, 1995).

away in the theology of religions and so will be returned to throughout the study. Although I have noted the negative consequences of an evangelical preoccupation with soteriology, in one sense such a preoccupation is predictable, understandable and justifiable; indeed, it would be a worrying sign if soteriological questions were not front and centre of an evangelical theology of religions. Both theologically and pastorally we are right to prioritize and have utmost concern in considering the eternal destinies of human beings, particularly given what evangelicals believe to be clear teaching on the only way of salvation in Christ together with the reality of judgment and hell for those who are outside Christ. That soteriological questions are not my first concern in this study is by no means to minimize their importance, but to indicate that, having looked in great detail at these questions in previous work, new and underdeveloped questions need to be investigated. For those interested in evangelical positions regarding the salvation of non-Christians and the fate of the unevangelized, I refer the reader to a previous work, which in particular focuses on the soteriology of the doyen of evangelical inclusivists, Clark Pinnock.[26]

Fifthly, in my theological construction of an interpretation of other religions I hope to draw upon and integrate various disciplines that are often compartmentalized in theological studies: systematic theology, exegesis, biblical theology and missiology. I am fully aware that this is an ambitious undertaking, but I am ideologically convinced that as evangelical scholars we need to break out of our specialized ghettoes and interact with each other, for our own sake as well as the health of the church for whom we write. Obviously, the danger of such cross-disciplinary work is that of superficiality and possibly 'amateurism'. I am well aware that my background is as a systematician rather than as an Old Testament scholar, New Testament scholar, biblical theologian or missiologist. I hope those scholars who come from those backgrounds will charitably recognize the integration I am trying to achieve and offer more rigorous contributions in the future, all with the aim of edifying God's church worldwide.

Sixthly, a number of sections in the book are knowingly both exegetically and theologically speculative in nature (e.g. religio-genesis, Babel and the role of the demonic) and are properly located in disciplines within the study of religion that are for all intents and purposes not simply unfashionable but 'extinct' (e.g. the 'history of religion'). Concerning these sections I recognize

---

26. See Daniel Strange, *The Possibility of Salvation Among the Unevangelised: An Analysis of Inclusivism in Recent Evangelical Theology* (Carlisle: Paternoster, 2001); 'General Revelation: Sufficient or Insufficient', in Christopher W. Morgan and Robert A. Peterson (eds.), *Faith Comes by Hearing: A Response to Inclusivism* (Nottingham: Apollos, 2008), pp. 40–77.

that Dr Johnson's words may well be apt: 'It is not done well; but you are surprised to find it done at all'. However, as above, one of the reasons for not remaining in the safety of the shallow end but paddling out into deeper and murkier waters is to encourage or even dare others not only to join me in discussing these areas, but to push on past me with stronger strokes. Critically, I am confident that these exegetical and theological speculations of which I am less certain are not so crucial that they could endanger the validity of my overall argument concerning the religious Other.

Seventhly, although I shall be illustrating my theology of religions with specific examples drawn from various religious traditions, this work does not seek to interpret any one religion in detail. Rather, it indicates the dogmatic existence of a biblical interpretation of religions and provides a skeletal framework that I hope and pray will be fleshed out by others.[27]

Eighthly, I recognize that for many evangelical Christians the practical 'so what' or 'cash value' of the theology of religions is its consequence for missiological application in terms of apologetics, contextualization, dialogue, and so on. This is where pastorally and ministerially the 'rubber hits the road'. Given the confessional nature of my tradition, I myself am eager to see the implications my theology of religions has in terms of application and praxis. However, a degree of patience will be required, for while this theological analysis provides a necessary and firm springboard for such missiological application, the detailed discussion of these issues will not be included here apart from a brief chapter, which provides merely a sketch.[28]

Ninthly, in a work about 'other religions' it will be helpful to indicate how I understand and deploy the terms 'religion' and 'religions' in this study. I am aware of the scholarly tussle over this word in terms of essentialist versus functionalist definitions. I am also aware of the ideological use of the terms, which carries with it the baggage of an Enlightenment post-Kantian division between the (private) noumenal world of values and the (public) phenomenal world of facts. For some theologians, particularly those in the post-liberal theological tradition, the term 'religion' is redundant because religion is not a genus.[29] If that were not enough, finally I am aware that

---

27. An analogy that could be drawn here would be a dogmatic framework similar to that of the Vatican II document *Lumen Gentium*.

28. I hope to cover these missiological questions in more detail in a subsequent volume.

29. See John Milbank, 'The End of Dialogue', in Gavin D'Costa (ed.), *Christian Uniqueness Reconsidered* (New York: Orbis, 1990), pp. 174–191; D'Costa, *Christianity and World Religions*, pp. 55–102.

[t]he student of comparative religion who turns to the Bible for guidance meets his first discouragement in the fact that 'religion' is not really a biblical word at all. The Bible is concerned, not with religious systems as such, but with man in his life on earth before God. All that man does, therefore in every sphere of life, including that which he calls 'religious', is judged in the light of his response to the Creator Redeemer God who is axiomatic to the whole sweep of Scripture.[30]

While 'religion' as a defined category is more 'Western' than biblical, the Bible is concerned with universally inclusive descriptions and prescriptions of reactions to divine revelation, 'faith', 'religiosity', the 'heart' and encounters between the people of God and the religious Other. There is a wealth of biblical material to reflect upon.[31] As will become apparent in the study, I have an inclusive definition that ties 'religion' to 'worldview' and 'culture' in terms of one's ultimate heart commitments and presuppositions concerning reality. More theologically, Clouser is right when he says 'a religious belief is any belief in something or other as divine',[32] but then quickly defines 'divine' as 'having the status of not depending on anything else'.[33] Such a definition, based on something or someone *a se*,[34] includes all 'religions', 'philosophies' and 'worldviews'. While the universal theological anthropology I set out in this study *can* and *should* be applied to worldviews and cultures not usually deemed to be 'religious',[35] my focus will be on what are often called 'world religions', recognizing not only these porous definitional boundaries, but also the distinction and dynamic between religious 'systems' and individual 'believers'. That said, if we understand 'other religions' to be 'other' in respect of Christianity, then what we are dealing with here are rival social realities (still flowing from inner personal heart commitments) that are competitors to Christianity. We shall understand these to refer to *social* or

30. Christopher J. H. Wright, 'The Christian and Other Religions: The Biblical Evidence', *Them* 9.2 (1984), pp. 4–15 (4).

31. See Terry Muck and Frances S. Adeney, *Christianity Encountering World Religions: The Practice of Mission in the Twenty-First Century* (Grand Rapids: Baker, 2009). The authors have calculated and then list 289 accounts of 'religious' encounters in the Old and New Testaments.

32. Roy Clouser, *The Myth of Religious Neutrality* (Notre Dame: University of Notre Dame Press, 1991), p. 21.

33. Ibid.

34. Self-sufficient, not depending on anything else.

35. E.g. atheism, pop culture. For an excellent example of the latter see Ted Turnau, *Popologetics: Popular Culture in Christian Perspective* (Phillipsburg: P & R, 2012).

*corporate* rather than *individual* realities, as this seems to be the dividing line in contemporary discourse between 'religion' (social) and 'spirituality' (individual) – although this is not a strict demarcation (nor could it be, as individuals exist only in societies, and societies are composed of individuals). And again, what I say of 'religions' will be seen to be more widely applicable, but my concern here is with the term 'religious' thus defined. In what follows I shall use the following terms interchangeably: 'other religions', 'non-Christian religions', 'world religions' and the 'religious Other'.

Tenthly, having said something about my use of the term 'religion', I need to say something about my use of the word 'Christianity'. First, and echoing the previous point, I wish to understand Christianity not simply in terms of a set of propositional beliefs, but as a wholistic worldview that produces cultural fruit. Secondly, I recognize that the one true and unique gospel of Jesus Christ critiques not only the religious Other (the thesis of this study), but any lived expressions of Christianity not keeping to the revealed pattern of sound teaching (2 Tim. 1:13) and ethically not living lives worthy of Christ. Here it is relevant to respond to Terrance Tiessen's criticism of an earlier embryonic articulation of my theology of religions, whereby he discerns the 'dangerous triumphalism that could ensue from Dan's failure to recognize (or at least to state) that Christianity, like other religions, is also an ambiguous response to God's revelation'.[36] On the one hand, Tiessen is correct in pointing out that even those who are truly regenerated by God, and confess Jesus as Lord, still battle with indwelling sin and idolatry. He is also correct that just as 'not all Israel are Israel' (Rom. 9:6), so not everything that calls itself Christianity is Christianity. The categories of orthodoxy, heresy and apostasy are biblical categories as relevant now as they were when the Bible was written. As Visser notes, quoting J. H. Bavinck:

> The Christian church must never lose sight of the fact that it too, had been guilty of suppressing and replacing the truth and 'that its guilt in this respect is much greater than that of the other religions, because it has often obscured the revealed and clear gospel of Jesus Christ behind all kinds of cunning human reasonings,' which have been overcome solely by God's grace. Nor is this process of repression and substitution within Christianity in any way a thing in the past alone: 'in the Christian too, the

---

36. Terrance L. Tiessen, *My Reflections on the Conversation Between Strange and D'Costa* (2012), available online at http://thoughtstheological.com/d-costas-critique-of-stranges-subversive-fulfilment-interpretation-of-other-religions (accessed 8 Oct. 2012).

pagan continues to live and breathe.' And this holds not only for the individual
believer but also for the church as a whole which has turned its entire history into a
drama of 'formation, deformation and never ending reformation.'[37]

However, while I recognize the finitude, failures and inconsistencies of God's
people, together with the terrible truth that judgment begins within God's household (1 Peter 4:17), I am still able to say that there is a fundamental, indeed
antithetical, difference in principle between *the* regenerated and Spirit-enabled
confession that Jesus is Lord (*only* to be found through the preaching and teaching
of Christians) and every other confession where Jesus is not Lord, and where
people remain dead in their sins. That is to say that genuine and authentic
Christianity is that which is 'built on the foundation of the apostles and prophets,
with Christ Jesus himself as the chief cornerstone' (Eph. 2:20).[38] Therefore,
there is an inextricable link between Christ himself, Christ's gospel and Christ's
bride (the church), consisting of Christ's people (Christians) and given sacred
historical, social and institutional expression in what we call the 'Christian faith'
and 'Christianity'.[39]

---

37. Visser, *Heart for the Gospel*, p. 179.

38. This is not to deny God's revealing and redemptive activity before Christ in the
people of Israel. Although I discuss the salvation of Old Testament believers later in
this book, I have written in detail on this subject elsewhere. See Strange, *Possibility of
Salvation*, ch. 6.

39. In stating this link, I recognize I am in serious disagreement with one of my heroes
in the theology of religions, Hendrik Kraemer. With something of a Barthian tinge
Kraemer notes, 'The Christian religion in its many historical manifestations shows
the same disturbing combination of sublime, abject and tolerable elements as non-
Christian religions. Seen from this angle, Christianity as a phenomenon in history
has to be considered as *a* form of religion just like the others, although also like
them, it has, of course, its peculiar emphases and concerns. This thesis must be
constantly repeated in order to avoid the frequent occurring identification or partial
identification of Christianity, one of the religions, with the Revelation of God in
Christ' (Hendrik Kraemer, *Religion and the Christian Faith* [London: Lutterworth,
1956], p. 82 [his italics]). Ironically, the other formative influence for my theology
of religions, J. H. Bavinck (and one also indebted to Kraemer in so many ways),
critiques Kraemer precisely on this point, arguing that, while empirical Christianity
does need to be distinguished from the gospel, the two are nonetheless closely
linked. For Bavinck, Kraemer's view rules out the possibility of theology, because
anything a Christian says about God's revelation becomes part of empirical,

Finally, and as a corollary to the previous point, while I intend this study to be a positive piece of theological construction, my conclusions concerning the nature of non-Christian religions are often negative. I hope such pronouncements do not give rise to the charge that I am guilty of the sins of malice or vainglory: it is imperative that the context for Christians engaging with religious traditions be one of grace. First, a constant acknowledgment that we ourselves as Christians have been saved by grace through faith and not because of any ethical or intellectual superiority. Secondly, an attitude of grace towards those we are ministering among. J. H. Bavinck calls this a 'meeting-in-love':

> Meeting-in-love includes the recognition of myself in the other person, a sympathetic feeling of his guilt and a sincere desire in Christ to do with this man what Christ has done with me. This is the meaning of that tremendous word of Peter 'that ye should show forth the praises of him that has called you out of darkness out of which Christ has called me.' In the proper approach there is always an awareness of being on the same level with a person and there is a real consciousness of our common guilt in the eyes of God. It is this which gives the approach a warm undertone.[40]

This book is divided into nine chapters. After this introductory chapter (where I shall shortly declare my overall thesis and method), chapter 2 will describe the theological anthropology that should underpin any Reformed evangelical theology of religions. Chapters 3 and 4 seek to complement these theological foundations by investigating and speculating on the *historical* origin of the

---

historical Christianity, and thus has no theological value. Furthermore, in Kraemer's view the church cannot be considered 'true', which fails to grasp the fact that the Spirit is at work in the church. The NT regularly represents the church (in which empirical Christianity is found) in highly positive terms (e.g. Eph. 3:10). For more on Bavinck's critique of Kraemer, see Visser, *Heart for the Gospel*, pp. 181–182. Visser sums up Bavinck's and my own position nicely here: 'However true it may be that Christian faith (and certainly Christianity in general) does not coincide with the gospel, it is not right, Bavinck asserted, to set them over against each other in this way' (ibid., p. 182).

40. J. H. Bavinck, *An Introduction to the Science of Missions*, tr. David H. Freeman (Phillipsburg: P & R, 1960), p. 126. Even with this caveat made, there are those who think that an imperialism and self-righteous superiority just cannot be avoided, however much I might protest against it. This certainly seems to be Paul Knitter's view of my theology of religions as expressed in his formal response to my position paper in D'Costa, Knitter and Strange, *Only One Way?*, pp. 160–166.

phenomena of the 'religions', what could be called a 'religio-genesis'. Such analysis will further inform us as to the anatomy of non-Christian religions, an anatomy 'fleshed out' in chapters 5 and 6, which, and within the context of Old Testament studies, trace biblico-theologically Old and New Testament attitudes to the religious Other, with particular focus on the pervasive category of idolatry. Chapter 7 will attempt to synthesize the material into a systematic whole, and introduce the central idea that the gospel of Jesus Christ is the 'subversive fulfilment' of the religious Other. As a postscript to chapter 7, chapter 8 will highlight the missiological implications of a 'subversive fulfilment' theology of religions. Finally, chapter 9 will move from the 'what' of the religious Other to the 'why' and their teleology in the sovereignty of God. As a guide, for any who might not have the time or even inclination to get bogged down in both the intra- and cross-disciplinary detail and debates of the earlier chapters, chapters 7–9 act as a kind of systematic executive summary, which pulls together the findings of the previous chapters.

## 3. Declaring the thesis and method of this study

### a. My theology of religions stated

> The theology of religion asks what religion is and seeks, *in the light of Christian faith*, to interpret the universal religious experience of humankind; it further studies the relationship between revelation and faith, faith and religion, and faith and salvation.[41]

As compared to the allegedly 'neutral' discipline of 'religious studies', a Christian theology of religions should be a self-conscious example of *fides quaerens intellectum*.[42]

In the next seven chapters I shall outline a tradition-specific Christian theology of religions, seeking to interpret the nature, meaning and purpose of non-Christian religions from within what might be labelled 'Protestant Reformed Orthodoxy' or alternatively 'Reformed evangelicalism'. Both methodologically and substantially the doctrinal 'grammar' from which I shall be articulating this Christian interpretation of religion seeks to be faithful to biblical revelation

41. Jacques Dupuis, *Toward a Christian Theology of Religious Pluralism* (Maryknoll: Orbis, 1997), p. 7 (his italics).
42. Anselm's dictum of 'faith seeking understanding'.

(supremely), but also the Ecumenical Creeds,[43] the five *solas* of the Reformation,[44] the creedal affirmations of Reformed orthodoxy,[45] and several
pan-evangelical statements and covenants that have appeared since the 1970s.[46]
Far from being constricting, such confessional limits give ample room for safe
theological exploration and creativity and act as much as firm foundations as
they do restrictive fences.[47]

The theology of religions I wish to justify over subsequent chapters can be summarized as follows: *From the presupposition of an epistemologically authoritative biblical
revelation, non-Christian religions are sovereignly directed, variegated and dynamic, collective
human idolatrous responses to divine revelation behind which stand deceiving demonic forces.
Being antithetically against yet parasitically dependent upon the truth of the Christian
worldview, non-Christian religions are 'subversively fulfilled' in the gospel of Jesus Christ.*

You will see that I have included in this definition a description of theological
method. Given the fundamental importance of the themes of 'revelation' and
'presuppositions' for the theology of religions in general, and my theology of
religions in particular, the lines between method and substance are somewhat
blurred. Therefore, in outlining in a little more detail than usual what might be
called 'theological method', I am not only describing introductory prolegomena
but starting my argument proper. To put it another way, as Naugle has demonstrated in his work on the concept of worldview, even defining the term
'worldview' depends upon one's worldview.[48] Describing a Christian worldview

---

43. The Apostles' Creed (third–fourth century), the Nicene Creed (381), the Athanasian
    Creed (fourth–fifth century) and the Creed of Chalcedon (451).

44. *Sola Scriptura, solus Christus, sola fide, sola gratia* and *soli Deo gloria.*

45. The Thirty-Nine Articles (1571, Anglican); the Westminster Confession of Faith
    (1643–46, Presbyterian); the so-called 'Three Forms of Unity', which consist of the
    continental creeds (the Heidelberg Catechism [1563], the Belgic Confession [1561]
    and the Canons of Dordrecht [1618–19]); the New Hampshire Baptist Confession
    (1833, Baptist); and the Baptist Faith and Message (1925/1963).

46. Particularly significant here are the Frankfurt Declaration (1970), the Lausanne
    Covenant (1974; the fruit of the International Congress on World Evangelization,
    originally initiated by Billy Graham) and the Manilla Manifesto (1989). For details
    and commentaries on these documents see John R. W. Stott (ed.), *Making Christ
    Known: Historic Mission Documents from the Lausanne Movement 1974–1989*
    (Carlisle: Paternoster, 1996).

47. Keeping to the pattern of 'sound' teaching and guarding the good deposit (2 Tim.
    1:13–14).

48. David K. Naugle, *Worldview: The History of a Concept* (Grand Rapids: Eerdmans, 2002).

or religion in contradistinction to all other worldviews or religions will be an important part of my argument, but even to describe a Christian world-view depends upon a Christian worldview. Again, method and content are inextricably linked.

### b. The elephant speaks: theological method

In your light do we see light.
(Ps. 36:9)

I have already mentioned Lesslie Newbigin's much-quoted critique of the pluralist use of the story of the blind man and the elephant, where he argues that rather than demonstrating an epistemic humility, what in reality is revealed is an epistemic arrogance. Having voiced disquiet towards those who would align themselves with the king in the story, there must be a recognition that a position like mine must reveal its own *pou stō* (place to stand):[49] the ultimate authority upon which one bases and builds one's theology of religions. For pluralism, it is the exclusive claims of Kantian modernity. But what about my own ultimate authority? Fundamental to my own position is a doctrine of revelation, an 'extracosmic base for knowledge and meaning'.[50] To continue the illustration, knowledge of the elephant is possible only because the elephant speaks and tells us who he is. Without this self-disclosure we may speculate, guess or dream, but we have no secure starting point for knowledge: we remain blind.

Expounding further the doctrine of revelation I espouse, the following may be said. First, although it may appear otherwise, and thoroughly subverting the Cartesian and Kantian epistemological paradigm known as the 'Enlightenment', revelation implies that ontology precedes epistemology, for 'before there can be revelation, there must be something to be revealed and someone or something to reveal it. Revelation can never be first, as if we or God depended on it. It always depends on God.'[51] While I shall shortly expound further the nature and actions of God, I note here that the self-attesting, personal and ultimate authority

49. Archimedes' looking for a base outside the world for his lever's fulcrum: 'Give me a place where I may stand and I will move the world.' Quoted by Pappus of Alexandria in the fourth century.

50. Robert Reymond, *A New Systematic Theology of the Christian Faith* (Nashville: Thomas Nelson, 1998), p. 111, n. 1.

51. James Sire, *Naming the Elephant* (Downers Grove: InterVarsity Press, 2004), p. 68.

of divine revelation is what it is, solely because it is derived from a God who is self-attesting, personal and absolute.

Secondly, given this metaphysics of knowledge, one can steer a safe passage without being devoured by the Scylla of modern and hubristic rationalism (which in reality always leads to scepticism[52]) or sucked into the Charybdis of postmodern and despairing irrationalism (which in reality is always made on a rationalistic basis).[53] The nature of human knowledge is a reflection of the creature's metaphysical total dependence upon, and distinction from, a totally independent Creator. It is neither 'univocal' knowledge, nor 'equivocal' knowledge, but 'analogous' in the sense of being a 'finite replica', image or reflection: 'We think God's thoughts after him, without presuming to think God's thoughts.'[54] Kreitzer calls this epistemology 'transcendent foundationalism'.[55]

---

52. For the finite human mind is not a stable starting point for knowledge and is certainly not omniscient.

53. The 'confidence' that we know that we don't know and that we can rationally communicate that we know we don't know.

54. Michael S. Horton, 'Consistently Reformed: The Inheritance and Legacy of Van Til's Apologetic', in K. Scott Oliphint and Lane G. Tipton (eds.), *Revelation and Reason: New Essays in Reformed Theology* (Phillipsburg: P & R, 2007), pp. 131–148. For more on this 'analogical' understanding of religious language see Frame, *Cornelius Van Til*, pp. 89–96.

55. Kreitzer summarizes it thus: 'The theory that agrees with immanent Foundationalism that certain, beginning points are necessary for all human knowledge. The beginning point, however, is not found with the observable creation or neutral human reason. All true thought begins within a relationship with the invisible Creator, his comprehensive truth system, and his true data points. All true data that come into human senses, thus, are not ordered by the human mind but by God's mind. None are neutral. All true data must also cohere to this system of truth which God is in himself and reveals in his creation, providence and Scripture (John 1:1–3; 14:6; Col. 1:15–17; 2:3, 8; Heb. 1:1). The triune God and his inherent wisdom is the transcendent foundation of all truth for every individual and every culture.

'Humans can perceive some true data and can discover some aspects of their coherency within the divine truth system, but never comprehensively. However, sin and incautious perception can distort perceived information. The Holy Spirit unbends and heals the distortion caused by sin. The Spirit-led reading of Scripture in all groups and ethnicities of humanity together limits our human finiteness. Therefore, facts exist that are not first interpreted by human minds. God is the

Two contemporary approaches to doing theology that take account of this epistemological stance are those of multi-perspectivalism and 'symphonic' theology, championed by Reformed theologians John Frame and Vern Poythress respectively.[56] In terms of theology, multi-perspectivalism argues that there are both continuities and discontinuities between God's knowledge and our own. Truth is one and yet only God is omniscient, seeing reality simultaneously from all possible perspectives. In summary, multi-perspectivalism recognizes that 'because of our finitude, we need to look at things first from one perspective, then another. The more different perspectives we can incorporate into our formulations, the more likely those formulations will be biblically accurate.'[57] Frame notes that the Bible presents doctrinal relationships perspectivally because this reflects the nature of the triune God:

> God is one God in three persons; He is many attributes in one God-head – the eternal one and many. None of the persons is prior to the other, all are equally eternal, ultimate, absolute, glorious. None of the attributes is 'prior to' any of the others; each is equally divine, inalienable, and necessary to God's deity.[58]

Poythress echoes this:

> Different perspectives, though they start from different strands of biblical revelation, are in principle harmonizable with one another. We as human beings do not always see the harmony straight away. But we gain insights in the process of trying to see the same material from several different perspectives. We use what we have gained from one perspective to reinforce, correct, or improve what we understood through the other. I call this procedure *symphonic theology* because it is analogous to the blending of various musical instruments to express the variations of a symphonic theme.[59]

---

original Creator and interpreter. Humans must think God's thoughts after him to know certain truth and factuality' (Mark Kreitzer, *The Concept of Ethnicity in the Bible: A Theological Analysis* [London: Edwin Mellen, 2008], pp. 426–427).

56. John M. Frame, *The Doctrine of God: A Theology of Lordship* (Phillipsburg: P & R, 2002), pp. 89–90, 191–194, 200–204, 235; Vern S. Poythress, *Symphonic Theology: The Validity of Multiple Perspectives in Theology* (Phillipsburg: P & R, 1987).

57. John M. Frame, 'Machen's Warrior Children', in Sung Wook Chung (ed.), *Alister McGrath: A Dynamic Engagement* (Grand Rapids: Baker, 2003), pp. 113–146 (142).

58. Frame, *Doctrine of God*, p. 192.

59. Poythress, *Symphonic Theology*, p. 43.

Thirdly, and as hinted at by Frame and Poythress, this understanding of the nature of revelation has implications for our doctrine of Scripture and the meaning of *sola Scriptura*. Although God's revelation of himself comes to us through various media (nature, history, word, person),[60] all of which are authoritative and consistent,[61] 'the Bible has a unique role in the organism of revelation',[62] as both a verbal and written revelation is understood to be necessary. As I shall elucidate, given the universal suppression and distortion of God's revelation, the gospel message, now exclusively revealed in the Bible (for Jesus has ascended and the apostles have died), is necessary to 'correct' our vision.[63]

That this revelation is *verbal* is necessary, given the specificity of the message contained within: 'The reality of the Trinity, and the purpose of the incarnation, crucifixion, resurrection and ascension are sufficiently complex that they cannot be mimed, or communicated through a religious impulse or sensation; they need to be spoken.'[64] That it is *written* is necessary, given not only the need for it to be preserved and propagated, but also the Bible's 'covenantal' and constitutional nature.[65]

As Scripture is the revelation of a triune God, we see within it both unity-in-diversity and diversity-in-unity.[66] The diversity within Scripture does not

---

60. Theologians often organize these various media into two categories: general revelation and special revelation.

61. See below on this point.

62. John M. Frame, *The Doctrine of the Christian Life* (Phillipsburg: P & R, 2008), p. 141.

63. One recalls Calvin here: 'Just as old or bleary-eyed men and those with weak vision, if you thrust them before a most beautiful volume, even if they recognize it to be some sort of writing, yet can scarcely construe two words, but with the aid of spectacles will begin to read distinctly; so Scripture, gathering up the otherwise confused knowledge of God, having dispersed our dullness, clearly shows us the true God' ( John Calvin, *Institutes of the Christian Religion*, ed. John T. McNeill, tr. Ford Lewis Battles, 2 vols., LCC [Philadelphia: Westminster, 1960], 1.6.1).

64. Timothy Ward, *Words of Life: Scripture as the Living and Active Word of God* (Nottingham: Inter-Varsity Press, 2009), p. 106.

65. Ibid. Ward writes, 'It is in line with the very nature of the covenant that God has established and revealed progressively through time that its stipulations and history, as witness to God's faithfulness to it, be written down. It was not an absolute necessity that it was, but it is highly appropriate to the nature of his chosen form of revelation and salvation that God ensured it was' (ibid., p. 107).

66. As Frame notes, 'Scripture, of course, is written by human authors together with the divine author. God reveals himself by inspiring human beings. He generally does not

entail internal contradictions and tensions that would compromise the unity of Scripture, thus rendering Scripture *in*sufficient to be the ultimate authority for Christian faith. Rather, it enhances the richness and depth of revealed truth. In a contemporary restatement of Chemnitz's conclusion in the sixteenth century, that the Gospels exhibited 'a very concordant dissonance', Timothy Ward draws upon the discipline of intertextuality in literary theory and scholars such as Plett, Bakhtin and Ricoeur, arguing for a 'canonically limited polyphony':

> To be up to the task of naming a triune God, Scripture must reflect him in this ontological respect: it must say genuinely different things in different places, which faith receives as harmonious. If it is appropriate to take this as the theological background against which all faithful biblical teaching is ultimately performed, then Walter Brueggemann, in his recent large work of Old Testament theology, is wrong to judge that 'interpretation, in the end, cannot overcome the *irascibly* pluralistic character of the biblical text,' for he fails to take account of a basic Christian belief about the peaceable nature of the divine reality communicated in the texts.[67]

As I hope to demonstrate, this polyphony is very much in evidence as we look at the Bible's understanding of other religions, and methodologically this will be demonstrated structurally in an awareness of both synchronic and diachronic approaches to the biblical text, as well as by an attempted integration of the concerns of systematic theology, biblical theology and Old Testament and New Testament studies.

Fourthly, and clearing up some common misconceptions, in adopting the Reformation slogan of *sola Scriptura* I am not *divinizing* the Bible, *distracting*

---

dictate, but rather enables them to write consistently with their own gifts, education, and personalities, that is, their own perspectives. And by such divine enablement, each author writes exactly what God wants him to write. And God often determines that his truth is best conveyed by multiple human perspectives rather than just one. In Scripture, all those human perspectives convey truth, and all are warranted by God's infinite perspective, though none is identical with that divine perspective. This is what we should expect, since God has created us as people who learn through multi-perspectival experience' (John M. Frame, *A Primer on Perspectivalism* [2008], available online at http://www.frame-poythress.org/a-primer-on-perspectivalism/ [accessed 9 Oct. 2012]).

67. Timothy Ward, 'The Diversity and Sufficiency of Scripture', in Paul Helm and Carl Trueman (eds.), *The Trustworthiness of God: Perspectives on the Nature of Scripture* (Grand Rapids: Eerdmans; Leicester: Apollos, 2002), pp. 192–218 (214, his italics).

from Christ, *dismissing* the role of the 'rule of faith' or *dichotomizing* Scripture from the other media of revelation. Ward is again helpful here on the first three. To the first charge he uses the discourse of 'speech act theory' to argue that God is 'semantically present' in the Bible:

> There is, then, a complex but real relationship between God and his actions, expressed and performed, as they are, through God's words. In philosophical terms, there is an ontological relationship between God and his words. It seems that God's action including his verbal actions, are a kind of extension of him.[68]

To the second charge, and while noting important distinctions, Ward can affirm both Christ and the Bible as the 'word of God' because 'the speech acts related in Scripture are the means by which Christ continues to present himself as a knowable person in the world'.[69] Hence *solus Christus* is not compromised but enhanced in *sola Scriptura*: all of Scripture points to him; he is the fulfilment and climax of all God's promises. To the third charge, Ward, along with others, is keen to distinguish *sola Scriptura* from 'solo *scriptura*', or 'nuda *scriptura*':

> The Reformers' conviction of *sola Scriptura* is the conviction that Scripture is the only *infallible* authority, the only supreme authority. Yet it is not the *only* authority, for the

---

68. Ward, *Words of Life*, p. 33. As I am so indebted to his theology of religions in general, I should note here a substantive difference I have with Hendrik Kraemer that relates to this point. Although Kraemer has been criticized for having too high a view of the Bible in his theology of religions (what Kraemer called 'biblical realism'), from an evangelical point of view Kraemer's doctrine of Scripture has a distinct 'neo-orthodox' feel, which might leave one uncomfortable. E.g. he writes, 'Revelation in the Bible is objective divine action in the person and work of Jesus Christ, "the 'Word made Flesh.'" Strictly speaking, the word should be confined to his basic divine history. It is, however, the custom, which is to a certain extent acceptable, to speak about the transmission of the *kerygma* regarding this history by means of persons and writings also as "revelation." This is "revelation" in a subjective secondary sense. Into this category falls the Bible, when we speak about this book as "God's Revelation." It is one of the most difficult tasks of theology to guard against a blurring of the distinction between revelation in the primary and in the secondary sense, or the substitution of Christ, who is the Word, and the Bible, which is a witness to the only word of God' (Kraemer, *Religion and the Christian Faith*, p. 345). For more of Kraemer's doctrine of Scripture see Perry, *Radical Difference*, ch. 5.

69. Ward, *Words of Life*, p. 75.

creeds and the church's teaching function as important subordinate authorities, under the authority of Scripture.[70]

Finally, to the charge of dichotomization. One set of relationships that will require careful delineation in my argument is the relationships between the various media in the organism of God's revelation, for these impinge upon the construal of universality and particularity, perennial themes within the theology of religions. While we must affirm the uniqueness of Scripture in the organism of God's revelation, we must be careful not to dichotomize Scripture from the other media of revelation (nature and history), but rather highlight their complementarity and unity. Although the common dogmatic distinction between general revelation and special revelation is generally useful, it can be a rather blunt instrument, especially in the usual categorization of 'history' as 'general revelation'. As Frame notes in his exposition of God's Word through nature and history:

> On the whole, my category of 'revelation given through nature and history' is identical to the traditional category of 'general revelation'. But there is a difference. Revelation given through nature and history, taken as a whole, includes both law and gospel, for the gospel is a segment of history, that segment we call redemptive history. But general revelation understood in the traditional way is that portion of God's revelation in nature and history that does not include the gospel. Redemptive history is hard to classify . . . Since God's revelation in redemptive history is revelation in event, rather than word, we are inclined to want to call it general. But since it has redemptive content, we are inclined to call it special. To some extent these are artificial categories, and it doesn't matter much which we use to describe

---

70. Ibid., p. 149 (his italics). Ward here is indebted to Keith A. Mathison, *The Shape of Sola Scriptura* (Moscow, Idaho: Canon, 2001). Mathison's is a detailed study carefully distinguishing between different understandings of the authority of Scripture and using Heiko Oberman's categories of tradition, in Heiko Oberman, *The Dawn of the Reformation* (Edinburgh: T. & T. Clark, 1986). 'Tradition I' is a one-source theory that sees 'a single exegetical tradition of interpreted Scripture' (Oberman, *Dawn of the Reformation*, p. 280); 'Tradition II' is a two-source theory that sees Scripture and tradition as equally authoritative sources of revelation; 'Tradition III' understands the real source of revelation to be the living magisterium of the church; 'Tradition . . . exalts the individual's interpretation of Scripture over and against that of corporate interpretation of past generation of Christians' (Ward, *Words of Life*, p. 150). In this chapter I am defending 'Tradition I'.

redemptive history. But we should be aware of the ambiguity of this category of revelation.[71]

We shall return later in the study to this set of relationships within the organism of revelation.

In summary, given that the authority of Scripture is shorthand for 'the authority of God as he speaks through Scripture', so the Bible is the Christian's ultimate authority in all metaphysical, epistemological, ethical and soteriological issues, and is totally trustworthy and consistent because it has been inspired (or better, 'breathed out') by a totally trustworthy and consistent God.[72] In terms of justification, the Bible is self-attesting because God is self-attesting, being ultimate and self-contained.[73] Philosophically such self-attestation is not fallaciously circular, for all *ultimate* commitments (Enlightenment rationalism included) must be self-attesting if they are not to be self-referentially incoherent.

---

71. Frame, *Doctrine of the Christian Life*, p. 136, n. 6. Leithart puts it helpfully this way: 'The Bible teaches that God reveals His character in creation, in history, and in Scripture. If we wish to know God, we have to seek Him as He has revealed Himself through these media. We cannot know God by peeking "behind" the screen of history and Scripture; we come to know Him *through* His words and works. History, Scripture and creation are the "books" of God, and if we would know Him we must open the books. There is fuller revelation in one or another of God's books. For example we know about God's provision in Christ from Scripture rather than from creation. Yet it is the same God who writes to us in each. Each book, in fact, is large enough to include the others. If we open God's book of creation, we realize that the creation is not static but in motion, that creation has a history; thus God's revelation in creation includes His revelation in history. And since Scripture exists in history, it too forms a chapter in God's book of creation and history. History is the story of God's actions, which manifest His character, and Scripture is largely a record of those actions, that story' (Peter Leithart, *Heroes of the City of Man* [Moscow, Idaho: Canon, 1999], pp. 33–34 [his italics]).

72. For contemporary defences of an evangelical doctrine of Scripture see Ward, *Words of Life*; Peter Jensen, *The Revelation of God* (Leicester: Inter-Varsity Press, 2002); D. A. Carson and John Woodbridge (eds.), *Scripture and Truth* (Leicester: Inter-Varsity Press, 1983); ibid., *Hermeneutics, Authority and Canon* (Leicester: Inter-Varsity Press, 1986); Mathison, *Shape of Sola Scriptura*.

73. See below for more on this description of God. Biblically, we see an example of this in Heb. 6:13, where God swears an oath by himself, for there is no greater authority by which to swear an oath.

Biblical authority and *sola Scriptura* mean that there is no brute factuality: all facts, including all extra-biblical facts, are interpreted in the light of God's light in Scripture.[74]

## Conclusion

Given the particular method just outlined, the importance of demonstrating 'biblical' justification for my theology of religions will be imperative. However, this might be seen to present an immediate obstacle, for as the history of the theology of religions demonstrates, all 'Christian' theologies of religions have to a lesser or greater extent claimed biblical support and justification for their position. Attempting now to summarize and synthesize a coherent and unified theology of religions that is faithful to the *whole* of biblical revelation and relevant to our contemporary 'religious' world would seem a presumptuous and insurmountable task. However, I believe such a task, while difficult, is not impossible, given the nature of divine revelation and my subscription to the Reformed theological tradition, which I believe to be the closest asymptotic approach to biblical revelation.[75]

---

74. 'The self-contained God is self-determinate. He cannot refer to anything outside that which has proceeded from himself for corroboration of his words . . . the mind of man is itself in all of its activities dependent upon and functional within revelation. . . . All the facts are through and through revelational of the same God that has made the mind of man. If then appeal is made from the Bible to the facts of history or of nature outside the Bible recorded in some documents totally independent of the Bible it must be remembered that these facts themselves can be seen for what they are only if they are regarded in the light of the Bible. It is by the light of the flashlight that has derived its energy from the sun that we may seek to answer the question whether there be a sun. This is not to disparage the light of reason. It is only to indicate its total dependence upon God. Nor is it to disparage the usefulness of arguments for the corroboration of the Scripture that comes from archaeology. It is only to say that such corroboration is not of independent power. It is not a testimony that has its source anywhere but in God himself. Here the facts and the principles of their interpretation are again seen to be involved in one another' (Cornelius Van Til, 'Introduction', in Samuel G. Craig [ed.], *B. B. Warfield, The Inspiration and Authority of the Bible* [London: Marshall, Morgan & Scott, 1951], pp. 36–37).
75. 'A curved line may approach a straight line asymptotically, never quite touching it but always getting closer . . . The model is useful precisely because it never touches

A multi-perspectival view of divine revelation could give way to a structural paralysis: as there are so many ways of ordering the biblical material on a given topic, it is difficult to know where to start. However, I have decided to structure my theology of religions in the following way. First, although my exposition will primarily be thematic and systematic, I shall strive to give consideration to the fact that the Bible is a metanarrative,[76] written in a variety of literary genres, by different writers at different times, but with a unified and distinct plotline (and with particular turning points and climaxes, etc.). These redemptive-historical features should not be flattened out. Therefore, I am roughly adopting a pattern that mirrors the creation–fall–redemption– consummation structure of the Christian metanarrative. Within each of these redemptive-historical moments I have chosen a particular scriptural *locus classicus* in the theology of religions from which to launch my exposition. These passages will act as gateways and springboards to move into related material both scriptural and extra-scriptural.

Secondly, I wish to model my claim that Reformed theology has the necessary resources out of which one can fashion a biblically nuanced and sophisticated theology of religions. Therefore, throughout my exposition I shall be referring to a number of explicitly Reformed theological doctrines that will be applied to the area of the theology of religions. While I shall give only a brief description of these doctrines, I have attempted to reference fuller doctrinal and creedal formulations in the footnotes.

---

the axis. In exactly the same way, we may not aspire to absolute knowledge of the sort only Omniscience may possess, but the "approximation" may be so good that it is adequate for placing human beings on the moon' (D. A. Carson, *The Gagging of God: Christianity Confronts Pluralism* [Leicester: Apollos, 1996], p. 121).

76. Indeed *the* metanarrative that includes and 'out-narrates' all other metanarratives.

## 2. *HOMO ADORANS*: REFORMED THEOLOGICAL FOUNDATIONS FOR INTERPRETING THE RELIGIOUS OTHER

### Introduction: on *not* reinventing the religious wheel

'Homo sapiens,' 'homo faber,' . . . yes, but, first of all 'homo adorans.'[1]

Paul then stood up in the meeting of the Areopagus and said: 'People of Athens! I see that in every way you are very religious. For as I walked around and looked carefully at your objects of worship, I even found an altar with this inscription: TO AN UNKNOWN GOD. So you are ignorant of the very thing you worship – and this is what I am going to proclaim to you.

'The God who made the world and everything in it is the Lord of heaven and earth and does not live in temples built by human hands. And he is not served by human hands, as if he needed anything. Rather, he himself gives everyone life and breath and everything else. From one man he made all the nations, that they should inhabit the whole earth; and he marked out their appointed times in history and the boundaries of their lands. God did this so that they would seek him and perhaps reach out for him and find him, though he is not far from any one of us. "For in him we live

---

1. Alexander Schmemann, *For the Life of the World: Sacrament and Orthodoxy* (New York: St Vladimir's Seminary Press, 1973), p. 15, quoted in David K. Naugle, *Worldview: The History of a Concept* (Grand Rapids: Eerdmans, 2002), p. 275.

and move and have our being." As some of your own poets have said, "We are his offspring."

'Therefore since we are God's offspring, we should not think that the divine being is like gold or silver or stone – an image made by human design and skill. In the past God overlooked such ignorance, but now he commands all people everywhere to repent. For he has set a day when he will judge the world with justice by the man he has appointed. He has given proof of this to everyone by raising him from the dead.'

(Acts 17:22–31)

So far in the preliminary stages of this study I have been anxious, some might say overanxious, to highlight the tradition-specific nature of my theology of religions. The main reason for bringing my own theological tradition into the foreground is born out of a concern that some may view the theology of religions as a radically new discipline requiring new theological methods and doctrines, as if one's previous methods and doctrines were somehow ill-equipped to answer the questions at hand. However, it is my contention that deeply sunk (and cherished) theological, epistemological and anthropological foundations should not be ignored or, worse, 'dug up' when faced with the religious Other. Rather, it is on these secure foundations that one should build one's theology of religions. Based primarily on Genesis 1 – 11, this chapter will describe these foundations. In order to reach this destination, however, I want us to stop briefly in Athens, starting with the *locus classicus* of the apostle Paul's address to the Areopagus.

Whether it is properly exegeted or improperly eisegeted, Acts 17:16–24 seems to have an almost magnetic quality in the way it is returned to and referenced in biblically based theologies of religions.[2] My theology of religions will be no different here and we shall have recourse to return to this passage throughout our study.[3] In the beginning, however, I want to use Paul's address as a theological hyperlink and 'anchor' to access and explore the beginnings of the book of beginnings, Genesis 1 – 11, which contains many fundamental theological distinctives of a Reformed Christian worldview, a worldview through which I

---

2. Adolf Deissmann called it 'the greatest missionary document in the New Testament . . . a manifesto of worldwide importance in the history of religions and of religion' (*Light from the Ancient East*, 2nd ed. [Grand Rapids: Baker, 1978; orig. 1927], p. 384, cited in John Span, 'The Areopagus: A Study in Continuity and Discontinuity', *SFM* 6.3 [2010], p. 517).

3. See esp. pp. 285–294 in this book.

shall seek to interpret non-Christian religions. Although I shall shortly justify my reasons for using Genesis, I should first justify my reasons for using Paul's Areopagus address in this way.

First, and in terms of situational background, what Paul was doing *then* in the first century (i.e. describing the unique contours of a Christian worldview in contradistinction to other worldviews) I am attempting to do *now* in the twenty-first century. Providentially, the 'religious' setting in which Paul gives his own thumbnail systematic theology is remarkably similar to our own, one of philosophical and religious diversity, not just a factual pluralism but often a cherished pluralism, be it henotheism, polytheism or syncretism.[4] This makes any claims to Christian distinctiveness and uniqueness all the more self-conscious and stark. Paul may refer to times of ignorance but he himself was not ignorant of the religiously plural world in which he lived. Given the similarity of context between Paul's world and our own, we would do well to observe and perhaps mirror those doctrinal loci the apostle chooses to emphasize.[5] This I hope will be evident in what follows.

Secondly, and the reason why Athens is a detour rather than a destination, is that behind Paul's address are the same primary revelatory resources that I see as foundations for my own theology of religions. As Richard Hays notes, Paul 'repeatedly situates his discourse within the symbolic field created by a single

---

4. See e.g. Richard S. Hess, 'Yahweh and His Asherah? Religious Pluralism in the Old Testament World', in Andrew D. Clarke and Bruce W. Winter (eds.), *One Lord, One God: Christianity in a World of Religious Pluralism* (Cambridge: Tyndale House, 1991), pp. 5–33; Bruce W. Winter, 'In Public and in Private: Early Christians and Religious Pluralism', in Clarke and Winter, *One Lord, One God*, pp. 125–148. Carson is right when he notes that the reason Paul outlines a Christian worldview is evangelistic and apologetic: 'In this context he has done so in order to provide a framework in which Jesus himself, not least his death and resurrection, makes sense. Otherwise nothing that Paul wants to say about Jesus will make sense' (D. A. Carson, 'Athens Revisited', in D. A. Carson [ed.], *Telling the Truth: Evangelizing Postmoderns* [Grand Rapids: Zondervan, 2000], pp. 384–398 [394]).

5. Having noted the context of religious pluralism for Paul's speech in Lystra and Athens, Winter notes that one of the central purposes of these speeches (together with 1 Cor. 8 – 10) is to model an evangelistic method without compromise. His conclusion is that 'the reason that the matter of religious pluralism was discussed in public preaching was simply that it was an essential component of the gospel presentation' (Winter, 'In Public and in Private', p. 142).

great precursor text: Israel's Scripture'.[6] Paul's own description of God, and of human beings, here is not a novel formulation, but is steeped in his Jewish background and worldview, albeit now 'fulfilled' and 'filled in' in the coming of Christ.[7] And as Pardigon states:

> The Areopagitica begins with creation and concludes with the Parousia, having alluded to the story of Babel and Noah as well as the Sinaitic covenant with Israel. It considers human religion from the perspective of God's original design, of post-Babel condition, of God's covenant of grace, including eschatological fulfilment and of final judgement.[8]

In terms of intertextuality, and my principle of 'canonically limited polyphony', in returning to the Old Testament from the New Testament I am being faithful to Paul, who gave the address, to Luke the redactor, who wrote it down, and to the triune God, who authoritatively supervised the entire process.

In structuring my overall argument, the decision to focus first on Genesis 1 – 11 allows me to organize my theology of religions into a unified whole. First, these chapters contain the theological DNA of a Reformed worldview not only in terms of metaphysics, epistemology and ethics, but crucially in terms of an embryonic gospel narrative: creation–fall–redemption. What we witness redemptive-historically throughout the rest of Scripture, while dynamic and complex, is a continuous and consistent revelation, a flowering of seed to tree. Having this worldview framework in place at the start of my exposition gives

---

6. Richard Hays, *Echoes of Scripture in the Letters of Paul* (London: Yale University Press, 1989), p. 15.
7. For Paul's use of Isa. 42 in his address see Greg Bahnsen, *Always Ready: Directions for Defending the Faith* (Nacogdoches, Tex.: Covenant Media, 1996), pp. 263–266; Steve R. Scrivener, 'Principles for Apologetics from Paul at Athens' (2009), available online at http://www.vantil.info/articles/Principles%20for%20apologetics%20from%20 Paul%20at%20Athens.pdf (accessed 4 Oct. 2013); G. K. Beale, 'Other Religions in New Testament Theology', in David W. Baker (ed.), *Biblical Faith and Other Religions: An Evangelical Assessment* (Grand Rapids: Kregel, 2004), pp. 79–105.
8. Flavien Olivier Cedric Pardigon, 'Paul Against the Idols: The Areopagus Speech and Religious Inclusivism', PhD diss., Westminster Theological Seminary, 2008. As I shall mention again in a later chapter, Pardigon, drawing on the work of David Pao, argues that the Areopagus speech is the climax of an anti-idol polemic, itself a subtheme of the overarching OT background of Luke-Acts, specifically that of an Isaianic New Exodus.

me both the theological boundaries within which to work and the theological tools with which to fashion my theology of religions. As with my use of Acts 17, I do not believe I am going 'against the grain' of the purpose of Genesis here, for, as well as probably functioning as an explanatory history of Israel in the wilderness, it serves a similar canonical function for the people of God throughout history. Knowing both the depth and diversity of reflection within the Reformed tradition, my treatment of these loci can be little more than fairly derivative revision notes,[9] although I shall glean relevant material pertaining to the theology of religions and foreshadow certain perspectives and trajectories that will be picked up later on in the study.

## 1. Creation: the Creator–creature distinction and the *imago Dei*

> The God who made the world and everything in it is the Lord of heaven and earth . . .
> 'We are his offspring.'
> (Acts 17:24a, 28b)

The first building block of a Reformed Christian worldview is a doctrine of creation *ex nihilo* that preserves the Creator–creature distinction.[10] Metaphysically, although we can never become God, nor can God lose his deity, we are made in God's image, built with the relational purpose of worshipping and glorifying the one who made us, and built for speaking and making under the authority of the ultimate Speaker and Maker. Metaphysically, we are dependent upon God ('in him we live and move and have our being'); epistemologically, we were created to depend upon and obey God's authoritative and benevolent revelation, both given in the medium of 'works' and 'words'. We are to think God's thoughts after him. With the help of the Reformed theologians Cornelius

---

9. I shall attempt to refer the reader to creedal formulations and seminal texts in footnotes.

10. 'As Van Til put it, the Christian worldview involves a "two-level" concept of reality. Van Til used to walk into class and draw two circles on the board, one under the other, connected by vertical "lines" of communication. The larger upper circle represented God; the smaller, lower circle represented the creation. All non-Christian thought, he argued, is "one circle" thought. It either raises man to God's level or lowers God to man's. In any case, it regards God, if it acknowledges him at all, as man's equal, as another part of the "stuff" of the universe' (John M. Frame, *Apologetics to the Glory of God: An Introduction* [Phillipsburg: P & R, 1994], p. 43).

Van Til and his student John Frame, let us first start with the divine side of this distinction.

### a. 'And God said . . . and it was so': the independent creator

The Christian God is distinctively a personal absolute and absolute personality. He is both transcendent (but not 'wholly other' to creation) in that he does not need anything, and immanent (but not identical to creation) in that 'he is not far from any one of us'.[11] I have already alluded to the personal nature of God in my comments on revelation: the living God 'speaks' ('And God said', Gen. 1:3) and is one with whom creatures can have a covenantal I–Thou relationship. The Bible is replete with personal names, personal descriptions and personal actions of this God. While, of course, we note the analogous and anthropomorphic nature of all such statements, it is significant that ultimate reality is not impersonal matter, principle or fate but a personal and living God, involved in the world and especially with his people.

Not only is the Lord personal, but he is absolute, or self-sufficient. There is a long theological tradition grounding description of God in the name Yahweh: 'That was the name that described his essence par excellence. God is the Existent One. His whole identity is wrapped up in the name: "I will be what I will be". All God's other perfections are derived from this name.'[12] Vos comments that the name Yahweh

> gives expression to the self-determination, the independence of God, that which, especially in soteric associations, we are accustomed to call his sovereignty . . . The name . . . signifies primarily that in all that God does for his people, He is from-within-determined, not moved upon by outside influences.[13]

---

11. Frame points out the epistemological problems if God is either 'wholly other' or 'wholly revealed': 'If God is "wholly other", then how can we say or know that He is "wholly other"? . . . And if God is indistinguishable from the world, why should the theologian even speak about God? Why not simply speak of the world? Is it faith that validates such talk? Faith based on what? Can such a faith be more than an irrational leap in the dark?' ( John M. Frame, *The Doctrine of the Knowledge of God* [Phillipsburg: P&R, 1987], p. 14).

12. Herman Bavinck, *Reformed Dogmatics*, ed. John Bolt, tr. John Vriend, 4 vols. (Grand Rapids: Baker, 2004), vol. 2, p. 151.

13. Geerhardus Vos, *Biblical Theology: Old and New Testaments* (Grand Rapids: Eerdmans, 1948; Edinburgh: Banner of Truth Trust, 1975), p. 134, quoted in Robert Reymond, *A New Systematic Theology of the Christian Faith* (Nashville:

It is worth dwelling a little more on God's 'self-existence' or aseity, for again in this description of God we are saying something *sui generis* about the Christian God. God can be described as the 'self-contained ontological Trinity': 'God is in no sense correlative to or dependent upon anything besides his own being. God is the source of his own being, or rather the term *source* cannot be applied to God. God is *absolute*. He is sufficient unto himself.'[14] From this Van Til connects and extrapolates a number of other descriptions and characteristics of God, all of which are key building blocks in a Reformed Christian worldview.

First, the connection between aseity and triunity, for God's triunity is not derived from or dependent upon a historical creation: 'Rather, he has his own unity and plurality, which is distinct from the unity and plurality of the universe'.[15] As Frame explains, a conception of God as 'abstract oneness' is necessarily dependent on or correlative to the world:

> Now orthodox Trinitarianism renounces such correlativism. On the orthodox view, God's unity is correlative only to himself, to the complexities and pluralities of his own being. The world also is a unity and a diversity, because God made it that way.
>
> Consider love, as an attribute of God. If God is a mere unity without Trinity, then what is the object of God's eternal love? Himself? But love in the fullest biblical sense by its very nature reaches out to another, not merely to the self. The world? Then God's eternal attribute of love depends on the world; it needs the world. On a Trinitarian basis, however, God's love is both interpersonal and self-contained: God's love is the love among Father, Son, and Spirit for one another and it is not dependent on the world . . . The Trinity guards aseity, for without it, God is relative to the world. The Trinity also guards the personality of God: he is not a blank unity, which would be impersonal. Rather, he is unity of persons.[16]

---

Thomas Nelson, 1998), p. 158. I have already mentioned in this study that I am defining the term 'religion' in terms of belief in something or someone *a se*.

14. Cornelius Van Til, *The Defense of the Faith*, ed. K. Scott Oliphint, 4th ed. (Phillipsburg: P & R, 2008), p. 9.

15. John M. Frame, 'Divine Aseity and Apologetics', in K. Scott Oliphint and Lane G. Tipton (eds.), *Reason and Revelation: New Essays in Reformed Apologetics* (Phillipsburg: P & R, 2007), pp. 115–130.

16. John M. Frame, *Cornelius Van Til: An Analysis of His Thought* (Phillipsburg: P & R, 1995), p. 65. Elsewhere Frame notes the difficulties if God is not triune: 'Since God is both three and one, he can be described in personalistic terms without being made relative to the world. For example God is love (1 John 4:8). Love of what? If we immediately answer "love of the world", then we have a problem. For on that

Secondly, the notion of God's unity:

Theologians traditionally distinguish God's unity of singularity (there is only one God) from his unity of simplicity (that he is not made up of parts or aspects that are intelligible in themselves, apart from the divine being as a whole) . . . If there is only one God, then there is nothing 'in' him that is independent of him. God's goodness, for example, is not something in his mind to which he brings himself into conformity. If it were, that goodness, an abstract quality, would be a second deity coordinate with God himself. Thus, denial of God's unity of simplicity violates God's unity of singularity.[17]

God's simplicity complements what I stated regarding God's personal nature in that God is not subject or subordinate to impersonal principles outside himself; he *is* goodness, holiness, righteousness, and so on.

Thirdly, God's aseity implies his sovereignty:

It is edifying to observe that only a personal God can be sovereign and only a sovereign God can be an absolute person. That is to say, only a personal being can make choices and carry them out, and only a sovereign God can avoid being subject, ultimately, to impersonal principles.[18]

Finally, the connection between aseity and creation *ex nihilo*:

If God is fully self-contained then there was no sort of half-existence and no sort of non-being that had any power over against him. There was therefore no impersonal law of logic that told God what he could do, and there was no sort of stuff that had as much even as refractory power over against God when he decided to create the world.[19]

---

account the divine attributes of love depend on the existence of the world. And to say that God's attributes depend on the world is to say that God himself depends on the world. This is the route to the "wholly revealed". Should we say then, that "love" is merely a metaphor for something mysterious? That is the route to the "wholly other" . . . But he is not mere one. He is one in three. His love is initially the love of the Father, Son and Spirit for one another (John 17). His love, therefore, like his being is self-existent and self-sufficient. It does not depend on the world (though it surely fills the world), and it need not be swallowed up in religious agnosticism' (Frame, *Apologetics*, p. 49).

17. Frame, *Cornelius Van Til*, p. 56.
18. Ibid., p. 60.
19. Van Til, *Defense of the Faith*, p. 247.

Such metaphysic, which links divine aseity to sovereignty and creation *ex nihilo*, would seem to be in direct opposition to those non-Christian worldviews,[20] together with certain Christian interpretations of a passage such as Genesis 1:2,[21] that posit some kind of *chaoskampf* – that is, a primordial chaos out of which creation is refashioned and shaped.[22] There are elements of dualism here that entail not only a denial of a creation *ex nihilo*, but also a denial of God's sovereignty and his aseity.

Looking forward, we can say that concerning who the triune God is (in terms of metaphysics), what the triune God says (in terms of epistemology and revelation) and what the triune God does (in terms of his sovereignty over both creation and redemption), there is no one like him. Christians are not defending bare theism, impersonal Being or non-absolute personal beings. *The* God *is* the living God of the Bible, the self-revealing, self-contained ontological Trinity. There is no ultimate reality or chaos that can claim divine aseity behind this God. It is this God, or no god. As we shall see in due course, there is either the worship of the Christian God, or the worship of idols that are nothing at all.

### b. 'Let us make mankind in our image, in our likeness . . .': the dependent creation

The first thing to note about God's dependent and good creation is that it constantly reveals its Creator (Rom. 1:20; Ps. 19:1–2), not merely in terms of bare information *about* God, but relational I–Thou knowledge, as God is a personal God.[23] While there may be disagreement as to both the precise objective content

---

20. E.g. as found in Hesiod, Ovid and the *Enuma Elish*.

21. 'Now the earth was formless and empty'.

22. E.g. Alistair McKitterick, 'The Language of Genesis', in Norman C. Nevin (ed.), *Should Christians Embrace Evolution? Biblical and Scientific Responses* (Nottingham: Inter-Varsity Press, 2009), pp. 27–42, observes that Walter Brueggemann affirms a version of *chaoskampf* in his affirmation of a personified *Nihil*. Brueggemann writes, 'That is, in the sovereign act of creation, whereby Yahweh orders chaos, Yahweh provisionally defeated the power of Nihil but did not destroy or eliminate the threat of chaos . . . Thus is posed a primordial dualism in which Yahweh has the upper hand but is not fully in control, and so from time to time creation is threatened' (Walter Brueggemann, *Theology of the Old Testament* [Minneapolis: Fortress, 1997], p. 153).

23. Once again, seeing the systematic connections, Van Til links this to God's sovereignty: 'This God naturally has an all-comprehensive plan for the created universe. He has planned all the relationships between all the aspects of created being. He has planned the end from the beginning. All created reality therefore

and also the subjective appropriation of such natural revelation (particularly after the fall), there is unanimity over its existence. One aspect of God's revelation in nature that I shall return to a little later on concerns the sufficiency of this revelation even before the fall. While I need to be careful with my terms here, it seems that accompanying, complementing and yet supplementing God's revelation of himself in nature is his 'positive' and 'supernatural' revelation of himself through direct theophanic communication.[24] Vos calls this 'pre-redemptive special revelation'.[25] Even in Eden God's 'words' are needed to understand and interpret God's 'works'.

The apex of God's creation is men and women created uniquely in God's image and likeness, 'the head and crown of the whole creation . . . both *mikrotheos* (microgod) and *microkosmos* (microcosm)'.[26] Here, once again, the Reformed tradition evidences a long history of discussion and a rich diversity of explanation, with a number of qualifying distinctions made, which seek not only to explain the precise meaning of these terms but to indicate continuity and discontinuity of 'image' and 'likeness' in pre- and post-lapsarian states. Three useful sets of distinctions are particularly well known within the tradition: that (1) between structural and functional aspects of the image; (2) between a broader ontological concept of the image, retained after the fall, and a narrower ethical

---

actually displays his plan. It is, in consequence, inherently rational' (quoted in Frame, *Cornelius Van Til*, p. 117). James Jordan does an interesting thought experiment here on the receptivity of this revelation: 'Suppose the only composer who ever lived was Johann Sebastian Bach. There is no music in this world except that of Bach. Whenever we hear music in this world, it sounds like Bach's music. It may be played well or played badly but the fundamental raw material is always Bach, only Bach, nothing but Bach. Now, since there is no other music to compare this music to, would we be able to "hear" Bach's personality in the music? Or would it be easy for us to forget about Bach, and assume that "music simply *is*"? The problem with hearing or detecting God's authorship of the world is just like this. There is no other world to compare God's world to. There is no "music" except God's. It can be played well or perversely, but there are no other raw materials at hand. God's personality is fully displayed in the world, but it is easy for us to become deaf to this fact. The Bible tells us that this deafness and blindess is sin' (James B. Jordan, *Through New Eyes: Developing a Biblical Worldview* [Brentwood, Tenn.: Wolgemuth & Hyatt, 1988], p. 21).

24. Also through prophecy and miracle.

25. Vos, *Biblical Theology*, p. 22.

26. H. Bavinck, *Reformed Dogmatics*, vol. 2, p. 531.

concept, lost at the fall; and (3) between the image as resembling the Creator, and the image as representing the Creator. For my purposes I wish to concentrate on the universal 'religious' nature of the image. The following interrelated characteristics are to be noted.

### i. The revelational
First, the *revelational* aspect of the image. Being created in the image of God means we are metaphysically 'analogues' of God: we are a revelation of him.[27]

Added to this, and still remembering the Creator–creature distinction, is the notion that the 'whole' person is the image of God: 'We reflect everything in God, and everything in us reflects God in some way'.[28]

### ii. The relational
Secondly, the *relational* aspect of the image. Bypassing usual ways of categorizing the *imago* with either essentialist or functionalist definitions, Lints argues that the triune relational identity of God is reflected in the creation of 'persons in relation', a move away from 'an ontology of human personhood as objects (substances) and toward a relational ontology of human personhood'.[29] While Genesis 1 and 2 indicate the existence of horizontal human–human relationships and

---

27. As Van Til states, 'By the idea of revelation, then, we are to mean not merely what comes to man through the facts surrounding him in his environment, but also that which comes to him by means of his own constitution as a covenant personality. The revelation that comes to man by way of his own rational and moral nature is no less objective to him than that which comes to him through the voice of trees and animals. Man's own psychological activity is no less revelational than the laws of physics about him. All created reality is inherently revelational of the nature and will of God' (Cornelius Van Til, *Christian Apologetics*, ed. William Edgar, 2nd ed. [Phillipsburg: P & R, 2003], p. 73).

28. John M. Frame, *Salvation Belongs to the Lord: An Introduction to Systematic Theology* (Phillipsburg: P & R, 2006), p. 88. As Naugle notes, 'As the image and likeness of God, people are animated subjectively from the core and throughout their being by that primary faculty of thought, affection and will which the Bible calls the "heart". As Gordon Spykman states, "the imago Dei embraces our entire selfhood in all its variegated functions, centred and unified in the heart"' (Naugle, *Worldview*, p. 267).

29. Richard Lints, 'Imaging and Idolatry: The Sociality of Personhood in the Canon', in Richard Lints, Michael S. Horton and Mark R. Talbot (eds.), *Personal Identity in Theological Perspective* (Grand Rapids: Eerdmans, 2006), pp. 204–225.

human–creation relationships (both captured in the 'cultural mandate'),[30] it is the vertical divine–human relationship that is most basic. As Hoekema notes:

> Man is a creature who owes his existence to God, is completely dependent upon God, and is primarily responsible to God. This is his or her first and most important relationship. All of man's other relationships are to be seen as dominated and regulated by this one.[31]

Such a construal is in keeping with the Creator–creature distinction, for transitory relational 'images' depend upon the permanence of independent 'originals'. Lints's proposal gives us, at this early stage, another insight into the trajectory of the argument to come:

> The argument or proposal to follow is that the substance of the reflection is the nature of the relation and the ground of the relation is the character of the reflection. This would further suggest that bare notions of sociality will not sufficiently ground personhood in the canonical soil. . . . The image stands in a peculiar relationship to a God who speaks and acts in peculiar ways. And it is those 'peculiar ways' that serve as a thread that holds the canon together and that thereby hold human identity together. *This proposal also claims that the perversion of this peculiar way is the very underside of the canonical witness regarding the imago Dei, namely that of idolatry. Idolatry is the conceptual 'turning upside down' of the originally intended relationship of image to origin.*[32]

In the light of the above point, is it possible to unpack the nature of this divine–human relationality in a little more detail? What precisely is the 'peculiarity' of this relationship? Here I want to focus on the recent work of Horton and

---

30. To 'fill the earth and subdue it' (Gen. 1:28), and 'to tend and keep' the garden (2:15).
31. Anthony A. Hoekema, *Created in God's Image* (Grand Rapids: Eerdmans, 1986), p. 75. Lints continues on the 'primacy' of this relationship: 'What is distinctive about a Christian anthropology is precisely the affirmation that it is a peculiar relation which in the end more clearly and adequately explains human personality – namely, the relation to the God who is in some ontologically prior sense, personal. It is this distinctive and particular relationship which most nearly captures the identity of human personhood. It is also appropriate to say, Christianly speaking, that relationship to God is not only that which gives identity to us as humans, but also that which constitutes our humanity. Our existing as personas is rooted in our relation to God' (Lints, 'Imaging and Idolatry', p. 208).
32. Lints, 'Imaging and Idolatry', p. 210 (my italics).

Niehaus. In his treatment of the *imago Dei* Horton organizes his material around the concepts of covenant and eschatology, distinguishing between the prerequisite characteristics for human image-bearing and the *imago* properly considered. The former are natural capacities 'uniquely suited among the creation to be covenant partners with God',[33] but cannot be identified as the *imago* proper: 'Rather, the image is to be understood in this account as an office or embassy, a covenantal commission with an eschatological orientation'.[34] While other gracious divine–human covenants are instituted after the fall, this 'creational' covenant remains in perpetuity, albeit in a distorted and perverted form:

> Thus, even after the fall, human existence remains intrinsically covenantal, even though divided between Cain's proud city (Gen. 4:17–24) and the City of God represented by Seth, whose descendants are distinguished by their invocation of the Great King for their salvation, 'At that time, people began to invoke the name of the Lord' (v. 26). Those who do not acknowledge God or embrace his covenant of grace are nevertheless included 'in Adam' under the original covenant. Intrinsic to humanness, particularly the *imago*, is a covenantal office or commission into which everyone is born; it is, therefore, as an equally universal phenomenon, the basis for God's righteous judgement of humankind, even apart from special revelation (Rom. 1&2). This is to say that 'law' – in particular, the divine covenant law – is natural, a *verbum internum* identified with the conscience. Hardwired for obedience, human beings fell from this state of rectitude through no ontological weakness (such as finitude or concupiscence) but through an inexplicable rejection of the reign of God.[35]

> The covenant of creation provides the basis for the unity of the human race and even after the fall the features of this original human creatureliness are not in any way altered but are employed in ways that are ethically subversive of their original intention.[36]

For those aware of the history of the Reformed tradition, talk of a 'creational covenant'[37] opens up a much discussed and disputed area, which has produced a fair amount of theological bloodletting. Fortunately for my thesis I do not

---

33. Michael S. Horton, 'Image and Office: Human Personhood and the Covenant', in Lints, Horton and Talbot, *Personal Identity in Theological Perspective*, pp. 178–203.
34. Ibid.
35. Ibid., p. 181.
36. Ibid., p. 200.
37. Otherwise known as a covenant of works or covenant of nature or law.

believe we have to become entangled in this very complex systematic theological web. However, there is one 'take' on this debate that is worth noting given the focus of this study. The Old Testament scholar Jeffrey Niehaus has argued against 'theologically constructed covenants', believing them to be foreign to the ancient Near Eastern context of the Bible and believing 'they import an alien construct into the discussion and use it as a hermeneutical key'.[38] Such a proposal does not 'do away' with the notion of 'covenant' in Reformed theology; rather, the concept is greatly strengthened being seen to be against naturalistic 'evolutionary models' in Old Testament studies, which 'are used to portray supposed (but unreal) relations between people and their gods'.[39] Niehaus argues that the covenant idea originates in the mind of God himself and is first evidenced in Genesis 1 and 2. Here we are back to relational definitions of the *imago Dei*. First, he notes that, as created beings in the image of God, all human beings are in God's family (Acts 17:28). Using the work of Gruenler and Kline, Niehaus notes that 'the social nature of the human family images the social nature of the triune God, and that is part of being in God's image'.[40] What is more, just as Adam was the 'son of God', so those 'in Adam' 'also share his family sonship to God, as Paul declares in Acts 17:28 . . . although only in a common grace way'.[41] Secondly, having established this familial basis, Niehaus attempts to demonstrate that this relationship is construed 'covenantally' in an Adamic covenant that has all the usual features of an ancient Near Eastern covenant. His point is that all these later examples of ancient Near Eastern divine–human covenants are derived from this Adamic covenant. Here it is worth quoting him at length:

> It should be clear that Gen. 1:1–2:3 (and 2:17) and other data (e.g. Ps. 47:2, Mal. 1:14) display the following facts about God: he is the Creator and Great King over all in heaven and earth; he has provided good things in abundance for those he created; he made the man and woman royalty ('subdue,' 'rule over') and gave them commands; he blessed them; and he pronounced a curse on them should they disobey his commands. These facts are the essence of covenant: a Great King in authority over lesser rulers, with a historical background in doing good to them, with commands and

---

38. Jeffrey J. Niehaus, 'An Argument Against Theologically Constructed Covenants', *JETS* 50.2 (2007), pp. 259–273 (273).

39. Jeffrey J. Niehaus, 'Covenant: An Idea in the Mind of God', *JETS* 52.2 (2009), pp. 225–246 (227–228).

40. Ibid., p. 229.

41. Ibid. For more on 'common grace' see below.

with blessings, but also a curse in case of disobedience. These facts about the Genesis creation material are the stuff of covenant, and primordially so. Some may not want to say that they constitute a covenant, but the creation data do tell us just what, later in history, would form the constituent elements of a suzerain–vassal treaty in the ancient Near East, and of a divine–human covenant in the Bible. Such things are expressions of God's nature, as that nature comes to us through the creation data. We know the workman by his works (cf. Rom. 1:19–20). God, then, from the beginning showed a nature that could be called covenantal, and he entered into relationships that could appropriately be called the same.

That understanding about the nature of deity was passed on through the generations. Human beings made in God's image were constituted for such relationships themselves, and entered into them in both family and, later, national forms. The late second millennium BC international treaty form was produced by humans as a legal articulation of the sorts of commitments that a covenant relationship should involve. That legal form arose out of a human nature made for such relationships, and that human nature was made in the image of God who was and is also supremely relational (or more particularly one might say covenantal). In his good time, God employed that historical/legal form as he acted in history and as his Spirit breathed forth Scripture (2 Tim. 3:16). Its elements appeared in narratives that reported divine–human covenants. But the original, archetypal covenant idea was part of God's very, relational nature, or, as we have said in the title of this article, an idea in the mind of God.[42]

*iii. The representational*
Thirdly, the *representational* nature of the image. I have already mentioned the 'cultural mandate' of Genesis 1:28 and 2:15, where Adam is told to 'fill' and 'subdue', and 'work' and 'take care' of his environment. As Leithart notes:

> God has revealed Himself as a Speaker and a Maker, and thus the immediate significance of being made in His 'image' is that Adam and Eve were created to speak and make . . . to be the image of God is to be a creative speaker and producer of 'cultural products . . .'[43]

Immediately, we see this mandate followed, as Adam, the son of God, founds both science and the arts in his classification of the animals (2:20) and in his 'poem' on the creation of Eve (2:23). What is to be noted here is that Adam and

---

42. Ibid., p. 233.

43. Peter Leithart, *Heroes of the City of Man* (Moscow, Idaho: Canon, 1999), p. 30.

Eve's vicegerency and dominion are still to be under God's authority, according to his norms and for his glory.[44]

But what has this to do with 'religion' and the 'religions'? The point to be made here, and one I shall elaborate on further, is that the 'relational' nature of the image in all three directions (divine–human, human–human and human–creation), while ethically and functionally distorted and marred at the fall (i.e. we do not create culture under God's norms or for his glory), remains structurally intact. Simply as being human we still image God in our speaking and making. We are still 'prophets', 'priests' and 'kings', although we may be subject(ed) to other lords and other gods. Two relevant implications of our representational nature can be drawn out here.

First, the opportunity at this early stage to demonstrate the inextricable links between 'culture', 'worldview' and 'religion'. These terms are notoriously difficult to define, both anthropologically and theologically. Indeed, some even question not only their continuing usefulness[45] but even their existence.[46] While

---

44. Both Frame and Van Til describe this with their own distinctive vocabulary. Frame writes, 'As vassal lord, Adam is to extend God's *control* over the world ("subdue" in Genesis 1:28). He has the right to name the animals, an exercise of *authority* in ancient thinking (Genesis 2:19ff; cf. 2:23; 3:20), where he also names his wife! And he is to "fill" the earth with his *presence*' (John M. Frame, 'Men and Women in the Image of God', in John Piper and Wayne Grudem [eds.], *Biblical Manhood and Womanhood: A Response to Evangelical Feminism* [Wheaton: Crossway, 1991], p. 233 [his italics]). And Van Til: 'Next to noting that man was created in God's image it must be observed that man was organically related to the universe about him. Man was to be prophet, priest and king under God in this created world. The vicissitudes of the world would to a large extent depend upon the deeds of man. As a prophet, man was to interpret this world after God, as a priest he was to dedicate this world to God, and as a king he was to rule over it for God' (Van Til, *Christian Apologetics*, p. 41).

45. E.g. James K. A. Smith argues that the use of 'worldview' as a concept overintellectualizes what orients us in the world as human beings, underplaying desires and imagination formed by 'ritual', which are far more unconscious and unreflective (James K. A. Smith, *Desiring the Kingdom: Worship, Worldview and Cultural Formation* [Grand Rapids: Baker Academic, 2009]).

46. E.g. Mario I. Aguilar, 'Changing Models and the "Death" of Culture: A Diachronic and Positive Critique of Socio-scientific Assumptions', in M. I. Aguilar and L. J. Lawrence (eds.), *Anthropology and Biblical Studies: Avenues of Approach* (Leiden: Deo, 2004), pp. 299–313.

each of these terms needs to be very carefully defined[47] to avoid misunderstanding, I believe all three terms are useful and are inextricably related to one another. As a starting proposal, I wish to argue that culture is worldview exteriorized, and worldview is culture interiorized, and both stem from the religion of the human heart. In other words, the specific contours of the products we use to 'make a home for ourselves' come from our understanding of the world, our *Weltanschauung*, and, as carriers of worldview, these cultural products (or 'texts') contour our consciousness along the lines of the worldviews they carry. Kevin Vanhoozer relates these two concepts by calling culture a '*lived* worldview'.[48] Cultures are dynamic shared worlds of meaning that communicate, orientate, reproduce and cultivate.[49] To bring in my third element of 'religion', as I have already indicated, these more 'horizontal' relationships and activities of culture and worldview are shaped by our 'vertical' relationship: that which we as human beings believe to be most basic, most ultimate, *a se*. We can define this commitment as one's 'religion', and our culture-making as 'religious', definitions that are able to include both essentialist and functionalist aspects. Religion defined as our covenantal heart relationship between God and man is at the centre of both culture and worldview. Frame makes this connection:

> Culture is both what society is and what it ought to be, both real and ideal. Culture is what a society has made of God's creation, together with its ideals of what it ought to make. Or maybe we should put the ideal first. People make things, because they already have a plan in view, a purpose, a goal, an ideal. The ideal comes first, then making things. First the norm, then the cultivation, the culture.
>
> So now we can see how culture is related to religion. When we talk of values and ideals, we are talking religion. In the broad sense a person's religion is what grips his heart most strongly, what motivates him most deeply. It is the value which transcends

---

47. For a detailed anthropological treatment of worldview as it impacts the field of missiology see Paul G. Hiebert, *Transforming Worldviews: An Anthropological Understanding of How People Change* (Grand Rapids: Baker, 2008). For a defence of 'worldview' as a concept see Michael W. Goheen and Craig G. Bartholomew, *Living at the Crossroads: An Introduction to Christian Worldview* (Grand Rapids: Baker Academic, 2008), pp. 11–30. In terms of 'culture' see Kevin J. Vanhoozer, 'What Is Everyday Theology? How and Why Christians Should Read Culture', in Kevin J. Vanhoozer, Charles A. Anderson and Michael J. Sleasman (eds.), *Everyday Theology: How to Read Cultural Texts and Interpret Trends* (Grand Rapids: Baker, 2007), pp. 15–60.

48. Vanhoozer, 'What Is Everyday Theology?', p. 26 (his italics).

49. Ibid., pp. 27–32.

all other values. . . . It is interesting that the Latin term *colere* . . . also refers to religious service, and comes into English as *cult, cultic* and so in. Culture and cult go together. If a society worships idols, false gods, that worship will govern the culture of that society. If a society worships the true God, that worship will deeply influence, even pervade, its culture. If, like ours, a society is religiously divided, then it will reveal a mixture of religious influences.[50]

It is important to note that while individuals qua individuals are in the *imago Dei*, and while every individual has a 'worldview' and 'relationship' with God, there is a *social* aspect of the image: 'It is not good for the man to be alone' (Gen. 2:18). If culture refers to 'shared meaning' in a society, then those with similar 'fundamental orientations' will build similar culture together. This means that generalizations and systematizations concerning worldviews, cultures and religions are not illegitimate tasks and have some useful functions. However, as J. H. Bavinck warns in his interaction with those of other faiths, 'each generalization, every systematization, carries within itself the danger that one will do injustice to the living person. I am never concerned with Buddhism, but with a living person and *his* Buddhism.'[51] Bavinck himself believes we need both a 'scientific awareness' and a 'living approach'.[52] In other words, to bear in mind anthropologically a 'human constancy', 'religion variability' and 'person variability'.[53]

Secondly, we note the creaturely *limitations* on our representational speaking and making that reveal the triune Creator, and once again evidence a structural similarity in God's image bearers. In what might be called his sketch of a 'theology of literature', Leithart, in the tradition of Frye and Lewis, reflects on archetypal literary patterns found throughout the history of literature. His contention is that the biblical story is 'mysteriously built into the structure of our minds and practices'.[54] Theologically, he justifies this claim first with a discussion on the limitations of human creativity. Although there is a sense in which we image God's inexhaustible creativity, our creativity is still that of a creature, which implies a dependence upon the Creator, meaning our creations are never abso-

---

50. John M. Frame, *The Doctrine of the Christian Life* (Phillipsburg: P & R, 2008), p. 857.

51. J. H. Bavinck, *An Introduction to the Science of Missions*, tr. David H. Freeman (Phillipsburg: P & R, 1960), p. 240.

52. Ibid., p. 241.

53. Or, to put it yet another way, we need to bear in mind both synchronic and diachronic perspectives on worldview and culture.

54. Leithart, *Heroes*, pp. 29–30.

lutely free. For Leithart, 'this helps to explain why storytellers from the beginning of time seem continually to be repeating the same stories, though repeating them differently'.[55]

At this point let me summarize. All human beings are created in the *imago Dei*, and 'sons of God' are created as 'religious' beings, revealing God, representing him, and built for relationship with him, with each other and with the rest of creation. This 'religious' nature, *sensus divinitatis* or *semen religionis*,[56] is not merely the capacity we have for relating to, worshipping, obeying or disobeying something or someone we consider ultimate, what we might call a *generic religiosity*,[57] but is rather a *particular religiosity*: our relationship, worship and obedience or disobedience to the self-contained ontological Trinity, *the* living God of the Bible. All humanity by virtue of being in the image of God is already and always in a covenantal relationship with this God:

> A man without 'religion' is a contradiction in itself. In his 'religion' man gives account of his relation to God. His religion is reaction upon the (real or pretended) revelation of God. Man is 'incurably religious' because his relation to God belongs to the very essence of man himself. Man is only man as man-before-God.[58]

The perpetuity of the image means the perpetuity of this kept or broken covenantal relationship. Even though I am about to describe the drastic nature of the fall, which brings great epistemological and ethical disruption and discontinuity, metaphysically and structurally the *imago Dei* remains intact, still

---

55. Ibid.

56. To use Calvin's terms.

57. See the quotation that opened this chapter, '"Homo sapiens," "homo faber," . . . yes, but, first of all "homo adorans"' (Schmemann, *For the Life*, p. 15, quoted in Naugle, *Worldview*, p. 275).

58. Johannes Blauw, 'The Biblical View of Man in His Religion', in Gerald H. Anderson (ed.), *The Theology of the Christian Mission* (London: SCM, 1961), pp. 31–41. Bahnsen too is helpful here: 'Man cannot cease being man, and to be a man is to be made in God's image. Man is the finite replica of God, being like him in every respect that is appropriate for the creature to resemble his Creator. Hereby no man can escape the face of God, for God's image is carried along with man wherever he goes – even into Hades. . . . Creation established forever that no man is beyond the touch of God's revelation; men have been created with the capacity to understand and recognize their Maker's voice' (Bahnsen, *Always Ready*, p. 47).

revealing God, and still evidencing a degree of continuity across all of human life and culture, including, of course, what we classify as formal 'religion'.[59]

## 2. The fall: de-creation and 'false faith'

Therefore since we are God's offspring, we should not think that the divine being is like gold or silver or stone – an image made by human design and skill.
(Acts 17:29)

---

59. It is worth noting that in the intra-evangelical debates concerning theistic evolution and creationism, and particularly the issue of a historical Adam, there are those such as Denis Alexander, *Creation or Evolution: Do We Have to Choose?* (Oxford: Monarch, 2008), who, in defending theistic evolution, wish to distinguish between universal man made in the image of God and a specific later time when, from the existing human population, God revealed himself for the first time to Adam and Eve, thereby humankind *only then* becoming *Homo divinus*. In his critique of Alexander, Michael Reeves notes the 'religious' implications of such a position, which he deems as deeply problematic. He writes, 'If, as Alexander maintains, being in the image of God is about having a personal relationship with God, then all those humans in God's image who had not received the revelation of what that meant must have been sinning. Created in God's image, to relate to God, they were not relating to God. In fact, though he does not use the word, the picture Alexander paints is one of humanity immersed in idolatry, for, he says, "religious beliefs existed before this time [of Adam and Eve], as people sought after God or gods in different parts of the world, offering their own explanations for the meaning of their lives." Thus the model has sin before the fall' (Michael Reeves, 'Adam and Eve', in Norman C. Nevin [ed.], *Should Christians Embrace Evolution? Biblical and Scientific Responses* [Nottingham: Inter-Varsity Press, 2009], pp. 43–56 [48]). For Reeves, if Alexander ignores this idolatrous worship, then this clashes with passages such as Rom. 1:18–32 and creates difficulties in explaining Adam's sinfulness before his fall, or alternatively difficulties in arguing for his temporary sinlessness. Reeves's conclusion has echoes with the point I made earlier regarding the doctrine of creation *ex nihilo*: 'The fact that God creates the opportunity for sin long before creating any opportunity to know him reflects what is perhaps most troubling about this synthesis, that there is a God somehow constrained to work in a less-than-ideal situation. Indeed, throughout the proposal, one gets the sense that God is having to work by someone else's rules, as if in someone else's universe' (ibid., p. 49).

To repeat, what I am trying to do in this section is to lay down the contours of a Reformed worldview, within which to interpret non-Christian religions. Using Genesis 1 – 11 I am plotting a creation–fall–redemption narrative seen in these chapters in embryonic form and expounded throughout the rest of the biblical revelation. As with the doctrine of creation, we come to the doctrine of the fall and its consequences 'perspectivally challenged' given the number of ways both Scripture and the Reformed tradition have chosen to describe this event. I wish to focus on the nature of sin generally in terms of the first sin in particular, 'from which the others flow as from a fountain'.[60] In continuity with what I have already said regarding the fundamental Creator–creature distinction established in Genesis 1, and looking ahead to what I am going to say regarding non-Christian religions and idolatry, I wish to analyse the fall in terms of a reversal of creation, and an act of 'false faith'. Ovey's analysis here is especially insightful and will be drawn upon.[61]

I have argued that a key metaphysical building block in a Reformed Christian doctrine of creation is the Creator–creature distinction: the triune God is self-contained and *a se*, and human beings are dependent upon the Creator both metaphysically and epistemologically. The archetypal sin of Adam and Eve in the garden, in which we are all federally included, and of which subsequent sins are repeated instantiations, involves a blurring of this Creator–creature distinction, a de-creation, whereby we pull God down to the level of the creature and push ourselves up to the level of Creator. Let us explore this in more detail.

In the act of creation itself Genesis 1 – 2 unveils to us certain characteristics of both Creator and creation. First, the lordship, sovereignty and benevolence of the Creator are revealed. God's word, 'it was so', is seen not only to be utterly effective but also truthful, 'in that it corresponds to reality, or more accurately reality corresponds to it'.[62] This effective and truthful word is also ethically 'good' and 'very good': God is a God who blesses his good creation. What is more, God not only has the might to create like this; he has the right: 'He rules because he made all. The relationship between making and ruling is sometimes explained in terms of ownership.'[63] Secondly, we see a God-ordained

60. Francis Turretin, *Institutes of Elenctic Theology*, ed. James T. Dennison Jr., tr. George Musgrave Giger, 3 vols. (Phillipsburg: P & R, 1992), vol. 1, p. 604.

61. Michael Ovey, 'The Cross, Creation and the Human Predicament', in David Peterson (ed.), *Where Wrath and Mercy Meet: Proclaiming the Atonement Today* (Carlisle: Paternoster, 2001), pp. 100–135.

62. Ibid., p. 107.

63. Ibid.

hierarchy established within the creation itself: God as Lord has authority over his vicegerent, Adam, helped by the 'flesh of his flesh', Eve, who are given dominion over the animals.

Starting with the creational pattern, we see a de-creational reversal in Genesis 3: first 'the snake invites the woman to accept him as her guide and familiar, and, under his influence, to dismiss the authority of God'.[64] A little later there is further disruption between Adam and Eve: 'The woman takes the initiative and offers "her husband" the fruit. By accepting, he completes the inverted chain of influence: snake, woman, man, God.'[65]

However, de-creation is also evidenced in the serpent's strategy to 'question' the characteristics of both the creature and the Creator himself. Ovey quotes Calvin at this point:

> Yet it is at the same time to be noted that the first man revolted from God's authority, not only because of Satan's blandishments, but also because, contemptuous of truth, he turned aside to falsehood. And surely, once we hold God's word in contempt, we shake off all reverence for him. For unless we listen attentively to him, his majesty will not dwell among us, nor his worship remain perfect. Unfaithfulness, then, was at the root of the Fall . . . Yet it was not simple apostasy, but was joined with vile reproaches against God. These assented to Satan's slanders, which accused God of falsehood and envy and ill will. Lastly faithfulness opened the door to ambition, and ambition was indeed the mother of obstinate disobedience; as a result, men having cast off the fear of God, threw themselves wherever lust carried them.[66]

The creational hierarchy of relationships is disrupted as the creature 'shakes off all reverence' for the Creator. The 'craftiness' of the serpent is very much in evidence here. First, he entices Eve and Adam to believe wrong things about themselves. As C. J. H. Wright notes:

> The strategy of the serpent was not so much to draw us into conscious, deliberate rebellion against God by implanting alien desires, but rather to corrupt and pervert

---

64. Jerome T. Walsh, 'Genesis 2:4b–3:24: A Synchronic Approach', *JBL* 96.2 (1977), pp. 161–177 (176).

65. Ibid., p. 176.

66. Ovey, 'Cross, Creation', p. 109 (quote from John Calvin, *Institutes of the Christian Religion*, ed. John T. McNeill, tr. Ford Lewis Battles, 2 vols., LCC [Philadelphia: Westminster, 1960], 2.1.4).

through doubt and disobedience a desire that was legitimate in itself. After all, what is more natural than for man to wish to be like God. Is it not the proper function and ambition of the image of God to be like the one who created him in his own image? The Satanic desire lay in the desire to be *as* God, 'the temptation of man to bring God and himself to a common denominator'.[67]

Tragically but judicially appropriate, as we are reminded in Psalm 90, the punishment of death, as promised by God in Genesis 2:17, is a revelatory reminder of the 'transitoriness' and 'dependence' of the image: 'Death is God's limit on creatures whose sin is that they want to be gods (Gen. 3:4–5; Rom. 1:18–32).'[68]

Secondly, the serpent entices Eve and Adam into disbelieving the truths about God that Genesis 1 and 2 have clearly established and that Adam and Eve had witnessed experientially since their own creation. So God is portrayed as being *not* benevolent (for he is actuated by envy); his words are *neither* truthful *nor* effective ('you will not die'). Like Calvin, Ovey notes here that this belief dimension has two aspects, a 'disbelief' or denial of who God is, and also a belief in falsehood about him (the 'vile reproaches').[69] Here he mentions a small

---

67. C. J. H. Wright, 'The Christian and Other Religions: The Biblical Evidence', *Them* 9.2 (1984), pp. 4–15 (5; his italics). Blaauw speaks of the temptation being a '(willingly accepted) suggestion that this privilege of being created as man in communication with and dependent upon God is not man's *treasure* but his *deficiency*' (Blaauw, 'Biblical View', p. 33 [his italics]).

68. D. A. Carson, *How Long, O Lord? Reflections on Evil and Suffering*, 2nd ed. (Grand Rapids: Baker, 2006), p. 99. He continues, 'The true God is holy; he is unique, and cannot, by his very nature, tolerate those who try to relativize him. We are not gods; and by death we learn that we are only human. Our pretensions are destroyed. We are cut off, and all our yesterdays "are one with Nineveh and Tyre". At the same time, we cry out against this limitation, not only because in our rebellion we still want to become gods, but because we have been made in the image of God. We are not mere mammals. We are persons. If we really believed that we were nothing more than accidental collections of atoms, moral outrage over anything would be irrational. But we want to live, even while our hubris means we have been cut off from him who alone gives life. That we are mammals means that our death has a physical side; that we are not merely mammals means that our death is God's determination to limit our arrogance' (ibid.).

69. Ovey, 'Cross, Creation', p. 109.

but felicitous phrase by Turretin, who in his own account of the fall speaks about Adam as 'engendering a *false faith* from Satan's lies'.[70] Ovey comments here:

> What this highlights so strikingly is that the distinction is not simply between those who have true faith and those who have not. Rather it is between those who have true faith and those who have false faith. Further, the truth or falsehood of the faith turns not on whether the person who has faith is sincere or not, but on whether the belief that person holds is true to the reality of the person of whom he or she believes it.[71]

To have 'false faith' is to believe lies about God, lies that are both rationally and ethically unjustified, 'both because it treats God as bad when he is shown to be good, and because God is treated as not having legitimate sovereignty when the process of creation shows that he does have such sovereignty, as Adam well knows'.[72] The decision to follow the serpent's interpretation is a somewhat blind 'leap of faith'[73] given their previous experience of God's truthfulness, effectiveness and benevolence, evidenced even in the fact that God's prohibition was not bare command but a loving warning.[74]

A number of relevant implications can be drawn here, and will be drawn out subsequently. First, there is further confirmation regarding what we have already noted about the perpetuity of the *imago Dei* meaning the perpetuity of a personal relationship with the triune God of the Bible. Turretin's 'false faith' and Calvin's 'unfaithfulness' re-enforce the permanent accountability of creature before Creator, the creature being universal metaphysically (as being in the *imago Dei*), legally (as covenant breakers) and federally (being *in* Adam). Post-lapsarian humanity may have a terribly broken relationship with this God, but it is never a non-existent relationship with him. Ironically, as C. J. H. Wright points out, it is 'religion' that highlights the breakdown of relationship:

> If religion is 'man giving account of his relation to God', it will be in the religious dimension of human life that we would expect to find the clearest evidence of the radical fracture of that relationship. If the immediate response of the fallen Adam

---

70. Ibid., quoting Turretin, *Institutes of Elenctic Theology*, vol. 1, p. 605 (Ovey's italics).
71. Ovey, 'Cross, Creation', p. 109.
72. Ibid., p. 110.
73. On this, Ovey notes that sincerity is not the issue (ibid., p. 109).
74. Francis Schaeffer, *Genesis in Space and Time* (Downers Grove: InterVarsity Press, 1972), p. 73.

in us is to hide from the presence of the living God, what more effective way could there be than through religious activity which gives us the illusion of having met and satisfied him? 'Even his religiosity is a subtle escape from the God he is afraid and ashamed to meet.'[75]

Secondly, given that this supreme instance of 'unfaithfulness' is between the unique self-contained triune God of the Bible and Adam and Eve (God being the only object of 'false faith' here), we are able to classify this first human sin as an act of idolatry.[76] Idolatry includes both physical and mental creations. Crucially, its scope includes not only *displacements* of the triune God, but also *distortions* and *denials*:

> Such idolatrous lies falsify a person, obscuring and distorting who the person is. The lie
> destroys true relationship as humans stop relating to God as he knows himself
> to be, instead treating him as they have fashioned him. Idolatry strongly expresses
> human sovereignty, but sovereignty at the expense of true relationship.[77]

The consequences of inappropriately relating to God as he has revealed himself to be are severe, and are witnessed throughout the remainder of the biblical narrative.

Thirdly, we need formally to note the satanic involvement and deception in this narrative, an involvement I shall have to account for in my theology of religions. While not taking away from the responsibility and culpability of Adam and Eve in their idolatrous 'false faith',[78] it is to be remembered that prior to

---

75. C. J. H. Wright, 'Christian and Other Religions', p. 5. The quotation 'Even his religiosity is a subtle escape from the God he is afraid and ashamed to meet' is from John R. W. Stott, *Christian Mission in the Modern World* (London: Falcon, 1975), p. 69.

76. Indeed, idolatry can be described as *the* sin: 'The principal crime of the human race, the highest guilt charged upon the world, the whole procuring cause of judgement, is idolatry. For although each single fault retains its own proper feature . . . yet it is marked off under the general account of idolatry' (Tertullian, *On Idolatry* 1, in *Ante-Nicene Fathers*, vol. 3, tr. S. Thelwall, ed. Alexander Roberts and James Donaldson [Peabody: Hendrickson, 1999], p. 61).

77. Michael Ovey, 'Idolatry and Spiritual Parody: Counterfeit Faith', *Cambridge Papers* 11.1 (Mar. 2002).

78. John Murray makes the important point that Satan's temptation was the *occasion* of man's fall, not the *cause* (John Murray, *Collected Writings of John Murray*, 4 vols. [Edinburgh: Banner of Truth Trust, 1977], vol. 2, p. 68).

this first human fall on earth has been an angelic fall in heaven. Telling lies about God in the garden has been prompted by 'the father of lies' (John 8:44). If Isaiah 14:12–15 is referring to the fall of Satan, then we have a familiar motivation for these lies: the grasping for equality with God.[79]

Lastly, we witness in this narrative an early example of quite complex biblical relationships: that of divine, human and satanic agency; that of the 'unholy trinity' of the world, the flesh and the devil; and finally the metaphysical, epistemological and ethical. First, the question of religious authority and supposed religious autonomy lies at the heart of the fall. Prompted by Satan, Adam and Eve believed they could have self-determination *metaphysically* ('you will be like God'), *epistemologically* ('like God, knowing good and evil') and *ethically* ('she took and ate . . . her husband ate', Gen. 3:5).[80] However, what they believe to be epistemological autonomy is in reality epistemological slavery.

Also, it is to be remembered that while there may be epistemological delusion on the part of both humanity and Satan (believing that a creature can attain 'Creator-hood'), metaphysically the Creator–creature distinction remains intact: God remains God, and creation remains creation. Therefore it is a mistake to view God's power and authority and Satan's power and authority symmetrically or, rather, dualistically: 'There is no common measure between his infinite power – one of his names is Pantokrator, Master of all – and the devil's limited power, the fact that the devil can act only on God's sovereign permission (Job!) highlights this radical breach of symmetry'.[81] Both created humanity and created Satan pre-fall and post-fall continually 'live and move and have their being' in God.

---

79. As Francis Schaeffer states, 'Satan the liar, the originator of The Great Lie, in his heart (that is within himself, from himself outward) says, "I will be greater than the rest, and I will be equal with God." The story of Satan in Isaiah is paralleled almost exactly in Genesis in regard to man's revolt. Satan wants to be equal with God, but the end of this is that he will be brought down into the abyss. In Genesis 3 the woman would be equal with God, but she ends in death' (Schaeffer, *Genesis in Space and Time*, p. 79). The Puritan Ralph Venning notes that 'sin goes about to unGod God, and is by some of the ancients called *Deicidium*, God-murder or God-killing' (Ralph Venning, *Plague of Plagues* [Edinburgh: Banner of Truth Trust, 1965], p. 30).
80. Reymond, *New Systematic Theology*, p. 446.
81. Henri Blocher, 'Agnus Victor: The Atonement as Victory and Vicarious Punishment', in John Stackhouse (ed.), *What Does It Mean to Be Saved? Broadening Evangelical Horizons of Salvation* (Grand Rapids: Baker, 2002), pp. 67–91 (62).

## 3. The promise of redemption: antithesis and restraint

From one man he made all the nations, that they should inhabit the whole earth.
(Acts 17:26)

Having made some comments regarding the *nature* of the fall, and relating this event to 'religion' and 'religiosity', we come to our final stop in this tour of a Reformed Christian worldview by focusing in a similar manner on the *consequences* of the fall as seen in God's pronouncement to the serpent, and to Eve and Adam (Gen. 3:14–19). I am especially interested here in the ways in which the narrative illuminates a theological anthropology, for this will form the spine of my theology of religions. From a background of both divine curse and divine blessing I shall highlight two distinctively Reformed doctrines: the doctrine of the 'antithesis', with its stress on separation and discontinuity, and the doctrine of 'common grace', with its stress on unity and continuity.

### a. The pronouncement of salvation: the protoevangelium

As before, there are a variety of ways Reformed theologians have expounded the multiple effects of the fall. Murray speaks of a series of immediate 'revolutions': *internally*, in terms of man's attitude to God, *in God's relation to man*, in terms of 'anger, reproof, retribution, curse and condemnation';[82] *cosmically*, in that the fall has implications for physical creation; *familially*, in ensuing dysfunctional human relationships; and finally, the distintegration in man's own constitution – physical and spiritual death (the fulfilment of Gen. 2:17).[83] More systematically and creedally there are the doctrines of 'original sin', 'total depravity', 'total inability' and real guilt.[84] These doctrines, albeit in a variety of interpretations, are all hamartiological 'givens' within Reformed theology.

What is to be remembered in these verses in Genesis, however, is that the depth and universality of human sin as intimated in these divine punishments and 'curses' are symbiotically related to deep and universal promises of God's blessing and grace. As H. Bavinck notes:

---

82. Murray, *Collected Writings*, vol. 2, p. 71.

83. Ibid., pp. 70–72.

84. For some standard Reformed treatment of these doctrines see Hoekema, *Created in God's Image*, pp. 112–186; Michael S. Horton, *The Christian Faith: A Systematic Theology for Pilgrims on the Way* (Grand Rapids: Zondervan, 2011), pp. 408–443; H. Bavinck, *Reformed Dogmatics*, vol. 3, pp. 75–125.

In the punishment that God pronounced after the transgression of the serpent,
the woman and the man, we hear the voice of God's mercy more than that of his
wrath. It is both punishment and promise . . . In it, accordingly, lies the origin and
guarantee of continued existence, the expansion and development, the struggle and
victory of humankind as a whole. Religion and morality, cult and culture have their
beginnings there.[85]

The decision of Adam and Eve to side with the serpent's interpretation of reality
created a deep division between God on one side and Satan and the fallen human
race on the other: 'The creature warred against the creator; evil against goodness,
darkness against light'.[86] In the pronouncement to the serpent, which 'bursts
upon us like a rising sun dispelling darkness, gloom and misery',[87] God himself
announces that he will break this unholy creaturely alliance by pronouncing to
the serpent that 'enmity' will be inserted at three levels:

> And I will put enmity
> > between you and the woman,
> > and between your offspring and hers;
> he will crush your head,
> > and you will strike his heel.
> (Gen. 3:15)

These verses have been called the *protoevangelium*, for they are seen to predict
the coming of Christ, who will crush the serpent, although through suffering:

In principle, Genesis 3 contains the entire history of humankind, all the ways of God
for the salvation of the lost and the victory over sin. In substance the whole gospel, the
entire covenant of grace, is present here. All that follows is the development of what
has been germinally planted here.[88]

Concerning the *protoevangelium* the following should be noted. First, this enmity
is divinely initiated and, although set in the context of punishment (i.e. towards

---

85. H. Bavinck, *Reformed Dogmatics*, vol. 3, p. 216.
86. Henry Stob, 'Observations on the Concept of the Antithesis', in Peter De Klerk and
Richard R. De Ridder (eds.), *Perspectives on the Christian Reformed Church* (Grand
Rapids: Baker, 1983), pp. 241–258 (243).
87. Hoekema, *Created in God's Image*, p. 134.
88. H. Bavinck, *Reformed Dogmatics*, vol. 3, p. 200.

the serpent), is a gracious act towards humanity, which is unmerited given the nature and seriousness of the fall. Predictably, an understanding of spiritual victory as a divine and sovereign act of grace in contradistinction to an under-standing of spiritual victory through works righteousness is a key distinction we shall have to return to at a later point.

Secondly, the revelation and reception of this promise. Reformed scholars are divided as to the specificity of the *protoevangelium*, especially concerning whether the third 'level' of enmity refers to a single individual (i.e. Christ), and how much Adam and Eve knew of this. Without entering into that debate here, there do appear to be hints in the subsequent verses that this grace has been understood and received in some measure.[89]

Thirdly, the universality of the promise. Those familiar with the theology of religions may have assumed that in the much-discussed areas concerning the relationships between themes of universality and particularity, and between exclusivity and inclusivity, a position like mine would stress the particularity axiom over and against the universality axiom.[90] However, both axioms are present here and need to be emphasized. As H. Bavinck states:

> The universal idea of the revelation of salvation does not get its due, when, in the covenant of grace in time, we immediately proceed to Israel and the church of the New Testament. Scripture, after all, does not move all at once from Adam to Abraham either; it does not abandon humanity as a whole but in broad brushstrokes describes its development up to the time of Abraham. Then, when out of the whole human race, Abraham and Israel are chosen, the bond with that mass of humanity is not severed. Israel does not float, like a drop of oil, on the sea of peoples, but remains connected by numerous ties to those peoples and to the end keeps expectation alive

---

89. Adam names the women 'Eve' (living); Eve later names Cain ('obtained', which is linked to the Lord), and then Seth (appointed). There is also God's making of garments for Adam and Eve in 3:21. As Schaeffer notes, 'Probably these were the first animals to die. This indicates, I believe, that man could not stand before God in his own covering. Rather he needed a covering from God – a covering of a specific nature – a covering that required sacrifice and death, a covering not provided by man but by God. One would want to be careful not to press this into dogma, but it is my opinion that this was the beginning of the Old Testament sacrificial system looking forward to the coming of the one who would crush Satan's head' (Schaeffer, *Genesis in Space and Time*, pp. 105–106).

90. Hence talk of the 'scandal of particularity', or epithets such as 'particularism' or 'restrictivism'.

also for them. In the fullness of time, Jew and Gentile were reconciled in the one
Man: humanity as a whole gathers around the cross; and the church, chosen from
that humanity, is closely united with it. Nature and grace, creation and re-creation,
must be related to each other in the way Scripture relates them. And when we do, we
note that the first promises of grace that are addressed to Adam and Eve after the fall
are totally universal and concern the whole human race.[91]

In both theological and missiological circles one pattern or principle often
mentioned in this regard which safeguards both sets of axioms is that of 'through
the one to the many'. God deals, either in blessing or curse, with one individual
or one nation, in a particular way that ultimately has significance or implications
for many individuals and many nations. The early chapters of Genesis are no
exception here; indeed, given the book's place in the biblical revelation and the
primordial nature of its subject matter, they are *sui generis*, for we see here
the beginnings of *both* themes of particularity and universality 'in one man'.

### b. The pronouncement of separation: the doctrine of 'the antithesis'
While the *protoevangelium* of Genesis 3:15 provides the hope of redemption in
the crushing of the serpent's head, God puts enmity between the 'seed of Satan'
and the 'seed of the woman'. Robertson identifies the seed of the woman in the
context of God's originating enmity 'within the heart of the natural descendants
of the woman':[92]

> By the process of natural birth the fallen woman brings forth a depraved seed. But by
> grace God establishes enmity within the heart of particular descendants of the woman.
> These individuals may be designated as the woman's seed. . . . The introduction of
> conflict on the level of the two 'seeds' anticipates the long struggle that ensues in the
> history that follows. 'Seed of woman' and 'seed of Satan' conflict with one another
> throughout the ages.[93]

Reformed theology has called this extreme opposition the 'antithesis'.[94] These
two streams of humanity diametrically opposed to one another can be traced

---

91. H. Bavinck, *Reformed Dogmatics*, vol. 3, p. 216.

92. O. Palmer Robertson, *The Christ of the Covenants* (Phillipsburg: P & R, 1980), p. 98.

93. Ibid.

94. From *antithēmi*, 'to set against'. The term 'antithesis' as used here does not refer to
    Hegelian thinking but is rather a technical theological term associated with Reformed
    theology and refers to the radical difference between believer and unbeliever.

throughout redemptive history. In Genesis this is immediately represented genea-logically in the two lines of Adam–Seth (who call upon the name of the Lord in Exod. 3:14) and Cain–Lamech (Cain who is of the evil one; cf. 1 John 3:12). Noah is set apart by God, and after the flood Shem is set apart from his brothers. Abraham is called out, and the line of Isaac is chosen over Ishmael. As we shall see, it is the 'antithesis' that accounts for the calls for Israel to be a 'holy' separate people, and for the often mutually hostile relationship between Israel and the surrounding nations. Into the New Testament, those who believe themselves to be children of Abraham are in reality children of the devil (John 8:44). The antithesis is seen in the stark contrasts drawn between belief and unbelief, good and evil, wisdom and foolishness, light and dark, death and life, those who are blind and those who can see, covenant keepers and covenant breakers, those in Adam and those in Christ. As Jesus says, 'Whoever is not with me is against me' (Matt. 12:30), and 'No one can serve two masters' (Matt. 6:24). It is within this context and spirit that Paul's command to cease yoking with unbelievers makes sense. How can there be a lasting and deep fellowship (of which marriage is but one example) between believer and unbeliever, between Christ and Belial (2 Cor. 6:14)? Eschatologically, the final separation between sheep and goats (Matt. 25:31–33, 40) confirms the irrevocability of the antithesis.

This antithesis applies to all areas of life, including the intellectual and epistemological as well as the ethical.[95] Moreover, looking again at the origins

---

95. Bahnsen draws this out well: 'Consider the words of Paul in Romans 8:7: "the mind of the flesh is enmity against God; for it is not subject to the law of God, neither indeed can it be." The mentality of those who are unregenerate (those who are in the flesh) cannot subject itself to the truth of God's Word. There is then, no peace between the mindset of the unbeliever and the mind of God (which believers seek to reflect, cf. John 15:15; 1 Cor. 2:16). They are rather at enmity with each other. Paul similarly describes the unregenerate, unreconciled spiritual condition of unbelievers in Colossians 1:21, when he says "they are alienated and enemies in their mind" (*enemies in their mind*) against God. The "enmity" is specifically one which is worked out "in the mind" or thinking of the unbeliever. The unbeliever is unable to be subject to the law's greatest command, which is to "love the Lord your God with all your heart, with all of your soul and with all of your mind" (Mt. 22:36–37). Instead, the unbeliever "hates the wisdom and instruction" of God, as Proverbs 1:7 puts it. Although the fear of the Lord is the beginning – the very starting point – of knowledge, there is no fear of God before the unbeliever's eyes (Rom. 3:18). He is, as such, kept from realizing any of the "treasures of wisdom and knowledge" which are deposited in Christ (Col. 2:3). The unbeliever's intellectual enmity against God is simultaneously his epistemological

of the antithesis in Genesis 3, we see that the concept is founded upon what we often call 'religious' questions, questions of ultimate commitment and authority, questions about the interpretation of reality, either God's authority and inter-pretation, or the serpent's. Such questions move us back once more into the area of worldview. Here we can build on what I said earlier concerning worldview by utilizing James Sire's helpful definition:

> A worldview is a commitment, a fundamental orientation of the heart, that can be expressed as a story or in a set of presuppositions (assumptions which may be true, partially true or entirely false) which we hold (consciously or subconsciously, consistently or inconsistently) about the basic constitution of reality, and that provides the foundation on which we live and move and have our being.[96]

Sire's definition here helps illuminate the 'religious' nature of the antithesis. First, both Sire and Naugle define worldviews 'kardioptically', noting that biblically, the heart is the centre of the human person.[97] Secondly, Sire notes the fundamental role of 'presuppositions' in their understanding of worldview.[98] Thirdly, and perhaps most significantly, is Sire's decision to include the phrase

---

undoing' (Greg Bahnsen, 'At War with the World: The Necessity of the Antithesis', *Antithesis* [1990], available online at http://www.cmfnow.com/articles/pao83.htm [accessed 25 Sept. 2013] [his italics]).

96. James Sire, *Naming the Elephant* (Downers Grove: InterVarsity Press, 2004), p. 122. This definition of Sire's is a revised one in the light of his reading of Naugle, *Worldview*.

97. As Frame puts it, 'The heart is the source of our fundamental commitment, either to God or to serve an idol. It governs our actions (Matt. 15:19), words (Matt. 12:34), and thoughts (Matt. 9:4; 15:19)' (Frame, *Doctrine of the Christian Life*, p. 325).

98. Sire defines 'presupposition' as 'assumptions which may be true, partially true or entirely false' (Sire, *Naming the Elephant*, p. 19). A more expansive definition is given by Bahnsen: 'A presupposition is an elementary assumption in one's reasoning or in the process by which opinions are formed . . . It is not just any assumption in an argument, but a personal commitment that is held at the most basic level of one's network of beliefs. Presuppositions form a wide-ranging, foundational *perspective* (or starting point) in terms of which everything else is interpreted and evaluated. As such, presuppositions have the greatest authority in one's thinking, being treated as one's least negotiable beliefs and being granted the highest immunity of revision' (Greg Bahnsen, *Van Til's Apologetic: Readings and Analysis* [Phillipsburg: P & R, 1998], p. 2, n. 4 [his italics]).

'fundamental orientation', for he wishes to incorporate in his definition of world-view something similar to Dooyeweerd's theological concept of 'religious ground motives' (*grondmotief*), which serves as the '*pre*-pretheoretical spiritual core of each human'.[99] Dooyeweerd writes:

> Since the fall and the promise of the coming Redeemer, there are two central mainsprings operative at the heart of human existence. The first is the dynamis of the Holy Ghost, which by the moving power of God's Word, incarnated in Jesus Christ, re-directs to its Creator the creation which had apostatized in the fall from its true Origin. This dynamis brings man into the relationship of sonship to the Divine Father. Its religious ground motive is that of the Divine word revelation, which is the key to the understanding of Holy Scripture: the motive of creation, fall, and redemption by Jesus Christ in the communion of the Holy Ghost.
>
> The second central mainspring is that of apostasy from the true God. As religious dynamis, it leads the human heart in an apostate direction, and is the source of all deification of the creature. It is the source of all absolutizing of the relative even in the theoretical attitude of thought. By virtue of its idolatrous character, its religious ground-motive can receive very diverse contents.[100]

Although one must account for person and culture 'variability' within each category,[101] the antithesis means that in reality there are only two categories of human beings that operate as bounded sets. Colossians 2:6–8 describes this binary demarcation when it speaks of those 'rooted and built up' (v. 7) in Christ as opposed to those not according to Christ but captive according to 'hollow

---

99. Sire, *Naming the Elephant*, p. 87 (his italics).

100. Herman Dooyeweerd, *A New Critique of Theoretical Thought*, tr. David H. Freeman and William S. Young (Phillipsburg: P & R, 1969), p. 61.

101. That is to say, and as I shall deal with in chapter 8, I recognize, indeed celebrate (as a feature of God's triune diversity as displayed in creation – his 'manyness'), that the Christian worldview is never to be equated and wedded to any one cultural context. See Andrew F. Walls, 'The Gospel as Prisoner and Liberator of Culture', in Andrew F. Walls (ed.), *The Missionary Movement in Christian History: Studies in the Transmission of Faith* (Maryknoll: Orbis, 1996), pp. 3–15. However, I equally affirm (as a feature of God's 'Oneness') with Carson that 'no truth which human beings may articulate can ever be articulated in a culture-transcending way – *but that does not mean that the truth thus articulated does not transcend culture*' (D. A. Carson, 'Maintaining Scientific and Christian Truths in a Postmodern World', *SCB* 14.2 [2002], pp. 107–122 [120; his italics]).

and deceptive philosophy, which depends on human tradition and the elemental spiritual forces' (v. 8).

Fourthly, if the above description is correct, the 'seed of the woman' and the 'seed of Satan' entail two antithetical and incommensurable worldviews, fundamentally oriented in the presuppositions of the heart, which are all-encompassing and hermetically sealed interpretations of reality. As such they do not allow for any epistemological or ethical neutrality, and *in theory* are organic, interrelated and inseparable 'systems' where, to use the illustration, as Jesus himself does, tree and fruit are related to one another (Matt. 7:15–20). As such, *in principle* these worldviews are 'seamless garments' that demand 'systemic' rather than 'atomistic' analysis. As Van Til notes, 'The unbeliever is the man with yellow glasses on his face. He sees himself and his world through these glasses. He cannot remove them. His interpretation of himself and of every fact in the universe relating to himself is, unavoidably a false interpretation.'[102]

The doctrine of the antithesis stresses the starkest of 'religious' contrasts and implies a radical discontinuity at all levels of human existence between those who worship the living God and 'think his thoughts after him', and those who do not worship this God, and believe they are thinking autonomously (when in reality they are captivated by Satan's interpretation of reality). It is a core anthropological theme that can be traced longitudinally throughout Scripture and that will naturally influence one's perception of non-Christian religions.

However, there is another essential doctrinal ingredient I must add to this anthropological mix, which does not *contradict* the antithesis but rather 'limits'[103] or 'supplements' it, giving within this default discontinuity a theme of continuity

---

102. Cornelius Van Til, *A Christian Theory of Knowledge* (Philadelphia: P & R, 1969), p. 259. Such an argument will bring to mind one of Hendrik Kraemer's most famous contentions concerning the incommensurability between religions: 'Every religion is a living indivisible unity. Every part of it – a dogma, a rite, a myth, an institution, a cult – is so vitally related to the whole that it can never be understood in its real function, significance and tendency, as these occur in the reality of life without keeping constantly in mind that vast and living unity of existential apprehension in which this part moves and has its being' (Hendrik Kraemer, *The Christian Message in a Non-Christian World* [London: Edinburgh House, 1938], p. 135).

103. Van Til adapts the term 'limiting concept' from Kant. Commenting, Edgar writes, 'For Van Til a Christian "limiting concept" means that one doctrine defines another so that no one doctrine can stand alone and govern the entire system' (Cornelius Van Til, *An Introduction to Systematic Theology*, ed. William Edgar, 2nd ed. [Phillipsburg: P & R, 2007], p. 68, n. 25).

and commonality. Without this accompanying theme my biblical anthropology is incomplete and I lay myself open to the inevitable charges of both 'reductionism' and 'fideism'. It is to this theme that I now turn.

### c. The pronouncement of long-suffering: the doctrine of common grace

As noted above, God's pronouncements to the serpent, woman and man in Genesis 3 contain both punishment and blessing. I have already spoken of the *protoevangelium* in terms of a gracious salvific promise to the seed of the woman, which Reformed theologians have called 'special grace', and the embryonic manifestation of a 'covenant of grace'. However, we also witness here a broader non-salvific manifestation of God's grace, which Reformed theologians have called 'common grace', remembering that at this stage in human history 'common grace and special grace still flow in a single channel'.[104] So, for example, in our passage in Genesis, the ground is cursed and Adam and Eve are banished from the garden, both of which are punishments; they are also tinged with blessing, for 'a divine act may have diverse grounds according to the aspect from which it is viewed'.[105] So Adam is still able to work the cursed ground, and Cain, while banished, is marked to prevent and restrain others from acting in the murderous way he himself acted.[106]

This idea of restraint is given a firmer covenantal context in the covenant with Noah, a covenant inextricably linked to the narrower salvific work of special grace and yet to be distinguished from it:

> This covenant with Noah (Gen. 8:21–22; 9:1–17), though it is rooted in God's grace and is most intimately bound up with the actual covenant of grace because it sustains and prepares for it, is not identical with it. It is rather a covenant of long-suffering made by God with all humans and even with all creatures.[107]

---

104. H. Bavinck, *Reformed Dogmatics*, vol. 3, p. 216.

105. Murray, *Collected Writings*, vol. 3, p. 99.

106. Here is H. Bavinck: 'There is nobility in labour. It preserves humans from moral and physical degradation, stimulates their energy, and heightens their activity. Though banished from paradise, humans are not consigned to hell. They are sent into the world in order to subdue and control it by burdensome and exhausting labour. Here lies the beginning and first principle of all culture. Human dominion is not totally lost but is expanded by labour (Ps. 8) . . . Even temporal death is not just a punishment but a benefit. God instituted death so that sin would not be immortal' (H. Bavinck, *Reformed Dogmatics*, vol. 3, p. 199).

107. Ibid., p. 218.

In this covenant God promises to sustain, preserve and restrain the world (Gen. 8:20–22) through his ordinary works of providence and by preserving and not exterminating creation.[108]

This sustaining, preserving and restraining will happen *through various means* (Gen. 9:1–7). The beginning of Genesis 9 parallels creation and cultural mandate but with a difference – sin has now darkened the scene. There is the call to procreate but also the issue of the protection from the animals (now being ruled by fear) and protection from fellow man. Finally, we begin to discern the divine purposes behind God's preservation and restraint and their inextricable relationship with his plan of salvation. As with Adam, we have at this point in world history Noah's representing both universal humankind in general, and redeemed humankind in particular. God's covenant with Noah is substantially different from but related to other 'covenants' within redemptive history. First, Noah is not the second Adam (who is Jesus Christ), and the antithesis between belief and unbelief continues through Shem, Ham and Japheth. Secondly, God's promises to Noah are not spiritual but physical. And yet Noah is saved by God, makes a bloody sacrifice to God that is pleasing to him, and through Noah's line comes Christ. The point here is that God does not relate to his creation through Noah apart from his ongoing program of redemption. Even the ordinary nature of the seasons must be understood within the framework of God's purposes for redemption. Sin is restrained in order that humanity might continue – the advancement of God's chosen people and the

---

108. What is the basis of this blessing? Here H. Bavinck makes an interesting if somewhat speculative suggestion in comparing Gen. 8:21 with Gen. 6:5: 'These words are strikingly similar to and yet are remarkably different from those of Genesis 6:5 . . . The words used in Genesis 6:5 are in consideration of the extirpation, those of Genesis 8:21 are in consideration of the preservation of the earth. In the first instance the emphasis falls on wicked deeds in which the corrupt heart of ancient man came to expression; in the second instance the stress is on the evil nature which always continues in man, also in post-diluvian man. It seems therefore as if the Lord in these last words wishes to say that He knows what to expect of His creatures if He were to leave them to his own devices. Then the heart of man, which always remains the same, would again burst out into all kind of gruesome sins, would constantly provoke Him to wrath, and move Him to destroy the world another time. And this He does not want to do. Hence He will now lay down fixed laws for man and nature, prescribe an established course for both, by which to limit and hem them in' (Herman Bavinck, *Our Reasonable Faith* [Grand Rapids: Baker Book House, 1956], p. 48).

coming of Christ. God understands that the sin problem will never be cured by judgment and curse. If the appropriate relief from sin's corruption is to appear, the earth must be preserved from devastating judgments until the appropriate time. In other words, God's covenant with Noah makes the continuance of history possible. All of creation is blessed for the sake of God's plan of redemption in Christ.

Collating the above points more systematically we note that common grace is 'common' because it is universal, and it is 'grace' because it is undeserved and given by a gracious God. As with my other foundational doctrinal loci, the formulation of this doctrine is extremely rich, complex and controversial, and I can highlight only some of the relevant points. The exposition of Murray is seminal.[109] Murray defines common grace as 'every favour of whatever kind or degree, falling short of salvation, which this undeserving and sin-cursed world enjoys at the hand of God'.[110] According to Murray, common grace has both a negative and a positive function. Its negative function is that of divine restraint: a restraint on sin, a restraint on wrath and its execution, and a restraint on the effects of sin. The positive function is that of divine favour, whereby creation receives divine blessing, non-Christians receive divine favour and goodness, 'good' is attributed to non-Christians, and non-Christians receive benefits from the presence of the gospel. It is important to note that with all of these functions, under the sovereignty of God, there can be a great deal of differentiation and variegation in terms of the amount of divine restraint and blessing within a particular society or period of history.[111]

While acknowledging the presence of common grace and its instruments, we must also note its limitations. Common grace is not special grace, the grace

---

109. Murray, *Collected Writings*, pp. 93–119.

110. Ibid., p. 96.

111. Concerning the instrumentality of this grace, Macleod notes that the instrumentality of God's common grace is many and varied. God's general revelation of himself externally in creation (Acts 14:17; Rom. 1:20, 32) and internally, the law 'written on their hearts' (Rom. 2:15), together with structures and organizations in society, can both restrain sin and promote good; e.g. the family unit, law and government, and public opinion (Donald Macleod, *Behold Your God* [Fearn: Christian Focus, 1995], pp. 149–150). Finally, there is the presence of the church in the world: 'At one level, the Christian community has an exemplary and illuminative function. It is the light in the world's darkness . . . At another level, Christians, individually and collectively, simply by being what they are, restrain and inhibit the depravity, dissoluteness and selfishness of the world around them. They are the salt of the earth (Matt. 5:13)' (ibid., p. 150).

of God that regenerates the heart and brings the Spirit-given ability not only to obey but also to delight in God's law. Similarly, in terms of quality and quantity, God's general revelation is not the special revelation revealed in Scripture:

> In a fallen world where natural revelation is suppressed in unrighteousness, special revelation is needed to check, confirm and correct whatever is claimed for the content of natural revelation . . . Moreover, there are no moral norms given in natural revelation that are missing from special revelation (2 Tim. 3:16–17); indeed the content and benefit of special revelation exceeds that of natural revelation (cf. Rom. 3:1–2).[112]

## Conclusion: *Homo adorans* – a complex anthropological mix

In this chapter I have attempted to lay some theological foundations from a Reformed Christian worldview. While there is variegation in both the expression and interpretation of these individual tenets, the Creator–creature distinction, the *imago Dei* and the doctrines of the antithesis and common grace are by and large uncontested doctrinal 'givens' and part of the grammar of the Reformed faith. However, in the history of Reformed theology the precise synthesizing of these doctrines into a coherent theological anthropology for application in areas such as apologetics and social theology has proved more complex, and as a result more controversial. It is precisely this area of theological anthropology, though, that cannot be avoided in our quest to understand the phenomena of human religion and religiosity.

In concluding this chapter I wish to pull together some of the areas already outlined, to give a preliminary sketch of a theological anthropology that will then be returned to and illustratively 'filled in' in later chapters. The synthesis that, to my mind, best 'holds together' and 'captures' these different elements is the theological anthropology underpinning the Reformed apologetic methodology known as 'presuppositionalism', associated with Cornelius Van Til and his students, especially Greg Bahnsen and John Frame.

Regarding the religious epistemic status of the unbeliever, there is something of an irony concerning Van Til and his followers. For, while scholars like Van Til, Bahnsen and Frame have the reputation not only for being intellectual polymaths, but also, either fairly or unfairly, for their theological dogmatism on

---

112. Greg Bahnsen, 'The Theonomic Position', in Gary Scott Smith (ed.), *God and Politics* (Phillipsburg: P & R, 1989), pp. 21–53 (p. 21, n. 1).

certain issues, all admit to a difficulty in perspicuity and articulation in this area. Bahnsen notes that 'the unbeliever is a very complicated, complex, and confusing person from a religious perspective'.[113] Van Til notes that 'we should admit that we cannot give any wholly satisfactory account of the situation as it actually obtains . . . All that we can do with this question . . . is to hem it in, in order to keep out errors and to say that truth lies within a certain territory.'[114] Frame notes that 'the question remains a very mysterious one . . . Scripture does not give us an epistemological elucidation in as many terms; that elucidation must be drawn carefully out of what Scripture says about other matters.'[115] Because of this complexity, and for the sake of clarity, the following description may appear somewhat more derivative and laboured than usual.

In my comments on the antithesis and its relationship to worldview, I was careful to note the 'theoretical' and 'principial' ways in which worldviews are interrelated, hermetically sealed and systemic interpretations of reality. As Sire includes in his own academic definition of the concept, and as is intuitively 'obvious', *in practice* people's worldviews are often inconsistent, particularly the less epistemologically conscious they are of their most cherished presuppositions. While Christians may be more epistemologically aware, it is part of their daily experience that men and women who are the 'seed of the woman', who in their hearts proclaim the lordship of Christ, who have been regenerated by the Spirit and who are united to Christ and receive all his benefits still struggle with indwelling sin as the 'old man' is torn down, and the 'new man' is built up. Given their spiritual presuppositional roots, Christians do not always produce the ethical and cultural 'fruit' they should. As theologian Jim Packer is fond of saying, Christians are 'men and women under reconstruction'. In the terms of our debate we can say that *practically* the 'antithesis' still runs through the believer's heart, although *principially* those born again are new creations.

In an analogous (rather than symmetrical) way,[116] the same can be said of those who are unbelievers, whom I have antithetically defined as the 'seed of Satan':

> As the Christian sins against his will, the natural man 'sins against' his own essentially Satanic principle. As the Christian has the incubus of his 'old man' weighing him down and therefore keeping him from realizing the 'life of Christ' within him, so

---

113. Bahnsen, *Van Til's Apologetic*, p. 443.
114. Van Til, *Introduction to Systematic Theology*, p. 64.
115. Frame, *Doctrine of the Knowledge*, p. 59.
116. For we are not saying that unbelievers are 'saved'.

the natural man has the incubus of the sense of Deity weighing him down and keeping him from realizing the life of Satan within him. The actual situation is therefore always a mix of truth with error. Being 'without God in the world' the natural man yet knows God, and, in spite of himself, to some extent recognizes God. By virtue of their creation in God's image, by virtue of the ineradicable sense of deity within them and by virtue of God's restraining general grace, those who hate God, yet in a restricted sense know God, and do good.[117]

While 'in principle' the antithesis between believer and unbeliever is stark in terms of ultimate commitments, ultimate motivations, ultimate eternal destinies, and while 'in theory' this should entail worldview incommensurability, and thus radical discontinuity, 'in practice' there are a number of supplementary factors that 'complicate' this antithesis and provide commonality between believer and unbeliever. Van Til names these factors as the *imago Dei* and common grace:

> After the fall, therefore, all men seek to suppress this truth, fixed in their being about themselves. They are opposed to God. This is the biblical teaching on human depravity. If we are to present the truth of the Christian religion to men we must take them where they are. They are: a) creatures made in God's image, surrounded by a world that reveals in its every fact God's power and divinity. Their antithesis to God can never be metaphysical. They can never be anything but image bearers of God. They can never escape facing God in the universe about them in their own constitution. Their antithesis to God is therefore an ethical one; b) because of God's common grace, this ethical antithesis to God on the part of the sinner is restrained, and thereby the creative forces of man receive the opportunity of constructive effort. In this world the sinner does many 'good' things. He is honest. He helps to alleviate the sufferings of his fellow men. He 'keeps' the moral law. Therefore the 'antithesis' besides being ethical rather than metaphysical, is limited in a second way. It is one of principle, not one of full expression. If the natural man fully expressed himself as he is in terms of the principle of ethical hostility to God that dwells in his soul, he would be a veritable devil. Obviously he is nothing of the sort. He is not at all as 'bad as he may be.'[118]

First, let us start with the *imago Dei*. In their act of 'false faith' and 'unfaith-fulness' Adam and Eve may have believed themselves to be independent and autonomous from God, but metaphysically they remained creatures both before and after the fall. Bearing in mind that as God holds all things together, without

---

117. Van Til, *Introduction to Systematic Theology*, p. 65.
118. Ibid., p. 45 (his italics).

him they would cease to exist: he is both sovereign and sufficient. In this sense, although sinful men and women think they are independent, in fact they are not and are just as dependent as they ever were, but will not accept it. To put it another way, in the words of the apostle Paul there is a difference and therefore dissonance between believing that we 'live, move and have our being' in an imagined worldview and actually living and moving and having our being in the reality of God's world: 'The unbeliever cannot change who he actually is, certainly not by verbalizing theories contrary to it.'[119]

The reality of the antithesis being ethical and not metaphysical, in other words what I earlier described as the perpetuity of the *imago Dei*, has profound implications for epistemology and in particular religious epistemology. In a similar manner to Satan himself, who at one level 'knows' God but on another does not 'know God', so the unbeliever who is captive to Satan is 'a living contradiction',[120] who simultaneously on the one hand *knows* the living God of the Bible (i.e. knows in 'personal relationship', not just 'knows about'), leaving her responsible and 'without excuse', and yet on the other hand *does not know* God. The following are some representative statements from Van Til on this matter:

> To be sure, all men have faith. Unbelievers have faith as well as believers. But that is due to the fact that they are creatures of God. Faith therefore always has content. It is against the content of faith as belief in God that man has become an unbeliever. As such he tries to suppress the content of his original faith . . . [W]hen this faith turns into unbelief this unbelief cannot succeed in suppressing fully the original faith in God. Man as man is inherently and inescapably a believer in God.[121]

> Every man, at bottom, knows he is a covenant-breaker. But every man *acts* and *talks* as though this were not so. . . . His conscience troubles him when he disobeys his Creator. . . . [Sinners] do not want to keep God in remembrance. They keep under the knowledge of God for fear they should look into the face of their judge.[122]

> The natural man does not know God. But to be thus without knowledge, without living, loving, true knowledge of God, he must be one who knows God in the sense of having the sense of deity (Romans 1).[123]

---

119. Bahnsen, *Van Til's Apologetic*, p. 438.
120. Ibid., p. 452.
121. Ibid., p. 444.
122. Ibid., p. 449 (his italics).
123. Ibid., p. 447.

The natural man is such a one as constantly throws water on a fire he cannot quench.[124]

The Prodigal cannot altogether stifle his Master's voice.[125]

If the *imago Dei* serves as a metaphysical 'check' to the reality of the antithesis, the restraint of sin by the Holy Spirit in common grace serves as an ethical 'check': 'Common grace is the means by which God keeps man from expressing the *principle* of hostility to its full extent . . . The very real accomplishments of unbelievers are not their own and cannot be accounted for apart from the grace of God.'[126] Given the unbelievers' worldview, which is constructed from the 'root' of a 'ground religious motive' or presupposition of a heart in rebellion against God, common grace does not imply a 'religious' neutrality but rather must be seen as a God-given 'inconsistency' or, to use Van Til's famous phrase, must be shown to be the 'stolen capital' of the Christian worldview.[127]

---

124. Ibid., p. 438.
125. Ibid., p. 459.
126. Ibid., p. 426 (his italics).
127. Van Til, *Introduction to Systematic Theology*, p. 152. It is also worth noting with Bahnsen that 'The foregoing considerations not only establish that there is no neutral ground between believers and unbelievers, but also that there is ever present common ground between the believer and the unbeliever. What must be kept in mind is that this common ground is God's ground. All men have in common the world created by God, controlled by God and constantly revealing God. In this case, any area of life or any fact can be used as a point of contact. The denial of neutrality secures rather than destroys commonality' (Bahnsen, *Always Ready*, p. 43).

# 3. THE CURIOUS CASE OF REMNANTAL REVELATION: GLEANINGS ON THE ORIGINS OF THE RELIGIOUS OTHER

It is doubtless, in many respects, a wise and commendable caution, which excludes the obscure domain of primeval beginnings from the sphere of history. It is however, a characteristic mark of our time, which holds it to be prudent to keep to the middle of things, and not to inquire into the beginnings and endings of them. At other times, the investigation of ultimate reasons and principles has been regarded as wisdom.

(C. A. Auberlen)[1]

In recent years many scholars have therefore asserted that basic to all religions – not only the ancient religions of Babylonia but all pagan religions – there was an original monotheism. As a matter of fact, one has to come to some such a conclusion if and as long as one believes in the truth and value of religion. In the religions one then has to distinguish between a pure and impure development. In other words a distinction must be made between true and false religion (even if one avoids the terms). Superstition in that case can no more be the primitive form and origin of pure religion than a lie can be the origin of truth, or vice the origin of virtue. Certainly the least one then has to acknowledge is that one must judge the essence of religion, not by its most primitive beginnings but by its later times of flourishing, just as one can only know the child from the mature adult

---

1. C. A. Auberlen, *The Divine Revelation: An Essay in Defence of the Faith*, CFTL 16 (Edinburgh: T. & T. Clark, 1867), p. 150.

and an acorn from the oak that grows from it. But then that highest point of
development must already have been inherent in the earliest beginning as its
leading idea and dynamic. And by analogy one is forced, whether one wants to
or not, to posit the idea of God, which is the foundation of all religion, not at the
end but at the beginning. Without God, without the acknowledgement of his
existence, his revelation and his knowability, one cannot satisfactorily explain the
origin and essence of religion.

(Herman Bavinck)[2]


## Introduction

In F. Scott Fitzgerald's whimsical short story *The Curious Case of Benjamin
Button*,[3] the eponymous central character is born an old man and dies a baby.
The 'curiosity' is at its most acute at the beginning and the end of the story, for
in this case the beginning is the end and the end is the beginning. As H. Bavinck
notes in the above quotation, the highest point of religious development has
within it the seeds of its beginning – 'its leading idea and dynamic'. It is these
beginnings that will concern us in the next two chapters.

Immediately, though, when it comes to speculating on the origins of religion
and the religions, our task would appear to many to be equally curious, often
fantastical and certainly fictional. Masuzawa's opening statement in her *In Search
of Dreamtime* is hardly the positive encouragement we need as we approach the
contents of this chapter, engendering not confidence but rather a fair amount
of authorial fear and trembling:

> It has been some time since the question of the origin of religion was seriously
> entertained. Today, there is little sign of the matter being resuscitated and once
> again becoming the focus of the lively debate of old. Looking back upon the bold
> speculations of their forefathers, contemporary scholars of religion seem to consider
> themselves to be in a new phase of scholarship, having learned, above all, not to ask
> impossible questions.[4]

---

2. Herman Bavinck, *Reformed Dogmatics*, ed. John Bolt, tr. John Vriend, 4 vols.
   (Grand Rapids: Baker, 2004), vol. 1, p. 317.
3. F. Scott Fitzgerald, *The Curious Case of Benjamin Button: And Six Other Stories*
   (London: Penguin Classics, 2008).
4. Tomoko Masuzawa, *In Search of Dreamtime: The Question for the Origin of Religion*
   (Chicago: University of Chicago Press, 1993), p. 1.

Unfortunately, Masuzawa is correct in her assessment; indeed, she heaps on further obstacles: 'It is the prerogative of origin itself that has come under suspicion in recent times, together with the assumption of the unity, simplicity and self-identity of absolute beginning'.[5] What is worse is that Masuzawa may have *understated* the situation for someone like me. For if these questions of origin are 'impossible' for those scholars of religion working from presuppositions of methodological naturalism, and who live, move and have their being within a climate of methodological naturalism, how much more 'impossible' to ask these questions today from my presuppositions of methodological supernaturalism? As I have already stated, the best a position like mine can hope for is to be viewed as historical curiosity, fine and fashionable in the seventeenth century but not in the twenty-first.

Perhaps the self-flagellation should stop and I should take some comfort, for given the primary audience and aims of this study, what those outside my confessional tradition think of my questions and answers is less problematic. Perhaps I can retreat into my evangelical community and discuss these questions of origin, which are surely still 'all the rage' here. Or perhaps not. Questions surrounding the origin of religion, while maybe not 'impossible', are still deeply problematic, for within my community, apart from some notable exceptions, these are questions that either don't seem to be asked at all or are 'relegated' to matters of historical theology where they can be 'described' without contemporary and constructive prescription and application. It is my contention that while these questions of origin remain 'difficult', answers to them, albeit tentative and speculative, can be attempted, for such answers contribute greatly to our overall task of providing a scripturally rigorous theology of religions. If we can say something concerning the origin of religion, we may be in a better position to speak both of the nature of other religions and their overall purpose in the economy of God.

In the previous chapter I used the early chapters of Genesis as a platform to describe the contours of a Reformed worldview, focusing particularly on how fundamental doctrinal loci such as the Creator–creature distinction, the *imago Dei*, the antithesis and common grace combine to produce a theological anthropology of *Homo adorans* that will be crucial in my development of a Reformed theology of religions. My contention has been that the beginning of the book of beginnings gives us in embryonic or 'seed' form a creation–fall–redemption metanarrative that has great import and significance as to the origin and nature of 'religion' and 'religiosity', and sets certain theological and anthropological patterns that, while significantly developed throughout the

5. Ibid.

rest of the Bible, are not then deviated from. The maturation of this theme will be seen in subsequent chapters as I focus on the pervasive biblical theme of idolatry, which is possibly *the* most significant theological category with which to interpret other religions. It also forms the core of my overall definition of the religious Other, which I seek to demonstrate in this study as follows: *from the presupposition of an epistemologically authoritative biblical revelation, non-Christian religions are sovereignly directed, variegated and dynamic, collective human idolatrous responses to divine revelation, behind which stand deceiving demonic forces. Being antithetically against yet parasitically dependent upon the truth of the Christian worldview, non-Christian religions are 'subversively fulfilled' in the gospel of Jesus Christ.*

As I seek to justify and fill out this definition, and, as an ideal complement or sequel to the previous chapter, the question I ask in this chapter is yet another question of 'origins'; not so much the *theological* origin of 'religion' and 'religiosity', as the *historical* origin of the phenomena of the 'religions'. I shall attempt to demonstrate a Reformed tradition that from this *Urgeschichte* of Genesis one can glean historically a 'religio-genesis'. Such analysis will further inform as to the anatomy of non-Christian religions. The spotlight of the next chapter will be on the table of nations (Gen. 10) and the tower of Babel (Gen. 11), but already waiting in the wings are two seemingly retired 'characters' who demand renewed attention, the *prisca theologia* and 'original monotheism'.

Before I get to the substantive section of this chapter, and knowing that the thesis of this chapter even within the context of evangelical theological studies may well be somewhat controversial and countercultural, some methodological housekeeping is once again in order.

Although I have already summarized my methodological espousal of both 'transcendent foundationalism' and *sola Scriptura*, some further comments are necessary to engender both confidence and caution concerning the task ahead in this chapter.

First, what I am attempting to do here in the realms of historiography and religious studies is unashamedly 'theological'. In contrast to the claim that an 'objective' study of other religions is incompatible with a theological reading, thus highlighting the often hermetically sealed worlds of 'confessional' theology and 'secular' religious studies, I agree with D'Costa's powerful critique of modernity's narrative concerning 'religion': 'The attempt to throw off one interpretative framework (Christianity) only results in new interpretative frameworks, which can be criticised by theology for failing to meet their own objectives'.[6] These

---

6. Gavin D'Costa, *Christianity and World Religions: Disputed Questions in the Theology of Religions* (Chichester: Wiley-Blackwell, 2009), p. 91.

objectives are the 'spurious' claims of neutral objectivity, which 'fail to tell the full truth of the phenomena in question – the full truth meaning speaking in the light of the triune God who is the fullness of truth. Only from this theological narrative can other religions be understood, simply because Christianity is true.'[7]

Similarly, Gerald McDermott in his analysis of Jonathan Edwards's historiography of other religions (an analysis I shall come to in due course) defends Edwards's methods against the criticisms of 'ideology' and 'subjectivity', by again noting the collapse of the Enlightenment model of unbiased history: there are no naked facts of history. A little later, and again in defence of Edwards, he partakes in an act of philosophical co-belligerence:

> Philosopher Richard Rorty, hardly a sympathizer with such a project of Edwards's, nevertheless warns us that the true distinction is not between subjective and objective reality but normal and abnormal discourse. Normal discourse, a generalization of Thomas Kuhn's notion of 'normal science', is any discourse (scientific, political or theological) which embodies agreed-upon criteria for reaching agreement; abnormal discourse is any which lacks such criteria. Rorty argues that the attempt of traditional philosophy to explicate 'rationality' and 'objectivity' in terms of conditions of accurate representation is a self-deceptive effort to eternalize the normal discourse of the day.[8]

Secondly, given my espousal of epistemological transcendent foundationalism (very much contra Rorty), that we are to 'think God's thoughts after him', I am able to 'provide both a unifying paradigm for acquiring theological and scientific knowledge, and a model for interdisciplinarity':[9]

> In summary then, because God has previously pre-planned and pre-designed every detail of the universe and of history, 'there are causal connections, meaning, and purpose to be discovered by man when he uses his powers of observation and applies his intellect to what he finds.' Except in those areas where Scripture gives direct information about nature and history, he cannot find 'God's thoughts regarding them [in Scripture].' Therefore, he must use his senses. 'Given the presuppositions of

---

7. Ibid.
8. Gerald R. McDermott, *Jonathan Edwards Confronts the Gods: Christian Theology, Enlightenment Religion, and the Non-Christian Faiths* (Oxford: Oxford University Press, 2000), p. 129.
9. Mark Kreitzer, *The Concept of Ethnicity in the Bible: A Theological Analysis* (London: Edwin Mellen, 2008), p. 47.

creation, providence, and revelation, empirical knowledge is both possible and important to man' (Bahnsen 1998, 241).[10]

Thirdly, and given the above, the question now becomes whether Genesis 1 – 11 gives us this 'direct information about nature and history'. The question of historiography is complex and cannot be examined in detail here.[11] Again we note that undergirding both 'minimalist' and 'maximalist' spectrums are commitments to presuppositions and interpretative paradigms, be they those of methodological naturalism or supernaturalism. Like epistemological neutrality, 'brute factuality' is a myth. More generally, I wish to affirm with Long that

> [j]ust as the best way to read a portrait and to grasp its significance is to combine historical interest with competent appreciation of the artistic medium employed, so the best way to 'read' the historiography of the Old Testament is to combine historical interest with competent appreciation of the literary medium employed.[12]

Of course, when we come to historiographical questions concerning the 'remoteness' of the *Urgeschichte*, we see these issues in an acute form. The intra-evangelical 'arena' for these discussions is that of the broader methodological questions concerning the relationship of theology and science and more substantially literal and historical interpretations of Genesis 1 – 11 as opposed to more literary or figurative interpretations. Here I know I must tread *very* carefully, aware of the strength of feeling often generated by these issues, together with a recognition that I am outside my area of expertise. On the one hand, I recognize that the strength of any conclusions reached concerning the historical origins of religions in these chapters will be tentative and provisional;

---

10. Ibid. The references to Bahnsen are taken from Greg Bahnsen, *Van Til's Apologetic: Readings and Analysis* (Phillipsburg: P & R, 1998). In a footnote Kreitzer continues, 'An excellent example of this singular methodology is the principles given for legal research in Dt 13:12–14; 19:15–18; 25:1–2. The Creator provides the epistemological meaning framework and upholds all the data details to be discovered by the judges' (Kreitzer, *Concept of Ethnicity*, p. 47, n. 62).

11. For a good introduction on these issues see V. Philips Long, 'The Art of Biblical History', in Moises Silva (ed.), *Foundations of Contemporary Interpretation: Six Volumes in One* (Leicester: Apollos, 1997), pp. 287–434.

12. V. Philips Long, 'Historiography of the Old Testament', in David W. Baker and Bill T. Arnold (eds.), *The Face of Old Testament Studies: A Survey of Contemporary Approaches* (Leicester: Apollos, 1999), pp. 145–175.

hence the term 'gleanings' in the subtitle. Even a scholar as conservative as
H. Bavinck notes, 'Every student of ancient history has his own chronology. It
is a labyrinth without a thread to guide the inquirer.'[13] I also am concerned
that for some, commitment to certain presuppositions and arguments in this
area might serve to distract or, worse still for others, invalidate my whole
theology of religions or certainly question its plausibility. I am very keen not
to promote either reaction. That said, given Bavinck's caution, he is still one
who can maintain that 'the first eleven chapters of the book of Genesis are
extremely important: they constitute the point of departure and the foundation
of the whole of world history'.[14] I do believe that these early chapters of Genesis
contain important theological *and* historical material concerning 'religion', and
while there is not the space to justify my presuppositions concerning these
chapters, it might be helpful here to state them explicitly, noting their interconnected nature.

First, and with McKitterick, while I shall have recourse to say much about
the narrative style and structure of this block, 'the language of these chapters
. . . is not less than chronological and historical, and to omit or deny this is to
lose a central aspect of the author's intention'.[15] He quotes theologian Gerhard
Hasel here:

> There is no doubt that time and its progression functions in a most profound way in
> the Bible. This is evident from the beginning. Genesis creation is intended to be the
> beginning or opening of history. History begins with time and space and consists of
> functions in time and space. The Genesis creation account is part of a history which
> contains numbers and time sequences.[16]

Secondly, and staying with McKitterick, I mention the very relevant discussion on the dependency and derivation of source material. McKitterick's overall
aim concerning the language of Genesis is a refutation of purely 'theological'
and 'literary' interpretations that deny logical and chronological sequence, and
thus accommodate a position like that of theistic evolution. What is most interesting here, though, is that the 'assumptions' McKitterick seeks to refute directly

---

13. H. Bavinck, *Reformed Dogmatics*, vol. 2, p. 522.

14. Herman Bavinck, *Our Reasonable Faith* (Grand Rapids: Baker, 1956), p. 45.

15. Alistair McKitterick, 'The Language of Genesis', in Norman C. Nevin (ed.),
    *Should Christians Embrace Evolution? Biblical and Scientific Responses* (Nottingham:
    Inter-Varsity Press, 2009), pp. 27–42.

16. Ibid.

relate to the theology of religions, those being that (1) Genesis is derived and dependent upon a Babylonian literary context, and (2) that Genesis has undergone a process of demythologization, making it a polemical document against Babylonian and Sumerian creation stories. Agreeing with McKitterick, I have already noted the potential problems of such a reading vis-à-vis creation *ex nihilo*. For reasons that will become clear shortly, I am persuaded by the work of Tsumura[17] and others (upon whom McKitterick relies) in denying the derivative and dependent parallel between Genesis 1 and Babylonian epics. That there are parallels is not in dispute, but I believe they are not construed in *this* particular relationship.

Finally, and with Lloyd, I adhere to three doctrines that are held for broader systematic theological reasons and 'their close relationship to the plotline of the Bible',[18] but have important scientific and historical implications; hence the context again being that of a refutation of neo-Darwinism, and an assertion of a monogenetic view of human origins: 'Adam as a historical individual from whom the whole human race is descended',[19] a global flood that destroyed all human and non-human life,[20] and 'No-agony-before-Adam'.[21] I touched upon the first and third of these in my discussion of the *imago Dei*. For the purposes of this chapter, the second is especially relevant given what I shall say about the table of nations and the tower of Babel. Lloyd stresses the importance of the universality of human death in the flood (save Noah and his family of course) and the universality of the post-flood promises:

> Noah is explicitly said to be the father of all the peoples of the earth (9:19). The universality of this statement is supported by the way Noah is portrayed as the new Adam commanded to 'Be fruitful and multiply, and fill the earth' (9:1,7) and to have dominion over creation (9:2). Noah is portrayed as a man of obedience (6:22; 7:5), but, like Adam he later disobeys. Just in case we missed the point: as the introduction

17. David T. Tsumura, 'Genesis and Ancient Near East Stories of Creation and Flood', in Richard S. Hess and David T. Tsumura (eds.), *I Studied Inscriptions Before the Flood*, SBTS (Winona Lake: Eisenbrauns, 1994), pp. 27–57.
18. Stephen Lloyd, 'Christian Theology and Neo-Darwinism Are Incompatible: An Argument from the Resurrection', in Graeme Finlay, Stephen Lloyd, Stephen Pattermore and David Swift (eds.), *Debating Darwin* (Carlisle: Paternoster, 2009), pp. 1–29 (3).
19. Ibid., p. 4.
20. Ibid., p. 9.
21. Ibid., p. 15.

to another story, that of Babel, which again uses universal language (Gen. 11:1), the author reminds us in Genesis 10:32 that the nations came from Noah's sons.[22]

## 1. The case for remnantal revelation

From the perspective of Reformed theology, out of what are non-Christian religions fashioned? Towards the end of the previous chapter I outlined the complex anthropological mix that makes up *Homo adorans*. On the one hand, all men and women *as creatures* in the *imago Dei* are metaphysically revelations of God, 'know' God, are responsible before God and so are without excuse. On the other hand, all men and women *as sinners* epistemologically suppress the truth, are guilty of 'false faith' and unfaithfulness and thus 'do not know' God. Given this teaching, and although we are still in the foothills of our theology of religions quest, one should be able to look up and see a trajectory that is heading towards a conclusion that non-Christian religions are fashioned out of a suppression and distortion of this 'natural' or 'general' revelation.

Certainly, within the soteriological debates that have been conducted within the evangelical theology of religions, those arguing, myself included, *against* a soteriological inclusivism have been at pains to distinguish clearly and demarcate a universal non-salvific general or natural revelation from a more particular special revelation.[23] After the fall, what sinners need is the regenerating power of the gospel to know God as Creator and Redeemer, and general revelation is an inappropriate vehicle because knowledge of the gospel of our Lord Jesus Christ is not contained in it: 'Man the sinner, as Calvin puts it, through the testimony of the Spirit receives a new power of sight by which he can appreciate the new light given in Scripture. The new light and the new power of sight imply one another. The one is fruitless for salvation without the other.'[24]

Soteriologically speaking, to say that general revelation is insufficient for salvation is, I believe, a sound thesis and to be defended. However, such a doctrinal assertion is a point of systematic theology and as a result is a somewhat artificial, generalized and redemptive-historically 'flat' reading. An even deeper

---

22. Ibid., p. 11.

23. See Daniel Strange, 'General Revelation: Sufficient or Insufficient', in Christopher W. Morgan and Robert A. Peterson (eds.), *Faith Comes by Hearing: A Response to Inclusivism* (Nottingham: Apollos, 2008), pp. 40–77.

24. Cornelius Van Til, 'Nature and Scripture', in Paul Woolley (ed.), *The Infallible Word: A Symposium* (Philadelphia: Presbyterian Guardian, 1946), pp. 255–293 (281).

complexity is manifested as we view this anthropological picture from a historical or phenomenological perspective, for here the 'categories' of general revelation and special revelation break down somewhat. *Homo adorans* is a complex *historical* mix.

This 'complexity' has already been alluded to in this study. First we noted Frame's dissatisfaction in classifying the category of 'history' as 'general revelation'.[25] Secondly, we noted H. Bavinck's comment on the *protoevangelium*, that 'the universal idea of the revelation of salvation does not get its due',[26] that concerning this period of world history 'common grace and special grace still flow in a single channel'.[27] Finally, that 'religion and morality, cult and culture have their beginnings there'.[28]

Given a monogenetic understanding of human origins, what is being posited here is a 'single-source'[29] theory of revelation and knowledge, when the whole of humanity was in proximity of redemptive-historical events and which therefore defies a simplistic categorization as either natural 'general' revelation or supernatural 'special revelation'. As well as the more usual 'media' and 'means' of 'general revelation', a number of Reformed scholars include specific and 'supernatural' knowledge preserved as 'tradition' and 'memory'. I wish to label this revelation as 'remnantal'. While such revelatory material is always sinfully corrupted, distorted and degenerates to the point of being salvifically useless,[30] it has to be factored into the phenomena of religion in general and therefore of the 'religions' in particular. I shall give two examples of this understanding in the writings of Van Til and H. Bavinck.

### a. Remnantal revelation in Van Til
In Van Til's exposition of the category of revelation he posits a highly complex schema where revelation is received from God, from the self and from nature, and whereby each of these sources reveals God, self and nature. Under the category of 'general revelation' he proceeds to comment on all these categories in prelapsarian humanity and then a number in post-lapsarian humanity before coming to his treatment of special revelation. First, he agrees with Vos that even

---

25. Frame, *Doctrine of the Christian Life*, p. 136, n. 6.
26. H. Bavinck, *Reformed Dogmatics*, vol. 3, p. 216.
27. Ibid.
28. Ibid.
29. Peter Harrison, *'Religion' and the Religions in the English Enlightenment* (Cambridge: Cambridge University Press, 1990), p. 131.
30. The result of God's 'giving people over' to sin (cf. Rom. 1:18–32).

before the fall Adam both needed and received supernatural revelation.[31] However, unlike Vos he does not call this pre-redemptive revelation 'special' but rather 'general': 'We do not use this term because we would reserve the term special revelation in order to use it interchangeably with redemptive revelation. Moreover, all the revelation given in Paradise was really general in the sense that it was given to all men.'[32] Secondly, after the fall, and within the category of 'revelation about nature from nature', Van Til includes here the category of tradition, which he believes is an added complexity in post-diluvian humanity. For Van Til, the existence of this tradition has to be included in the establishment of men and women's responsibility before God:

> Finally the matter of tradition must be considered. The tradition of the creation story and of man's residence in paradise was, no doubt, handed down in the generation of Cain as well as the generation of Seth. Moreover, the revelation of God's redemptive purpose came to Cain just as well to Abel. With respect to the generations immediately following Cain, when Adam and Eve were still alive to tell the story to their grandchildren, even if Cain studiously avoided telling it to them, we may hold that they 'knew' the truth intellectually as fully as did the children of God. All this was carried forth to the nations. At the time of the flood the whole human race was once more brought into immediate contact with God's redemptive revelation. The tradition of the flood, no less than the tradition of creation lived on and on. This tradition was distorted, however as time passed by. The creation myths and flood myths that have been discovered among the nations prove that the original story was greatly distorted. The result has been that those who came many generations after the time of Noah, and who lived far away from the pale of redemptive revelation as it appeared in Israel, did not have as clear a tradition as the earlier generations had had. This brought further complexity into the situation for them.[33]

> No concrete case exists in which man has no more than the revelation of God in nature. It is no doubt true that many have *practically* nothing else, inasmuch as in their case the tradition of man's original state has not reached them and no echo of the redemptive principle has penetrated to their vicinity. Yet it remains true that the race

---

31. What Vos calls 'pre-redemptive special revelation' (Geerhardus Vos, *Biblical Theology: Old and New Testaments* [Grand Rapids: Eerdmans, 1948; Edinburgh: Banner of Truth Trust, 1975], p. 22).

32. Cornelius Van Til, *An Introduction to Systematic Theology*, ed. William Edgar, 2nd ed. (Phillipsburg: P & R, 2007), p. 126.

33. Ibid., p. 141.

as a whole has once been in contact with the living God, and that it was created perfect. Man remains responsible for these facts. Back of this arrangement is the Creator, the sovereign God.[34]

Finally, in the category of 'revelation about God from God', Van Til argues that after the fall there is a change in the content of God's communication with human beings but that in tradition a knowledge of this prediluvian communication remains:

> After the entrance of sin, the supernatural revelation of God to man ceased. It was only through the tradition of it that it lived on at all. This tradition was undoubtedly very clear at first. Cain knew it as well as Abel. But, because natural man is at enmity with God, he perverted this tradition rapidly. Accordingly, the generations that came thousands of years later had nothing but a greatly obscured tradition, if they had any tradition at all. The obscuration due to sin was, in this instance much greater than it was in the case of the revelation in nature and in man.[35]

> This direct revelation to man stopped after the entrance of sin insofar as it was an original loving communication. God did often speak to man after the entrance of sin, but it was always either in judgement of sin or in mercy for the purpose of the removal of sin. Thus God spoke to Cain and Abel in order to reveal to them the way of sacrifice, the way of redemption. Then, again he spoke to Cain afterward by way of judgement on his rejection of the sacrifice. In both cases, we may say that there is a new revelation of the plans and purposes of God. The revelation as it was originally given, that is, a loving self-communication of God to his creature as creature, could not be continued. If God was to continue his communication with his creation, it was to be either by condemnation or by atonement. So then we must single out this original communication of God to man and say that after the entrance of sin, only the tradition of it remained. Man was, of course, responsible for this tradition.[36]

### b. Remnantal revelation in H. Bavinck

Herman Bavinck in a less abstruse fashion comments in a number of places regarding an original knowledge of God that was preserved by tradition and memory but was gradually distorted. First, he comments on the close proximity of general and special revelation at this stage in world history:

---

34. Ibid., p. 147 (his italics).
35. Ibid., p. 171.
36. Ibid., p. 188.

What deserves attention immediately is that general and special revelation, although distinguished, do not stand in isolation alongside of each other, but rather in constant inter-relationship, and that both of them are directed to the same people, that is, to mankind as it then existed. Special revelation was then not yet given to a few individuals, not limited to a single people, but was distributed among those who were then alive. The creation of the world, the forming of man, the history of paradise and of the fall, the punishment for sin, and the first announcement of God's grace (Gen. 3:15), as well as public worship (Gen. 4:26), the beginnings of culture (Gen. 4:17), the flood, and the building of the tower of Babel – these all are treasures which mankind has carried along as part of its equipment in its journey though the world. Hence it need cause no surprise that traditions of these events, be it often in very distorted forms, turn up among the various peoples of the earth. The history of mankind has one common beginning and is built up on a common broad basis.[37]

Secondly, he comments on the 'supernatural elements' within general revelation:

But, according to Scripture, this general revelation is not purely natural; it also contains supernatural elements. The revelation that occurred immediately after the fall bears a supernatural character (Gen. 3:8ff) and via traditions becomes the possession of humankind. For a long time the original knowledge and service of God remains intact in a more or less pure state . . . Pagan religions, accordingly, do not rest only on the acknowledgement of God's revelation in nature but most certainly also on elements that from the most ancient times were preserved from supernatural revelation by tradition even though that tradition was frequently no longer pure . . . Hence the distinction between natural and supernatural revelation is not identical with the distinction between general and special revelation. To describe the twofold revelation that underlies pagan religions and the religion of Scripture, the latter distinction is preferable to the former.[38]

Hence the distinction between general and special revelation does not consist primarily in the fact that the latter consistently and in all parts bears a strictly supernatural character; the difference is evidenced fundamentally and primarily by the fact that special revelation is a revelation of special grace and this brings into existence the salvific religion known as Christianity.[39]

---

37. H. Bavinck, *Our Reasonable Faith*, pp. 45–46.
38. H. Bavinck, *Reformed Dogmatics*, vol. 1, p. 311.
39. Ibid., vol. 1, p. 342.

Again it needs to be reiterated that in positing this 'remnantal' revelation I am not saying it has any 'salvific' potential; rather, at this stage, I want to note the fact of its existence alongside the ever-present internal revelation of the *imago Dei* and the external revelation within creation.

## 2. Support for remnantal revelation

Does this idea of a remnantal revelation of God, disseminated and preserved universally in humanity but distorted and degenerated over time, first, have any precedent within the Reformed theological tradition itself, and secondly, receive any support outside the discipline of theological studies? In support of this theory and in an attempt to increase its plausibility I wish to focus briefly on two older traditions that have been somewhat neglected but in recent years have been championed by evangelical scholars. The first is Jonathan Edwards's use of the *prisca theologia*, resurrected and then utilized by the theologian Gerald McDermott. The second is the rehabilitation of the anthropologist Wilhelm Schmidt and his theory of 'original monotheism', currently being undertaken by the scholar of religion Winfried Corduan. Edwards and Schmidt make an interesting comparison. In one sense they appear to have little in common, Edwards operating in the infancy of the Enlightenment, Schmidt in its dotage; Edwards, the confessional systematic theologian, Schmidt, the 'scientific' cultural anthropologist; Edwards, the staunch Calvinist, Schmidt, the Catholic priest. However, in their particular versions of a 'remnantal' revelation with regard to religion and 'religions', both were subversive as they sought to combat rival theories – rival theories that, as we shall see, have some family resemblance of, for Edwards, the deists and, for Schmidt, the evolutionary model of religious origin and development. I shall deal with each in turn.

### a. The prisca theologia *and comparative mythology*
It is somewhat ironic that concerning their etymology it appears the first use of the terms 'religion' and 'religions' in the sixteenth and seventeenth centuries originated out of much discussion as to the historical origination of religion and the religions.[40] Harrison has argued that the seeds of the so-called 'scientific' study of religion, *Religionwissenschaft*, were present here, and not in the nineteenth, as often thought: 'The whole comparative approach to religion

---

40. See D'Costa, *Christianity and World Religions*, pp. 61–65. D'Costa's account is heavily reliant upon Harrison, *'Religion' and the Religions*.

was directly related to confessional disputes within Christianity'.[41] Although he appears to depart from Harrison's overall conclusions, D'Costa uses Harrison's analysis to argue that in the debates between Protestant Scholastics, Cambridge Platonists and deists, one has the 'typological anticipations of exclusivism, inclusivism, and pluralism',[42] the subject being a familiar one to the theology of religions: the scandal of particularity. In a little more detail this could be described as the fairness and justice of God in his provision of salvation, given factual religious diversity (then increasingly being discovered), and the relative roles of reason and revelation in religion. In this analysis Calvinist and Lutheran Protestant scholastics maintained soteriological predestinarianism and a thoroughly negative and disinterested attitude towards other religions. The Cambridge Platonists, however, built upon the heritage of earlier Renaissance scholars such as Marsilio Ficino (1433–99) and were much more interested in and were able to talk about a common 'genus' of religion. They

> turned to 'religions' to show that natural religions did render the truths established by revelation . . . this meant that either they discovered the doctrine of the trinity almost everywhere in other religions . . . or they were pushed to play down various supernatural truths not found elsewhere.[43]

D'Costa notes that although the Cambridge Platonists often chose the former option, it was the deists who decoupled 'reason as a mode of revelation',[44] arguing that reason was a natural property of all humanity:

> The deism of Lord Herbert of Cherbury perfectly exemplifies this move, found in a mature form in *De Religione Gentilium* (1663). Here, morality alone counts, even though morality is based on belief in God, a belief found in all religions. Belief and ethics are what religion is about. Revelation, in the form of trinity and incarnation, is unnecessary.[45]

Out of this context and transcending these general categories comes Jonathan Edwards, or rather Gerald McDermott's, championing of 'a strange new Edwards . . . fascinated by other religions and religious others'.[46] Before outlining certain

---

41. Harrison, *'Religion' and the Religions*, p. 3.
42. D'Costa, *Christianity and World Religions*, p. 65.
43. Ibid., p. 63.
44. Ibid., p. 64.
45. Ibid.
46. McDermott, *Jonathan Edwards*, p. 3.

discontinuities between Edwards and his Reformed Scholastic heritage, McDermott still maintains that in his overall judgment regarding other religions Edwards fundamentally remained in continuity with the Protestant Scholastic heritage. He writes:

> Edwards's Reformed predecessors, the seventeenth-century orthodox scholastics resisted this trend to conceive of historical religions as derived from a common religion-in-general. For these Calvinists, historical religions were either the true (Christian) religion of grace and revelation or pagan heresy, which arose from human corruption. They used the Latin word *religio*, which means to 'bind back or re-attach' only for the true religion, which they thought was the only way for humans to be brought back – or reattached to God. Religion-in-general was excluded because it did not contain the historical particularities of the Christian faith, which alone could reconcile sinners to a holy deity. The religions could not be placed on a continuum with Christianity because without those historical particularities their nature and direction were fundamentally different. While in orthodox Christianity, a holy God reaches down to save helpless sinners, in all other religions sinful humans try unsuccessfully to be reconciled to a holy God.[47]

However, drawing largely from Edwards's *Miscellanies*, McDermott argues that for Edwards the greatest threat to the Christian faith at this time came from the religion of the Enlightenment: deism. McDermott's thesis is that Edwards fought the deists by responding to the 'scandal of particularity' in subversively using the deists' own evidence against them: 'His principal purpose was to show, against the Deists, that nearly all humans have received revelation, and therefore all knowledge of true religion among the heathen is from revelation rather than the light of natural reason'.[48] Here we come to the *prisca theologia* and comparative mythology, both of which were implications of a single-source theory of revelation. Regarding the *prisca theologia* McDermott picks up the story:

> Many of the writers whom Edwards reads, particularly Skelton and Ramsey, understood other religions in terms defined by what was called the *prisca theologia* (ancient theology). This was a tradition in apologetic theology, resting on misdated texts (the Hermetica, Chaldean oracles, Orpheia, and Sybilline oracles), that attempted to prove that vestiges of true religion were taught by the Greeks and other non-Christian religions. Typically it alleged that all human beings were originally

---

47. Ibid., p. 88.
48. Ibid., p. 94.

given knowledge of true religion (monotheism, the Trinity, *creatio ex nihilo*) by the Jews or by traditions going back to Noah's good sons (Shem and Japheth) or antediluvians such as Enoch and Adam. This knowledge was subsequently passed down to Zoroaster, Hermes Trismegistus, Brahmins and Druids, Orpheus, Pythagoras, Plato, and the Sybils.

The *prisca theologia* was developed first by Clement of Alexandria, Origen, Lactantius, and Eusebius to show that the greatest philosophers had borrowed from the chosen people. It was revived in the Renaissance by Marsilio Ficino and Pico Della Mirandolo to reconcile Neoplatonism and Christian dogma. In the seventeenth and eighteenth centuries it was taken up again by the 'Jesuit figurists', who tried to win acceptance for their mission in China by claiming that China worshiped the true God two thousand years before Christ, and by a number of other, mostly Protestant, thinkers, four of whom Edwards read carefully and took quite seriously.[49]

Edwards picks up this tradition and contextualizes it within a more theologically orthodox framework. The result looks remarkably similar to the systematic argument concerning 'remnantal revelation' I have outlined above:

> In his own appropriation of the *prisca theologia*, Edwards said that the heathen learned these truths by what could be called a trickle-down process of revelation. In the 'first ages' of the world the father of the nations received revelation of the great religious truths, directly or indirectly, from God himself. These truths were then passed down, by tradition, from one generation to the next. Unfortunately, there is also a religious law of entropy at work. Human finitude and corruption inevitably cause the revelation to be distorted, resulting in superstition and idolatry.[50]

Regarding historiography, McDermott notices that although Edwards rejected cyclical interpretations of history, 'he saw in redemption history a number of recurring patterns: recurring regeneration, periodic revival, and the repeated use of jealousy as a catalyst, and leadership by an eminent person':[51]

> Throughout the work of redemption, degeneration set in whenever progress was made. By what I have called religious entropy, the revelations given to human beings were

---

49. Ibid., p. 93.
50. Ibid., p. 94.
51. Ibid., p. 96.

immediately and then continually attacked by corruption and distortion. God's intermittent recharging of the battery of revelation, as it were, was inevitably followed by loss of religious energy. The final result of thousands of years of such renovation and destruction was an entire world of heathen peoples hopelessly lost in idolatry.[52]

Accompanying the *prisca theologia* and, according to Harrison,

another offshoot of the single-source theory which enjoyed considerably more vogue, was comparative mythology. Like ancient theology, this approach stressed the derivative nature of all gentile mythologies, most often by reducing them to variants of Hebrew History.[53]

Harrison points out that scholars such as Samuel Schuckford, in his *Sacred and Profane History of the World Connected* (1728), developed a history of religious (de)evolution that linked linguistic diversity and religious diversity. Two analytical tools were used to uncover the original unified single source of religion: 'Etymology and euhemerism could together show that despite appearances, pagan myths were all about the same thing, namely important events in the first Ages of the world.'[54] In terms of etymology, as one deity could be given various names, 'linguistic diversity led in turn to an apparent religious diversity which in turn became actual'.[55] According to the older theory of euhemerism, the gods of ancient mythology were deified human heroes. This tradition may originally have been used to argue for the naturalistic origin of religion, but had been utilized by the early Christian apologists and patristic fathers with an added 'theological' element: 'The standard Patristic version of euhemerism was that the names of the pagan gods were those famous rulers or inventors of whom statues were made, and these were inhabited by deceiving demons who wished to be worshipped.'[56] As Augustine stated in *The City of God*, 'The deceitful spirits are glad to allow them to be fictitiously ascribed to divinities, so that men may

---

52. Ibid., p. 97.
53. Harrison, *'Religion' and the Religions*, p. 139.
54. Ibid., p. 140.
55. Ibid.
56. D. P. Walker, *The Ancient Theology: Studies in Christian Platonism from the 15th to the 18th Century* (Ithaca, N.Y.: Cornell University Press, 1972), p. 7. Seznec calls this the 'historical tradition' (Jean Seznec, *The Survival of the Pagan Gods: The Mythological Tradition and Its Place in Renaissance Humanism and Art*, tr. Barbara F. Sessions [New York: Harper, 1961], pp. 11–36).

suppose they have sufficient authority, as it were by heaven sent revelation, for the perpetration of abominable crimes'.[57]

As with the *prisca theologia*, Edwards, much like the early fathers, appears to have read and appropriated contemporary writings on comparative mythology in his own theology of religions. As McDermott helpfully summarizes:

> From Ramsay, Edwards learned that the breakdown was caused in part by the problem of language. All original people – even the Gauls, Germans and Britons – shared hieroglyphs with the Egyptians to present divine things taught by Noah. Over the course of time, pagans dissociated the symbol from its referent. 'Men attached themselves to the letter and signs without understanding the spirit and the thing signified' (Misc. 1255). This accounted for idols and 'vile superstitions' (ibid.). It also accounted for the similarity between the stories of Christ's sufferings and applied to their own champions. By this mechanism and others the original purity of truth was continually breaking down, corrupted by profane and demonic admixtures (Misc. 986).[58]

> Edwards followed Vossius, Gale, and Shuckford in postulating a migration of gods from Israel through Phoenicia and Egypt to Greece (and later to Rome) by three vehicles: 1) euhemerism (the notion that pagan gods are inflated versions of historical figures), 2) linguistic confusion (conflating several different figures into one because of a similarity of words, or dividing exploits of one person among several new names because of verbal similarities), or 3) hermeneutical confusion (attributing the works of a human figure to God because of failure to understand the biblical text). The result was a profusion of deities and myths, all betraying derivation from Hebrew biblical legends. So the God of Israel was given new names when his legends were taken abroad, and the stories of his people in Canaan took on new life and ontological meaning (humans often became divinities) when they travelled through the Mediterranean world.[59]

At *this* point in my argument I do not feel a need to comment on the validity or otherwise of the actual phenomenological evidence Edwards (or anyone else for that matter) uses for his version of the *prisca theologia* and comparative mythology. Rather, my more modest aim is to highlight the theoretical theological existence of the *prisca theologia* and comparative mythology to demonstrate that they have some precedent in Reformed historical theology. Significantly, historians

---

57. Augustine, *Concerning the City of God Against Pagans*, tr. Henry Bettenson, Penguin Classics (London: Penguin, 2003), 2.10.
58. McDermott, *Jonathan Edwards*, p. 95.
59. Ibid., p. 190.

such as Harrison and Walker, who at times reveal a very different set of pre-suppositions from those of Reformed theology,[60] make the theological links I am attempting to make and ask the theological questions I am attempting to answer:

> This single-source theory is, of course, nothing more than a strict, and perhaps extreme, application to human culture of the monogenetic view of human origins. . . . In this more restricted form, it was closely allied with the thesis of the 'ancient theology . . .' that the religion of all lands must originally have been that of the parent culture.[61]

> If a Christian wishes to believe in the existence of a series of Ancient Theologians who in some measure foreshadow the Christian revelations, he must assume or accept as a historical fact the following: Either that the only or main pre-Christian revelation was the Jewish one; but that this filtered through to the Gentiles, the usual channel of communication being Egypt, where Moses had taught the priests or left books. Or that there were partial pre-Christian revelations other than that given to the Jews.[62]

### b. Wilhelm Schmidt and original monotheism

The second strand of evidence in supporting what I have called 'remnantal' revelation concerns the voluminous ethnographical research of the polymath Wilhelm Schmidt (1868–1954).[63] The doyen of the 'science of religion' Mircea Eliade recognized Schmidt to be a giant in this field alongside those more well-known names of Durkheim, Freud, Jung and Pettazzoni. Indeed, Eliade believed the publication of Schmidt's monumental twelve-volume *Der Ursprung Der Gottesidee*[64] marked 1912 as the beginning of the discipline. In a similar vein to the earlier and more rudimentary work of Andrew Lang, Schmidt's ethnological conclusion was of an original ethical monotheism in the most primitive human societies, which subsequently devolved, but most probably originated from an *Uroffenbarung* (a primeval revelation). Given the then strongly hegemonic model of evolutionary religious development, of which Schmidt's thesis was a direct contradiction, his conclusions were highly disputed. Moreover, it was not only Schmidt's conclusions that courted controversy. As contemporary evangelical

---

60. See Harrison, *'Religion' and the Religions*, pp. 173–175; Walker, *Ancient Theology*, p. 193.

61. Harrison, *'Religion' and the Religions*, p. 132.

62. Walker, *Ancient Theology*, p. 20.

63. For a detailed biography of Schmidt, see Ernest Brandewie, *When Giants Walked the Earth: The Life and Times of Wilhelm Schmidt SVD*, SIA 44 (Fribourg: Fribourg University Press, 1990).

64. Published between 1912 and 1955.

religious scholar and champion of Schmidt's work Winfried Corduan points out, Schmidt's *method* of ethnohistory and *kulturekreis* ('culture circles', which later became known as the 'Vienna school') was as revolutionary and important as his actual conclusion:

> It is a common misunderstanding that Schmidt's argument is a cumulative case based on the fact that some recognition of a Creator god is found in numerous cultures. This wide distribution of a possible vestigial monotheism is certainly true, and it constitutes a phenomenon that should not be ignored. For example, it is difficult to find an African traditional religion that does not include some conception of a Supreme God, at least in memory. But again, left to itself, this reality would not amount to a very strong case. In addition to compiling all of these data based on anthropological accounts from all over the world, Schmidt established a chronological sequence by which one can distinguish between cultures that reflect earlier stages of development and later ones. Without such a tool, we would, indeed, never be able to break the tie score between those who advocate an original monotheism or an original animism. But Schmidt put an original monotheism on sound footing by being able to demonstrate that those societies that manifested a solid monotheism along with a solid moral code, with relatively little ritual, magic, or reference to the spirit world, were in fact those societies that reflect the earliest stages of human development. This methodology is called ethnology or the 'culture-historical method,' and it was already being practiced by some scholars before Schmidt refined it and applied it unequivocally to the question of the origin of religion.[65]

Despite the controversial nature of his work, Schmidt remains a 'giant' (if somewhat sleeping) within the discipline, but whose legacy is difficult to assess because, as Corduan points out, Schmidt's success in demonstrating original monotheism 'turned out to be not a general acceptance of his conclusion, but the dropping of the question'.[66]

Eager to reassert the question for today, Corduan's recent monograph *In the Beginning God*[67] is to date the most detailed and substantial demystification and

---

65. Winfried Corduan, 'In the Beginning, God: Ethnology and Original Monotheism', plenary paper, International Society of Christian Apologetics, Kansas City, Mo., 2–3 June 2007, pp. 5–6.

66. Ibid., p. 2. We shall encounter the evolutionary model of religious development again in the next chapter.

67. Winfried Corduan, *In the Beginning God: A Fresh Look at the Case for Original Monotheism* (Nashville: Broadman & Holman, 2013).

apologetic for both Schmidt's ethnohistographic method and Schmidt's conclusions of an original monotheism.[68] Moreover, his study also serves as an apologetic
against the evolutionary theories of religion so prevalent among Schmidt's

---

68. It is important to note that the task of synthesizing and incorporating the findings
of Schmidt's research into a more Reformed theological framework was attempted
during Schmidt's own lifetime (and midway through the writing of *Der Ursprung
Der Gottesidee* [1912–54]) by the pioneer Reformed missiologist Samuel Zwemer,
in his own work on the origin of religion. Given my overall concerns in this
chapter, Zwemer's own summation, hugely dependent on Schmidt, and dedicated
to him with Schmidt's permission, is a helpful guide as to the importance of this
material (noting Zwemer's final comments here, regarding the non-biblical source
of this knowledge, a point I shall return to shortly): '1. The history of the history of
religion reveals two theories, the one theistic, the other anti-theistic, and these are
in conflict. It is important, therefore, for all who believe in God and his revelation,
not to omit the Bible as source book in the study of religions; 2. The origin of the
idea of God is not by any process of evolution, but by instinct or by an objective–
subjective revelation; 3. The evidence for primitive monotheism is found, not only
in every area of primitive culture, but also found in the earlier forms of the great
ethnic religions; 4. The widespread Creation-myths regarding the origin of the
world and of man, the so-called Golden age and the entrance of death, all point to
a common tradition regarding man's Creation and the fall, strangely parallel to the
Scriptures; 5. Prayer and sacrifice are religious rites of such antiquity and
universality that their significance and persistence point to a common origin,
namely, in man's desire to restore a lost communion and propitiate God; 6. The
origin of fire is mysterious and it is everywhere associated with religion and
sacrifice. In primitive religion and in ethnic faiths it is a symbol of deity, and object
of worship or a method of communion. The universality of this symbolism and its
antiquity point to a common primitive tradition; 7. Taboos and totemism, together
with the laws against incest, witness to the early sanctity of marriage and its
monogamous character over against the evolutionary theory of early promiscuity.
There are evidences of faith, hope and charity in primitive religions, which can only
be explained on the basis of a primitive revelation; 8. Finally, belief in the
immortality of the soul is universal among primitives and in nearly all of ethnic
religions this otherworldly character of man's religious outlook is also a proof of
primitive revelation. The argument outlined above is based, however, not primarily
on the Scriptures nor on any dogmatic preconceptions, but on the historical
method of investigation' (Samuel M. Zwemer, *The Origin of Religion* [London:
Marshall, Morgan & Scott, 1935], p. 13).

contemporaries[69] and also those who have been, and continue to be, responsible for the ambiguation of 'historical investigation' and what this does to the meaning and validity of the concept of 'origins'. Corduan's own conclusions are, I believe, relatively modest. At the very least he wishes to show that 'the hypothesis of an original monotheism stands so far unfalsified'.[70] More positively, and he admits the risk of overstatement, 'I would suggest that the standing of original monotheism is . . . supported by data based on a strong, though admittedly not infallible, method, and its most formidable competing hypotheses are – well, absent.'[71]

Corduan's work on Schmidt merits careful study.[72] If Schmidt's conclusions (refracted through someone like Corduan) are correct, then they provide confirmatory extra-biblical support to the exegetical and theological arguments I am advancing from the Genesis account. But is Schmidt's evidence 'inadmissible'? Here we return, albeit briefly but tenaciously, to an issue of method. Brandewie, who has produced the most detailed work on the life and work of Schmidt, comments that

---

69. Which still exist in OT studies; see chapter 5.

70. Corduan, *In the Beginning God*, p. 337.

71. Ibid., p. 338. Apologetically, Corduan is careful not to claim too much in his argument, although as an anthropological and ethnographical support for the theological arguments put in this chapter, they serve us well: 'a) We have *not* proven the theory of original monotheism beyond all conceivable doubt. We have, however, shown that it is true beyond any reasonable scientific doubt, which acknowledges the truth of the source material. b) We have *not* demonstrated that all supreme beings contained in cultures with an original monotheism are real. We have however indicated that the fact that the oldest cultures consistently manifest a monotheism lets us establish a high probability that they experienced something real. c) We have *not* shown that all the supreme beings are identical with each other. Still, by looking at their attributes, they all fit into the category of deity and, therefore, share a likeness on a very foundational level. d) Finally, we did *not* argue that the supreme being of original monotheism was necessarily the God of the Bible. However, insofar as he is real, and since there can only be one being with all of the attributes of the one and only God, he must be identical with the biblical God. The attributes of the god of many monotheisms today are such that we can say pretty confidently that they all may have a common origin with the one true God, but they are not necessarily identical with the one true God when we consider all of their natures' (ibid., p. 353 [his italics]).

72. And is certainly a great primer for non-professionals interested in the world of ethnology.

often he is not understood, usually not read, yet cursorily dismissed, a dismissal which often included some brief reference to his being a Roman Catholic priest 'and therefore . . . ,' as if this makes his work, for that specific reason, suspect, if not totally invalid.[73]

What kind of a scholar was Schmidt? An overt 'objective' ethnological scientist, or a secret theologian who wished to demonstrate the basic historicity of the Genesis account of origins and who offered 'a sixth proof of the existence of God, an ethnological proof, to supplement the five proofs of St Thomas Aquinas'?[74] After noting a number of commentators who believed Schmidt to be biased and to be clericalizing ethnology, 'dominated by the necessity of reconciling the findings of anthropology with scriptural precedent',[75] Brandewie notes that 'Schmidt never tried to hide his Catholicism. He wore it on his sleeve. He felt it gave him, and others like him, an advantage.'[76] He offers some illuminating comments from Schmidt himself on the matter: 'It is the duty alike of the believing and of the unbelieving investigator not to let their views of the universe, their philosophy and their resultant judgements as to truth and value in any way influence their setting forth of the historical facts.'[77]

Here and there only the amusing simplicity of some reactionary imagines that an unprejudiced view of the science of religion is the privilege of the unbeliever.[78]

Missionaries, however, should be careful to describe the facts as they know them accurately and exactly. Everything must be handled with religious relevance: nothing must be glossed over or 'prettified'. If missionaries describe the facts falsely, they falsify the ways of God and put obstacles in the way of deriving any great benefit from their description.[79]

---

73. Ernest Brandewie, *Wilhelm Schmidt and the Origin of the Idea of God* (Lanham: University Press of America, 1983), p. 1.

74. Ernest Brandewie, 'The Exile of Wilhelm Schmidt, S. V. D. from Austria', *Academici* (2008), available online at http://www.academici.net/blog.aspx?bid=4559 (accessed 25 Sept. 2013).

75. Brandewie, *Wilhelm Schmidt*, p. 12.

76. Ibid.

77. Ibid.

78. Ibid.

79. Ibid., p. 13.

Whether or not Schmidt believed he was simply dealing in brute 'historical facts', and whether or not one believes this is actually possible, certainly his conclusions towards the end of the final volume of *Der Ursprung Der Gottesidee* do have a strong theological and apologetic flavour, as, quoting Job 38:4–7, he speaks of God as the only witness of creation and says that

> [o]nly from the Creator Himself could man have gotten such a detailed, reliable, living and appealing account of creation, of the creator, and of the creatures that were made, among them as the peak and in the first place, man himself. This is exactly what we encounter in the oldest, commonly held religion of mankind. This point is made even more clear to us inasmuch as all of the earliest ancient (*Ur*) cultures unanimously state that the Creator himself lived with men on earth and taught them all these things as he discoursed intimately with them. This testimony which resounds from ancient cultures which are spread all over the globe cannot be ignored or passed over for another reason. The content of their religion also states clearly, as we have seen, that they have not gotten this from their own thinking and desire.[80]

But is Schmidt's confessionalism a problem? Here we return to perennial methodological issues in the study of religions surrounding the relationship between 'objectivity' and 'subjectivity', and between 'interpretative frameworks' and 'data'. Given my earlier methodological comments and commitments, especially the 'interpreting' nature of presuppositions, it will come as little surprise that I do not believe Schmidt's research to be necessarily invalid because he comes from a particular confessional tradition. Here it is instructive to return to D'Costa's 'reinterpretation' of the rise of the 'science' of religious studies, with its spurious claim to 'neutrality' and 'objectivity': 'The religious "scientists" simply promoted different interests with alternative "pious sentiments", not pure objectivity'.[81] Ironically, and given my brief analysis of Schmidt, D'Costa may be unfair to him when he categorizes his work as an example of a 'principled secular reading' (PSR), alongside figures such as Muller, a school of interpretation D'Costa 'outs' as a false claim to epistemic neutrality and objectivity. More

---

80. Ibid., p. 285. In his own study of Schmidt's method Corduan helpfully describes Schmidt's belief in an original revelation, although it is important for Corduan to stress that 'Schmidt does not base his ethnological conclusions on divine revelation. Instead, his ethnological conclusions entailed that the monotheism of the *primitive* tribes must have been due, at least in part, to the fact that God revealed himself to them' (Corduan, *In the Beginning God*, p. 223 [his italics]).

81. D'Costa, *Christianity and World Religions*, p. 94.

sympathetically, it may be that Schmidt is better positioned within the camp
that both D'Costa and myself espouse, a legitimate 'comparative theological'
reading of religion, or alternatively a 'theological religious studies' that is able
to (and in the best place to) incorporate both 'insider' and 'outsider' interpretations (and that interestingly D'Costa himself traces back to tradition such as
the *prisca theologia* in the sixteenth and seventeenth century). Echoing Schmidt's
own advice to missionaries quoted above, D'Costa comments on this theological
reading:

> The point I want to stress is that regardless of their respective theological verdicts
> on the religions, what we see is that a good initial understanding is required of what
> is then theologically praised or criticized, or declared as being bewilderingly complex.
> Understanding, to the best of one's ability, is a prerequisite to any form of judgement.
> Of course this understanding is not neutral, as it is structured by particular research
> questions, interests and methods. Some philosophers of science agree this is true of any
> research paradigm (Kuhn 1970) and this has been applied in the arts and social
> sciences as well (see Polanyi 1962; McGrane 1989; Asad 1993).[82]

## Summary

I started this chapter by asking the question 'Out of what are non-Christian
religions fashioned?' Although some theologians place it under the category of
'general' revelation, and others 'special' revelation, as well as the ever-present
dynamic revelation of God in nature, there is a historical *remnantal* revelation
within religious traditions, which, though entropically distorted over time,
through for example the mechanisms of etymology or euhemerism, gives us a
comparative theological explanation of 'commonalities' and 'continuities'
between religious traditions, for example certain events, themes and archetypes.
Schmidt's ethnographic work on an original monotheism gives extra-biblical
corroboration to this thesis. Such 'single-source' theory still enables us to speak
of 'religion' as a genus while being able to trace a devolutionary descent from
'pure' original to distorted copy – a theme to which I shall return when we look
at the biblical category of 'idolatry'.

---

82. Ibid., p. 93.

# 4. TOWARDS A RELIGIO-GENESIS: BABEL AND THE NATIONS IN THE DEVELOPMENT OF THE RELIGIOUS OTHER

> From one man he made all the nations, that they should inhabit the whole earth; and he marked out their appointed times in history and the boundaries of their lands.
>
> (Acts 17:26)

> If the modern reader finds this incredible, that reflects a materialism that tends to doubt the existence of spirits, good or ill. But those who believe the creator could unite himself to a human nature in the Virgin's womb will not find the story intrinsically beyond belief.
>
> (Gordon Wenham)[1]

## Introduction

In arguing for a revelatory 'single-source' theory as to both the theological and historical origin of religion and the religions, does the *Urgeschichte* provide us with any more detail or explanatory 'mechanism' as to the pattern of religion that begins with an original divine disclosure but that, due to human sin, and without divine preservation, ends in a derivative religious degeneration and decay as God

---

1. Commenting on Gen. 6:1–4, Gordon J. Wenham, *Genesis 1–15*, WBC (Waco: Word, 1987), p. 140.

'gives people over' to idolatry? In this chapter I wish to concentrate on the table of nations (Gen. 10) and the tower of Babel (Gen. 11), believing them to be foundational in providing us with further details of a 'religio-genesis'. After making some background comments, I shall describe a number of thinkers who in their own exegeses of these texts have brought out, in varying degrees, material that can be added to our building of a biblical theology of religions. Finally, and on the back of this description, I shall offer my own speculations as to the role that these events play. Concerning this last section in particular, but more generally the whole chapter, I wish to reiterate the 'health warning' I gave in chapter 1 and at the beginning of the previous chapter regarding the admittedly speculative nature regarding some of my exegetical decisions and theological constructions in what follows in this part of the study. While a less risky editorial strategy might have been not to dabble in these areas at all, I still think it worth commenting here, however in a provisional and tentative way. The safety net I believe I have in place here is that the overall thrust of my theology of religions exegetically, systematically or missiologically does not depend upon these constructions, which remain more at the periphery than in the centre. With this caveat in place we can now dive in.

Predictably, the amount of literature pertaining to Genesis 10 – 11 is vast, as are the vastly differing exegetical and theological interpretations, even among Reformed scholars. In order not to drown under this material, and to give some already synthesized 'relief', I have decided to 'piggyback' the recent work of the Reformed theologian Mark Kreitzer in his important monograph *The Concept of Ethnicity in the Bible*.[2] Coming out of his political and ecclesiological experiences in pre- and post-apartheid South Africa, Kreitzer's work is an ambitious technical and cross-disciplinary study that not only attempts to provide a biblical theology of 'ethnicity', but does so fully aware of and seeking to integrate contemporary social-scientific perspectives. Both the table of nations and the tower of Babel provide crucial material for Kreitzer, and he provides a detailed study of these chapters, again fully cognizant of the most recent academic treatments of these texts. I shall summarize Kreitzer's understanding of these two chapters before complementing his primary focus on 'ethnicity' with my own, on 'religion'.

First, and methodologically, I have already mentioned Kreitzer in some of my earlier remarks, having found his work helpful in articulating a Reformed theological method. Kreitzer self-consciously defends his interdisciplinary method,

---

2. Mark Kreitzer, *The Concept of Ethnicity in the Bible: A Theological Analysis* (London: Edwin Mellen, 2008).

again under the influence of Van Til. In critiquing the popular epistemological stance known as 'critical realism', Kreitzer adopts a transcendent foundationalist epistemology, which he calls 'Trinitarian Creationism'.[3]

Secondly, and more particularly concerning Genesis 10, Kreitzer rejects the claim that the *Völkertafel* is a late political polemic, and/or has a limited Hebrew ethno-horizon, arguing rather that it describes the 'ethno-geography of singular humankind':[4]

> The 'carefully crafted genre' of the proto-history is 'historical narrative' (Mathews 1995, 432). The redactor uses polemic and other literary techniques to distance the source material from the 'common ancient Near Eastern fare of legend or the sort' (Mathews 1995, 432; see Wenham 1987).[5]

> The Table of Peoples, in context, provided the Israelites a socially constructed 'verbal "map" of the [human] world' (Brueggemann 1982, 91). It gives a tripartite division based upon the three sons of Noah. As such, it demonstrates the extraordinary insight for the ancient Near East of 'unity' (Von Rad 1962, 161) and 'brotherhood' of mankind (Custance 1975, 57).[6]

Thirdly, and concerning the literary context and structure of these chapters within the rest of Genesis 1 – 12, a number of 'recursions' need to be borne in mind, recursions I have already noted in the previous chapter: (1) the pattern of creation, de-creation and re-creation as seen in the strong parallels between the first creation and post-flood 'creation', especially the 'scatter command' both to Adam and then to Noah to 'fill the earth'; (2) the pattern of a divine action being simultaneously *both* an act of divine judgment and an act of divine grace following human disobedience and rebellion, seen, for example, in the expulsion from Eden; and (3) the inextricable relationships (founded upon the nature of God, both sovereign and triune) between universality and particularity, and human unity and human diversity – that through the one, many will be blessed.

These patterns are evidenced in Genesis 10 – 11: (1) Babel's attempt at hubristic unification as an act of de-creation against the creational mandate to scatter, setting the scene of Abraham's calling, another act of divine re-creation; (2) the divine scattering at Babel, acting as judgment and blessing, 'this scattering

---

3. Ibid., p. 7.
4. Ibid., p. 11.
5. Ibid., p. 104.
6. Ibid., p. 112.

was gracious in that it prevented man from further collective evil and gracious in that it caused humanity to obey, albeit externally, the command to diversify and fill the earth';[7] (3) 'the essential interconnectedness of the human family despite present diversity of genealogical descent, language, geography and political alignment':[8]

> Ethno-linguistically diverse yet singular humanity is then of equal value. All people
> are to be blessed by Abraham's one family . . . Johannes Verkuyl gives a preview of
> the rest of Scripture: 'No one can fail to see that the world of the nations mentioned
> already in Genesis 10 is the final goal – not the point of departure – of all God's
> subsequent efforts.'[9]

Fourthly, and in turning to Genesis 10 – 11 in particular, Kreitzer, along with a number of other recent commentators, takes both the table of nations and Babel to be a single literary unity and ordered dischronologically. Although there are various strands of structural and literary evidence for such a reverse (or better, interspersed) chronological order,[10] for Kreitzer such an order is theologically important, for it gives justification to one of his major contentions throughout his study that ethno-linguistic diversity is itself a naturally occurring creational ordinance and blessing, rather than a judgment and curse, a 'negative' impression that would be created if the Babel pericope had come first in the narrative:

> As it stands now, the Table functions to fulfill the post-diluvial command, which in
> turn repeats the original Creation Mandate or Dominion Covenant (9:1; 1:28) (Clines
> 1976, 494). Thus the scattering of the sons of Noah indicated the blessing of fertility
> and filling the earth (Gen. 9–10). However the judgement upon hubris (Gen. 11)
> was to stop the building of the city and tower. The scattering was an unmitigated
> good because it resulted in obedience to the divine command, which is the definition
> of good.[11]

> At the tower of Babel, then, the Creator accelerated a built-in creational process of
> linguistic divergence that resulted from geographic separation. Yahweh created the

---

7. Ibid., p. 108.
8. Ibid., p. 114.
9. Ibid., p. 115.
10. Ibid., pp. 115–120.
11. Ibid., p. 116.

'seventy people' (Gen. 10) . . . , an ethnolinguistic mosaic upon the earth (Gen. 10:5, 20, 31; 11:9). This destroyed man's pretensions of collective deity and hubris.[12]

Hence, for Kreitzer, diversity is not abolished in the 'reversal' at Pentecost.

## 1. Babel and the origin of religious diversity

I believe that Kreitzer's analysis of these two chapters within the *Urgeschichte*, together with his broader thesis concerning the centrality of the scattering motif and the 'goodness' of ethno-linguistic diversity, is persuasive. However, although the primary focus of Kreitzer's attention is that of 'ethno-genesis', implicit in his argument are implications for both religion and religions; in other words, a 'religio-genesis'. On a number of occasions Kreitzer links 'religion' to 'ethnicity'. First, in his detailed chapter concerning the biblical words pertaining to ethnicity (*'ām, gôy, ethnē, laos*) Kreitzer lists 'religious covenant' with divinities (whether idols or Yahweh) as being a core characteristic of a *gôy*:

> The word normally describes the ethno-national or ethno-political entities as idolatrous peoples of the world (see e.g., Gen. 10:5, 20, 21, 31, 32; Dt 28:36, 49–51; 2 Sm 7:23). However, Israel as an ethno-political entity is also termed a *gôy* in Genesis 12:3, 35:11, Deuteronomy 4:7–8, 34, 32:28, etc. This seems to indicate that behind territorial, lingual-cultural, and socio-political elements is a religious covenant with divinities, either the gods of the *gôyîm* or Yahweh of Israel.[13]

Kreitzer's comments here have some important affinities to the relationship between religion, culture and worldview as outlined in chapter 2, particularly the 'religious ground motive' or 'heart' orientation behind worldview and its exteriorization in culture. Towards the end of this definitional chapter, and synthesizing a number of Old and New Testament terms, Kreitzer comes to a general definition of 'ethnic solidarities' (ESOLs), which he believes are permeably bounded, centred sets, thus including insights from *both* 'primordial' and 'instrumentalist' perspectives:

> ESOLs then are relatively intermarried (endogamous) groups of families of similar religion, custom, language and geo-history who define themselves in respect to the

---

12. Ibid., p. 136.
13. Ibid., p. 76.

Other, that is dissimilar groups in ever changing internal and external contexts throughout time.[14]

Kreitzer summarizes the 'religious' nature of ESOLs, touching on some familiar themes:

> Both the Old and New Testaments view the *ta ethnē* and *gôyîm* as groups that worship idol-gods (see e.g. Dt 12:2, 30; 29:18; Jos 23:7; 2 Sm 7:23; 1 Kgs 11:1–2; 2 Chr 32:15; Pss 9:17; 135:15; Is 36:18–20; 45:20; Ez 23:30; 1 Pt 4:3). Hence there exists an implicit covenantal unity under the rulership of that/those idol(s), and/or ancestors (or civil religion) (see e.g. Block 2000). These idols are actually empowered by demons (1 Cor 10:20–21; see Lv 1:7 NASB; Deut 32:17 NASB; Ps 106:37; Rv 9:20). Israel itself was a covenanted solidarity of families under the monarchy of El-Yahweh (1 Sm 8–12).[15]

> Scripture always sees the ethnies (*gôyîm*) as being religious. No people and certainly no ethno-law are a-religious or neutral. Therefore, Israel is constantly warned not to follow the idol gods of the nations (Dt 12:2–8, 30; 29:18). These idolatrous peoples follow abominable laws and customs, which flow from their religion. Of course this does not mean that there is not a great remnant of common grace in these statutes, customs, and laws of the *gôyîm* . . . I will tentatively conclude again that this principle remains valid today.[16]

Secondly, although Kreitzer may argue for the creational 'goodness' of ethno-linguistic diversity, he notes that 'religiously' God's prescriptive will is that of a faithful unity of confession rather than religious diversity and pluralism:

> If post-diluvial humanity had obeyed the Creator, they would have developed distinct lingual-cultural groups, yet they would have remained in unity because of their confession and ethics from Yahweh. However, this did not occur, as we shall see. Yahweh thus fast-forwarded the process of creating languages to prevent the evil of a unified, collective humanity to prevail (11:6).[17]

> Instead to the false dilemma of a simple either/or proposition in which a false unity is based on the sin of hubris and the scattering on God's curse, Brueggemann proposes a

---

14. Ibid., p. 400.
15. Ibid., p. 99.
16. Ibid., p. 210.
17. Ibid., p. 102.

'three-factored' counter-proposal . . . 1) Unity of the city is a rebellion to the cultural mandate. 2) Scattering over the face of the earth was indeed a punishment. 3) A true unity was expressed by 'dispersion all over the earth' in loyal obedience to God . . . This model is correct. God judged a false attempt at unity that rejected the Creator's will for true diversity. On the other hand, God judged autonomous diversity as well. The Creator desires a world 'community genuinely loyal to the creator and dependent upon God's gifts and purposes.' This community has different languages attending to the distinctive needs, yet the community is not divided in its primary loyalty.[18]

What is implicit in Kreitzer can be stated more explicitly as a developing redemptive-historical pattern instantiated at both meta- and micro-levels, and revolving around 'faithful' expressions of human unity and diversity, and 'faithless' expressions of human unity and diversity. These can be summarized as follows:

Creation:
- *What God intended*: unity of true religion and ethnic diversity.

Fall:
- *What humankind sinfully wanted*: unity of false religion and ethnic unity.
- *What God gives in both blessing and punishment*: diversity of false religion and ethnic diversity.

Redemption:
- *What God intends (of which the church is a proleptic expression)*: unity of true religion and ethnic diversity.

My contention concerning the Babel incident in particular is that we have here both a historical and a theological account, not simply of the origin of 'religion', nor even the origin of 'false' religion, but rather the origin of the *diversity* of false 'religions'. As Pardigon notes:

Genesis 1–11 does *not* contain any trace of polytheism and paganism, in spite of man's unrelenting and increasing rebellion and failures. All religious activity prior to Babel is immediately related to God, whether in a covenant-keeping and obedient/humble way (demonstrating a true 'seeking' and 'knowing' of Yahweh as God and Lord), or in a covenant-breaking and mutinous manner. In the case of Cain and Abel, for example,

---

18. Ibid., p. 130.

both are addressing their worship to the same God. And yet, only one sacrifice finds favor in Yahweh's eyes. The fact that Abel's is accepted and agreeable seems to be due to both the attitude of his heart and the form of the sacrifice (the latter expressing externally the former).[19]

Given that I have argued that idolatrous 'false faith' was behind the first sin, in Babel we see a new development in the history of idolatry.

I recognize that this is a perspective on the Babel story that needs some justification, not least because the majority of contemporary commentators do not seem to discern such a 'religious' theme. My hope is that this relative neglect is not because this 'religious' reading is an example of tenuous eisegesis, but rather it has not been brought into the foreground of late because, as I have outlined above, questions on the historical origin of religion are unfashionable, a fact compounded when integrated with historical claims concerning the *Urgeschichte*. Therefore I shall attempt to demonstrate some exegetical evidence for such a claim. However, first I want to demonstrate, as I did with the *prisca theologia*, that there is a *historical* precedent in Reformed theology in linking Babel and 'religion'.

### a. Reformed historical precedent

Surveying a number of what appear to be more or less 'speculative' attempts to show a relationship between 'religion' and the origin of language, Harrison speaks of the importance of the Babel incident for seventeenth- and eighteenth-century scholars as follows:

> Whatever difference there might have been between them, sacred historians, comparative mythologists, and champions of the ancient theology all agreed that along with the Fall and the Deluge, the events that took place at Babel had an irreversible effect upon the history of religion. Babel led to dispersion – travel into different geographical areas which in one way or another had shaped religious beliefs and practices. Babel had, moreover, severed that link of communication between the earliest patriarchs and their descendants, effectively halting the transmission of ancient divine truths. Finally, because different names of God had arisen, Babel had led to an appearance of religious pluralism, which, it was generally agreed, led to a *de facto* pluralism.[20]

---

19. Flavien Olivier Cedric Pardigon, 'Paul Against the Idols: The Areopagus Speech and Religious Inclusivism', PhD diss., Westminster Theological Seminary, 2008, p. 277, n. 178 (his italics).

20. Peter Harrison, *'Religion' and the Religions in the English Enlightenment* (Cambridge: Cambridge University Press, 1990), p. 146.

This relationship between Babel and religion continues into the nineteenth and early twentieth century. I shall focus on three representative examples, Delitzsch, Auberlen and Candlish, and finally again Herman Bavinck.

### i. Franz Delitzsch

In a number of places Franz Delitzsch speaks of the 'sin' of Babel, in terms of false worship and God's punishment, acting as both curse and blessing. In his commentary on Genesis he notes that the tower is built to secure them 'against the dissolution of their unity':[21]

> The unity which heretofore had bound together the human family had been the acknowledgement and worship of one God, one and the same religion, and the mode of thought and action resulting therefrom. This unity does not suffice them, they exchange it for an external self-made and therefore ungodly unity, from which the dispersion, which it was to prevent, proceeds as the punishment.[22]

> The name Babel was a significant retrospect of the Divine judgment interwoven in the origin of the world city, and of that tendency to anti-godly unity peculiar to it.[23]

Seeing the danger of this ungodly unity, God destroys their plans:

> Sin has taken possession of this association, it must therefore be destroyed. This destruction is not merely the demand of righteous retribution, but at the same time a wise educational arrangement designed to check the fearful apostasy, to which such spurious unity would lead.[24]

This idea is repeated in his Old Testament history of redemption:

> The breaking up of the united race into peoples with different languages was a divine act for the good of man; for by this means a barrier was made against sin, which without this separating of the wall of the language, would have attained a terrible intensity. Now, however, the immoral and irreligious products of one nation are not equally destructive to another; and many false religions are better than one,

---

21. Franz Delitzsch, *A New Commentary on Genesis* (Edinburgh: T. & T. Clark, 1888), p. 350.
22. Ibid.
23. Ibid., p. 352.
24. Ibid., p. 351.

since they paralyze one another. Even war, which arises from the selfish character
of nationalities, is better than the idle peace of universal estrangement from God,
for the demon of war arouses the peoples and drives them to God.[25]

For Delitzsch, the result is both the loss of a united language and the loss of
united religion: 'But then the linguistic unity of mankind was lost, together with
unity of their religious consciousness, a splitting up devoid of unity and a falling
into fragments devoid of combination took the place of diversity in unity'.[26]

## ii. C. A. Auberlen

In his work *The Divine Revelation* C. A. Auberlen gives an unbroken three-page
quotation from F. W. J. von Schelling's *Philosophy of Mythology* (1856), noting
that 'though we do not bind ourselves to them in detail, or in all their consequences, we agree with them on the whole'.[27] Certainly, some of Schelling's
idealism and proto-panentheism can be detected here, but his comments are
still worth noting. First, though in more rudimentary fashion, he sees the link
between *gôyîm* and religion: 'There are just as many religions as there are nations,
for every nation has its own gods'.[28] Secondly, and moving on to Babel, Schelling
notes that behind the confusion of language must have been a confusion of
intellect (we might say worldview):

> This disturbance must have affected the mind most vitally and profoundly, in its very
> roots . . . it must be a movement which should shatter the bonds which had hitherto
> held men together: that mental force must give way, which had hitherto resisted every
> tendency to separate development.[29]

Schelling continues:

> This force could only be a God who filled the whole consciousness of the soul, who
> was common to all the race; a God who, as it were, comprehended and drew them
> into His own unity. Polytheism, spreading then as ever, made a continuance in this

---

25. Franz Delitzsch, *Old Testament History of Redemption* (Edinburgh: T. & T. Clark,
    1888), p. 39.
26. Delitzsch, *New Commentary on Genesis*, p. 354.
27. C. A. Auberlen, *The Divine Revelation: An Essay in Defence of the Faith* (Edinburgh:
    T. & T. Clark, 1867), p. 163.
28. Quoted in ibid., p. 159.
29. Quoted in ibid., p. 161.

unity of the race impossible. This cause of the actual change is indeed not actually mentioned in Genesis; but by naming the next cause, the confusion of language, it at least indicates the remote and final cause, the rise of polytheism.[30]

Thirdly, the result of this division, and for Schelling the origin of mythology and language ('found at a point of transition when a people have not yet risen into separate existence as a nation, but are just on the point of dividing and becoming such'),[31] still evidences an innate desire for unity, which points us back to 'that remote age':[32]

> Not an outward impulse, but the thorn of inward rest, the feeling that they are no longer the whole of the human race, but only a part of it – that they no longer belong to the absolutely ONE, and have become subject to some particular God or Gods: this was the feeling that drove them from land to land, from coast to coast, until each saw itself alone, separated from all that was foreign to it, and found itself in the place destined for it, and appropriate to it (cf. Deut xxxii.8). This fear lest the unity of man should be entirely lost, and with that, all truly human consciousness, suggested to them not only the first institutions of a religious kind, but even their first municipal arrangements, the purpose of which was no other than to preserve whatever remnants of pristine unity had been saved, and to save them from further disintegration.[33]

Auberlen adds to Schelling's commentary, concluding that the human pride of Babel had radical implications for humankind's relationships and noting a gradual devolution into idolatry:

> While mankind, by their pride in building the tower of Babel, have departed from God, and have lost God, they at the same time have lost themselves. Only in God, who as the source and upholder of all created life, is the bond of union to all, could they be truly one amid diversity. . . . There was, in real truth, no longer a humanity; there were only detached nations, whom God suffered to walk in their own ways (Acts xiv.16). Every apostasy from God is at the same time a subjection to the world and its princes. So it was here. The nations left to themselves, to go no further into the demonic background of heathenism, came more and more under the dominion

---

30. Quoted in ibid.
31. Quoted in ibid., p. 162.
32. Quoted in ibid.
33. Quoted in ibid., p. 163. Notice the reference here to Deut. 32:8, a verse I shall return to below.

of natural forces, climate, soil etc. which they could no longer counterbalance with a spiritual power.[34]

### iii. Robert Candlish

Candlish, in his *The Book of Genesis*, holds that it was Eber (Gen. 10:21) who was given a commission from God to divide the tribes and families,[35] and that, directly rebelling against this mandate, Nimrod and his 'swarm' planned to 'hive' in Shinar:

> Such was, 'the beginning of Nimrod's kingdom' – such was the building of Babel. It was an act of rebellion against God most high; and in particular, against his prerogative of dividing the nations their inheritance; being avowedly intended for the purpose of preventing the orderly dispersion which God had manifestly appointed. It was, moreover, an act of apostasy from the primitive worship and the first open avowal of heathenism or idolatry. The building of the tower 'unto heaven' had undoubtedly religious meaning. What name they were to make, what gods they intended to worship.[36]

### iv. H. Bavinck

Finally, Bavinck, who references Delitzsch and Auberlen, speaks of Babel in a passage on general revelation, its being 'the stable and permanent foundation'[37] of pagan religions whose origins are that of apostasy from pure knowledge of God. Referring to Romans 1:18–32, he notes the objectivity of general revelation (both nature and history) and the subjective suppression of this revelation. He then supplements this by saying, 'In addition, the confusion of tongues and the dispersion of the peoples (Gen. 11) were certainly also of great influence for the development of polytheism.'[38] Noting the 'ethno-religious' nature of *gôyîm* he continues:

> At the breakup of the human race into separate peoples, the oneness of God and hence the purity of religion was lost. Every people or nation acquired its own national god.

---

34. Ibid., p. 165.
35. Robert S. Candlish, *The Book of Genesis: Expounded in a Series of Discourses* (Edinburgh: A. & C. Black, 1868). He bases this on Eber's naming of Peleg (division).
36. Ibid., p. 174.
37. Herman Bavinck, *Reformed Dogmatics*, ed. John Bolt, tr. John Vriend, 4 vols. (Grand Rapids: Baker, 2004), vol. 1, p. 314.
38. Ibid., p. 315.

Once the concept of the unity and absoluteness of God had been lost, other powers could gradually be recognized and venerated as gods alongside the national god. As the idea of the divine became impure and declined, the various forces of nature came to the fore and increased in importance. The boundary between the divine and creaturely was erased, and religion could degenerate into animism and fetishism, sorcery and magic. According to Scripture, therefore, the character of pagan religions consists in idolatry.[39]

## b. Contemporary treatments

Moving on, we come to three more contemporary commentators and theologians who offer an interpretation of Babel that includes a religio-genesis theory, and who generally engage more closely with the text itself: the Reformed scholars Meredith Kline, James Jordan and James Montgomery Boice. Their expositions of the *Urgeschichte* offer an interesting comparison, for while all are agreed on Babel as originating and typifying universal religious rebellion, the details of their respective interpretations are markedly different. I shall outline their treatments of the Babel pericope before offering some evaluative comments highlighting familiar themes I have already commented upon, namely the sovereignty of God, the agency of Satan and the demonic, the close relationship between religion and culture, and a true and 'pure' revelation of God idolatrously corrupted and perverted by sin. What must be remembered here is that concerning these questions of theological and historical ethno-genesis, while I might want to be more dogmatic in generalities, and while I affirm the hermeneutical principle of Scripture interpreting Scripture, my conclusions as to some of the details must be measured and more tentative, especially given that I shall be referring to a number of notoriously opaque texts, all of which, arguably, are related to the Babel narrative, namely Genesis 6:1–4 and Deuteronomy 4:19; 32:7–9, 15–17, 21.

### i. Meredith Kline

Noting both the common curse and grace of the nations scattering in Genesis 10, Kline understands the Babel account to be a representative and local appendation: 'Here the emphasis shifts from the outward aspects of man's worldwide expansion to the inner spirit and religious character of the movement. In this respect too post diluvian history resumed the prediluvian pattern.'[40] A number of relevant points should be noted. First, Kline makes strong thematic links

---

39. Ibid.
40. Meredith Kline, *Kingdom Prologue: Genesis Foundation for a Covenantal Worldview* (Oregon: Wipf & Stock, 2006), p. 272.

between Babel and the infamously cryptic passage of Genesis 6:1–4. Kline interprets the *běnê hā'ělōhîm* (sons of the gods) in 6:1 as human kings who blasphemously claim divine prerogatives and identity in a continuation of the dynasty of Cain.[41] Secondly, although Kline rejects the view that the *běnê hā'ělōhîm* are non-terrestrial angelic or demonic beings,[42] he still notes that the cult of divine kingship retains a strong satanic and demonic element: 'Demons should not, then, be substituted for the human kings in the reconstruction of the event but rather the demonic element should be kept in subordination to the fundamental reality of the earth's rulers' revolt against heaven'.[43] For Kline, Babel is 'a revival, with crusading fervor, of the ideology of the city of man'.[44]

Thirdly, although physically Kline believes the *migdāl* (tower) to be a ziggurat, he rejects the theory that the Babel narrative is derivative from the mythical Mesopotamian ziggurat tradition, arguing rather for Babel's historical facticity. Interestingly, Kline argues that these traditions represent 'the historical continuation of the inner apostate spirit of the Babel enterprise',[45] for in the mythological accounts the celebrating of the achievement of Marduk in the building of the tower and the recasting of the building as a 'creation-event' demonstrate that 'there is a guilt suppression of the ugly fact of man's violation of his covenantal troth to his Creator and a devilish attempt to identify the abnormal conditions of man's fallen state with the pristine order that came from the hand of God'.[46] He continues:

> In their oblique way, the Mesopotamian traditions of the origin of Babylon and ziggurats attest to the nature of the Genesis 11 event as a human effort to do the divine work of establishing the cosmic force. Babel was an idolization of man. Inspired by the spirit of human autonomy and omnipotence, the Babel builders would soar above their geophysical entrapment . . . 'There' (*šām* v. 2) at the place they chose in *šin'ār* (v. 2), they determined to establish the foundation-platform of their mutinous mountain and to launch their temple-pinnacle into the 'heaven' (*šāmayîm* v. 4). Sound plays tie things together: the project to its purpose, the foundation to the heaven-summit, and all to the quest for a name. The old temptation to be like the gods entranced the builders. They covet an immortal name.[47]

---

41. Ibid., p. 186.

42. The 'majority' contemporary interpretation.

43. Kline, *Kingdom Prologue*, p. 186.

44. Ibid., p. 272.

45. Ibid., p. 274.

46. Ibid.

47. Ibid.

Finally, the figure of Nimrod links Genesis 6, 10 and 11: 'Like those ancient dynasts, Nimrod is called a *gibbôr* (Gen. 10:8).'[48] In what might be called the first case of euhemerism, Kline notes that 'claims to deity by Nimrod possibly lie behind the mythological tradition that the gods built Babylon with its stage-tower for the majesty of Marduk. (Some have argued the equivalence of the names Marduk and Nimrod.)'[49]

### ii. James Jordan

James Jordan's fullest exposition of Babel comes in his recent commentary on the book of Daniel, where he seeks to provide a context for understanding the Babylon of Nebuchadnezzar in Daniel 1 – 6.[50] However, certain elements of his exegesis have appeared elsewhere in other contexts. First, as with my earlier conclusions based on the work of Kreitzer, Jordan believes ethno-diversification to be what God *originally* intended for his creation, a reflection of God's triune character, seen now in the unity of the worldwide church; God has established Christianity to establish a true unity of confession (lip), among all nations and peoples, but this unity will not destroy the diversity of languages. Rather, each nation will praise him in its own tongue (Rev. 7:9). Thus the scattering of language at the tower of Babel was not a curse. Rather, it was the multipli-cation of pagan religions that showed God's judgment against the builders of the tower.

Secondly, in contrast to Kline, but again contextually relevant to his under-standing of the Babel pericope, Jordan takes the more 'traditional' interpretation of *běnê hā'ělōhîm* in 6:1, believing them to be Sethites (the elect seed of the woman) who have intermarried with the Cainites (the non-elect seed of Satan), resulting in great apostasy and God's decision not to strive with humankind but to send the flood. Jordan contends that this illegitimate union occurs again in the Babel project, as he believes the 'they' who journeyed from the east in Genesis 11:2 are the Joktanites mentioned in Genesis 10:30, who dwelt in the east. For Jordan this is significant:

> We already know however that Nimrod and the Cushite Hamites were also involved in the Babel Project, but it is specifically the apostasy of the priestly line that is in focus in the Babel incident. This is important, because it

---

48. Ibid., p. 276.

49. Ibid.

50. James B. Jordan, *The Handwriting on the Wall: A Commentary on the Book of Daniel* (Powder Springs, Ga.: American Vision, 2007).

focuses us on the religious rather than the political or cultural aspect of the
Babel affair.[51]

Because of the representative function of the priestly line, 'the sin of a priestly
people affects the whole human race, just as the sin of Adam did. Though not
all of humanity was present at Babel, the scattering of religions and languages
affected all humanity because of the sin of their representatives'.[52] However, like
Kline, for Jordan, the sin of the Babel builders is that 'they rejected the command
of God in Genesis 9:1 to spread over the whole earth. Also, by making a "name"
they were rejecting God as their Namer . . . The idolaters make a false name that
will be the center of their civilization.'[53]

Thirdly, for Jordan this 'religious' component of the Babel story is directly
referred to in the text. Rather than seeing 'language' and 'lip' in 11:1 as a
hendiadys, Jordan translates 'lip' (*śāpâ*) not as language (as in *lāšôn*) but as
'religious confession' as evidenced elsewhere in Scripture (e.g. Job 27:4; 33:3;
Pss 12:2–4; 16:4; 40:9; 45:2; 51:15; Isa. 6:5, 7; Mal. 2:6–7). He writes:

> 'Lip' means religious confession. For instance, alluding to the Tower of Babel, the
> prophet Zephaniah wrote: 'For then I will restore to the peoples a pure lip, that they all
> may call on the name of Yahweh' (3:9). The only other place in the Bible where the
> *saphah* is generally mistranslated as 'language' is Psalm 81:5 where it clearly refers to
> religious confession, not to a foreign language:
>
>> v. 4. For this is a *statute* for Israel,
>> And a *law* of the God of Jacob.
>
>> v. 5. This He established in Joseph for a *testimony* when
>> He went throughout the land of Egypt
>> Where I heard a *language* that I did not understand.
>
> Notice that the word *lip* is parallel to *statute, law,* and *testimony* in the preceding
> phrases. It clearly refers to a religious confession, not just to Egyptian vocabulary
> and syntax.[54]

---

51. Ibid., p. 89.
52. Ibid., p. 91.
53. Ibid., p. 95.
54. Ibid., p. 90. Jordan has said more on this in a previous work: 'It is important to see
    that it was not a simple unity of language that gave these men power. Rather, they

Again, we note the close associations between language, culture and religion. For Jordan the chiastic structure in verses 1–9 and the parallel of the builders communicating to each other in verse 3a with God's confusing them in verse 7b re-enforces the notion that the desire of the builders to make a name for themselves is cemented by a common ideological purpose:

> We can see that this speaking or communication is not merely linguistic, using a common language, but religious having the same ideology. People of various languages can and do combine in ideological projects, the true version of which is Christianity. Thus, speaking to one another is not the idea of conversation but the communication of a common goal.[55]

God's scattering of the builders meant the tower building had to stop: 'The city was the culture that would unify the people at the secondary level. God destroyed the city by destroying the tower project, the primary unifying component. Religious diversity meant cultural disunity.'[56]

Finally, Jordan tentatively presents one more exegetical possibility within the text in his decision to follow the Jewish commentator Samson Hirsch in translating 'confuse' (*bālal*) in 11:7 as 'wither' (*yābal*):

---

> all thought the same way. They had a common ideology, a common religious faith. Without this anti-God unity, they could not have cooperated. In order to shatter this unity, God did not simply divide their languages. First and foremost, He shattered their ideologies. What the story of the Tower of Babel tells us is that there was originally only one, anti-God religion in the world. At the Tower of Babel, God acted to diversify paganism. All the heathen religions in the world have the same basic ideas, but each is slightly different from the rest . . . If it seems strange that God Himself would act to create these different pagan religions, we have to remember that according to Romans 1:18–32, God punished sin by giving people over to it. Idolatry is destructive to human life, and if men rebel against God, He will give them over to worse and worse forms of idolatry, until they repent or are destroyed. The punishment fits the crime. According to Genesis 11:1, all the people not only had a common ideology (lip), they also had the same language (speech). The passage clearly implied that God also confounded their languages so that they would not understand one another. Not only were their religions in conflict, but they couldn't understand one another's speech either' (James B. Jordan, *The Bible and Nations: A Syllabus* [Niceville, Fla.: Biblical Horizons, 1988], pp. 11–12).

55. Jordan, *Handwriting on the Wall*, p. 50.
56. Ibid., p. 101.

What in fact happens with false religions is that over time they lose the power to grip men's souls, they wither. The withering leads to scattering. The way this passage is usually translated, we get the impression that God all at once confused the religion and languages and within 24 hours the people were moving away from one another. The concept of withering, however, indicates that the development of conflict and the decay of the project probably took a generation or two. This withering of the core religion leads to religious and cultural fragmentation.[57]

The withering is at the level of religion, not of language. As we have seen, linguistic and cultural confusion is also entailed, but is not the explicit focus of the judgement. It is rather that there will no longer be one unified false religion in operation among men. The withering of the original false religion produces the multiplication of false religions. Hirsch argues that God did not confuse their religion, so that it became internally contradictory, but that he withered it, so that it no longer operated for them.

From an objective perspective, the various religions of the ancient world look very much alike, but to their servant they were not the same. Baal warred with Chemosh, and Chemosh with Molech, and Molech with Zeus, etc.[58]

### iii. James Montgomery Boice

Boice's thoughts on the Babel pericope are to be found in his more 'popular' expositional commentary on Genesis. They do, however, offer an interesting and suggestive reading of the narrative that merits further investigation. First, and 'completing the set' of main interpretative options for Genesis 6:1–4, Boice believes the běnê hā'ělōhîm to be 'fallen angels', an interpretation in line with many modern commentators.[59] While his lines of argument for this view are fairly standard in this discourse, two interesting remarks should be noted. Boice notes that the Nephilim in verse 6 are the result of a union between fallen angels and humans, and makes an observation that would support what I have called 'remnantal revelation':

What would be more natural than that this union would produce the 'mighty men' of antiquity? Since this verse refers to the 'heroes of old,' what would be more probable than that this is the origin of those stories of half-human-half-divine figures present in virtually all ancient mythologies? The stories of Homer and other writers would be

---

57. Ibid., p. 99.
58. Ibid., p. 100.
59. See Wenham, *Genesis 1–15*, p. 139.

embellished, of course, but they probably reflect memories of these ancient
outstanding figures of the pre-flood period.[60]

Boice also remarks that taking a more 'natural' interpretation of Genesis 6 loses
an important theme in these early chapters of Genesis. For while the 'Sethite'
reading contrasts the godly and ungodly lines, what about the other contrast
concerning the role of Satan in the *Urgeschichte*?

> If Genesis 6 does not refer to demonic activity, Satan apparently fades out of the
> picture entirely after chapter 3. But if Genesis 6 refers to a further attempt by Satan
> to pervert the race, then we have a reminder of his continuing hostility not only to
> God but to ourselves as well.[61]

For Boice, although the ensuing flood is a great judgment upon all of humanity,
it is also a great blessing, for Satan's attempt at 'infecting the entire race',[62] with
the implications of this for redemption (the promised Saviour and deliverer
could not come from a 'demon-possessed mother'), is thwarted and God's plan
of salvation remains intact through Noah and his family.

Fast-forwarding to Genesis 11, Boice keeps the 'satanic' and 'demonic' themes
in the foreground. He agrees with my analysis that Babel has a religious meaning
and justifies this claim in a series of interlocking points largely dependent on
the writings of Henry Morris. First, he notes the significance of Babylon throughout Scripture as being the origin of false religion, not just theologically (cf. Rev.
17:5) but also historically. He quotes Morris: 'The essential identity of the various
gods and goddesses of Rome, Greece, India, Egypt, and other nations with the
original pantheon of the Babylonians is well established. [In fact], Nimrod
himself was apparently later deified as the chief god ("Merodach" or "Marduk")
of Babylon.'[63]

Secondly, Boice focuses on the tower itself, believing that the builders' aim
was not literally to 'reach' the heavens but rather 'in, on, with, or by' the heavens:
'This could mean that the top was dedicated *to* the heavens as a place of worship
(the view of Morris) or even that it had a representation *of* the heavens (a zodiac)

---

60. James Montgomery Boice, *Genesis: An Expositional Commentary*, 3 vols. (Grand
    Rapids: Zondervan, 1982), vol. 1, p. 248.

61. Ibid.

62. Ibid., p. 249.

63. Ibid., p. 340 (quote from Henry Morris, *The Genesis Record* [Grand Rapids: Baker,
    1974], p. 264).

upon it'.[64] Here he notes the origins of astrolatry as being Babylonian and the later Old Testament denunciations that link such practices with demonism and Satanism. His conclusions once again echo the theme of an original 'pure' revelation distorted though rebellion:

> The religion of the tower was actually a Satanic attempt to direct the worship of the human race to himself and those former angels who, having rebelled against God, were now already demons. No doubt as Morris suggests, 'This project was originally presented to the people in the guise of true spirituality. The tower in its lofty grandeur would symbolize the might and majesty of the true God of heaven. A great temple at its apex would provide a centre and an altar where men could offer their sacrifices and worship to God. The signs of the zodiac would be emblazoned on the ornate ceiling and walls of the temple signifying the great story of creation and redemption, as told by the antediluvian patriarchs.' But God was not in this worship. Satan was. Thus, the forms of religion became increasingly debased, and the worship of the devil and his hosts became more noticeable. 'From some such beginning soon emerged the entire complex of human religion – an evolutionary pantheism, promulgated via a system of astrology and idolatrous polytheism, empowered by occultic spiritism and demonism.' Satan is a great corruptor, so it is even possible that this system of religion was a perversion of an earlier, true revelation in the heavens of God's plan of redemption. It has been suggested with considerable evidence that the formations of the stars were originally named by God (or the godly patriarchs) as a reminder of godly things, perhaps even to the point of forecasting the coming of the great Deliverer, who would crush the head of Satan.[65]

## 2. Evaluation and synthesis

What are we to make of these respective interpretations of the Babel pericope? Although all three scholars interpret these passages within their wider redemptive-historical contexts and commitments (remembering that Kline's and

---

64. Ibid., p. 341.
65. Ibid., p. 342. The notion of the 'gospel in the stars', an original revelation of God in creation that has been demonically perverted and counterfeited, has had a number of advocates. See E. W. Bullinger, *Witness of the Stars* (Grand Rapids: Kregel, 1967); Joseph A. Seiss, *The Gospel in the Stars* (Grand Rapids: Kregel, 1979). The most recent is D. James Kennedy, *The Real Meaning of the Zodiac* (Fort Lauderdale, Fla.: Coral Ridge Ministries, 1989).

Jordan's respective 'frameworks' possibly represent the 'bookends' on a covenantal Reformed spectrum),[66] given the infamous opacity of a passage such as Genesis 6:1–4, all three have their particular strengths and weaknesses, and are at times more or less plausible in their exegetical detail. The student of Scripture can weigh the evidence given for some of these proposals and hold to them with more or less certainty. What unites all three, and what places them within a Reformed interpretative tradition, is their concern, shown in their own construals, to see Babel as a 'religious' event, and a supreme theological and historical instantiation of what has already been observed concerning the nature of God and his revelation, the nature of humanity and their rebellion, and the nature of Satan and his deception.

In what remains of this chapter I wish to offer my own theological construction of the Babel incident, which I believe further confirms, consolidates and synthesizes the various strands outlined in this and the previous chapter: (1) the case for remnantal revelation, evidenced in the *prisca theologia*, comparative mythology and 'original monotheism', and (2) the connection between Babel and the origin of the diversity of religion supported by a number of historic and contemporary Reformed commentators.

Without wanting to labour the point unnecessarily I wish to stress once again the tentative and more speculative nature of my argument at this point, knowing full well that what is being presented has the look and sway of an edifice more teetering than rock solid. To reiterate, if on later reflection it were all to come crashing down, I do not believe my overall theology of religions is at peril, particularly because the area of the demonic we shall be focusing on is, as I say later on, a 'dark margin'[67] in my definition of the religious Other. However, given the reality of Scripture in front of us and the need to offer some understanding of religions and their relationship to one another, I believe that what I am about to present is plausible and worthy of consideration.[68]

---

66. Kline's covenantal biblical theology represents a more discontinuous framework, and Jordan's a more continuous one.

67. Hendrik Kraemer, *Religion and the Christian Faith* (London: Lutterworth, 1956), p. 379.

68. It is worth noting Corduan's comments here: 'Some hypotheses are more important than others because they constitute the fountainhead of further truths. Furthermore, there are degrees of plausibility, and when I say that hypothesis A is more plausible than hypothesis B, the difference in meaning may range all the way from 1) "All things considered, I'm more inclined towards A than B," to 2) "A is clearly supported by the best evidence, and B stretches one's credulity to the breaking point." In the latter case we're clearly not merely expressing a subjective preference between two hypotheses of almost equal standing, but a rather well-grounded theory and a highly

In what might be facilely labelled hermeneutical 'good news', a number of scholars have noted a later biblical intertextual 'commentary' on the nature and meaning of the Babel narrative. The hermeneutical 'bad news' is that these texts in their own right are notoriously difficult both textually and interpretatively. My contention is that a 'triangulation' of all of them may aid overall perspicuity. The texts I am speaking of here alongside the Babel narrative are Deuteronomy 4:19 and sections of Deuteronomy 32:7–8, 15–17, 21:

> And when you look up to the sky and see the sun, the moon and the stars – all the heavenly array – do not be enticed into bowing down to them and worshipping things the LORD your God has apportioned to all the nations under heaven.
> (Deut. 4:19)

> Remember the days of old;
>     consider the years of many generations;
> ask your father, and he will show you,
>     your elders, and they will tell you.
> When the Most High gave to the nations their inheritance,
>     when he divided mankind,
> he fixed the borders of the peoples
>     according to the number of the sons of God.
> (Deut. 32:7–8 ESV)

> But Jeshurun grew fat, and kicked;
>     you grew fat, stout, and sleek;
> then he forsook God who made him
>     and scoffed at the Rock of his salvation.
> They stirred him to jealousy with strange gods;
>     with abominations they provoked him to anger.
> They sacrificed to demons that were no gods,
>     to gods they had never known,
> to new gods that had come recently,
>     whom your fathers had never dreaded.
>         (Deut. 32:15–17 ESV)

> They have made me jealous with what is no god;

---

dubious attempt at an alternative to it' (Winfried Corduan, *In the Beginning God: A Fresh Look at the Case for Original Monotheism* [Nashville: Broadman & Holman, 2013], p. 337). In what follows I wish to locate myself far nearer to A than to B.

they have provoked me to anger with their idols.

So I will make them jealous with those who are no people;

   I will provoke them to anger with a foolish nation.

(Deut. 32:21 ESV)

What is immediately interesting about these texts is that, even without the possible allusion to Babel, they are well-known 'argued over' texts within the theology of religions and require attention in their own right. For example, some even within the evangelical tradition use Deuteronomy 4:19 to argue for a theological tolerance of or, even stronger, a version of, inclusivism. As Clark Pinnock writes, ' "With liberality Yahweh permitted the nations to worship him in ways not proper for Israel to do" (Dt. 4:19).'[69] Recognizing the weight of other biblical texts strongly denouncing idolatry, and not wanting to jeopardize the unity of Scripture, many evangelical and Reformed commentators usually end up exegeting this verse in two ways, both of which are 'possible' interpretations. C. J. H. Wright offers both interpretations for consideration. Either the verse refers to a 'provisionality' in God's assignment and allotting 'to be replaced by the true worship of the living God presently entrusted to Israel. This would then be another dimension of Israel's role as the agent of God's blessing the nations';[70] or the verse is not speaking at all of God's positive *intention* that sun, moon and stars be worshipped; rather, these bodies have been given to all nations with the purpose of acting as lights (Gen. 1:14–18), and so are not to be abused as objects of worship.[71]

Deuteronomy 32:8–9 is a *locus classicus* of Old Testament textual criticism, the main question revolving around the translation and identity of the party in verse 8. Although the Masoretic Text speaks of the *běnê yiśrā'ēl* (sons of Israel), both the Septuagint and Qumran fragment 4Q have *běnê hā'ĕlōhîm*, meaning heavenly beings.[72] Although the majority of scholars today believe the LXX 4Q text to have priority, there appears to be a 'theological' subtext to this textual debate, with those who still persist in adopting the more 'naturalistic' variant being accused by some of rationalization and demythologization or, more

69. Clark Pinnock, *A Wideness in God's Mercy: The Finality of Jesus Christ in a World of Religions* (Grand Rapids: Zondervan, 1992), p. 101.

70. Christopher J. H. Wright, *Deuteronomy*, NIBCOT (Peabody: Hendrickson, 1996), p. 52.

71. Ibid.

72. Daniel I. Block, *The Gods of the Nations: Studies in Ancient Near Eastern National Theology*, 2nd ed. (Leicester: Apollos, 2000), p. 27.

charitably, of 'protecting God' and the Old Testament from affirming a more
'opaque' construal of monotheism or, worse, of admitting to the reality of henotheism or polytheism. However, and an issue to which I return in the next
chapter, a more 'supernatural' reading does not entail a denial of biblical
'monotheism'.

Here we return to Babel.

In his study of the relationship between ancient Near Eastern nations and
their deities, Daniel Block's most important piece of evidence for a prior
and primary association with deity and people is Deuteronomy 32:8–9. After
describing these verses' complex textual and interpretive history, he notes that
'we should associate Deut. 32:8' with the tradition that provides the background
to the table of nations in Genesis 10:

> If one assumes the originality of the tradition reflected by LXX and the 4Q
> fragment renderings of Deut. 32:8–9, the chronological sequence of events seems
> to have run as follows: 1) Originally the heavenly court consisted of Yahweh, the
> presiding deity, and a host of lesser beings identified variously as the *běnê 'ělōhîm*,
> 'the sons of God,' princes, or angels. 2) God divided humankind (*běnê 'ādām*) into a
> series of peoples/nations whose total corresponded to the number of members in the
> heavenly court. One of the latter was designated as the patron and guardian
> over each of the former. 3) Israel, however, received special treatment inasmuch as
> Yahweh selected her for his own direct care; she would need no intermediary patron.
> 4) For each of the nations Yahweh allocated a specific geographical region to be
> possessed and occupied.[73]

Given the literary unity of Genesis 10 – 11, we can shed further light on this
connection by bringing Babel into our analysis. In his commentary on Deuteronomy the Jewish scholar Jeffrey Tigay believes 4:19 and 32:8–9 to be a
description of Babel and the biblical origins of polytheism:

> The worship of idols and celestial beings, including the heavenly beings, began
> when God divided humanity into separate nations after it built the tower of Babel.
> Evidently this view assumes that, as punishment for man's repeated spurning of His
> authority in primordial times (Gen. 3–11), God deprived mankind at large of true
> knowledge of Himself and ordained that it should worship idols and subordinate
> celestial beings, such as heavenly bodies. Then, He selected Abraham and his
> descendants as the objects of His personal attention to create a model nation

---

73. Ibid., p. 32.

and show the others the blessing He bestowed on those who acknowledge His authority.[74]

However, at this point Tigay takes a wrong turn when he says that because polytheism is a result of God's will, 'it is no sin for other nations to worship idols and heavenly bodies; it is considered sinful only when done by Israel, to whom God revealed Himself and forbade the worship of these objects'.[75] Again, as I shall demonstrate in the next chapter, there are major exegetical and theological problems in affirming either innocence and/or ignorance to the nations.

A much better conclusion in my mind is that of Michael Heiser, who has studied Deuteronomy 32:8 in some detail. Like Tigay, he links both Deuteronomy 32:8–9 and 4:19 to Babel, noting various difficulties in linking the Masoretic 'sons of Israel' reading to Genesis 10 – 11. However, unlike Tigay, his understanding of God's apportioning supports the theological framework I have been outlining in this study:

> The point of verses 8–9 is that sometime after God separated the people of the earth at Babel and established where on the earth they were to be located, He then assigned each of the seventy nations to the fallen sons of God (who were also seventy in number). After observing humanity's rebellion before the Flood and then again in the Babel incident, God decided to desist in His efforts to work directly with humanity. In an action reminiscent of Romans 1, God 'gave humanity up' to their persistent resistance to obeying Him. God's new approach was to create a unique nation, Israel, for Himself, as recorded in the very next chapter of Genesis with the call of Abraham (Gen. 12). Hence each pagan nation was overseen by a being of inferior status to Yahweh, but Israel would be tended to by the 'God of gods,' the 'Lord of lords' (Deut. 10:17).
>
> According to Deuteronomy 4:19 this 'giving up' of the nations was a punitive act. Rather than electing them to a special relationship to Himself, God gave these nations up to the idolatry (of which Babel was symptomatic) in which they wilfully persisted. Seeing these two passages together demonstrates this relationship.[76]

---

74. Jeffrey H. Tigay, *Deuteronomy*, ed. Nahum M. Sarna, JPSTC (Philadelphia: Jewish Publication Society, 1996), p. 435.

75. Ibid.

76. Michael S. Heiser, 'Deuteronomy 32:8 and the Sons of God', *BSac* 158 (2001), pp. 52–74 (71).

Meredith Kline echoes this interpretation:

> A more general interpretation . . . is that God assigned over each nation a 'son of El',
> these being understood as the heavenly 'princes' of specific nations. Like Persia and
> Greece, mentioned in Daniel 10:13,20,21 and 12:1. It would then evidently be this
> relationship viewed from the reverse perspective of the peoples' idolatrous worship
> of such gods that is referred to in Deuteronomy itself, in 4:19,20 and 29:26, passages
> linked to Deuteronomy 32:8,9 by their common use of key terminology. So
> understood, Deuteronomy 32:8,9 would assert the national election of Israel as God's
> own covenantal proprietorship (32:9; cf. Deut. 4:20), with the concomitant claim to
> Israel's worship, and the abandonment of the other nations to the service of creature
> gods, heavenly princes though they were (32:8; cf. Deut. 4:19; Rom. 1:21–25).[77]

My contention therefore is that what we have in these verses in Deuteronomy
is a divinely revealed 'God's-eye view' of the Babel incident that illustrates the
usual Reformed compatibilist reading of divine sovereignty and human responsibility. God's sovereignty is seen in his apportioning of the nations to be ruled
by members of the heavenly host, but, far from being an 'endorsement' of such
worship, it is a judgment, a 'giving up' to idolatry. This would accord well with
Jordan's understanding of God's confusing or withering the ideological 'lip' of
the people.

Given that these Deuteronomic texts give us a 'peek behind the scenes' of the
Babel incident, are we now able to say any more about the specifics of the nature
of idolatrous 'religion' that God punished and dispersed? Tentatively, I suggest
the following connections and associations, which possibly have the closest
similarities with elements of Boice's reading and draw on the doctoral research
of Mody.[78]

First, if Deuteronomy 4 and 32 are to be read together as perspectives on
Babel, then there would appear to be a connection between astrolatry – the
worship of the heavenly bodies, which God strongly denounces in 4:19 – and
the allocation of heavenly beings (*běnê hā'ĕlōhîm*) to the nations in Deuteronomy

---

77. Kline, *Kingdom Prologue*, p. 290.
78. Rohintan Mody, 'The Relationship Between Powers of Evil and Idols in
    1 Corinthians 8:4–5 and 10:18–22 in the Context of the Pauline Corpus and
    Early Judaism', PhD diss., Aberdeen University, 2008. See also the more popular
    dissemination of his thesis, Rohintan Mody, *Evil and Empty: The Worship of Other
    Faiths in 1 Corinthians 10:18–22 and Today*, Latimer Studies 71 (London: Latimer
    Trust, 2010).

32:8–9. The connection between the heavenly host and heavenly bodies is one made elsewhere in Scripture. As Jordan comments, astral bodies 'are associated with the heavenly host, the angelic and human array around the throne of God. This also follows from the fact that they are positioned in heaven. They represent the angelic host in Judges 5:20, Job 3:7, Isaiah 14:13.'[79]

Secondly, we may possibly be more specific that the objects of idolatrous worship at Babel, either directly or indirectly, through the worship of astral bodies, are 'fallen angels', that is to say that the *běnê hā'ělōhîm* are in reality demons.[80] In Deuteronomy 32 this connection is certainly made (and also by Pss 96:4–5; 106:27, 37):

> But Jeshurun grew fat, and kicked;
>> you grew fat, stout, and sleek;
> then he forsook God who made him
>> and scoffed at the Rock of his salvation.
> They stirred him to jealousy with strange gods;
>> with abominations they provoked him to anger.
> *They sacrificed to demons that were no gods,*
>> *to gods they had never known,*
> *to new gods that had come recently,*
>> *whom your fathers had never dreaded.*
> (Deut. 32:15–17 ESV; my italics)

Poston notes that the 'characteristic' of fallen demons is the desire to be worshipped:

> What we know about demons accords very well with a presentation of themselves as gods and goddesses. They are in league with Satan, who desired to be exalted like God (Isaiah 14:13–14; Ezekiel 28:15–18), and who demanded the worship of Jesus Himself (Matthew 4:9). Thus it is certainly plausible that his minions would have similar goals for themselves . . . in several passages in both the Old and New Testaments, the gods which are worshipped in connection with these idolatrous practices of Biblical people are either equated with or closely connected to demons or demonic activity. (Deut 32)[81]

---

79. James B. Jordan, *Through New Eyes: Developing a Biblical Worldview* (Brentwood, Tenn.: Wolgemuth & Hyatt, 1988), p. 55.

80. See Mody, 'Relationship', pp. 76–91.

81. Larry Poston, 'The Bible and the Religions', in *The Narrow Gate* (unpublished manuscript, n.d), pp. 68–82 (72).

Thirdly, there may be one more level of specificity regarding the nature and character of these demons if we bring back into focus the founder of the city, Nimrod, and his possible eventual 'deification'. We remember that in his exposition of Genesis 6:1–4 and his decision to take the 'supernatural' interpretation of *bĕnê hā'ĕlōhîm*, Boice wishes us to remember the satanic and demonic element in false religion and apostasy. Although Boice does not explicitly make the connection, if we, first, take the Nephilim or Gibborim of Genesis 4 – 6 to be the 'gigantic' hybridized offspring of the de-creational divine or supernatural marriages and, secondly, take the cryptic phrase of Genesis 6:4, 'The Nephilim were on the earth in those days, and *also afterwards*', to mean that these illegitimate unions restarted after the flood, then Nimrod's instrumental founding of the city would bring together many of these themes. While I shall return to this argument in later chapters, when we come to 1 Corinthians 10:20–21,[82] this interpretation of Babel becomes a supreme example of Poston's conclusion concerning the originating role of demonic angels in non-Christian religion and religions:

> In the case of some faith-systems, demonic angels assume the role of various deities for the purpose of receiving worship themselves and keeping people from the knowledge of the One true God. In exchange for this adoration, they dispense certain kinds of 'power' and provide so-called 'revelations'. The Bible indicates that these foundational deceptions are received by human beings and expanded further because of the sinful, rebellious nature of humankind.[83]

While immediately fantastical to our modern sensibilities,[84] the postulation that demons are connected with the dead and the underworld, and particularly the spirits of dead giants, is not without merit exegetically and theologically,[85] and of course is a major theme in non-canonical early Jewish apocalyptic writings such as *1 Enoch*, *Jubilees* and *Liber Antiquitatum Biblicarum* (Pseudo-Philo). In

---

82. 'No, but the sacrifices of pagans are offered to demons, not to God, and I do not want you to be participants with demons. You cannot drink the cup of the Lord and the cup of demons too; you cannot have a part in both the Lord's table and the table of demons.'

83. Poston, 'Bible and the Religions', p. 78.

84. See the comment by Wenham that begins this chapter.

85. For such an unnatural union between human beings and non-human beings would be yet another instantiation of 'de-creation' and rebellion against the creative order.

these works there is far less reticence in their identification of the *bĕnê hā'ĕlōhîm* and the development of demonology, especially the watcher angels who produce the Nephilim.[86]

Finally, we are able to posit in Deuteronomy 32, but also elsewhere in passages such as Psalms 96 and 106, a relationship between idolatry and demons. For Mody, Deuteronomy 32 is a microcosm of his overall thesis, which argues that demons 'stand behind' and 'co-opt' idols:

> In Deuteronomy 32 the relationship between *daimonia* and idols can be characterized as between two distinct entities; *daimonia* are powerful personal supernatural beings who are the supernatural rulers over the pagan nations, and the idols are spiritually unreal and lifeless cult images of pagan gods. The *daimonia* 'stand behind' idols, and co-opt and appropriate for their own use the sacrifices intended for the idols. The sacrifices to the idols of the nations are the means for Israel coming under the sphere of influence of the *daimonia*.[87]

I shall return to this relationship in a little more detail in subsequent chapters when we come to 1 Corinthians 10:20.

## Conclusion

Given my methodological commitments concerning *sola Scriptura*, and the 'difficulties' of these passages, I do not believe one can be dogmatic regarding this interpretation of Babel. However, and bringing together some of the major themes in this and the previous chapter, I finish with some extra-biblical historical support for such a reconstruction in the form of the *prisca theologia*, with its close connections to Gnosticism. The perennial *prisca theologia* tradition, which can be traced from antiquity to the contemporary world, accords with many of the aspects of the Babel story that I have been keen to highlight. What is more, though, this tradition *in itself* is an example of an original revelation,

---

86. See A. T. Wright, *The Origin of Evil Spirits* (Tübingen: Mohr Siebeck, 2005); L. T. Stuckenbruck, 'Giant Mythology and Demonology', in A. Lange, H. Lichtenberger and K. F. D. Romheld (eds.), *Die Dämonen: Die Dämonologie der israelitisch-jüdischen und frühchristlichen Literatur im Kontext ihrer Umwelt* (Tübingen: Mohr Siebeck, 2003), pp. 318–338. Interestingly, some astral connections are made; e.g. *1 Enoch* 18, where fallen angels are associated with the seven stars.

87. Mody, 'Relationship', p. 120.

distorted and perverted over time, where Creator–creature distinctions have been blurred. In closing, a few historical snapshots will suffice.

First, Jean Seznec in his classic work *The Survival of the Pagan Gods* traces how the gods of ancient mythology were gradually 'integrated' in the worldview of the medieval period and the Renaissance. I have already mentioned what Seznec calls the 'historical tradition' in the varied use made of the euhemeristic tradition. Seznec also speaks of the 'physical tradition' that divinized the stars, and so saw the absorption of the gods into astral influences: 'The stars are alive: they have a recognized appearance, a sex, a character, which their name alone suffices to evoke. They are powerful and redoubtable beings, anxiously prayed to and interrogated, since it is they who inspire all human action.'[88] Noting the nuanced negativity towards this tradition by the early Christian apologists, Seznec notes the following:

> Even when the apologists and Fathers interpret astrology in this way, and even when they condemn it – they leave untouched the underlying belief in demons in which it is rooted. The existence of evil angels is an article of faith with them all, as it is for the Church; but the gods of pagan fable are now combined with the demons mentioned in the Bible in confused rabble of malevolent spirits. 'The things which they sacrifice, they sacrifice to devils and not to God', says Paul, speaking of the Gentiles . . . It is through the stars and through astrology that these demons often act. In former times, for man's temptation and perdition, they taught him to read the stars. Now, scattered through the air (*aeria animalia*, as St. Augustine says), they make use of the heavenly bodies to aid them in their evil dominion.[89]

Secondly, although deism may immediately be associated with an incipient rationalism and naturalism, Frances Yates and D. P. Walker in their seminal work on the *prisca theologia* have highlighted much more strongly than either McDermott or Harrison the mystical and 'magical' strand within the tradition, even within a largely 'Christian' cultural milieu. As Walker argues, 'The dividing line between magic and religion, between theurgy and theology, is a hazy one, and the two overlap and interact'.[90] In his chapter on Lord Herbert of Cherbury, one of the most celebrated deists, Walker describes Cherbury's history of religion:

---

88. Jean Seznec, *The Survival of the Pagan Gods: The Mythological Tradition and Its Place in Renaissance Humanism and Art*, tr. Barbara F. Sessions (New York: Harper, 1961), p. 41.

89. Ibid., p. 45.

90. D. P. Walker, *The Ancient Theology: Studies in Christian Platonism from the 15th to the 18th Century* (Ithaca, N.Y.: Cornell University Press, 1972), p. 3.

The ancients 'anxiously' investigated the created world to find something 'eternal' but, realizing they would not find it in this transitory and corruptible earth, they lifted their eyes to the heavens. From the study of the stars they came to attribute all earthy phenomena to astral influences; and this 'perspicacious opinion' of theirs induced them to venerate the stars and planets, not as the 'supreme divinity' but as His chief ministers, to which they therefore gave the names of gods. . . . This was the most ancient, and once the only, religion.[91]

Walker notes that Cherbury believed that such star-worship was legitimate, describing it as a *cultus symbolicus*, not a *cultus proprius*, which it later became through priestcraft:

Verily indeed, if they are alive, they can be worshipped with some sacred and religious cult, such as is fittingly given to holy men; which is the opinion of a most learned Jesuit in his 4th dissertation on the heavens, since those things that are higher seem to deserve greater honour and worship than those that are lower, the eternal than the corruptible, especially among people who considered that, after this life is over, sempiternal felicity is enjoyed in the heavens and stars.[92]

Other contemporaries of Herbert, like Vossius, were less charitable in their reading of star worship: 'Vossius never once suggests that the worship of the sun and stars was symbolic; indeed, his whole book is designed to show, on the basis of Rom. 1:20–28, that the pagans, though some of them had some knowledge of God, always worshipped the creature instead of the Creator.'[93]

Finally, in his recent comprehensive survey of contemporary spirituality in the West, *The Re-Enchantment of the West*, the religious studies scholar Christopher Partridge mentions the *prisca theologia* tradition in his survey of contemporary 'occulture' and in particular the origins of the occultic practice:

Historically, the term 'occult' can be traced back several centuries and concerns that which is hidden or concealed. . . . In 1633 it is enriched with new meaning and related to ancient knowledge and the secrets of antiquity. Hence, in developing this enriched meaning of the term, from a religio-cultural perspective, 'occult' became a broad,

---

91. Ibid., p. 175.

92. Ibid., p. 179. Note that Walker a few pages later (p. 187) says that Herbert changes sources here.

93. Frances A. Yates, *Giordano Bruno and the Hermetic Tradition* (London: Routledge & Kegan Paul, 1964), p. 187.

multi-faceted concept referring to arcane and restricted knowledge. . . . Subsequent occultism, particularly in the nineteenth century, can be described as a subculture of various secret societies and 'enlightened' teachers involved in disciplines concerned with the acquisition of arcane, salvific knowledge (*gnosis* and *theosophia*), the experience of 'illumination', the understanding of esoteric symbolism (often related to occult interpretations of the Kabbalah), the practice of secret rituals and initiatory rites, and particularly the quest for a *prisca theologia, philosophia occulta* or *philosophia perennis* – a tradition of divine *gnosis* communicated, it is believed, through a line of significant individuals, including Moses, Zoroaster (Zarathustra), Hermes Trismegistus (the mythical author of the *Hermetica*), Plato, Orpheus, and the Sibyls. Much time is invested by numerous individuals and groups in interpreting the 'true' meaning of occult material (e.g. the Enochian system famously communicated to Elizabethan magician John Dee) in order to gain access to, it is believed, profound and powerful natural and supernatural knowledge. In short, such occultism is concerned with the understanding of *gnosis* concealed within a complex symbolism and enigmatic alchemical formulae.[94]

This perennial pursuit for secret knowledge is religiously significant and provides a helpful final illustration in this chapter on the origin of religion and the 'religions'. Still under this broad category of occulture, Partridge speaks of both paganism and Satanism, arguing that, while they are separate religions, there are 'areas of significant convergence'.[95] Concerning paganism's contribution to occulture, he mentions the traditional methods of divination, and particularly that of runes:

> Runes are symbols . . . which, for Heathens, are more than simply tools for 'fortune telling' in the modern sense of that term. That is to say, using the runes is more about spiritual guidance, achieving wholeness, communicating with non-human beings and listening to deities, and less about finding out what a person's future might hold.

> If you have come to the realization that you have forgotten your presence on the Earth, the Runes can be used to restore that memory. By using the Runes as gateways, you descend to the underworld to regain lost knowledge and find the spiritual tools that will enable you to carry out the task that you remember. . . .

---

94. Christopher Partridge, *The Re-Enchantment of the West: Alternative Spiritualites, Sacralization, Popular Culture and Occulture*, 2 vols. (London: T. & T. Clark, 2004), vol. 1, p. 68.

95. Ibid., p. 83.

> Runes can . . . help us towards achieving wholeness and act as a mouthpiece for the
> gods, goddesses, ancestors and non-human beings who will help us with the task of
> environmental regeneration.

> This quotation touches on several other important aspects of occulture which
> Paganism is helping to shape and promote, the most important of which are the
> emphases on the ancients, the Goddess, the environment and 'other-than-human
> persons'.[96]

The above quotation brings us back full circle to a single-source theory of
religion, issues of general and special revelation, their distortion and degeneration
as humankind seeks autonomy from God, and the presence of a darker spiritual
influence. We return too both to Van Til and Bavinck, who argue that the media
of special revelation, theophany, prophecy and miracle are counterfeited in
general revelation, thus evidencing, as Edwards posited, a certain continuity
even with radical discontinuity:

> In the second place there is *prophecy*. In Paradise man knew himself to be a
> reinterpreter of God's interpretation. When sin entered the world, man sought to
> be his own ultimate interpreter. Hence in special revelation God had to reappear
> to him as his ultimate interpreter and he himself has constantly felt that there is
> something lacking in all his interpretations of the universe. He has felt something
> of the need of an ultimate interpreter. Hence, we have false prophecy or *divination*
> as a caricature of true prophecy.[97]

> In the case of general revelation in nature and history, we can already speak analogically
> of the appearance, speech, and working of God (Pss. 19:2; 29:3; 104:29).
>     But the correspondence comes to light especially when in view of general
> revelation we include the different world religions in our purview. Not only do these
> religions exhibit a variety of resemblances to the religion of Israel and Christianity
> so that together they belong to one genus – for all religions have a dogma, a code of
> ethics, a cult, a temple and altar, sacrifice and priesthood, etc., but special revelation
> also employs the extraordinary means whose analogues occur in the various religions.
> It employs theophany, prophecy and miracle and does not even disdain the use of lot,
> dream and vision. The divine descends so deeply in the human that the boundaries

---

96. Ibid.
97. Cornelius Van Til, *An Introduction to Systematic Theology*, ed. William Edgar, 2nd
    ed. (Phillipsburg: P & R, 2007), p. 204.

between special revelation and analogous phenomena are sometimes hard to draw. Divine speech and oracle, prophecy and mantic, miracle and magic, prophetic and apostolic inspiration on the one hand, poetic and heroic inspiration on the other, seem frequently to approximate to one another. On a peripheral and atomistic view, it is even difficult in each special case to clearly point out the difference between them. But the person who positions himself squarely in the center of special revelation and surveys the whole scene from that perspective soon discovers that, for all the formal similarity, there exists a larger material difference between the prophets and the fortune-tellers of the Greeks, between the apostles of Christ and the envoys of Mohammed, between biblical miracles and pagan sorceries, between Scripture and the holy books of the peoples of the earth. The religions of the peoples, like their entire culture, show us how much development people can or cannot achieve, indeed not without God, yet without his special grace. But the special grace that comes to us centrally in Christ shows us how deeply God can descend to his fallen creation to save it.[98]

---

98. H. Bavinck, *Reformed Dogmatics*, vol. 1, p. 343.

## 5. NO OTHER GODS BEFORE ME: THE IDOLATRY OF THE RELIGIOUS OTHER IN THE OLD TESTAMENT

For although they knew God, they neither glorified him as God nor gave thanks to him, but their thinking became futile and their foolish hearts were darkened. Although they claimed to be wise, they became fools and exchanged the glory of the immortal God for images made to look like a mortal human being and birds and animals and reptiles.

(Romans 1:21–23)

### Introduction

If Paul's address to the Areopagus in Acts 17 is a *locus classicus* in constructing a theology of religions, then vying for equal attention is the apostle's teaching in Romans 1:18–32. What we are confronted with in this passage is a stark distillation of the universal human religious response to a universal divine revelation. It is this pericope that J. H. Bavinck chooses to confine himself to in his description of 'human religion in God's sight', the centrepiece of his analysis concerning the 'perilous exchange' that takes place when 'the human mind as the *fabrica idolorum* (Calvin) makes its own ideas of God and its own myths'.[1] While for many, such analysis will appear offensive and/or irrelevant, and while we may seek to offer

---

1. J. H. Bavinck, *The Church Between Temple and Mosque* (Grand Rapids: Eerdmans, 1966), p. 122.

nuance, depth and qualification, it is, I contend, out of this pervasive biblical theme of *idolatry*, so seminally summarized in Romans 1, that we must interpret the religious Other and out of which we hew our theology of religions: *From the presupposition of an epistemologically authoritative biblical revelation, non-Christian religions are sovereignly directed, variegated and dynamic, collective human idolatrous responses to divine revelation behind which stand deceiving demonic forces. Being antithetically against yet parasitically dependent upon the truth of the Christian worldview, non-Christian religions are 'subversively fulfilled' in the gospel of Jesus Christ.*

Although much maligned as a tool for theological analysis, it will be argued that *idolatry* is perhaps *the* hermeneutical master key with which to unlock the nature of non-Christian religion and religions. I shall return to Bavinck's own exegesis of Romans 1 in the next chapter, for it provides both a consolidation of material covered in this chapter as well as giving a vantage point from which to offer a panoramic and systematic summary as to the nature of religion and the religions in chapter 7.

In order to reach this summit there lies before us a considerable trek (and for the systematician one both arduous and perilous) as I seek to give biblical theological justification to the bald thesis stated above by focusing on the history of the people of God and their attitudes to the religious Other, as inscripturated in the Old Testament. However, as we begin this ascent (or maybe better 'plunging descent') it is crucial to remember, and continuing the analogy, that we begin our climb neither unprepared nor unaware, for we have already travelled some distance and set up a substantial 'base camp' in the first chapters of this study. In chapter 2 I not only outlined the contours of a Christian worldview but did so, first, from the location of Eden in the early chapters of Genesis and, secondly, introduced there, at the beginning of history, the fundamental creation distinction between the *a se* Creator and finite creature, together with the de-creative *idolatrous* blurring of this distinction in Adam and Eve's 'false faith' – a rebellious and *religious* act of displacement, distortion and denial. In chapters 3 and 4 we gradually moved east and located ourselves in Babel, there witnessing an epic act of human apostasy and the origination of a religious plurality behind which we discovered the influence of the demonic. What is first seen in embryonic microcosm in Eden, developed at Babel and then later summarized by Paul to those in Rome is seen to be instantiated, illustrated and 'incarnated' in the history of Israel: what Kuyper describes as 'the canvas upon which He embroidered the revelation of redemption for us'.[2]

---

2. Abraham Kuyper, *The Work of the Holy Spirit*, tr. Henri De Vries (1900; Grand Rapids: Eerdmans, 1941), p. 52.

Finally, and as we start out, we should acknowledge that we shall have with us a travelling companion for most of our journey through this material. The missiologist and Old Testament scholar C. J. H. Wright has covered this terrain on many occasions and his work is influential among contemporary evangelicals.[3] As will be seen, on many matters I consider him to be a profound and expert guide to be followed. However, on some other matters I wish to question his sense of direction and whether he might misguide.

## 1. An open-and-shut case or an open verdict? Pluralisms and presuppositions in the study of Old Testament attitudes to the religious Other

Tucked away as a footnote in his little monograph on the meaning of the divine name in Exodus 6:2–3, Alec Moyter makes an observational comment which is at the same time both 'throwaway' and profound: 'It is worth remarking that the Bible knows nothing of different "names" of God. God has only one name – Yahweh. Apart from this, all the others are titles or descriptions. This fact is often imperfectly grasped.'[4] How God chooses to reveal himself, to whom God chooses to reveal himself, and the implications for humanity in *not* choosing to relate to God as he chooses to reveal himself are questions that lie at the heart of a biblical theology of religions, questions I have already been indirectly addressing in the previous three chapters.

In the opinion of some, while there may be a number of *missiological* implications that need teasing out, *theologically* these questions are easily answered and do not require much attention. As part of the warp and woof of this Old Testament canvas, one of the most prominent and unifying threads, a thread picked up later by New Testament writers, is that of the Shema: 'Hear, O Israel: the LORD our God, the LORD is One' (Deut. 6:4). Driver rightly calls this 'the

---

3. John E. Goldingay and Christopher J. H. Wright, '"Yahweh Our God Yahweh One": The Oneness of God in the Old Testament', in Andrew D. Clarke and Bruce W. Winter (eds.), *One God, One Lord: Christianity in a World of Religious Pluralism* (Grand Rapids: Baker, 1992), pp. 43–62; Christopher J. H. Wright, 'The Christian and Other Religions: The Biblical Evidence', *Them* 9.2 (1984), pp. 4–15; *Deuteronomy*, NIBCOT (Peabody: Hendrickson, 1996); *The Mission of God: Unlocking the Bible's Grand Narrative* (Nottingham: Inter-Varsity Press, 2006).

4. J. A. Motyer, *The Revelation of the Divine Name* (London: Tyndale, 1959), p. 31, n. 18.

fundamental truth of Israel's religion'.[5] This positive confession of lordship has
many significant implications for a Christian interpretation of other religions,
perhaps the most important being the Shema's negative corollary, the exclusivity of the first commandment, 'You shall have no other gods before me' (Exod.
20:3 NIV), and the explicit emergence and then pervasive presence of the category
of *idolatry*. As Nikides writes:

> If there is any theme suffusing the Old Testament, surely it is the gracious way in
> which God's redemptive intentions work through a covenant people in opposition to
> every form of *idolatry* and *false religion*; these are set in contradistinction to the one
> true faith of Abraham, Isaac and Jacob who are the recipients of singular grace. . . .
> marked and set off by the law for holiness as a witness to the nations.[6]

On this negative aspect Poston is bold in his assertions. First, he states that
'The Bible *never* speaks of the religious expressions of people outside of God's
covenant line in any other than a negative sense. The very first command of the
Ten Commandments speaks to this issue, forbidding the worship of any god
other than Yahweh.'[7] Secondly, on the punishment for idolatry in Deuteronomy
13:6–11[8] he writes:

---

5. S. J. Driver, *A Critical and Exegetical Commentary on Deuteronomy*, ICC (Edinburgh:
   T. & T. Clark, 1895), p. 89. More recently and from the discipline of systematic theology,
   Frame echoes this statement when he notes that the Shema is the 'fundamental confession
   of the people of God in the Old Testament' (John M. Frame, *Salvation Belongs to the Lord:
   An Introduction to Systematic Theology* [Phillipsburg: P & R, 2006], p. 7).
6. Bill Nikides, 'A Response to Kevin Higgins' "Inside What?" Church, Culture, Religion
   and Insider Movements in Biblical Perspective', *SFM* 5.4 (2009), pp. 92–112 (his italics).
7. Larry Poston, 'The Bible and the Religions', in *The Narrow Gate* (unpublished
   manuscript, n.d.), p. 68 (his italics).
8. 'If your very own brother, or your son or daughter, or the wife you love, or your
   closest friend secretly entices you, saying, "Let us go and worship other gods" (gods
   that neither you nor your ancestors have known, gods of the peoples around you,
   whether near or far, from one end of the land to the other), do not yield to them or
   listen to them. Show them no pity. Do not spare them or shield them. You must
   certainly put them to death. Your hand must be the first in putting them to death,
   and then the hands of all the people. Stone them to death, because they tried to turn
   you away from the LORD your God, who brought you out of Egypt, out of the land
   of slavery. Then all Israel will hear and be afraid, and no one among you will do such
   an evil thing again.'

The wording of this command sounds particularly harsh to those of us who have been raised in a culture of 'tolerance.' But the fact that we are horrified by the rigor here only serves to show how radically our Christian sub-cultures have departed from the mind and heart of the One True God. Never in Scripture does He excuse the followers of the non-Christian religions. Never does He 'tolerate' them or see them as simply 'naïve' or 'ignorant.' His attitude is that of a stern Judge who condemns them for their unbelief.[9]

In the Old Testament is there such a transparent uniformity of confession together with a uniform negativity towards the religious Other? Is this a simple 'open and shut' case demanding little more of our attention?

Unfortunately not, for from the perspective of much contemporary academic biblical studies there remains an open verdict or, probably more accurately, a verdict where all appeals to uniformity are laughed out of court. I am very aware of the 'default setting' within contemporary Old Testament biblical criticism, which on the subject of ancient Israelite religion plays a particular theme in countless variations of varying sophistication. First, concerning the text itself, the view that while later redactional conformity may have been attempted, seen negatively by some as religiously oppressive and positively by others as religiously progressive, there are enough textual clues to show us that what we have before us is a composite collection of discordant writings that show the pluralistic character of the biblical text on the subject of religious pluralism. Secondly, the methodological separation between history and theology and the attempt to 'go behind the biblical text' to reconstruct with the help of archaeological and epigraphic evidence the historical origins of monotheism in ancient Israel.[10]

---

9. Poston, 'Bible and the Religions', p. 81.

10. To reiterate an important point of theological method, *sola Scriptura* means that Scripture interprets history and not the other way around. As John Sailhamer puts it, 'The meaning assigned to the things (*res*) referred to by the words of Scripture is found in the meaning of those words (*verba*) as parts of the ancient biblical language. The biblical words point to and assign meaning to the extrabiblical things (*res*) in the real (*res*) world' (John H. Sailhamer, *The Meaning of the Pentateuch: Revelation, Composition and Interpretation* [Downers Grove: InterVarsity Press, 2009], p. 88). Therefore, while it will be necessary to engage in a certain amount of historical speculation in this chapter (in order to uncover and question unwarranted presuppositions of others in this area), I do not want to imply methodologically that the Bible is to be treated as 'a kind of repository of the religious beliefs and practices of . . . early saints' from which '[r]emnants of early pentateuchal religion

Thirdly, the favoured version of the reconstruction itself, which presupposes an evolutionary model of religious development from polytheism *via* henotheism to mono-Yahwism, typically that 'Israelite religion was originally indistinguishable from Canaanite religions, and that exclusive Yahwism was a late development of the monarchical period'.[11]

What is our immediate response to these approaches to the Old Testament? At one level, given the theological method and doctrine of Scripture presupposed and espoused in this study, we need not spend too much time on many of these constructions, as they ultimately evidence very different presuppositions and so are immediately ruled out of court. We are fortunate on this occasion to be able to circumvent this particular jungle, recognizing that there are those intrepid souls with presuppositions similar to ours whose vocation it is to try to cut through (or, in some cases, slash and burn) this terrain. That said, and from a position of relative safety, it is still instructive to make a general methodological point concerning such approaches. The desire to 'get behind' the biblical text to find the 'real' history, the resulting chasm posited between the two, often believed to be 'confirmed' by extra-biblical sources, and the resulting speculative nature of the whole enterprise juxtaposed with often quite dogmatic ideological, even theological, conclusions, must be questioned.

As Bauckham writes:

> The conclusion that exclusive Yahwism did not exist until the late monarchical period results mainly from treating the biblical texts not just with historical scepticism but with historical scepticism based on very considerable ideological suspicion of the texts, along with the use of religio-historical models for interpreting the non-biblical evidence and making a plausible story out of it. Such models are inescapable in any history of religions, and the smaller the amount of evidence and the more ambiguous it is, the more it is the models that control the conclusions from the evidence. Once the biblical texts have been discounted as reliable evidence, not only because of the very late datings given them but also because they are so ideologically shaped, the remaining evidence is, it must surely be admitted, rather easily malleable according to the models and analogies employed. While the historical reconstruction may indeed fully respect the integrity of this evidence, it is not so easy to tell whether an

---

and revelation [have] . . . to be "discovered"' (ibid., p. 568). Rather, 'we must understand [the patriarchs'] beliefs only as the Pentateuch describes them to us' (ibid., p. 570).

11. Richard Bauckham, *Jesus and the God of Israel: God Crucified and Other Studies on the New Testament's Christology of Divine Identity* (Cambridge: Eerdmans, 2008), p. 72.

alternative historical reconstruction might not do so just as well. Ironically, there is a clear danger of historiography that is not less ideologically shaped than it considers that of the Deuteronomists to have been. In particular, most such reconstructions seem controlled by a developmental model, however nuanced, that envisages a series of steps that advance by stages towards full monotheism and cannot reckon with serious departure from monotheism once it has been attained.[12]

In short, behind this evolutionary model can be found not epistemological 'neutrality', but the historical-critical presuppositions of the Enlightenment driven by some form of naturalism or deism.

While this methodological critique of presuppositions might enable us to cut through a swathe of Old Testament criticism and cut out from the root a number of illegitimate constructions regarding religion in the Old Testament, there is not yet a clear road ahead of us. There still remain a number of thorny Old Testament issues concerning Old Testament religion and Old Testament attitudes to the religious Other. While we may question his overall method in a similar fashion to those criticisms just aired, let us take the Jewish scholar Robert Goldenberg's study *The Nations That Know Thee Not*[13] as a typical example. Goldenberg's sole focus concerns ancient Jewish attitudes towards other religions. His study begins with a chapter on the Hebrew Bible. While he notes that the canon is virtually unanimous regarding the exclusivity of Israel's worship of Yahweh, he argues that there is no such uniformity to related questions, including whether this demand of exclusivity to Yahweh extended to other people. He writes:

> [W]hy was it wrong in the first place for Israelites to worship other divinities? If the demand for Israelite monolatry was based on an appeal to covenantal loyalty, then presumably such an appeal had no relevance to the lives of other nations who did not share in Israel's covenant with YHWH. If, however, the prophet's claim was to be understood as implying the unreality of other divinities altogether – if the worship of other deities was understood as involving a truly cosmic error, if the worship of other gods was wrong because those gods were false – then other nations too had to be weaned of [*sic*] of such worship: intellectual integrity and simple human decency demanded no less.
>
> On this matter, the biblical canon taken as a whole has no consistent point of view. Some passages unequivocally deny the existence of all deities other than YHWH and

---

12. Ibid., p. 73.
13. Robert Goldenberg, *The Nations That Know Thee Not: Ancient Jewish Attitudes Toward Other Religions* (New York: New York University Press, 1998).

denounce the worship of such deities by anyone at all. In the long run, such a denial of other deities was taken up in post-biblical Jewish and Christian thought, both of which projected it back onto Scripture as a whole as the biblical view of idolatry. This course of development, however, obscured an alternate view, preserved in many other passages of the Hebrew Bible, that saw nothing wrong with gentiles continuing to honor their ancestral deities just as the Israelite prophets wanted their compatriots to honor theirs.[14]

Therefore Goldenberg proposes that Israelite sacred literature evidences a plurality of views:

> In the end the Bible was canonized and accepted among Jews and Christians everywhere as the word of God, with the result that diverse attitudes toward the religious traditions of gentile nations were preserved side by side in the texts of Scripture. Taken as a whole, Israel's sacred literature now endorsed pluralism, whether neighbourly or competitive, and vehement missionary exclusivism at the same time; followers of the God of Israel might adopt either stance toward the religions of their gentile neighbors.[15]

He marshals a number of pieces of evidence to make his case.

First, he looks at the response of the people to Jeremiah's judgment on their idolatry in Jeremiah 44, where they determine not to listen to the prophet but to continue making offerings to the queen of heaven. Goldenberg argues that this dispute revolves around not whether another god exists but the power of this god in comparison to Yahweh. His point is that those who continue to worship the queen of heaven do not necessarily cease to worship Yahweh, nor do they repudiate their nations' covenant with Yahweh. Therefore they must not be charged with either apostasy or abandonment:

> By implication, they reject one point only: they cannot accept Jeremiah's demand they worship YHWH and YHWH alone; they cannot believe their covenant with YHWH requires this. We have tried that, they say, with disastrous results; we are too frightened to try again.[16]

Secondly, Goldenberg highlights a number of texts (Judg. 11:23–34; Deut. 4:19; 29:25; Dan. 10; Mic. 4:5) that required Israelite loyalty to Yahweh but 'no

---

14. Ibid., p. 9.
15. Ibid., p. 10.
16. Ibid., p. 14.

necessary quarrel with his counterpart divinities'.[17] For Goldenberg there is implied in these texts

> no urgent desire to put an end to polytheism and idolatry; it was enough to keep Israelites away from them. It was not implied that all humanity ought to worship the same deity; every nation had its own divinities, and the world worked according to plan when every nation remained loyal to its own proper gods.[18]

To elaborate this point further, Goldenberg focuses on three characters: Ruth, Rahab and Naaman. Regarding Ruth 1:15–16, Goldenberg does not equate Naomi's *'ĕlōhîm* with Israelite monotheism:

> There is no hint that any of the three women believed that acceptance of Israelite identity demanded the acceptance of monotheism, or indeed that Israelite religious conceptions were in any way closer to monotheism than their Moabite counterparts. The issue between Ruth and Naomi is not the truth and falsity of various divinities but rather the religioethnic loyalty that will shape the rest of their lives.[19]

Rahab's confession of Yahweh in Joshua 2:9–11 is one

> elicited more by the frightening power of the invading Israelite horde than by any intellectual analysis of the nature of the divine; it places in the mouth of a simple Canaanite woman the fundamental idea that no nation can achieve worldly power unless its tutelary deity rules the earth on its behalf, and acknowledges YHWH's ability to dominate the present situation.[20]

Although Naaman makes a bold profession of faith in Yahweh (2 Kgs. 5:15), Goldenberg remarks that the general wishes to return to Aram and to continue

---

17. Ibid.

18. Ibid., p. 15. Cf. Tigay here on his exegesis of Deut. 4:19; 32:8: 'This view of polytheism reflects the assumption that if the rest of mankind does not worship the true God, that must be God's will. For this reason, it is no sin for other nations to worship idols and the heavenly bodies; it is considered sinful only when done by Israel, to whom God revealed Himself and forbade the worship of these objects' (Jeffrey H. Tigay, *Deuteronomy*, ed. Nahum M. Sarna, JPSTC [Philadelphia: Jewish Publication Society, 1996], p. 435).

19. Goldenberg, *Nations That Know Thee Not*, p. 16.

20. Ibid., p. 17.

worshipping Rimmon: 'One can easily imagine Naaman will say kind words to the prophet but then go home and reconfirm his fealty to the Aramean god who has made him great'.[21] Goldenberg's conclusion here is that 'these stories, despite the bold assertions of Yahweh's greatness, do not reflect that assumption that gentiles worship false gods and should be encouraged to stop doing so'.[22]

Thirdly, Goldenberg notes the difficulty in distinguishing 'between theological assertion that means what it says and national pride in the form of exaggerated praise for the national deity'.[23] The biblical writers believed their God was the strongest among a pantheon of other honoured deities. However, by the time these texts are redacted, the fear of a reversion to ordinary polytheism meant that such a view is hidden: 'Widely reflected beneath the surface of the final canon, it receives clear expression almost nowhere'.[24] The denigration of other gods eventually becomes a denial of their divinity, as seen in Elijah's battle with the prophets of Baal and the exclusive statement of Isaiah 40:18–19, 25:

> Extending a favourite point of Yehzkel Kaufmann this position can be said to involve a kind of wilful misunderstanding of polytheism, as though the only choice were between one candidate for the title of 'God' and another, as though there were no real possibility that both YHWH and Baal could be gods, albeit rival gods contending for the loyalty of the fold. This sense that loyalty to YHWH requires denial of his rivals' very entitlement to the name 'god' is the matrix out of which Judeo-Christian monotheism emerged.[25]

What are we to make of a thesis like that of Goldenberg? Clearly, Goldenberg is not an evangelical scholar, and so does not hold to the presuppositions of Scripture (especially concerning its unity) espoused in this study. But before he is dismissed out of hand, we must recognize that many of the issues and examples he uses *have* been raised by evangelicals (who therefore hold the same methodological presuppositions as I do), and so demand attention. Later on in this chapter I shall focus on two specific questions: the alleged anomaly concerning the religion of the patriarchs, and whether in some cases there is an 'interim acceptance' of idolatry among the nations. For now, I wish to offer some more general observations.

---

21. Ibid.
22. Ibid.
23. Ibid., p. 18.
24. Ibid., p. 20.
25. Ibid., p. 22.

Concerning both the internal consistency of the biblical text and the relationship between the text and extra-biblical evidence, I wish to contend that what is often heard as dissonance and discord is actually the complex but unified 'canonically limited polyphony' I have argued for in chapter 1. Apparent contradictions in the biblical texts that may result in wilful neglect, eisegesis or crass harmonizations are avoided when we properly distinguish and differentiate among

- an Enlightenment conception of monotheism as opposed to the more dynamic biblical conception;
- normative or 'official' *prescriptions* of Israelite religion from various *descriptions* of aberrant and popular religious practices;
- Yahweh's exploitation of idolatrous religion without the giving of his assent;
- the progress of revealed redemptive history as opposed to syncretistic and evolutionary modes of religion from polytheism to monotheism.

Each of these merits a study, but let me now summarize each in turn.

### a. Enlightenment monotheism versus Yahweh's transcendent uniqueness

In a previous chapter I argued that the Creator–creature distinction is a fundamental building block of a Christian worldview, with God's *aseity* being central to the preservation of this distinction. I also mentioned the tradition in Christian theology of linking *aseity* with the meaning of the divine name. Whether or not there is a direct link between the two, my contention is that the meaning of the central Old Testament confession of the Shema together with the first two commandments imply and illustrate God's *aseity* and the Creator–creature distinction, thus implying and illustrating the Christian worldview. As I shall explain, the ramifications of this teaching for my theology of religions are far-reaching.

In understanding what we might call the 'doctrine of God in the Old Testament', Richard Bauckham's analysis in his essay 'Biblical Theology and the Problems of Monotheism' is a helpful starting point; indeed, it is something of a *tour de force*.[26] Bauckham starts by covering familiar ground, with a strong

---

26. The essay was first published in Craig Bartholomew (ed.), *Out of Egypt: Biblical Theology and Biblical Interpretation* (Milton Keynes: Paternoster, 2004), pp. 187–232. I am referring to its republication in the more recent work by Bauckham, *Jesus*, pp. 60–106.

critique of the evolutionary model of religious development in Israel, in particular the work of Robert Gnuse.[27] However, Bauckham's main interlocutor is Nathan MacDonald in his monograph *Deuteronomy and the Meaning of 'Monotheism'*.[28] MacDonald argues that the employment of the term 'monotheism' by many Old Testament scholars is not the confession of Israel enshrined in the Deuteronomic Shema, but rather a rationalized, intellectualized construction of Enlightenment origin imposed upon the text and leading to various evolutionary reconstructions of Israelite religion. The authentic 'monotheism' of Deuteronomy has been obscured. While appreciative of much of MacDonald's thesis, Bauckham is critical of MacDonald's understanding of Yahweh's uniqueness, particularly as MacDonald appears to reduce this uniqueness to the relationship Yahweh has with Israel, thereby making uniqueness primarily a soteriological rather than an ontological claim.[29] Having expertly cleared the ground, Bauckham proposes his own understanding of Jewish monotheism, recognizing the importance of this understanding for a Christian '"pan-biblical" theology':[30]

> For Jewish monotheism, the one God has a unique name, YHWH, and a unique relationship with his chosen people Israel, to whom he has revealed not only the supreme power he exercises in mighty acts of salvation and judgement in relation to Israel, but also moral dispositions . . . that characterise his dealings with Israel. All these elements of YHWH's particular identity as the God of Israel are essential to Jewish monotheism, as are the requirements of Israel summed up in the first commandment of the Decalogue and in the Shema, which make Israel's monotheism no mere matter of intellectual belief but a matter of distinctive cultic practice and living obedience that encompasses the whole of life.[31]

For Bauckham, central to Jewish monotheism is the claim of Yahweh's 'transcendent uniqueness':

> The essential element in what I have called Jewish monotheism, the element that makes it a kind of monotheism, is not the denial of the existence of other 'gods', but an

---

27. Robert Karl Gnuse, *No Other Gods: Emergent Monotheism in Israel*, JSOTSup 241 (Sheffield: Sheffield Academic Press, 1997).

28. Nathan MacDonald, *Deuteronomy and the Meaning of 'Monotheism'*, FAT 2.1 (Tübingen: Mohr Siebeck, 2003).

29. Bauckham, *Jesus*, pp. 62–71.

30. Ibid., p. 83.

31. Ibid.

understanding of the uniqueness of YHWH that puts him in a class of his own, a wholly different class from any other heavenly or supernatural beings, even if these are called 'gods'. I call this YHWH's transcendent uniqueness. (Mere 'uniqueness' can be what distinguishes one member of a class from other members of it. By 'transcendent uniqueness' I mean a form of uniqueness that puts YHWH in a class of his own.) Especially important for identifying this transcendent uniqueness are statements that distinguish YHWH by means of a unique relationship to the whole of reality: YHWH alone is Creator of all things, whereas all other things are created by him; and YHWH alone is the sovereign Lord of all things, whereas all other things serve or are subject to his universal lordship.[32]

What precisely is Bauckham saying here? The evolutionary model of Old Testament religion has often seen an internal redactional struggle between texts that affirm the relative claim of the incomparability of Yahweh (none *like* him) that imply a polytheistic context, in contrast to an affirmation of God's oneness (no *other* God).[33] We saw this tension outlined in Goldenberg's work. Bauckham's understanding of 'transcendent uniqueness' brings both of these elements together into a unified and consistent whole. Commenting on 1 Kings 8:60, 'so that all the peoples of the earth may know that the LORD is God; there is no other' (NRSV), he writes:

> The conclusion . . . can surely not mean that all the peoples of the earth will know that YHWH is the only god *for Israel*. What they will recognize is that YHWH alone is 'the God'. They need not deny that there are other gods, but they will recognize the uniqueness of YHWH as the only one who can be called 'the God'. It is in this category that 'there is no other.'[34]

He continues:

> The 'incomparability texts' usually say that YHWH is incomparable among 'the gods' (though sometimes the comparison is more generally with any creature at all) and so seem superficially polytheistic, in the sense of admitting the existence of other heavenly beings. In fact, however, they are expressions of the 'monotheizing' dynamic that is

---

32. Ibid., p. 86.
33. These are C. J. H. Wright's terms, in Wright, *Mission of God*, p. 82. Wright refers to numerous biblical texts to prove this claim; e.g. 2 Sam. 7:22; Ps. 86:8, 10; Isa. 46:9; 1 Kgs. 8:23, 60.
34. Bauckham, *Jesus*, p. 70 (his italics).

constantly driving a line of absolute distinction between YHWH and other 'gods'. The effect of 'there is none like YHWH' is precisely to put YHWH in a class of his own, exactly as the first category of texts do in denying that there is any 'other' besides YHWH. Whether the existence of other gods is denied or whether YHWH is simply said to be in a class of his own by comparison with them is of small importance to the general sense of all these texts. This is confirmed by the fact that examples of the two kinds of text sometimes occur in close association with each other, for example:

'There is none like you, and there is no god besides you' (2 Sam. 7:22).

'I am God, and there is no other; I am God, and there is no one like me' (Is. 46:9).[35]

It bears repeating that belief in the existence of other heavenly beings *does not* jeopardize Yahweh's transcendent uniqueness; indeed, it confirms it. A passage such as Nehemiah 9:6, 'You are the LORD, you alone; you have made heaven, the heaven of heavens, with all their host, the earth and all that is on it, the seas and all that is in them. To all of them you give life, and the host of heaven worships you' (NRSV), believed by some not to be a monotheistic text, is now shown to be strongly monotheistic:

By attributing to YHWH the creation of all other reality, by emphasizing that all creatures without exception have been created by YHWH, this text is making an absolute distinction between the unique identity of YHWH and all other reality. The fact that other heavenly beings, YHWH's retinue, 'the host of heaven', are included does not qualify the uniqueness of YHWH but, on the contrary, serves to underline YHWH's uniqueness by making it unequivocally clear that YHWH does not belong to a class of heavenly beings that include him with the host of heaven, but is absolutely distinguished from the host of heaven in that he created them. This text makes the transcendent uniqueness of YHWH as clear as could be.[36]

For Bauckham, when the Hebrew canon speaks of other 'gods', the reference falls into one of two categories. On the one hand, these 'gods' are created beings who are 'members of YHWH's retinue, serving his rule, or they are impotent non-entities':[37]

---

35. Ibid., p. 90.
36. Ibid., p. 87.
37. Ibid., p. 88.

In the former case, they are called by a variety of terms (gods, sons of gods, sons of the Most High, holy ones, watchers, the host of YHWH, the host of heaven) . . . The general point is that these 'gods' are not independent powers but servants of YHWH who no more qualify his unique status than do human beings who worship and obey YHWH. The other category of 'gods' is the gods of the nations reduced to the status of powerless non-entities by the biblical texts' insistence on YHWH's uniquely supreme power and ridiculed as 'non-Gods' and 'nothings.' Again the monotheizing dynamic is apparent, not in absolutely denying their existence, but in denying them
the status that could conceivably detract from YHWH's transcendent uniqueness.[38]

Bauckham is not alone in positing such an understanding of biblical monotheism. In a more recent article, which explores the issue of divine plurality in the Hebrew Bible, Michael Heiser comes to a similar conclusion:

My own view is that Israel believed in the existence of other gods, but that Yahweh was 'species unique.' That is, Yahweh was an *elohim*, but no other *elohim* was Yahweh – *and never was nor could be*. Yahweh was ontologically superior to and distinct from all the other gods. As Isaiah 43:10 and 44:6–8 affirm, Yahweh alone is pre-existent and uncreated. He in fact created all the divine members of the heavenly host. Their life derives from him, not vice versa. By virtue of His ontological superiority, Yahweh alone is sovereign and thus deserving of worship. Interestingly, species uniqueness is the basis for God's distinction from the other gods in later Jewish writers.

One could object that the idea of 'species uniqueness' is unintelligible with respect to divine beings, perhaps by analogy to the human world. I am human, yet no other human is me, but all humans share the same species status. Hence one can be unique in properties, but *species* uniqueness is a fallacy. The analogy with humankind is flawed, however, since no such claim as pre-existence before all humans is seriously offered. An attribute shared by no other member in the species makes for species uniqueness.[39]

---

38. Ibid.
39. Michael S. Heiser, 'Monotheism, Polytheism, Monolatry, or Henotheism? Toward an Assessment of Divine Plurality in the Hebrew Bible', *BBR* 18.1 (2008), pp. 1–30 (29; his italics). This article seems to be a summary of his doctoral thesis. See Michael S. Heiser, 'The Divine Council in Late Canonical and Non-Canonical Second Temple Jewish Literature', PhD diss., University of Wisconsin – Madison, 2004, available online at http://digitalcommons.liberty.edu/cgi/viewcontent.cgi?article= 1092&context=fac_dis (accessed 4 Oct. 2013).

At this point it merits saying that 'transcendent' or 'species' uniqueness chimes with many themes already mentioned in this study. First, these terms are just another way of affirming the divine *aseity* and the Creator–creature distinction, defined earlier as a foundational building block in a Christian worldview. Secondly, the 'transcendent' aspect recognizes the universality of Yahweh's dominion, and the covenantal accountability *all* humans have towards him, which I named as a perpetual *particular religiosity*. After the fall, the relationship between all humans and Yahweh remains, yet is now one of 'false faith'. This is a definition of idolatry. Thirdly, transcendent uniqueness allows for the existence and activity of other created supernatural beings, beings already encountered in the discussion of the *běnê hā'ělōhîm* in Genesis 6 and Deuteronomy 32, and their involvement in the genesis of the religious diversity from Babel.

### b. Prescription versus description

The second distinction to be made concerns the normative or 'official' *prescription* of Israelite religion from various *descriptions* of aberrant and popular religious practices. One typical example of both description and prescription side by side and clearly differentiated in the text is 2 Chronicles 15:16–18:

> King Asa also deposed his grandmother Maakah from her position as queen mother, because she had made a repulsive image for the worship of Asherah. Asa cut it down, broke it up and burned it in the Kidron Valley. Although he did not remove the high places from Israel, Asa's heart was fully committed to the LORD all his life. He brought into the temple of God the silver and gold and the articles that he and his father had dedicated.[40]

---

40. Daniel Block gives two other examples here: 'While Jephthah may have gotten his facts wrong, according to his response to the Ammonites in Judges 11:24, he seems to recognize the actual involvement of Chemosh in Ammonite affairs, as on a par with Yahweh's activity in Israel's: "Should you not possess what your god Chemosh gives you to possess? And should we not be the ones to possess everything that Yahweh our God has conquered for our benefit?" It should be remembered, however, that Jephthah embodies all that is wrong with Israel at this time. With his self-interested perspective on his own office and in particular his sacrificing of his daughter in fulfilment of a stupid vow to secure the favour of Yahweh, Jephthah's syncretism is typical of the recidivist Israelites in the dark days of the judges. Consider, too, David's response to Saul in 1 Samuel 26:19, when he tells him to "Go, serve other gods." Surely David's faith and religious commitment at this point is impeccable. The problem evaporates, however, when it is recognised that David is

Richard Hess's work is helpful in illuminating this distinction.[41] First, he discerns four distinct types of religious outlook in the northern and southern kingdoms, of which only the first is the prescribed view. Carson neatly summarizes this typology:

> a) The religion of the prophets insisted that Yahweh alone be worshipped, and that the covenant between Yahweh and his people be honoured. b) Many of the kings compromised such exclusiveness, tolerating and sometimes participating in the cults of the neighbouring pagan states, and entering into marriage alliances with the royals of those states. c) Doubtless for many ill-taught ordinary Israelites Yahweh was the official or state deity, recognized to be more or less supreme, while they themselves sought out local deities, not least the local manifestations of Baal and Asherah, and sometimes also assorted household gods. d) In certain more extreme cases, foreign deities were imported, and (at least temporarily) forced on the nation by compromised and compromising royalty.[42]

Next, Hess looks at a range of extra-biblical inscriptional evidence, and concludes that there is confirmatory support for this variegated biblical picture.[43] What is more, there appears to be confirmation of the normative or official 'exclusive' view, evidenced not only in the discovery of particular inscriptions, but also in the lack of evidence found in Hess's fourth type:

> According to the biblical text, this is the one type of religion we are least likely to find. This is because it seems to have existed for relatively brief periods of time. More importantly, the absence of attestation would be expected from the strong condemnation of the practice expressed by the biblical writers. If it had been practiced at one time, later rulers would have sought to obliterate all traces of it.[44]

---

quoting cursed men who have been trying to drive him away from Yahweh' (Daniel I. Block, 'Other Religions in Old Testament Theology', in David W. Baker [ed.], *Biblical Faith and Other Religions: An Evangelical Assessment* [Grand Rapids: Kregel, 2004], pp. 43–78 [65]).

41. Richard S. Hess, 'Yahweh and His Asherah? Religious Pluralism in the Old Testament World', in Clarke and Winter, *One God, One Lord*, pp. 5–33.

42. D. A. Carson, *The Gagging of God: Christianity Confronts Pluralism* (Leicester: Apollos, 1996), p. 249.

43. He looks at the Kuntillet Ajrud Blessings, the Khirbet el-Qom Tomb inscription and the Jerusalem Pomegranate.

44. Hess, 'Yahweh and His Asherah?', p. 42.

In summary here, the distinction between normative and illegitimate religious practices within Israel is particularly illustrative of a legitimate biblical and extra-biblical 'diversity' concerning ancient Israelite religion, fully consonant with the ebb and flow of divine revelation and human response I have articulated in previous chapters, where we see *both* religious degeneration and preservation even within God's chosen nation.

### c. Divine exploitation without divine assent

My third distinction recognizes many examples of Yahweh's, in his providence and sovereignty, adopting and exploiting elements of idolatrous pagan religions for his own divine purpose, while neither assenting to nor approving of such practices. Daniel Block delineates four categories here, all meriting a brief mention: pagan practices, pagan perceptions, the role of pagan gods, and pagan divine epithets.[45]

First, concerning pagan practices, Block lists a catalogue of forbidden practices undertaken by various non-Israelites (e.g. divination and hepatoscopy[46]), and even Israelites (e.g. Saul's consultation of the medium of Endor),[47] practices described as being effective and thereby furthering Yahweh's purposes. Although admittedly puzzling, Block notes, and this is crucial, that these examples do not merely demonstrate Yahweh's sovereignty and freedom to communicate with pagans and apostate Israelites, 'but this is more than mere accommodation; in doing so he also exposes the folly of their perception'.[48]

Secondly, concerning pagan perceptions, although something like Ezekiel's inaugural vision has many familiar features of ancient Near Eastern iconography, in communicating this picture Yahweh is able to subvert and challenge ancient Near Eastern iconography and thus demonstrate his character and supremacy:

> Whereas Yahweh has chosen 'the lip of Canaan' (Isa. 19:18) as the vehicle of verbal intercourse in an earlier revelatory moment, now he adopts the art of Mesopotamia as his method of ocular communication. And in doing so he beats the pagans and their gods at their own game.[49]

---

45. Block, 'Other Religions'.
46. Ezek. 21:21.
47. 1 Sam. 28:3–25.
48. Block, 'Other Religions', p. 49.
49. Ibid., p. 50.

Thirdly, Yahweh exploits the roles given to pagan gods— for example, fertility function of a Baal (Deut. 7:13–14), and an Ishtar/Astarte. Noting the certain rare words used in the description here, Block comments:

> The extent to which the Israelites in Moses' audience caught the links between the words he chose to use and the religion of the Canaanites is uncertain. However, his preference for these rare expressions seems to represent a deliberate stab at the jugular of Canaanite religion. Not these pagan deities, but Yahweh, the God of Israel, is Israel's only guarantee of safety.[50]

Finally, and returning to the point made above concerning Yahweh's transcendent uniqueness, the 'biblical authors exploit pagan mythological motifs for rhetorical purposes, either to expose the folly of Israelite syncretism or to declare the supremacy of Yahweh'.[51] So Moses, in a rhetorical gesture indicating the superlative nature of Yahweh, declared him to be 'God of gods, Lord of lords, the El' (Deut. 10:17).

### d. Religious devolution versus evolution

The final distinction to be made is between the progress of revealed redemptive history and the regress of idolatrous religion, as opposed to syncretistic and evolutionary modes of religion from polytheism to monotheism. To address this point we first need to take a step back.

So far in this biblical theology of religions I have spent nearly all my time concerning myself with matters of theological prolegomena, and then just the first eleven chapters of the first book of the Bible. Has this been time well spent or an unnecessary *longueur* (a tedious passage)? The method in this seeming madness is a belief in the adage that careful preparation is often the key to the success of any project: method and foundations matter. The theological and historical insights gleaned from these chapters in Genesis, the themes identified and the patterns established not only provide the context in which we approach the relationship between the nation of Israel and other religions, but enable us to 'short-circuit' (as opposed simply to ignore) a number of differing and, I believe, incorrect approaches to this material.

Rather than speculatively attempting to 'get behind the text' to reconstruct Israelite religious history on an a priori evolutionary model, or alternatively deciding not to address historical questions at all, my work in Genesis on the

---

50. Ibid., p. 51.
51. Ibid., p. 56.

nature of religiosity and the origin of religion enables me to offer a far more plausible and faithful 'reconstruction' that can bridge the gap between theological and historical concerns, as well as accounting for the unified yet complex picture of religious attitudes we see in Israel. This picture, to use a photographic analogy, while progressively defined and developed, is but a continuation and development of the original Genesis 'negative'. In other words, ancient Israel is *not* created *ex nihilo*, neither does it emerge from some primeval polytheistic chaos (as I shall argue below), but has a rich history that can be traced in the biblical revelation back to the universal history of Genesis 1 – 11. Importantly, and again a point I shall develop below, these early chapters are not to be detached from what follows – they serve a purpose in the literary unity and integrity of Genesis and the Pentateuch.[52]

For example, three 'patterns' I identified in these early chapters of Genesis can immediately be discerned in Israelite religion. The first are certain universal themes even within religious particularity, for example the pattern where God gives blessing and curse 'through the one to the many'. The second is the identification, on the one hand, of a certain anthropological similarity and continuity between Israel and the other nations in terms of religiosity, while, on the other hand, still upholding Israelite dissimilarity, discontinuity, indeed uniqueness, from the surrounding nations. Finally, and blatantly contradicting much contemporary Old Testament scholarship on the history of ancient Israelite religion, while much Old Testament scholarship assumes an evolutionary model of religious development, one discerns a *devolutionary* model of religious development, which posits degeneration from an original revelation of God into henotheism and polytheism and thus requiring constant divine preservation and regeneration.

Encouragingly, while the evolutionary model of religion still holds sway in Old Testament scholarship, the position I am articulating is not unknown in the literature, as Arnold points out in his comment on D. L. Petersen's typology concerning theories regarding the history of monotheism – evolution, revolution and devolution:

> From an ancient and positively valued religious conception (monotheism), there developed a less sophisticated and ignoble one, polytheism. Few indeed are the Old Testament scholars who have argued for such an ideological dissolution, *though the primeval history traditions may be interpreted to portray such a process.*[53]

---

52. And, of course, the OT and the entire canon.

53. Bill T. Arnold, 'Religion in Ancient Israel', in David W. Baker and Bill T. Arnold (eds.), *The Face of Old Testament Studies: A Survey of Contemporary Approaches*

Daniel Block is one senior Old Testament scholar who recognizes that there are 'fundamental common denominators between Yahwistic faith and extra-biblical religious perceptions',[54] noting both shared beliefs and shared religious practices. His conclusion is as follows:

> Although a previous generation of critical scholars tended to interpret these links in ideology, custom and design as evidence for Israelite borrowing from other cultures, now we are more prepared to recognise parallel developments and/or Yahwists' adoption of familiar symbols to communicate divine truth. An evangelical perspective proposes that these common features originate in some pristine revelation, that in the hands of pagans was garbled almost beyond recognition, but whose purity was secured in Israel through the inspirational work of the Holy Spirit.[55]

## 2. Problems and perplexities in Old Testament attitudes towards the religious Other

Having made these general observations, I now wish to home in on two areas of Old Testament religion that have interested a number of evangelical scholars: the nature of patriarchal religion in Genesis 12 – 50, and later passages that suggest an interim acceptance of idolatrous worship among the nations. After describing these issues, I shall offer comment, critique and construction.

### a. Ecumenical bonhomie? The 'problem' of patriarchal religion

The issue that concerns us regarding the so-called 'patriarchal narratives' (Gen. 12 – 50) is the nature of *patriarchal* religion, in particular its continuity or discontinuity with (1) other ancient Near Eastern religions existent at that time, and (2) what might be called exclusivistic Mosaic Yahwism from the exodus onwards. I shall engage primarily with C. J. H. Wright here, who has articulated this reconstruction in a number of places and who draws on a number of other

---

(Leicester: Apollos, 1999), pp. 391–420 (410; my italics). Petersen's typology can be found in D. L. Petersen, 'Israel and Monotheism: The Unfinished Agenda', in G. M. Tucker, D. L. Petersen and R. R. Wilson (eds.), *Canon, Theology, and Old Testament Interpretation: Essays in Honour of Brevard S. Childs* (Philadelphia: Fortress, 1988), pp. 92–107.

54. Block, 'Other Religions', p. 45.
55. Ibid., pp. 46–47.

scholars who have written on this topic, most importantly Walter Moberly and Gordon Wenham.

Wright's contention is that 'there is a marked difference between the religious faith and practice of the fathers of Israel in Genesis, and the developed cult of Israel after the exodus and Sinai covenant'.[56] In support of this thesis he draws on Walter Moberly's *The Old Testament of the Old Testament*.[57] Moberly's argument is worth summarizing.

Having rejected the modern historical-critical 'documentary hypothesis' construction for diversity and divergence in these narratives, Moberly seeks to account for and understand the theological and canonical reasons behind the Yahwistic narrator's preservation and to some extent legitimization of patriarchal religion. This religion, while showing continuity with later Mosaic Yahwism, is in other ways distinctive and superseded by Mosaic Yahwism. Concerning patriarchal monotheism, Moberly contends that the exclusivity of religious choice seen in Exodus 20:3 is absent from Genesis 12 – 50: 'There is no implied opposition to the worship of other gods'.[58]

> Genesis depicts no antagonism between the patriarchs and the religious practices
> of the native inhabitants of Canaan. Admittedly, little is actually said in Genesis
> about the religion of the inhabitants of Canaan, but the silence suggests a lack
> of polemical intent.[59]

> Although Mosaic Yahwism made exclusive demands on Israel and could be strongly
> polemical against other, especially Canaanite, religious systems, Mosaic Yahwism has
> no polemic against patriarchal religion even though patriarchal religion is open toward
> the Canaanites and appears to have certain affinities with Canaanite religion.[60]

Concerning the cultic practices of the patriarchs compared with Mosaic Law, Moberly notes that 'they are probably similar to the cultic practices of the inhabitants of Canaan which the Old Testament elsewhere opposes'.[61] This can be seen in the lack of a cultic centre, the role of trees (e.g. Gen. 12:6–7; 13:18;

---

56. C. J. H. Wright, 'Christian and Other Religions', p. 5.
57. R. W. L. Moberly, *The Old Testament of the Old Testament: Patriarchal Narratives and Mosaic Yahwism*, OBT (Minneapolis: Fortress, 1992).
58. Ibid., p. 87.
59. Ibid., p. 89.
60. Ibid., p. 163.
61. Ibid., p. 91.

21:33) and pillars (Gen. 28:18, 22; 31:45; 35:14), which are later strongly condemned (Deut. 16:21–22); and the lack of the call to observe Sabbath, dietary restrictions and circumcision. Finally, concerning the moral content of patriarchal religion, Moberly notes that 'generally speaking, patriarchal religion lacks moral content or at least moral emphasis in a way that contrasts with the strong moral content enjoined upon Israel by the covenant at Sinai'.[62] So there are 'no warnings of judgement for disobedience to God', and, referring to Sodom and Gomorrah, which might be an exception here, 'the overall ethos of the story, particularly with regard to Abraham, Isaac and Jacob, entirely lacks the emphasis upon sin and judgement and the corresponding need for moral choice that is characteristic of Mosaic Yahwism'.[63]

C. J. H. Wright agrees with Moberly's overall contention that 'the patriarchal era is an Old Testament within the Old Testament, standing in the same "dispensational" relation to Mosaic Yahwism as Mosaic Yahwism in turn stood to Messianic Christianity'.[64] For Wright, central to this claim is the contrast in use of the divine names, for although the redactor of Genesis clearly identifies Yahweh as the one who addresses the patriarchs, he is careful to note that at that time these believers knew this God only under the title El with its Mesopotamian and West Semitic heritage. This is supported by two specific 'incidents'. The first is God's words to Moses in Exodus 6:3, which Wright (and Moberly) interpret as meaning that the name Yahweh was unknown to the patriarchs.[65] The second is Abram's encounter with Melchizedek in Genesis 14 where Abraham's conjoining of the name Yahweh and El Elyon seems to imply 'that Abram and Genesis itself recognise that Malkisedeq [sic] (and presumably other people in Canaan who worship El under one manifestation or another) does serve the true God but does not know all there is to know about that God'.[66]

---

62. Ibid., p. 97.

63. Ibid., p. 98.

64. Christopher J. H. Wright, 'Editorial: P for Pentateuch, Patriarchs and Pagans', *Them* 18.2 (1993), pp. 1–2.

65. The insertion of the name Yahweh before Exod. 3 being anachronistic.

66. Goldingay and Wright, 'Yahweh Our God', p. 48. It is worth noting how Goldingay himself expands a little more on this incident in more recent work. First, in his *Genesis for Everyone* commentary he notes, 'In connection with the story about Melchizedek, the more immediate question is, What do you assume about the existent religious insight of the adherents of another faith (in our world, the question might arise with people such as Muslims)? Do you assume they are totally benighted? Abraham does not seem to assume this with Melchizedek, though he

Wright is insistent that he is not supporting a religious 'syncretism' but what he calls 'assimilation' or 'accommodation':

> The Pentateuchal tradition is better described as a case of accommodation and assimilation. The living God who would later reveal the fullness of his redemptive name, power and purpose, prepared for that fuller revelation by relating to historical individuals and their families in terms of religious rites, symbols and divine titles with which they were already culturally familiar – i.e. accommodating his self-revelation to their existing religious framework, but then bursting through that framework with new and richer promises and acts.[67]

----

does imply there is something Melchizedek needs to know' (John E. Goldingay, *Genesis for Everyone, Part 1: Chapters 1–16* [London: SPCK, 2010], p. 161). And again, 'Melchizedek comes out to celebrate with Abraham and bless him because Melchizedek is "priest of God Most High," which raises the question of what else he needs to know about God . . . Muslims refer to God as "Allah" which is simply the Arabic word for God, related to the Hebrew word *elohim*. It would be misleading to suggest that Muslims worship and think of God in a way totally different from the way Christians or Jews worship and think of God. Christian witness builds on what people know rather than requiring them to start again from scratch. At least, this is implied by Abraham's interaction with Melchizedek' (ibid., p. 164).

Secondly, and in what is a slightly revised and expanded version of the earlier 1991 chapter co-authored with Wright, Goldingay adds a new ending to the section that deals with Melchizedek: 'It has been suggested that biblical faith emerged in the context of multiple religious options. That is too Californian a way to put it. People did not think in terms of options, and these options were not multiple. Abraham lived in the context of one faith in Babylon and another in Canaan. He was summoned out of the first in order to begin a different narrative. He is then content to live that narrative alongside Canaanites such as Melchizedek who live their own narrative. What to do with the difference between these narratives is God's business. In the context of premodernity, people had one religious option that they recognized was the truth but accepted that other people lived by other narratives. In the context of modernity, people did not allow others to live by different religious options. In the context of postmodernity, everybody has a story and all stories are equally valid' ('How Does the First Testament Look at Other Religions?' in John Goldingay, *Key Questions About Christian Faith: Old Testament Answers* [Grand Rapids: Baker, 2010], pp. 248–265 [252]).

67. C. J. H. Wright, 'Christian and Other Religions', p. 6.

In summary, it can be seen that there are a number of correspondences between Yahweh and El as the Canaanites know him, but these correspondences do not constitute identity. They do not indicate that Canaanite faith and Israelite faith are identical, or equally valid alternatives depending on where you happen to live. From the perspective of the historical development of religions, it might be feasible to see Yahwism as a mutation from Western Asian religion, as Christianity was a mutation from Judaism, but this does not imply that the mutation is of similar status to its parent; rather the opposite. Canaanite religion had its insight and limited validity, but what God began to do with Abram was something of far reaching significance, even for the Canaanites themselves. The process was not merely syncretistic in a natural development of human religious insights. The biblical view is that the living God, later disclosed as Yahweh, accommodated his dealings with the ancestors of Israel to the names and forms of deity then known in their cultural setting. . . . The end result of what God began to do through Abram was of significance for the Canaanites precisely because it critiqued and rejected Canaanite religion.[68]

Finally, C. J. H. Wright refers to Joshua 24:14–15:[69]

The inference here is that however God may have initially accommodated his relationship with their previous worship and concepts of deity, as was necessary in the period historically prior to the exodus, now that their descendants have an unambiguous knowledge of Yahweh in the light of the exodus, Sinai and conquest, such concepts are inadequate and indeed incompatible with covenant loyalty. This text shows something of the strains in practice arising from Israel's polytheistic environment and pre-history. But the answer was not a tolerant syncretism but a radical rejection of all but the God known through his acts of revelation and redemption up to that point in history.[70]

It is worth noting that for Wright there are contrasting implications for the theology of religions arising from the nature of patriarchal religion. First, and

---

68. Goldingay and Wright, 'Yahweh Our God', p. 49.

69. 'Now fear the Lord and serve him with all faithfulness. Throw away the gods your ancestors worshipped beyond the River Euphrates and in Egypt, and serve the Lord. But if serving the Lord seems undesirable to you, then choose for yourselves this day whom you will serve, whether the gods your ancestors served beyond the Euphrates, or the gods of the Amorites, in whose land you are living. But as for me and my household, we will serve the Lord.'

70. C. J. H. Wright, 'Christian and Other Religions', p. 7.

contra readings that would legitimate a religious pluralism, he notes that *if*
there is a degree of openness in patriarchal religion or, as Wenham puts it, 'an
ecumenical bonhomie which contrasts with the sectarian exclusiveness of the
Mosaic age and later prophetic demands',[71] then this is relativized after Sinai:
'The dispensational progress of history and redemptive revelation does change
things. Those who knew God as Yahweh in the light of the exodus and within
the demands of the Sinai covenant could no longer live as though those things
were unchanged from patriarchal days':[72]

> So the patriarchal experience certainly allows us to believe that God does address
> and relate to men in terms of their existing concept of deity (as, e.g., in the case of
> Cornelius). But we must presume that such initiative is preparatory to bringing
> them to a knowledge of his historic revelation and redemptive acts (which, in our
> era, means knowledge of Christ). It does not allow us to assert that worship of other
> gods is in fact unconscious worship of the true God, nor to escape from the task of
> bringing knowledge of the saving name of God in Jesus Christ to men of other
> faiths.[73]

Secondly, however, Wright appears to reopen the soteriological debate:

> In the discussion whether it is possible to be saved without knowledge of Jesus,
> it can be pointed out that if Wenham, Moberly and others are right in taking
> Exodus 6:3 in its natural meaning and interpreting Genesis in light of it, then
> Abraham was saved not only without knowing Jesus but also without knowing
> about Yahweh.[74]

After mentioning other figures in a similar position to Abraham, his tentative
conclusion here is that 'a case could be argued biblically, it seems to me, for the
view that the criterion of salvation is not how much you do know about God,
but how you respond to what you know. And equally on the same grounds, that
ultimately only God holds the key to that criterion.'[75]

--------

71. Gordon J. Wenham, 'The Religion of the Patriarchs', in A. R. Millard and D. J.
    Wiseman (eds.), *Essays on the Patriarchal Narratives* (Leicester: Inter-Varsity Press,
    1980), pp. 157–188.
72. C. J. H. Wright, 'Editorial', p. 3.
73. C. J. H. Wright, 'Christian and Other Religions', p. 7.
74. C. J. H. Wright, 'Editorial', p. 3.
75. Ibid.

## b. Interim acceptance?

For C. J. H. Wright, while there may be an 'ecumenical bonhomie' within patri-archal religion, there is a definite 'change of atmosphere' witnessed in the 'unambiguous exclusiveness of the first commandment':[76]

> From this point on, the faith of Israel was dogmatically mono-Yahwistic, whether or not the monotheistic implications of that faith were as yet consciously understood. Israel was forbidden either to worship other gods or to attempt to worship Yahweh in the ways those gods were worshipped (Dt. 12:30f). The facts of this matter are quite unmistakable and need not to be tediously listed in detail. In the law (e.g. Dt. 7, 13, etc.), in the prophets (e.g. Jer. 2), in the narratives (e.g. 2 Ki. 17), in the Psalms (e.g. Ps. 106), even in the Wisdom tradition (e.g. Jb. 31:26) the overwhelming message is of the exclusiveness of Israel's faith – Yahweh alone.[77]

> The dominant concern of the opening eleven chapters of Deuteronomy is with idolatry. The ultimate claim on Israel was that they should acknowledge Yahweh alone as the living God. The monotheism of the shema (Deut. 6:4) was no armchair philosophy but a monumental challenge to all human polytheisms and still is. The severity of the warnings against idolatry is not some hangover from primitive religion (to which culturally pluralized western confusion consigns them) but are born of graphic awareness of what idolatry does to a society. It is not just an argument over how many gods exist. The shema does not say 'There is only one God,' but (in effect), 'Yahweh alone is that one God,' Yahweh as he is characterized in the rest of the OT, and specifically in the redemptive history of Israel recounted and celebrated in Deuteronomy. Once that living God and his claims are rejected, then the resulting vacuum is filled with gods that are destructive and cruel.[78]

However, in a number of places, and particularly in Wright's essay co-authored with Goldingay, he notes that such prescribed worship for Israel *does not* neces-sarily imply a uniform negativity or conflictual attitude towards the nations and their gods outside the covenant community.

The analysis of Old Testament attitudes to other religions by Goldingay and Wright is important in that it seeks to apply Israelite perspectives on religious diversity to a contemporary evangelical theology of religions. Within the Old Testament canon they note an implicit openness towards the religious Other,

---

76. C. J. H. Wright, 'Christian and Other Religions', p. 7.

77. Ibid.

78. Christopher J. H. Wright, 'Deuteronomic Depression', *Them* 19.2 (1994), pp. 1–3.

as well as more conflictual and guarded elements: exclusive and universal themes. As we have already observed in their treatment of patriarchal religion, from Exodus onwards they discern a progressive continuity between worship of El and of Yahweh: 'It is still the God worshipped within these other religions who is more fully known here, and it is apparently assumed that Israel can still learn from these other religions.'[79] This 'adaptation' can be seen in the use of Canaanite models and patterns for worship: 'This is not to say that these institutions, ideas, or texts are unchanged when they feature within Yahwism, but that it was able to reach its own mature expression with their aid'.[80] One example cited by Goldingay and Wright is (under the title *'ĕlōhîm*) God's decision to listen to the cries of the sailors who throw Jonah overboard. Similarly, the familiar texts of Deuteronomy 4:19 and Deuteronomy 32:8–9 are further evidence of an acceptance of the worship of other deities and of tension between this 'acceptance' and the ultimate purpose that all people should come to acknowledge Yahweh. This tension is resolved somewhat by recognizing the 'interim' nature of this acceptance that, with fuller revelation of Yahweh, shows up the inadequacy of this other 'worship'. These times come under the 'times of ignorance' Paul mentions in Acts 17:27–31: 'The knowledge of Christ requires repentance even from things God had previously overlooked'.[81] Having noted this inadequacy, though, they then make the following point:

> The Hebrew Bible does not explicitly base its condemnations of other peoples on the grounds that they believe in the wrong gods. Condemnation of the nations, where reasons are given, is usually based on their moral and social behaviour (see the oracles against the nations, e.g. Amos 1–2; Isa. 13–23). Condemnation of religious deficiency is reserved for the people of God (cf. Amos 2). The gods of the nations are regarded as simply impotent. Worship of them is not so much culpable as futile.[82]

For Goldingay and Wright, this 'moral dimension'[83] is a key determining factor in the level of 'conflict' seen between Israel and the surrounding nations: 'We can discern again a differential response to other religions related to the kind of social and moral characteristics they foster among their adherents'.[84] Elijah's

---

79. Goldingay and Wright, 'Yahweh Our God', p. 50.

80. Ibid.

81. Ibid., p. 51.

82. Ibid., p. 52.

83. Ibid., p. 57.

84. Ibid., p. 58.

vehemence against the Baalism of Jezebel 'was not simply over what was the right religion, but what was a right and just society for Naboth to live in. Baal religion undergirded – or at least imposed no restraint on – the way Ahab and Jezebel treated Naboth.'[85]

Finally, a number of extrapolations made by Goldingay and Wright based on their reading of the Old Testament canon. First, although other religions may be 'starting points' in recognizing the uniqueness of Yahweh, they can never be 'finishing points', 'because they are not witnesses to the deeds of the God who saves'.[86] Secondly, because Israel's and the church's function is that of a witness to these deeds, the charge of religious arrogance is muted:

> The gospel is not something we invented or can take any credit for. We merely bear
> witness, as messengers and stewards, to what God had done in the whole biblical
> story, culminating in Christ himself. We do not so much say 'We have the gospel',
> but 'There is a gospel'.[87]

Thirdly, the argument that 'the moral, social and cultural effects of a major religious tradition do give us some grounds for a discriminating response to it . . .'[88]

> Perhaps openness to the influence of other religions can be an enrichment or
> a perversion according to whether it allows a religion to come to full flowering
> as Yahweh's nature is more clearly grasped and Yahweh's lordship more fully
> acknowledged, or whether it turns it into something other than itself and leads
> to the ignoring of Yahweh's nature and expectations.[89]

### c. Evaluation and critique
What are we to make of Wright's arguments here regarding the alleged ecumenical bonhomie of patriarchal religion, together with later instances of the 'interim acceptance' of pagan worship? I hope it is clear that in many other matters I am heavily indebted to Wright's analyses.[90] I also concur with Wright's call for evangelicals to reflect deeply on these Old Testament texts, and his com-

---

85. Ibid.
86. Ibid., p. 54.
87. Ibid., p. 55.
88. Ibid., p. 58.
89. Ibid., p. 59.
90. E.g. in his superlative exposition of idolatry that I shall draw upon below.

184

mendation of scholars such as Moberly who 'point us to unexplored subtleties in the texture of the biblical tapestry – stories, texts, affirmations, that we may have either ignored or tended to subordinate under other control beliefs'.[91] In my own analysis I do not want to flatten the contours of biblical theology by denying the development and gradual 'dawning' of God's revelation of himself and his work in the history of his covenant people. Nor do I wish to ignore a number of complex and knotty texts and issues that arise from the patriarchal narratives and that 'test' the polyphonic harmony of the canon to the verge of dissonance.

That said, on the more *inclusive* nature of patriarchal religion and the assertion of an 'interim *acceptance*' of pagan religion, I am far less convinced. Wright and Moberly are, I think, correct to note *both* continuity or commonality and discontinuity or difference between, on the one hand, different dispensations of the history of God's chosen people and, on the other, between this history (of God's covenant people) and the history of those outside this line of revealed religion. However, my contention is that Wright et al. have skewed the internal balance of these axioms, which results in an overemphasis on discontinuity or difference between the different dispensations of God's revelation *within* the covenant community, together with an overemphasis on continuity or commonality between the covenant community and those *outside* this community.[92]

The main reason for this imbalance, and to reiterate a general criticism I have already articulated above, is that although Wright's and Moberly's readings are self-confessedly 'canonical' in their methodology, I question whether in practice they are canonical enough. Their analyses do not appear to take sufficient account of the theological and historical foundations of the nature and origin of religion and the religions as outlined in Genesis 1 – 11 that set a different balance and that provide the overarching pattern and hermeneutical 'key' in which to understand the ensuing drama. This is not to say that Wright and Moberly do not deal with creation and fall, but rather that even after their respective expositions there is still a theological and historical disconnect between themes established in Genesis 1 – 11 and the call of Abraham onwards. For example, Wright states that 'the story of God's redemptive work in history begins with the call of Abraham and the covenant with him and his descendants',[93] but, as I have argued, the story of God's redemptive work in history

---

91. C. J. H. Wright, 'Editorial', p. 3.
92. I would like to thank one of my postgraduate students, Steffen Jenkins, for his helpful insights in this section.
93. C. J. H. Wright, 'Christian and Other Religions', p. 3.

goes right back to Adam and the *protoevangelium*. Similarly, we must keep in mind all I have said concerning the following: the fall as unfaithfulness and 'false faith', the enmity between the seed of Satan and the seed of the woman, which creates a fundamental bifurcation within the human race, 'remnantal revelation' and its entropic degeneration, and the origin of religions in the Babel incident. *All* these need to be factored in as we come to understand the patriarchal narratives. The mood, or as Moberly says, 'ethos', created by this backdrop is *not* one of 'ecumenical bonhomie', or even a context that would allow 'accommodation' and 'assimilation', but one of revelation, idolatry and its judgment; in other words, of an *exclusivity* in keeping with the exclusivity of Mosaic Yahwism. Significantly, though, within this *exclusivity* is contained a broader missional theme of inclusive universality. Kreitzer sums this up well:

> 'Patriarchal history . . . is inseparable from universal history', and is 'expressly inaugurated' by God, 'for mission' to all peoples (Carroll 2000, 27). The background for this mission to the world is the implicit fact that though God creates the peoples, the peoples are always collectively regarded after Babel as the heathen *gôyîm*, that is as idol worshipping peoples. . . . There is 'a universal monotheistic era . . . thought of as coming to an end with the generation of the dispersal of mankind' because the 'appearance of idolatry is coeval with the rise of [the] nations' (Sarna 1970, 69). This idolatry and pagan nature of humanity is the source out of which God calls Abraham, a worshipper of idols (Jos. 24:2–3), whose wife was barren.[94]

If Genesis 1 – 11 does evidence such exclusivity, what are we to make of these patriarchal narratives, for there is much initial evidence to suggest that there *is* indeed a difference in ethos between these narratives and the Mosaic Yahwism that follows. How do we account for this difference? On the one hand, we could assume that the patriarchal narrative gives us the heart of the picture (ecumenical bonhomie), while Exodus layers exclusivism on top of that. The major deficiency in this approach is that the patriarchal narrative is *not* a text. Genesis is a text and

---

94. Mark Kreitzer, *The Concept of Ethnicity in the Bible: A Theological Analysis* (London: Edwin Mellen, 2008), pp. 165–166. Note Jonathan Edwards comments here, 'God raised up Abraham because true religion had gradually been corrupted after Babel, just as after the Flood when God had to start over with Noah's family. But after the Flood, degeneration resumed. So after attempting to cultivate religion in general humanity, God embarked on a novel procedure – the isolation of a chosen people' (Gerald R. McDermott, *Jonathan Edwards Confronts the Gods: Christian Theology, Enlightenment Religion, and the Non-Christian Faiths* [Oxford: Oxford University Press, 2000], p. 102).

should be read and understood as an integral unity. Whatever *literary* divisions there are within Genesis, chapters 1–11 versus 12–50 are not among them: those divisions are artificially imposed on the text. There is a break here, but it is on a par with many similar breaks within both 1–11 and 12–50, for example the *tôlĕdôt* structure. Genesis does not present itself as a book in two parts to be read separately. Just as we may not isolate Genesis 1 – 11, so we may not treat the patriarchal narrative without due attention to its place in Genesis and the Pentateuch. As soon as we ask the question of how Genesis works as a whole book, we notice that the same difference in ethos between Genesis 12 – 50 and Exodus is also evident between Genesis 12 – 50 and Genesis 1 – 11, as analysed earlier in this book. Equally, the story of Genesis makes good redemptive-historical sense of this difference and does not suggest inclusivism as the norm from which Exodus departs. Or, to put it more accurately, the norm from which Genesis 1 – 11 and the rest of the Torah and the rest of the Prophets and the Writings depart. Wenham warns that we need to see the stance of the whole book before we attempt to understand the ethics of the author and before we can take lessons from particular stories within the book.[95] This does not allow a partitioning of 1 – 11 and 12 – 50. What is more, it is crucial to see that the opening chapters' vision for humanity constitutes the blessing of later chapters, including 12 – 50.[96]

*i. Promise and fulfilment*

I would contend that the differences we see in the patriarchal narratives are 'redemptive historical' rather than 'religious'. Superficially, there is certainly a difference in the mode of revelation in which God chooses to reveal himself. In patriarchal religion there appears to be more direct and frequent communication with a number of individuals through theophany and angelic visitation, even with those outside the chosen people. God's communication with the nation of Israel is more mediated and structured.

More substantive is the difference between promise and fulfilment, from seed to tree. The many instances of small, partial fulfilment of the promises highlight for us that the promises are in large measure *not* fulfilled by the end of Genesis.[97] That is the plainest explanation for the difference in ethos between the patriarchal narratives and both later and earlier history.

---

95. Gordon J. Wenham, *Story as Torah: Reading Old Testament Narrative Ethically* (Edinburgh: T. & T. Clark, 2000), p. 17.

96. Ibid., pp. 22–24.

97. Ibid., p. 22.

We come here to the metaquestion regarding the purpose and polemic of the book of Genesis. I wish to contend that the book of Genesis intends to teach its readers that it was God's plan for Israel to leave Egypt and possess Canaan. Under this broad headline are several sophisticated subthemes that must be recognized. Although Wenham may be right that one of these major thrusts is the justification of 'peaceable relations with the Canaanites in the land',[98] does this justify his earlier claim of an 'ecumenical bonhomie' and Moberly's claim of a more laissez-faire attitude to religious 'toleration'? Wenham himself notes that 'tolerance with the Canaanites does not extend to intermarrying with them',[99] as well as noting the important condition that the Israelites 'should not be afraid to make agreements with the surrounding nations when they seek peace'.[100] As we have already noted, the patriarchal narratives are concerned with *unfulfilled* Abrahamic promises.[101] Part of what is 'unfulfilled' is the conquest that is explicitly tied to the sin of the Amorites not being filled up yet (Gen. 15:16). Therefore, although there may well be instances of cooperation, one of the reasons for this cooperation was that this was not the time for war, although there are some hints of this throughout the patriarchal narratives. Furthermore, Genesis 1 – 11 introduces the antithesis and how Abraham and his descendants are part of this 'seed' theology (cf. Gen. 3:15).

The major shift at Genesis 12 is a narrowing focus of God's means of blessing; whereas previously the blessing to the world was to be through universal humankind (whether Adam's or Noah's descendants), now one single idolater is chosen and *very slowly* built up into a family (he was ninety-nine years old before he was promised even one son). He is told that the blessing will be focused on one land, rather than the whole world, and even that will not be his in his lifetime. The antithesis that ran through Genesis 1 – 11 is now replanted as a seed that, when mature, will be one nation of promise among nations that may or may not receive blessing, depending on their attitude to Abram's seed.

If Abram and his first few generations of descendants do not behave in the way that the Exodus legislation describes, that is because the Sinai covenant is the mandate to a mature nation to conquer and live in a land, whereas Abram's family is a clan of merely seventy by the end of the book of Genesis, living in a land that is not theirs. The two circumstances are not comparable, while the patriarchs' behaviour is consistent with Mosaic Yahwism: even at the height of

---

98. Ibid., p. 41.
99. Ibid., p. 39.
100. Ibid.
101. Ibid., pp. 22–24.

the monarchy there is no mandate to invade Egypt or Babylon, but a clear mandate to show no mercy to any worshippers of Ra or Baal in the land, and the patriarchs are *not* in the land. What we see is the difference between, on the one hand, a constituted nation living in a land that is to be kept pure from idolatry (which includes that the land will vomit Israel out if they follow other gods), with a divine commission to do the purifying, and, on the other hand, 'a wandering Aramean' (Deut. 26:5) and a family waiting for that commission, woefully ill-equipped to carry it out (Gen. 34:30).

An example here is one of Moberly's discrepancies between patriarchal religion and the later law, noted above: there is no cultic centre to the worship of the patriarchs, which falls foul of the Deuteronomic law. But let us examine the law in question, Deuteronomy 12:8–11:

> You are not to do as we do here today, everyone doing as they see fit, since you have not yet reached the resting place and the inheritance the LORD your God is giving you. But you will cross the Jordan and settle in the land the LORD your God is giving you as an inheritance, and he will give you rest from all your enemies around you so that you will live in safety. Then to the place the LORD your God will choose as a dwelling for his Name – there you are to bring everything I command you: your burnt offerings and sacrifices, your tithes and special gifts, and all the choice possessions you have vowed to the LORD.

Had the patriarchs worshipped at a central site, they would have broken the law of Deuteronomy. The law clearly states that it is not operative until Yahweh chooses a central site, which he will not do until Israel has entered the land *and* been given rest from all of their enemies. Only *then* will they go to a central sanctuary. To say that something that was later added distinctively to Israel (central sanctuary) was lacking in both Israel and the Canaanites *before being added to Israel* hardly establishes a connection between the two. Indeed, the centralization of worship is explicitly predicted as a future ordinance in Deuteronomy 12:8–9, meaning that not even Mosaic Yahwism has a central place before a future date.

Taking Genesis as a whole, therefore, I believe a different interpretation emerges from the one given by Wright and Moberly. Here I shall offer a few more representative examples of this interpretation.

### ii. Morality and worship

Gordon Wenham coaches us in deriving ethics from the narrative of Genesis and brings together two things: the explicitly described creation ideal of chapters 1–2, alongside which is the behaviour of the later narrative that may implicitly be commended.[102] In applying this to the patriarchs, he notes that their behaviour is mixed, and they are uniformly neither to be copied nor to be avoided.[103] There are implicit lessons of the narrator to which we must pay attention: in the patriarchal narratives we *do* witness characters who intermarry with pagans, *but we then see them faring badly.* In their own genre-specific way these texts are strongly didactic and prescriptive.

Regarding a laissez-faire patriarchal attitude towards the worship of other gods, what Moberly counts as evidence is not what might be called hard evidence, for example instances of patriarchal worship at Canaanite shrines, but is often the silence of the text or the descriptively 'neutral' character of the text in comparison to the normative and 'exclusive' evidence seen in later Yahwistic religion.

Added to this are a number of occasions where Moberly himself notes prescriptive exceptions to this ethos. Regarding the 'undefined' significance of trees and pillars, Moberly admits that 'Abraham builds an altar beside a tree rather than plants a tree beside an altar, and the tree is not described as an Asherah.'[104] Regarding the lack of the observance of circumcision, he notes a more Yahwistic understanding of the rite in the massacre of the Shechemites after the rape of Dinah (Gen. 34:13–24).[105] Regarding religious 'toleration', he notes for example Genesis 35:2, where Jacob tells his family, 'Get rid of the foreign gods you have with you, and purify yourselves and change your clothes.' Finally, regarding the lack of moral content, he notes Genesis 13:13, where the men of Sodom are described as 'wicked, great sinners against the LORD' (ESV), and Genesis 15:16, which speaks of the iniquity of the Amorites.[106] Moberly's response here is that these are exceptions that prove the rule, occasions 'when apparently the narrator does not preserve the patriarchal perspective but tells the story in his own Yahwistic terms'.[107] While this is of course possible, to my mind a better construction that takes into account Genesis 1 – 11 is that these exceptions are in fact the rule, but need to be contextualized within their stage in redemptive history. Within this overarching story from Genesis 1 onwards it is therefore the exclusive 'exceptions' that Moberly acknowledges become all the more prominent and speak all the louder: as soon as Abram discovers that he is in

---

102. Ibid., p. 3.
103. Ibid., p. 107.
104. Moberly, *Old Testament*, p. 92.
105. Ibid., p. 93.
106. Ibid., p. 90.
107. Ibid., p. 89.

the Promised Land, he builds altars (Gen. 12:7–8); he does not join in with worship at whatever local site is available, but invades the land in this small way by setting up true worship. He takes great pains to *own* Sarah's tomb in the land, rather than merely being given use of it for free (Gen. 23), and Joseph is adamant that he must be buried in the land and not in Egypt (Gen. 47:29–31). Where we see partial fulfilment of the promises, it is often precisely in line with the antithesis.

Even the more explicit and positive examples of patriarchal ecumenism and affirmation of the religious Other need to be recast within the larger hermeneutical framework. For example, let us take Abraham's encounter with Abimelech (Gen. 20). Remember that at this stage of world history Babel is a recent event with fresh religious memory. I have called this 'remnantal revelation'. If I am right that God's variegated letting go of the nations after Babel was a gradual degeneration into idolatry via such mechanisms as euhemerism and etymology, then we are at an early stage where knowledge of the true God and his actions was still widespread. This factor, coupled with God's choice to communicate more directly with individuals at this time, may well account for Abimelech's faith in his interaction with Abraham. Moreover, however we regard the origin and nature of Abimelech's faith and morality, coupled with Abraham's dubious actions, a major point of the narrative is that it is still Abimelech who has to be blessed by the prophet Abraham, God's blessing bearer and intercessor.

Similarly, one could posit that Joseph's engagement with Egypt displays a more open attitude to the religious Other. As Moberly notes:

> The overall 'ecumenical' ethos of the storyline is exemplified in the way that the Egyptian Pharoah and the Hebrew Joseph respectively dream dreams whose content is given by one and the same God – consistently, the generic term for deity, *'ĕlōhîm*, is used in this context (Gen. 41). The main religious difference between the Pharaoh and Joseph is the quality of their dreams.[108]

However, the constant refrain in this narrative is that Yahweh was with Joseph, together with his victory over the local soothsayers, his intrinsic opposition to the priests, whose land he does not own, and the surprising blessing of Pharaoh *by* Jacob. How 'open' and ecumenical is the narrative here? God does indeed give the dreams to Pharaoh (just as he did to the cupbearer and baker), but purely so that Joseph will interpret them and rise up within Egypt, higher than all the local

---

108. R. W. L. Moberly, *The Theology of the Book of Genesis*, OTT (Cambridge: Cambridge University Press , 2009), p. 136.

priests. The significant fact is that *only* Joseph can interpret any of them and we are pointedly told that no one whom Pharaoh can access is able to. This is not 'degrees of insight here', but no insight as opposed to full insight. The point of all the dreams is to cause history to move for the benefit of Jacob and his family, in every case (the first gets Joseph to Egypt, the next couple get him out of jail, and the last gets him to be prime minister of Egypt so he can bring Jacob in).

Finally, we return to the significance of common religious rites and customs between God's covenant people and the surrounding nations. Similarity in structure does not necessarily mean similarity in meaning. Although referring to later Israelite society, Carson's point is equally applicable to patriarchal religion:

Certainly some of the institutions and ideas that characterized Israelite religion were shared with the surrounding pagan religions. That is almost inevitable: unless some group retreats into a hermitage and self-consciously sets out to do quite different things (and even then it will be unlikely that every base will be covered), common rites (e.g. circumcision) and the like are not unlikely. But the question to be asked is what those rites symbolize in each religion, and how common beliefs function within the structure of their respective systems.[109]

---

109. Carson, *Gagging of God*, p. 250. Looking forward, and as I shall argue more thoroughly and systematically in subsequent chapters, the recognition that certain words and rites may have unhelpful connotations is true of any religious language, and missiologically inevitable: 'By employing such terminology I inadvertently swallow a number of pagan conceptions at every moment' (J. H. Bavinck, *An Introduction to the Science of Missions*, tr. David H. Freeman [Phillipsburg: P & R, 1960], p. 138). Moreover, given the systemic nature of worldviews and the 'totalizing' nature of idolatry, the parallels between the genuine religious system and language and that of the idolatrous pagan system and language are not the result of neutral, or even positive, human instincts that can be learned from. Rather, all false religions are intricate systems, and the rites and terminology used within them 'are all understood in a fundamentally different sense, and applied in a quite different connection' to those of God's people (J. H. Bavinck, 'General Revelation and the Non-Christian Religions', *FUQ* 4 (1955), pp. 43–55 [54]). Using similar language and rites to those of pagan peoples, then, is not to endorse their systems, but is an example of how the Christian life 'takes [heathen forms of life] into possession and thereby makes them new . . . [Christ] fills each thing, each word, and each practice with a new meaning and gives it a new direction . . . it is in essence the legitimate taking possession of something by him to whom all power is given in heaven and on earth' (J. H. Bavinck, *Introduction*, pp. 178–179).

For example, the 'undefined' patriarchal use of trees and pillars in worship does not necessarily mean that the patriarchs were involved in 'pagan' practices, especially considering the rich symbolism of both objects throughout Scripture. Could these not be 'appropriate' cultic uses of these creations at this time? However, given the later counterfeit and abusive use of these symbols in Canaanite worship, the later Deuteronomic prohibition against their use is entirely appropriate to a people prone to falling into idolatry (cf. Num. 21:9 with 2 Kgs. 18:4).

We come back to Moberly's distinctive 'ethos' regarding the nature of patriarchal religion. Moberly is fully aware of the methodological complexities surrounding his approach, which is another variation, albeit one more 'reverential' to Scripture, of attempting to 'get behind' the finished text and reconstruct a particular history.[110] His response is that there is a distinctiveness here that was recognized and respected by the writers of Genesis and that

> the real test must be empirical, inductive and heuristic. If there is sufficient evidence
> in the text to build up a cumulative case and reasonably consistent picture of a distinctive
> tradition about the patriarchs, and this can illuminate a reading of the Pentateuch in
> appropriate ways, then the hypothesis can reasonably be claimed and well founded.[111]

I am arguing that the evidence is not strong enough to prove Moberly's case, especially considering the backdrop of Genesis 1 – 11.

*iii. The divine name*
The issue of the divine name and God's revelation in Exodus 6:2–3 has achieved legendary status in the history of biblical studies. These verses are seen as constituting key evidence in the justification of the 'documentary hypothesis' of the Pentateuch, a source-critical theory far less fashionable today but still in existence, and a theory that has been seen to bolster an evolutionary understanding of biblical religion.

Both C. J. H. Wright and Moberly reject this documentary hypothesis, yet they posit a reconstruction in which before Exodus 6 the redactors or redactor

---

110. 'If we are looking for a tradition of a religion distinct from Mosaic Yahwism and yet recognise that the material has already been in some way assimilated to the perspectives of Mosaic Yahwism (at least in the use of the name YHWH), how can we know that any given item genuinely belongs to patriarchal religion rather than Mosaic Yahwism?' (Moberly, *Old Testament*, p. 83).

111. Ibid., p. 84.

anachronistically use or uses 'a familiar name in a surprising context: God is called YHWH because that is how Israel knows God';[112] 'the patriarchal stories use the name YHWH, because the patriarchal traditions are being told from the perspective of Mosaic Yahwism'.[113]

As both Wright and Moberly mention in their respective works, there are other possible translations of this verse that would not indicate such radical newness in the revelation of the divine name and would allow the harmonization of Exodus 6 and the use of the name Yahweh prior to this revelation.[114] One alternative interpretation is that of Motyer in his monograph on these verses, *The Revelation of the Divine Name*.[115] Motyer's retranslation of Exodus 6:2–3 reads as follows: 'And God spoke to Moses, and said to him: I am Yahweh. And I showed myself to Abraham, to Isaac, and to Jacob in the character of El-Shaddai, but in the character expressed by my name Yahweh I did not make myself known to them.'[116] His contention is that the patriarchs knew the name 'Yahweh' but not the inner significance of this name, thus allowing for progressive revelation as an alternative to the then prevalent documentary hypothesis.[117]

Much of Motyer's study is taken up with lexical issues concerning the Exodus verses themselves. However, in his final section he looks for contextual support for this translation in the Genesis accounts. While he recognizes the majority of references to 'Yahweh' could be classed as a 'redactor's' or 'historian's use', 'there are forty-five cases which undoubtedly display patriarchal knowledge of the name, either because they themselves use it, or because it is used by God or

---

112. Moberly, *Theology*, p. 134.

113. Moberly, *Old Testament*, p. 78.

114. See Duane A. Garrett, *Rethinking Genesis: The Sources and Authorship of the First Book of the Pentateuch* (Fearn: Christian Focus, 2000), pp. 16–19.

115. Motyer, *Revelation of the Divine Name*.

116. Ibid., p. 12.

117. This is also the view of Vos: 'It is *a priori* improbable that Moses should have been sent to his brethren, whom he had to recall from forgetfulness of the God of their forefathers, with a new, formerly unknown, name of this God on his lips. Then there is the fact that Moses' mother bears a name compounded with Jehovah, in its abbreviated form, *Jo*, viz. *Jokhebed* . . . Closely looked at, Ex. 6:3 does not require absolute previous unknownness of the word. The statement need mean nothing more than that the patriarchs did not as yet possess the practical knowledge and experience of that side of the divine character which finds expression in the name' (Geerhardus Vos, *Biblical Theology: Old and New Testaments* [Grand Rapids: Eerdmans, 1948; Edinburgh: Banner of Truth Trust, 1975], p. 115).

man in addressing them'.[118] In arguing for progressive revelation, Motyer notes that the name 'Yahweh' was known, but that the revelation of the meaning of the name is unknown and remains unknown until the mighty redemptive acts of the exodus. Rather, the patriarchs knew God as 'El' and its epithets, titles that have their own meanings regarding the character of God and that, with regard to the title 'El Shaddai', 'undergirded that which later was shown to be at the very centre of the nature of God'.[119]

Given the background of Genesis 1 – 11 that I have described previously, and the embryonic revelatory knowledge of the gospel from Genesis 3:15 onwards, Motyer's reading is by no means fanciful. If some knowledge of God's saving and redemptive purposes was known to antediluvian saints and to the patriarchs, albeit in embryonic form, and these acts of God are linked to God's name, more fully revealed in the exodus, then is it not conceivable that rather than some references to Yahweh's being anachronistically written into the patriarchal narratives, they were mere reportage of instances when the divine name was used by the patriarchs themselves?[120]

---

118. Motyer, *Revelation of the Divine Name*, p. 25.

119. Ibid., p. 30. See also Garrett, who writes, 'The phenomenon of the interchange of Yahweh and Elohim can be explained far more satisfactorily and simply without resort to source criticism. Umberto Cassuto makes the point that the two names bring out different aspects of the character of God. Yahweh is the covenant name of God, which emphasizes his special relationship to Israel. Elohim speaks of god universally as God of all the earth. . . . Perhaps it is best to speak of Yahweh and Elohim having semantic overlap. In a context that emphasizes God as universal deity (e.g. Gen. 1), Elohim is used. In a text that speaks more of God as covenant saviour (Ex. 6), Yawheh is more likely to be utilized. In other cases, in which neither aspect is particularly stressed, the names may be alternated for variety or indeed for no specific reason' (Garrett, *Rethinking Genesis*, p. 17).

120. Interestingly, Motyer himself, at the end of his study, notes at least one exception to his rule: 'But as so often in the Bible, the light which will shine in fullness only at some future date is too strong wholly to be restrained from earlier ages, and here and there breaks through in hints and suggestions which are only appreciated when at last the moment of unveiling comes. Once in Genesis such a beam of light fell. When Abraham, on the mountain, found that God had indeed provided a sacrifice, and when he offered the ram in manifest substitution for his son, then, for a brief second he caught and expressed the truth, "Yahweh sees, Yahweh provides." Here only is the divine name elaborated in pre-Mosaic religion and Yahweh is declared to be the God who meets His people in their extremity, when the chosen seed is at the

If the name Yahweh was known to the patriarchs, then what Wright et al. posit as a development of religion from pagan 'El' worship to 'Yahweh' worship (albeit admitting discontinuity also) might be better described in terms of progression of revelation, where the divine titles and name are gradually filled out as God performs his mighty redemptive acts. Patriarchal knowledge of the name Yahweh and hints towards its meaning would also question Wright's soteriological point that Abraham was saved, ignorant of the Name.

However, *even if one is not convinced* by Motyer's thesis, although the description of God as El may well have been idolatrously corrupted by apostate religions and subsequently used as a description of a god, this does not invalidate its specially revealed character or show the uniform polytheistic prehistory of Israel. We might say that what God was doing in his divine calling and regenerating was not 'accommodating' or 'assimilating' a foreign title but rather 'reclaiming' or 'repossessing' his own self-revealed one. Commenting on the characteristics of Shemitic faith in comparison to those outside this line, Vos notes both the revealed nature of the divine descriptions, *as well as their degeneration*:

> It is plain that the traits on which we have dwelt lie rather on the line of a downward rather than of an upward movement. Outside of Israel we find them in historic times not on the increase but decidedly on the decrease. Within Israel itself we can trace the downward shift of this Shemitic faith, not merely in the struggle with alien influences, but also in a gradual internal decline. What existed, and continued to keep alive, was the remnant of a purer knowledge of God, preserved from extinction by God himself. As to the other point, that the higher religion of the Old Testament is not a simple evolution from low beginnings, it is sufficient to point out that nowhere else in the Shemitic world has a similar higher type of religion made its appearance except in Israel. The only reasonable explanation for the uniqueness of Israel in this respect is that here another factor was at work, the factor of supernatural revelation. The connection of subsequent revelation and this ancient Shemitic religion is shown in the two oldest and common divine names, *El* and *Elohim*. The biblical usage in regard to the word 'name' differs considerably from ours. In the Bible the name is always more than conventional sign. It expresses character or history. Hence a change in either respect frequently gives rise to a change of name. This applies to the names of God likewise. It explains why certain names belong to certain stages of revelation. They serve to sum up the significance of

---

point of extinction, and Himself provides the ransom price' (Motyer, *Revelation of the Divine Name*, p. 30).

the period. Therefore they are not names which man gives to God, but names given to God by Himself.[121]

This 'gradual internal decline' even within Shemitic religion is a description of gradual degenerative devolution, *not* a prescription that speaks of legitimization, validity and accommodation. It is a demonstration of the need of God's continual preservation and regeneration, seen in the call of Abraham. As Calvin notes, 'We know that at that time, religion was corrupt everywhere since Abram himself, who was descended from the sacred race of Shem and Eber, had been plunged into the profound vortex of superstitions with father and grandfather.'[122] This context makes better sense of Joshua 24:2, which, I suggest, is negative in its reference to illegitimate worship of the gods Joshua's fathers served. There is no indication in the text here that there is an evaluative distinction between the assessment of idolatry of 'the gods your fathers served in the region beyond the River' and 'the gods of the Amorites in whose land you dwell'. Regarding the faith of Abraham, Vos writes:

> Abraham's faith had an important bearing on the practical monotheism of patriarchal religion. Such a reliance upon God left no room for the cultivation of or interest in any other 'divine' numen that might have been conceived as existent. It is true, monotheism is nowhere theoretically formulated in this account. But God monopolized Abraham to the extent of the exclusion of all others. One motive for calling him out of his original environment was the prevalence of polytheism there; this much we learn from later Old Testament statements, e.g. Joshua 24:2, 3; among the branch of Abraham's family that remained in Haran the worship of other gods continued, alongside that of Jehovah [Gen. 31:19]. And according to Genesis 35:2, Jacob, on arriving in Canaan, charged his household to put away the foreign gods that were among them.[123]

### iv. Melchizedek
We return to Abram's meeting with Melchizedek in Genesis 14. None other than Von Rad notes that 'such a positive, tolerant evaluation of a Canaanite cult outside Israel is unparalleled in the Old Testament'.[124] I have dealt in some detail with this passage elsewhere, especially as this example of the Old Testament 'pagan

---

121. Vos, *Biblical Theology*, pp. 63–64.

122. John Calvin, *Genesis*, ed. Alister McGrath and J. I. Packer, CCC (Nottingham: Crossway, 2001), p. 129.

123. Vos, *Biblical Theology*, p. 87.

124. Gerhard von Rad, *Genesis: A Commentary* (London: SCM, 1961), p. 175.

saint' par excellence is used by evangelicals such as Clark Pinnock as strong evidence in his support of religious inclusivism.[125] While not proposing an inclusivism as bold as say a Pinnock, there are a number of what might be called 'provisionalist' readings of this encounter,[126] readings that share the view that God made *provision* for Melchizedek's genuine worship (under the name of a Canaanite deity), even though God's acceptance of that worship was *provisional*.[127]

---

125. Daniel Strange, *The Possibility of Salvation Among the Unevangelised: An Analysis of Inclusivism in Recent Evangelical Theology* (Carlisle: Paternoster, 2001), pp. 179–189. More recent on the Melchizedek incident is the Pentecostal inclusivist theologian Amos Yong: 'Inasmuch as Melchizedek was priest of El 'Elyon, can it also be said he was "the High-priest of the cosmic religion," and in that way have represented and foreshadowed how the religious longings and perhaps even beliefs and practices of all people are orientated towards God? Might we even be able to go further and suggest that Melchizedek's "eternal priesthood, consummated in the ministry of Christ, lies behind the church's calling as a witnessing community among and for – not against – other witnessing communities"? Can Melchizedek symbolize the stranger with whom we have more affinity than we realize, and can his religion be the religion of the stranger that is preserved, however obliquely, in the wisdom of the cultures and traditions of the ancient Near East and that anticipates the religion of Christ witnessed to in the many tongues of the Spirit?' (Amos Yong, *Hospitality and the Other: Pentecost, Christian Practices, and the Neighbor* [New York: Orbis, 2008], p. 117).

126. I am indebted to Nathan Weston for this term and for some of the following comments. Although by no means monolithic, the following could be cited as falling into this category: Goldingay, *Genesis for Everyone*; Goldingay and Wright, 'Yahweh Our God'; Gerald R. McDermott, *Can Evangelicals Learn from World Religions? Jesus, Revelation and Religious Traditions* (Downers Grove: InterVarsity Press, 2000); Don Richardson, *Eternity in Their Hearts*, 2nd rev. ed. (Ventura: Regal, 1981).

127. The missiological trajectory here (applied in varying levels of certainty) is that this incident is illustrative, analogous and even paradigmatic for those throughout history who have not come into contact with Christianity, a 'God-given starting point on their way to recognising that the definitive act and revelation of God are found in the story of Israel which comes to climax in Jesus' (Goldingay and Wright, 'Yahweh Our God', p. 43). At the very least, many of these readings seek to demonstrate how Gen. 14 is evidence that interfaith encounter can be a two-way process. So just as God accommodated his dealings with the patriarchs to the names and forms of deity known in their cultural setting, so 'one would expect the church to continue to grow in understanding . . . perhaps aided by revelations God has provided outside the church' (McDermott, *Can Evangelicals Learn?*, p. 117).

What are we to make of both these provisionalist readings and the mysterious encounter itself? Rather than isolating the incident, it is important to see it in its surrounding context, both in Genesis and within the canon, and as part of the unfolding narrative of redemptive history. When this is done, then more provisionalist readings are seen to be more and more unlikely.

First, while we do see Abram joining forces with pagan kings in order to rescue Lot, and then joining in with worship from a foreign priest, there is a rather more obvious and shocking contrast within this story (Gen. 14:17–24). After the battle, the king of Sodom approaches Abram (v.17). Before we are told his intentions, Melchizedek appears (v.18), identified as a foreign priest. Abram shares a meal (the height of fellowship), he accepts Melchizedek's blessing, and, on hearing that it is *Melchizedek's* God (El Elyon) who has given Abram victory, does not argue the point or ascribe the victory to Yahweh, but rather tithes into this foreign God's coffers (vv.18–20). When the king of Sodom, not a priest, states his business and merely wishes to divide the spoils (what one might call a safe secular activity), Abram refuses point-blank. Abram now shows that he was *not* engaging in interfaith worship, but identifies Melchizedek's God as *his* God, Yahweh. Melchizedek's blessing and Abram's declaration emphasize that Abram is copying Melchizedek's formula verbatim. It could not be clearer: Melchizedek worships El Elyon, the Most High God, the creator of heaven and earth, and Abram tells us that this God is Yahweh, El Elyon, the Most High God, the creator of heaven and earth, to whom Abram makes oaths. And what is the content of this oath? To accept *nothing* from the pagan king of Sodom. Here is exclusive Yahwism at its starkest. Moreover, that Abram copies Melchizedek's formulation throws into question the assertion 'that Abram and Genesis itself recognise that Malkisedeq [*sic*] (and presumably other people in Canaan who worship El under one manifestation or another) does serve the true God but does not know all there is to know about that God'.[128]

Secondly, there appears to be an intentional connection that can and should be made between the name given to Yahweh by Abram and Melchizedek, 'Creator of heaven and earth' (14:19, 22), and the land of Canaan that Abraham was promised by Yahweh back in the previous chapter (13:15, 17). It is Yahweh's land: *he*, not any other rival god in Canaan, possesses it. If this connection is to be made, then it would seem perverse shortly after receiving this promise, and what it teaches Abram about Yahweh's sovereignty, for Abram now to accept Melchizedek's worship of the Canaanite El under the explicit title of 'Creator of heaven and earth'.

Thirdly, and at the level of canonical context, we need to understand the

---

128. Goldingay and Wright, 'Yahweh Our God', p. 48.

incident in the light of what I have affirmed methodologically in terms of Scripture's unity, including an espousal of the *sensus plenior*. Written in a period 'safely' acknowledged to be exclusively Yahwistic, Psalm 110 confers upon the promised King (who is later revealed to be Jesus Christ; Matt. 22:44–45; Acts 2:34–36) the eternal priesthood in the order of Melchizedek. It would seem totally at odds with this exclusivity and Yahwistic 'purity' if such a paradigmatic promise were seen by the covenant community to be 'tainted' with Canaanite associations.[129] Does this imply that the community recognized the authentic Yahwism of Melchizedek? Similarly, moving into the New Testament, for Jesus' priesthood to be recognized as one that brings 'perfection' (Heb. 7:11), does this not mean that the criteria established with Melchizedek (a priest-king with the appearance of eternality, superior to Abram, outside the priest of Levi) theologically necessitate that his priesthood be properly Yahwistic?

Coming back to Genesis 14 itself, the Melchizedek incident is once again an instantiation and foretaste of the universalistic principle that Abraham is to be a blessing to nations.[130] It highlights once again that if we are to account for the

---

129. Although his own solution is thoroughly unsatisfactory, Hermann Gunkel notes that '[i]t is very unlikely that the later community, opposed to everything pagan . . . will have sought the pattern for the high-priesthood in a Canaanite' (Hermann Gunkel, *Genesis* [Macon: Mercer University Press, 1997], p. 280).

130. This is Vos's understanding, as it is John Owen's, who believes Melchizedek was from the line of Japheth: 'This signal prefiguration of Christ to the nations of the world, at the same time when Abraham received the promise himself and his posterity, gave pledge and assurance to the certain future call for the Gentiles unto an interest in him and participation in him' (John Owen, *An Exposition of Hebrews*, 4 vols. [Marshallton, Del.: National Foundation for Christian Education, 1969], vol. 3, p. 300). In a similar vein John Sailhamer notes that both Melchizedek and Jethro (priests outside the covenant community) have encounters with Abram and Moses respectively before God establishes his covenant with them, so fulfilling his creation purposes through special covenantal (and not general) revelation: 'Melchizedek's reference to "the Most High God" of creation shows that the author of the Pentateuch wants to trace God's plan for the nations back to God's plan for creation. This is the first real link between creation and covenant, or creation and redemption in the covenant in the Pentateuch . . . Melchizedek's words to Abraham reveal his understanding of the creation blessing that Abraham is about to inherit. Melchizedek reintroduces into the Pentateuch the notion that God will use the nations of the world to further his plans of blessing through the "seed" of Abraham. In those plans God's intent is to bless "all the nations" (Gen 12:1–3)' (Sailhamer, *Meaning of the Pentateuch*, p. 372).

difference between the patriarchal and the Mosaic administrations, rather than locating this difference in the relaxation of the fundamental antithesis between the seed of the woman and the seed of the serpent, we must focus on the wider geographical boundary in the former, which later would be confirmed and fulfilled in the coming of Christ:

> The history of the patriarchs is more universalistic than that of the Mosaic period. When the people were organized in a national basis and hedged off from the other nations by the strict seclusive rules of the law, the universalistic design was forced somewhat into the background. Further, through the conflict between Egypt and the Hebrews the real relation to the outside world became one of conflict. In the patriarchal period the opposite to this was true. Little was done to make the life of the people of God, even in an external religious sense, different from that of their environment. No ceremonial system on a large scale was set up to stress this distinction. Circumcision was the only rite instituted, and since this was also practiced by the surrounding tribes, even it did not really differentiate. And positively also, the principles on which God dealt with the patriarchs were of a highly spiritual nature, such that would make them universally applicable. The reasoning [Gal. 3:15] is in substance as follows: through the *diatheke* with Abraham the relation between God and Israel was put on a foundation of promise and grace; this could not subsequently be changed, because the older arrangement remains regulative for later institutions [v. 15], and the law was by no less than 430 years later than the Abrahamic *berith*. The revealed religion of the Old Testament in this respect resembles a tree whose root system and whose crown spread out widely, while the trunk of the tree confines the sap for a certain distance within a narrow channel. The patriarchal period corresponds to the root growth; the freely expanding crown to the revelation of the New Testament; and the relatively constricted form of the tree trunk to the period from Moses to Christ.[131]

It is right to be cautious in speculating on Melchizedek's background, given not only what I have said about trying to 'get behind' or 'go further than' the text of Scripture,[132] but also the theological importance of his enigmatic

---

131. Vos, *Biblical Theology*, p. 79.

132. As Meeter notes, 'The important thing to notice is the brevity of the record. Nothing is told us, either here or elsewhere, of his previous or subsequent history. We know nothing of his birth, or of other incidents of his life, or his death. As a picture in a diorama, so the picture given of Melchizedek in Genesis comes from the unseen, fills the eye for the moment, only to pass away again into the region of the unseen' (H. H. Meeter, *The Heavenly High Priesthood of Christ: An Exegetico-Dogmatic Study* [Grand Rapids: Eerdmans, 1915], p. 57).

character in Hebrews 7:3. However, rather than speculating upon and then highlighting Melchizedek's pagan background and so Abraham's 'endorsement' of his religion in his combination of 'Yahweh, El Elyon', another, and I believe equally plausible, account takes into consideration again the religious context of Genesis 1 – 11. We can note both the revealed nature of this divine description together with a recognition that at this stage in human history knowledge of God, creation, fall and flood was still fresh in certain strands of humanity. Taking these into account we may say that although Melchizedek was not 'in the circle of election recently formed', nonetheless he 'was a representative of earlier, pre-Abrahamic knowledge of God. His religion, though imperfect, was by no means to be identified with the average paganism of the tribes.'[133] Calvin says of him that 'amid the corruptions of the world, he alone in that land was an upright and sincere cultivator and guardian of religion'.[134] Melchizedek is therefore not a recipient merely of general revelation, but of special 'remnantal' revelation possibly handed down by oral transmission.[135] Alternatively, in a time where direct revelation from God was normative and received through various channels, Melchizedek could have received some kind of revelation that caused him to begin worshipping Yahweh, just as Abram did (Gen. 12:1). Neither of these options can be proved conclusively, but neither deserves to be

---

133. Vos, *Biblical Theology*, p. 77.

134. Calvin, *Genesis*, p. 130.

135. This too is Carson's position when commenting on Wright and Goldingay: 'When the Melchizedek passage is placed within the developing narrative of the book of Genesis, one can no longer think of monotheism emerging after endless struggles with pagan polytheism. It is far more natural in reading the account to suppose that there were still people who believed in the one true God, people who preserved some memory of God's gracious self-disclosure to Noah, people who revered the memory of the severe lesson of Babel. That Melchizedek should designate "God Most High" as "Creator of Heaven and Earth" points in the same direction: he was either a monotheist or a henotheist. Of course, Abram was the one who still received the special call to follow God and head up the race that would prove a blessing to all the nations of the earth. But that doesn't mean he was the only one who believed in the one true God' (Carson, *Gagging of God*, p. 250). See also the Jewish commentator Nahum Sarna here: 'He [Melchizedek] is patently regarded as a monotheist, one of the few select non-Israelite individuals who, in the scriptural view, preserved the original monotheism of the human race in the face of otherwise universal degeneration into paganism' (Nahum M. Sarna, *Genesis*, JPSTC [New York: Jewish Publication Society, 1989], p. 109).

ruled out a priori, and in the context of Genesis and canon would certainly make more theological sense.

Abram's routing and plundering of the other kings, together with his fellowship with Melchizedek, point to the special status of this priest-king. Given the later theological significance given to Melchizedek in the history of redemption, it would seem far more plausible that his background was not pagan and polytheistic but rather that he legitimately worshipped the one true God under the legitimate and revealed title and description of El Elyon, God Most High.[136]

*v. Interim acceptance*

The themes I have highlighted above can be restated variously as we move from the patriarchal narratives to the rest of the history of Israel in the Old Testament.

First, there are some outstanding questions to be asked of those who wish to demonstrate (albeit in a qualified way and not wanting to ignore a conflictual dimension) *continuities* between Israel and other nations, for example in terms of 'correspondences' between Yahweh and the gods of these nations, such that Israel could learn from those outside and 'was able to reach its own mature expression with their aid',[137] and that similarities between El and Yahweh meant that

> [t]he high god El could more easily become the sole God Yahweh than would be the case with the subordinate Baal; worship of Baal implied worship of other gods than Yahweh, rather than worship of Yahweh as Baal. The historical power of El was that shown in Israel's key experiences of exodus from Egypt and conquest of Palestine – even if the nature of El, not least as one failing to exercise real control in heaven, would need redefining in the light of those experiences.[138]

But just how exactly is El like Yahweh? Metaphysically, El is not considered to be transcendently unique, nor does he have the power and sovereignty of Yahweh.

---

136. El being the common appellative for 'god', and the adjective 'most high' being one used elsewhere in the OT, its meaning consonant with what I said earlier concerning Yahweh's transcendent uniqueness. It should be noted that though some are quick to equate El Elyon as head of the Canaanite pantheon, the phrase 'El Elyon' does not appear outside Gen. 14 in either the OT or Canaanite literature. See Bruce K. Waltke, *Genesis: A Commentary* (Grand Rapids: Zondervan, 2001), p. 233.

137. Goldingay and Wright, 'Yahweh Our God', p. 50.

138. Ibid., pp. 46–47.

Morally, Cross describes El as 'a vigorous and prodigiously lusty old man',[139] who is described in texts as becoming drunk and passing out,[140] seducing multiple wives in order to give birth to the gods,[141] marrying his sisters and emasculating his father.[142] Moreover, what are the precise criteria for evaluating what is acceptable and what is not? Goldingay and Wright say that the influence of other religions can be 'enrichment or a perversion according to whether it allows a religion to come to full flowering as Yahweh's nature is more clearly grasped',[143] but this is rather vague and indeed circular. If a foreign god could cause an Israelite to *more clearly grasp* Yahweh's nature, then on what basis does he or she determine that the deity does not *ignore* Yahweh's nature? In other words, if other deities can redefine Yahweh, how did the Israelites know whether or how to redefine *them*?

Secondly, and more generally, there appear to be numerous texts that reaffirm the patterns laid down in Genesis 1 – 11 concerning the universality of Yahweh's sovereignty over all people and nations: 'Yahweh is always proclaimed as the present reigning King of the whole earth, and all its people are his possession. . . . Every people is thus collectively responsible to seek and turn to Yahweh God (Ps. 2; 96; Is. 45:22–25; Ez. 14:12–20).'[144] There is much textual evidence to conclude that idolatry is forbidden not just for Israel but for *all* peoples, and in *all* epochs of redemptive history (Deut. 26:18; 32:8; Ps. 86:9). Contrary to Wright and Goldingay, therefore, I would suggest that polytheism has never been appropriate or acceptable worship.[145] The antithesis between true faith and false faith remains prominent and unbroken throughout the Old Testament. To reiterate, 'transcendent uniqueness' recognizes the universality of Yahweh's dominion, and the covenantal accountability *all* humans have towards him, which I have named as a perpetual *particular religiosity*.

Therefore if we wish to speak of 'difference', then we must not confuse or conflate an exclusivity of *focus* on Israel at this epoch within salvation (who are of course blessed to be themselves a blessing) with a divine neglect or even tolerance of humanity and their false religiosity outside Israel:

---

139. Frank Moore Cross, *Canaanite Myth and Hebrew Epic* (Cambridge, Mass.: Harvard University Press, 1973), p. 24.

140. Ibid., p. 39.

141. Ibid., p. 22.

142. Ibid., p. 42.

143. Goldingay and Wright, 'Yahweh Our God', p. 59.

144. Kreitzer, *Concept of Ethnicity*, p. 237.

145. I shall deal with the meaning of the 'times of ignorance' in the next chapter.

Although the Hebrew Bible does not normally address the pagans and tell them that they are worshipping the wrong gods, the impression Goldingay and Wright leave (perhaps unwittingly) is that it is acceptable for pagans to worship their own gods, provided that there is a reasonable amount of justice in the land. But the real reasons for biblical restraint when addressing the pagan nations are surely more nuanced. The primary locus of God's redemptive activity at that time . . . was Israel. And the Israelites are repeatedly told not only that Yahweh and Yahweh alone is their God, but that he is the only God, and the gods of the nations are impotent idols.[146]

J. H. Bavinck boldly states a similar thesis:

The idea of creation naturally implies God's jurisdiction over the whole world. . . . Although it might appear as if God had abandoned the nations to their fate, actually such is in no wise the case. The other peoples are also the continuous subjects of God's concern; he is also their righteous judge. It is striking how frequently the other nations are called upon in the Psalms to recognise and honour God, and how complete is the witness of the prophets against the nations surrounding Israel. God does not exempt other nations from the claim of his righteousness; he requires their obedience and holds them responsible for their apostasy and degeneration.

This is also why the service of the other gods is so strongly forbidden. The prophets repeatedly insist that the gods of the other nations are idols . . . It is just because the Bible is so earnest in holding that the Lord is the only God that it contains such strong possibilities for mission . . .

The separation of Israel did not change the situation. On the contrary, the latter was regarded as a temporary division, necessary in the divine plan of salvation, but one which would be abolished in God's due time. When Abraham was called from Ur he was assured that in him 'all the nations of the earth would be blessed' (Genesis 12:3). And this same promise was emphatically reiterated in connections with Abraham's seed (Genesis 22:18). Israel's awareness of the separation was never forgotten; it became rather the germ of the prophecies of the salvation of the nations, so characteristic of the late prophetic writings.[147]

Thirdly, and more specifically, the examples often cited to demonstrate a more positive evaluation of the religious Other may not be able to carry the inter-religious freight put upon them. We have already looked in some detail at Melchizedek, and also Deuteronomy 4:19 and 32:8–9. Given the ethos I have

---

146. Carson, *Gagging of God*, p. 251.
147. J. H. Bavinck, *Introduction*, p. 13.

outlined in this chapter, the narrative in 2 Kings 5:15–19 might initially raise an exclusivist eyebrow. On hearing of Naaman's dilemma in having to bow at the temple of Rimmon, Elisha's response is that he can 'Go in peace.' Is Elisha sanctioning idolatrous worship here?[148] From Naaman's perspective this is doubtful. First, there is his pronouncement in verse 15 that 'there is no God in all the world except in Israel'. Secondly, his intention to take Israelite earth on which to make burnt offering and sacrifices when he gets home. Thirdly, he asks for forgiveness from the prophet. Finally, the recognition that, given Naaman's own description, it is possible that his own 'bowing' will be nothing more than the physical movement of his aiding his elderly master to bow. Although details are scant here, these factors may well have determined Elisha's response.[149]

### 3. Idolatry as the primary Old Testament categorization of the religious Other

Although I appear to have covered a lot of ground in this chapter, in reality much of this has been ground clearing. It is only now towards the end that I am able to concentrate fully on my primary descriptor of the religious Other in the Old Testament. If Jewish monotheism's affirmation of Yahweh's 'transcendent uniqueness' is a historical articulation of the essential preservation of divine aseity and the Creator–creature distinction, then the 'de-creational' act of the

---

148. This is Pinnock's understanding: 'Some question whether God would put up with a religion that was grossly deficient. Would God accept people whose beliefs fall far short of complete truth? Yes I think he would. For Scripture often hints at how merciful he is, even in the realm of religion. . . . God allowed Naaman the Syrian leper, after his healing, to worship in Rimmon's temple because of the delicate circumstances he was in (2 Kings 5:18)' (Clark Pinnock, *A Wideness in God's Mercy: The Finality of Jesus Christ in a World of Religions* [Grand Rapids: Zondervan, 1992], p. 101).

149. Leithart's conclusion is interesting here: 'Elisha's apparent indifference to idolatry is a puzzle. Naaman is a Gentile, and Elisha would likely not have given the same permission to a Jew. Further Naaman does not consider bowing at the temple of Rimmon morally indifferent; he asks for pardon not mere permission. Even with these qualifications and explanations, Elisha's response is remarkable and shows something of God's gentleness in dealing with believers in tricky moral and political circumstances' (Peter J. Leithart, *1 and 2 Kings*, ed. R. R. Reno [London: SCM, 2006], p. 195).

blurring of this distinction and its consequences are articulated within the Old Testament category of idolatry and its strong prohibition. It needs to be remembered that while the focus of this prohibition often concerns the covenant community, this does not excuse the false religious expressions of those outside this covenant community, who universally remain related to Yahweh. Although I shall return again to this theme of idolatry in the final chapters, for now let me finish here by noting some of the distinctive Old Testament teaching on idols in terms of their composition, characteristics and consequences. For the final time I return to Chris Wright, whose exposition of idolatry is especially insightful.[150]

### a. The composition of idols and idolatry

Wright too is dependent upon Bauckham's formulation of 'transcendent uniqueness', and this enables him to answer the question as to the composition and nature of idols: What exactly are they? Wright's answer is to reject a neat linear and evolutionary view that posits a gradual shift from an earlier belief in the existence of other gods alongside Yahweh to a more mature declaration of their non-existence. Rather, belief in Yahweh's transcendent uniqueness recognizes that idols are 'nothing in relation to Yahweh' (cf. Heiser's 'species uniqueness'), but 'if the question is asked in relation to those who worship the other gods, whether the nations who claim them as their own national deities or even in relation to the temptation Israel faced to "go after" them – then the answer can certainly be something'.[151] What then is this 'something?' Wright notes three ways the Old Testament categorizes idols: as objects within the visible creation,[152] as demons,[153] or as the product of human hands.[154] The first two categorizations we have encountered previously in my discussion of astrolatry and the bĕnê hā'ĕlōhîm. There is little I wish to add here, except to say that Wright makes the important point that the scarcity of references to the demonic is theologically significant in not distracting us from recognizing that idols are human constructs

---

150. I would also point the reader to Daniel Block's discussion of Yahwistic hostility to idols and the worship of other gods, 'expressed in four principal ways: (1) pejorative designations for idols and the gods they represent; (2) explicit prohibitions of idolatry; (3) hostile actions against idols; (4) polemical portrayals of idols and idolaters' (Block, 'Other Religions', pp. 60–75).

151. C. J. H. Wright, Mission of God, p. 139 (his italics).

152. Ibid., pp. 142–144. He mentions astral worship here.

153. Ibid., pp. 144–146 (here he references Deut. 32).

154. Ibid., pp. 147–161.

for which humans are responsible. It is this understanding of idols as the 'work of human hands' that Wright sees as being the most 'pervasive and typical'[155] category in the Old Testament, and on which he himself spends most time. On this categorization he is critical of those who posit that Israelites committed to aniconic worship viewed pagan worship as fetishism – that 'Israel could not understand or appreciate the subtlety of iconic worship they saw around them. The real spiritual and psychological dynamic was not grasped by the Israelites, so they simply mocked what they did not understand.'[156] Wright counters this view by arguing that there are many examples where the Israelites were fully cognizant of this distinction in pagan worship; indeed, this was the basis for their polemic and satire:[157]

> The Israelites, fully aware of what *idols* were supposed to signify among those who bowed down before them, nevertheless castigated them as 'the work of human hands.' What then did this signify for the *gods* that the idols represented? The radical conclusion has to be that the psalmists and prophets make no distinction between images and the gods they represent – *not because they did not know that such a distinction was there in the minds of pagan worshipers but because ultimately there was no such distinction in reality.*[158]

### b. The characteristics of idols and idolatry

When we turn to the question of what idols are like, two characteristics can be brought out at this stage. First is their parasitic nature. Because idols are fashioned out of created matter, rather than *ex nihilo*, something good is taken from creation and turned into a god. Wright notes four Old Testament things from which gods are manufactured: things that entice us, things we fear, things we trust and things we need. His point is that it is only Yahweh who can ultimately provide for us:

> The one who has set his glory above the heavens is the only one before whom we should tremble in awe and worship. To live in covenantal fear of the Lord as sovereign Creator and gracious Redeemer is to be delivered from the fear of anything else in creation – material or spiritual. As the Rock, he is the utterly secure place to invest all our trust in all the circumstances of life and death, for the present and the future. And

---

155. Ibid., p. 147.
156. Ibid., p. 149.
157. He gives the example of Isa. 46:1–2, which speaks of Bel and Nebo.
158. C. J. H. Wright, *Mission of God*, p. 151 (his italics).

as the Provider of all that is needful for all life on earth, the God of the covenant with Noah and our heavenly Father, there is no other to whom we need to turn, to plead, placate or persuade, for the needs he already knows we have.[159]

Following on from this we note the counterfeit nature of idolatry. Idolatry and false worship show a similarity to true worship because they copy not only Yahweh's character but also his promises. Isaiah 36:13–20 is a great example of this mimicry:

> Then the commander stood and called out in Hebrew, 'Hear the words of the great king, the king of Assyria! This is what the king says: do not let Hezekiah deceive you. He cannot deliver you! Do not let Hezekiah persuade you to trust in the LORD when he says, "The LORD will surely deliver us; this city will not be given into the hand of the king of Assyria."
>
> 'Do not listen to Hezekiah. This is what the king of Assyria says: make peace with me and come out to me. Then each of you will eat fruit from your own vine and fig-tree and drink water from your own cistern, until I come and take you to a land like your own – a land of corn and new wine, a land of bread and vineyards.
>
> 'Do not let Hezekiah mislead you when he says, "The LORD will deliver us." Have the gods of any nations ever delivered their lands from the hand of the king of Assyria? Where are the gods of Hamath and Arpad? Where are the gods of Sepharvaim? Have they rescued Samaria from my hand? Who of all the gods of these countries have been able to save their lands from me? How then can the LORD deliver Jerusalem from my hand?'[160]

### c. The consequences of idols and idolatry

Finally, we come to the consequences of idolatry: What do idols bring to their followers? Chris Wright brings out the relational impact of idol worship. First, and most importantly, 'idols deprive God of his proper glory'.[161] A recurring theme throughout Scripture is that Yahweh is rightly jealous of his own name, and acts for the sake of his name and reputation, because his name is inextricably

---

159. Ibid., p. 171.
160. For more on the characteristics of idolatry see Richard Keyes, 'The Idol Factory', in Os Guinness and John Seel (eds.), *No God but God* (Chicago: Moody, 1992), pp. 29–48. Keyes's main thesis is that, counterfeiting the original human drives of dominion and dependence, idols 'come in pairs': a 'near idol', which is our need to dominate, and a 'far idol', which gives us meaning and legitimacy.
161. C. J. H. Wright, *Mission of God*, p. 171.

linked with his glory – the recognition of God as he truly is in all his perfections:[162]

> I am the LORD; that is my name!
>> I will not yield my glory to another
>> or my praise to idols.
> (Isa. 42:8)

> Therefore say to the Israelites, 'This is what the Sovereign LORD says: it is not for your sake, people of Israel, that I am going to do these things, but for the sake of my holy name, which you have profaned among the nations where you have gone. I will show the holiness of my great name, which has been profaned among the nations, the name you have profaned among them. Then the nations will know that I am the LORD, declares the Sovereign LORD, when I am proved holy through you before their eyes.'
> (Ezek. 36:22–23)

Rosner notes that '[t]he jealousy of God lies at the heart of the Old Testament's conflictual stance towards other religions (and more to the point, other gods) . . .'[163] When God's glory is taken away by false worship, there is holy indignation and divine retribution.

Secondly, the 'radical self-harm' of idolatry:

> *Idolatry is radical self-harm.* It is also radically, terribly ironic. In trying to be as God, we have ended up less human. The principle affirmed in several places in the Bible that you become like the object of your worship (e.g., Ps. 115:8; Is. 41:24; 44:9) is very apparent. If you worship that which is not *God*, you reduce the image of God

---

162. Bauckham writes, 'We may have difficulty with this picture of God desiring and achieving fame for himself, something we would regard as self-seeking vanity and ambition if it were said of a human being. But this is surely one of those human analogies which is actually appropriate uniquely to God. The good of God's human creatures requires that he be known to them as God. There is no vanity, only revelation of truth, in God's demonstrating his deity to the nations' (Richard Bauckham, *The Bible and Mission* [Carlisle: Paternoster, 2003], p. 37). To this we must add that there is no narcissism here, as God's triune and self-contained nature means that the persons of the Trinity seek one another's glory from eternity.
163. Brian Rosner, '"No Other God": The Jealousy of God and Religious Pluralism', in Clarke and Winter, *One God, One Lord*, pp. 149–159 (149).

in yourself. If you worship that which is not even *human*, you reduce your humanity still further.[164]

Idol worship brings only destruction, disillusionment and despair: 'The worship of false gods is the fellowship of futility, the grand delusion whose destiny is disappointment'.[165] Jeremiah evocatively brings out the tragedy of idolatry:

'Has a nation ever changed its gods?
      (Yet they are not gods at all.)
But my people have exchanged their glorious God
      for worthless idols.
Be appalled at this, you heavens,
      and shudder with great horror,'
declares the LORD.
'My people have committed two sins:
They have forsaken me,
      the spring of living water,
and have dug their own cisterns,
      broken cisterns that cannot hold water.'
(Jer. 2:11–13)


## Conclusion

In this long chapter I have attempted to argue that the Old Testament's positive affirmation of Yahweh's transcendent uniqueness reveals a corollary negative assessment of the religious Other, witnessed in the strong denouncement of idolatry. While much of the focus of the Old Testament is on Israel, the themes of transcendent uniqueness and idolatry have implications for the nature and status of religious worship among the *gôyîm* of the world. These themes are but a continuation and exemplification of universal themes laid down in

---

164. C. J. H. Wright, *Mission of God*, p. 172 (his italics). The idea that we become what we worship is the main theme of Greg Beale's major study *We Become What We Worship: A Biblical Theology of Idolatry* (Nottingham: Apollos, 2008). For a more popular but no less insightful analysis of idolatry and its implications for contemporary society, see Timothy J. Keller, *Counterfeit Gods: When the Empty Promises of Love, Money and Power Let You Down* (London: Hodder & Stoughton, 2010).

165. C. J. H. Wright, *Mission of God*, p. 176.

Genesis 1 – 11: the Creator–creature distinction, the sovereignty of God and the antithetical nature between true faith and false faith. As I hope to show in the next chapter, this antithesis continues into the New Testament's teaching.

However, in closing here, I wish to make a few concluding remarks I hope will tie off some loose ends concerning this portrayal of the religious Other in the Old Testament.

*First*, in developing a contemporary theology of religions there needs to be some hermeneutical bridge built that connects the assessment of the religious Other of the Old Testament to the assessment of the religious Other of the twenty-first century. I am aware that the Bible does not mention Allah or Muhammad, Krishna or Vishnu, Guru Nanak or Brahman, but Ashtoreth, Baal of Peor, Marduk, Bel, Nebo, Chemosh, Molech, Adrammelech and Rephan. However, I would contend that this bridge has already been established. First, what connects these variegated religious expressions are the anthropological universals archetypally laid down in Genesis 1 – 11 of *imago Dei* and the 'false faith' evidenced in the fall. Although human history witnesses not just to person variability but 'religious' variability, it also witnesses to a 'humanity constancy' that permeates all cultures and at all times.[166] Secondly, if the divine function of God-breathed Old Testament Scripture is to teach Christians *now* through the history of Israel *then*, then we should take seriously the Old Testament assessment of the religious Other and draw relevant applications. Thirdly, there may well be ways in which one can trace phenomenologically a historical lineage between the localized deities of the Old Testament and particular gods worshipped today. As Poston notes:

> The deities of the 'world-class religions' all began as primal, localized deities. The evolution of Varuna, Rudra, and the other gods of early Vedic Hinduism into Vishnu, Shiva and other modern deities is clearly traced in the history of religions. Mahayana Buddhism absorbed many local Asian deities, which resulted in new groupings of spirit beings known as Manushi Buddhas, Dhyani Buddhas and Bodhisattvas. The same kind of development is seen in nearly all of the modern faith systems. There is thus no intrinsic difference between the gods spoken of in the Old Testament and those of contemporary polytheistic religions.[167]

---

166. As will be seen shortly in my exposition of Rom. 1:18–32.

167. Poston, 'Bible and the Religions', p. 70. For a detailed account of these developments see Mircea Eliade, *A History of Religious Ideas*, 3 vols. (Chicago: University of Chicago Press, 1978–85).

*Secondly*, in keeping with the focus of this study, I recognize that my primary concern has been theological rather than missiological. In other words, my aim has been to look at what the religious Other *is* in the Old Testament, as opposed to what the people of God are to *do* in the light of what the religious Other is. Often, though, these two questions are inextricably linked. One consequence of the transcendent uniqueness of God is a secondary affirmation of the incomparability and uniqueness of Israel. There is no other covenant community like them, and there is no other community with a history like theirs because the incomparable and unique God has covenanted with them alone and intervened salvifically on their behalf alone. However, and as I hope I have made clear in this chapter, such exclusivity should never lead to vainglory or malice. Israel is chosen by the sheer grace of God to display his glory, and as such they have a unique responsibility and calling to be a light to the nations in both word and deed. As the book of Jonah clearly teaches, to neglect and abuse such a calling is an abuse of this delegated authority and power and leads to greater culpability.[168] On a related point, I would also want to note that just as I described and analysed the nature of the 'religious Other' among the nations from these texts, a parallel study would be to describe and analyse apostate religion from within the boundaries of Israel.[169]

*Thirdly*, I have described the Old Testament portrayal of the religious Other negatively in terms of antithesis and conflict, and described the relationship between Yahweh and Israel as one of particularity and exclusivity. However such a theological antithesis between prescribed religion and proscribed religion must be held in tandem, not merely with the broader themes of Israel's missionary mandate whereby eventually all nations will be blessed through them, but with the social-ethical themes of inclusion, diversity and tolerance, *seen in the history of Israel itself*, for example attitudes towards the alien and stranger, attitudes towards ethnic diversity, including the eschatological hope of God's people being drawn from all nations and languages, God's universal care and sustenance of

---

168. I recognize that there is a debate within missiological studies as to whether the nature of Israel's mission was purely inwardly and passively *centrifugal*, or whether it was centrifugal *and* outwardly and proactively *centripetal*. In terms of those I have referenced in this chapter, Chris Wright defends the former, Mark Kreitzer the latter. See C. J. H. Wright, *Mission of God*, pp. 500–505; Kreitzer, *Concept of Ethnicity*, pp. 171–190, 241–323. See also Walter C. Kaiser, *Mission in the Old Testament: Israel as a Light to the Nations* (Grand Rapids: Baker, 2000).

169. As indicated in chapter 2 I would broadly include this within the category of idolatry in terms of 'distortion'.

creation, and so on. Again there are rich and complex social-ethical norms and paradigms set out in Israel's history that can aid Christians in their reflection on more public theological issues.[170]

*Finally*, the more negative descriptions of the religious Other in terms of antithesis and idolatry do not admit to an *absolute* depravity concerning the religious Other. While the Old Testament often evidences the strong relationship between the worship of idols and the bad ethical fruit that is produced from such worship, 'this does not of course mean that there is not a great remnant of common grace in the statutes, customs, and laws of the *goyim*'.[171] The *gôyîm* are still made in the *imago Dei*. It is the fact of common grace that helps discern different levels of association, engagement and even cooperation between Israel and the surrounding nations. Interestingly, in his explanation of common grace Van Til uses an Old Testament example:

> The biblical analogy that serves our purpose here is that of Solomon hiring foreign help for the building of the temple. In the case of the Samaritans who wished to help the Jews rebuild the temple, it was the business of the true Jew to reject the offer. In the case of the Phoenicians, it was the privilege and the duty of the true Jew to accept the service. The difference is simply that in the case of the Samaritans there was an effort to have a voice in the interpretation of the plans of God for his temple. On the other hand, in the case of the Phoenicians there was no such attempt. There it was no more than a case of skilled workmanship. And skilled workmanship is often, by God's common grace, found more abundantly in the camp of the antitheists than in the camp of the theists.[172]

---

170. For a further exploration of these themes see Christopher J. H. Wright, *Old Testament Ethics for the People of God* (Leicester: Inter-Varsity Press, 2004); Jonathan Burnside, *God, Justice, and Society: Aspects of Law and Legality in the Bible* (Oxford: Oxford University Press, 2011); *The Status and Welfare of Immigrants* (Cambridge: Jubilee Centre, 2001); Nick Spencer, *Asylum and Immigration* (Carlisle: Paternoster, 2004).

171. Kreitzer, *Concept of Ethnicity*, p. 210.

172. Quoted in Greg Bahnsen, *Van Til's Apologetic: Readings and Analysis* (Phillipsburg: P & R, 1998), p. 433. The original quotation comes from Van Til, *Defense of the Faith*, vol. 2 (Philadelphia: P & R), p. 217 (this is the edition Bahnsen quotes from).

## 6. THE PERILOUS EXCHANGE: THE IDOLATRY OF THE RELIGIOUS OTHER IN THE NEW TESTAMENT

> [H]ow you turned to God from idols to serve the living and true God.
>
> (1 Thessalonians 1:9)

### Introduction

> 'Ah, all things come to those who wait,'
> (I say these words to make me glad),
> But something answers soft and sad,
> 'They come, but often come too late.'

Although it has been hijacked in the twenty-first century to promote a well-known Irish dry stout, 'all things come to those who wait' begins the last stanza of Violet Fane's nineteenth-century poem concerning unrequited love.[1] In our quest to understand the nature of the religious Other, the promise made at the beginning of the previous chapter was that after a lengthy trek through the Old Testament we would eventually find relief by coming to the seminal New Testament text of Romans 1:18–32. This passage, it was promised, will both

---

1. 'Tout vient á qui sait attendre', in Violet Fane, *From Dawn to Noon: Poems* (London: Longmans, Green, 1872), p. 85. Fane was the literary pseudonym of Mary, Baroness Currie.

confirm and further consolidate my thesis concerning the centrality of the category of idolatry through which we are to interpret the religious Other. That wait is nearly over.[2]

However, as we move from Old Testament to New Testament, it would be myopic in the extreme not to set these verses from Romans within their proper redemptive-historical context.

As Christians we are glad that the New Testament reveals that contra our poet, far from coming too late, 'at just the right time' (Rom. 5:6) and 'according to the definite plan and foreknowledge of God' (Acts 2:23 ESV), the 'all things' waited for in the Old Testament are now over. We start, and indeed finish, with Jesus Christ.[3]

---

2. The other seminal passage, Paul's address to the Areopagus in Acts 17, will be dealt with in the next chapter.

3. It is worth noting Andreas Köstenberger's caution regarding a NT biblical theology of religions in the General Epistles and Revelation: 'The presence of other worldviews and religious beliefs is presupposed rather than addressed directly. To what extent can one therefore speak of a contribution made by these [NT] books to a biblical theology of religions? Foremost of all, one should avoid overstating one's case by claiming that they reflect a consciously worked out Christian theology and response to religious pluralism in their day – in the opinion of this writer they do not. Conflicting truth claims are rather brought to the fore by religious persecution and the challenge of formulating a believing approach to it. The New Testament data should not be intellectualized, and one should not claim a greater degree of deliberateness or sophistication than the evidence bears out. Moreover, owing to the occasional nature of these writings, much of the relevant material is incidental rather than systematic, so that many insights can be gained on the level of inference or implication rather than by explicit reference or direct injunction' (Andreas Köstenberger, 'The Contribution of the General Epistles and Revelation to a Biblical Theology of Religions', in Edward Rommen and Harold Netland [eds.], *Christianity and the Religions: A Biblical Theology of World Religions*, Evangelical Missiological Society Series 2 [Pasadena: William Carey Library, 1995], pp. 113–140 [113–114]). In his own NT theology of other religions, Greg Beale uses the same Köstenberger quotation, but applies this caveat more generally to the whole of the NT. See G. K. Beale, 'Other Religions in New Testament Theology', in David W. Baker (ed.), *Biblical Faith and Other Religions: An Evangelical Assessment* (Grand Rapids: Kregel, 2004), pp. 79–105 (91). Finally, here it is worth reiterating a point made to me by one of my former students, Tim Edwards, that because they are largely confined to the lost sheep of the house of Israel, the Gospels show little engagement with religiosity per se. Jesus' confrontation

## 1. Jesus Christ our Lord

> ...regarding his Son, who as to his earthly life was a descendant of David, and who
> through the Spirit of holiness was appointed the Son of God in power by his resurrection
> from the dead: Jesus Christ our Lord. Through him we received grace and apostleship
> to call all the Gentiles to the obedience that comes from faith for his name's sake.
> (Rom. 1:3–5)

In the person and work of Jesus Christ we reach the 'Omega' point not only of
the biblical revelation and redemptive history, but of the Reformed tradition,
where the great *solas* coalesce most explicitly. The question of Jesus also remains
the crux for the theology of religions, for any credible biblical theology must be
Christocentric. As Netland notes:

> No serious discussion of the relation of Christianity to other faiths can proceed very far
> without coming to grips with the towering figure of Jesus. Sooner or later, the blunt
> question put by Jesus to his followers – 'Who do people say I am?' (Mark 8:27) – must
> be confronted.[4]

Given my tradition-specific context and presuppositions, together with my definition of God as the 'self-contained ontological Trinity', it is predictable that I
wish to defend and promote a 'high' Chalcedonian Christology together with a
constitutive soteriology.[5] It might also be predictable as to some of the general
themes and specific texts in the New Testament I might refer to, for even a

---

with the Pharisees and leaders of the Jewish nation are better seen as engaging with
corrupted forms of biblical religiosity (analogous to, say, Jeremiah's confrontations
with the prophets of his day). And where Jesus is engaging with Gentiles they seem
either to be God-fearers (such as the centurion who asked to have his servant healed),
and thus on the edges of biblical religiosity, or they are less obviously 'religious' – an
example would be Pilate, who seems concerned only with the political. While there
are implications from one sphere to the other, they are implications that we have to
make and not ones that the text makes.

4. Harold A. Netland, *Dissonant Voices: Religious Pluralism and the Question of Truth*
(Leicester: Apollos, 1991), p. 235.

5. 'High' here meaning an affirmation of Jesus' divinity; 'constitutive' meaning that
Jesus' life, death and resurrection ontologically 'constitute' salvation as opposed to
merely 'representing' salvation; 'Chalcedonian' referring to the classic Christological
statement of AD 451.

pluralist like Alan Race in his seminal book on the theology of religions writes, 'Not even the most detached reader of the New Testament can fail to give the impression that the overall picture of Christian faith which it presents is intended to be absolute and final.'[6]

However, and with much of the groundwork now complete, I wish to articulate the relevance of such a Christology within the context of the themes I have developed in previous chapters and why indeed 'there is no other name under heaven given to mankind by which we must be saved' (Acts 4:12). Concerning the following points, I hope we can quicken our pace somewhat from now on, as I have already established a number of important themes in this study, and have dealt with similar material in detail in previous writing.

### a. Jesus' transcendent uniqueness

First, concerning Christ's person, I wish to highlight the New Testament writers' deliberate equating of the identity and action of the historical Jesus of Nazareth with *the* God of Israel, Yahweh. Jesus Christ is Lord. Citing example after example, Chris Wright's avalanche of evidence concludes thus:

> For the Old Testament texts clearly did not mean that YHWH was one unique god among many within the species 'gods'. Rather, in what Bauckham calls 'transcendent uniqueness,' YHWH stood *sui generis*, entirely in a class of his own as *the* God, the sole Creator of the universe, and Ruler, Judge and Saviour of the nations. And the New Testament repeatedly makes the same affirmation about Jesus of Nazareth, putting him in the same exclusively singular, transcendent framework and frequently quoting the same texts to do so.[7]

> Jesus then, according to the consistent witness of many strands in the New Testament documents, shares the identity of YHWH, the Lord God of Israel, and performs functions that were uniquely and exclusively the prerogative of YHWH in the Old Testament. These include especially God's role as Creator and owner of the universe, Ruler of history, Judge of all nations and Saviour of all who turn to him. In all of these dimensions of God's identity and activity, New Testament believers saw the face of Jesus, spoke of him in exactly the same terms and worshipped him accordingly.[8]

---

6. Alan Race, *Christians and Religious Pluralism: Patterns in the Christian Theology of Religions* (London: SCM, 1983), p. 10.

7. Christopher J. H. Wright, *The Mission of God: Unlocking the Bible's Grand Narrative* (Nottingham: Inter-Varsity Press, 2006), p. 131.

8. Ibid., p. 122.

This identical association is part of what can be called a 'Christology from within', which focuses on Jesus as the person who brings fulfilment. Jesus is the antitype to the many Old Testament types.[9] All the Scriptures are about him (John 5:39); he is a 'Yes' to God's promises (2 Cor. 1:20): 'Jesus is not merely the agent through whom the knowledge of God is communicated (as any messenger might be). He himself is the very content of the communication.'[10] Indeed, within the probable context of some Jewish and pagan syncretism in Colossae, Paul's statements concerning the finality, exclusivity and even exhaustiveness of God's revelation in Christ are at their starkest:

> Christ himself is the mystery (2:2), the storehouse of wisdom and knowledge (2:3), the *pleroma* of deity (2:9), the reality over against the shadow (2:17), the head from whom these believers are in jeopardy of losing connection (2:19) . . . Far from seeking common ground with the incorporationist religions of Colossae the Apostle is intent on driving them out of the church through his explication of the unrivaled supremacy of the person of Jesus Christ. Instead of rapprochement or accommodation there is displacement.[11]

Gathering together several strands I have described in previous chapters is Bauckham's own interesting exposition of the Shema in the New Testament. One of three seminal texts with which he seeks to show how New Testament writers *Christologically* appropriated the Shema is 1 Corinthians 8:1–6 and 10:19–20. Here, not only does Paul affirm Yahweh's transcendent uniqueness in the context of the now familiar categories of idols and demons,[12] but he does so by drawing heavily on Deuteronomy 32.[13] Referring to 1 Corinthians 10:22, 'Or are we

---

9. Calvin famously understands the person and work of Christ as the fulfilment of the roles of prophet, priest and king (*triplex munus*). See John Calvin, *Institutes of the Christian Religion*, ed. John T. McNeill, tr. Ford Lewis Battles, 2 vols., LCC (Philadelphia: Westminster, 1960), 2.15.1.

10. C. J. H. Wright, *Mission of God*, p. 123.

11. Don N. Howell, 'The Apostle Paul and First Century Religious Pluralism', in Edward Rommen and Harold A. Netland (eds.), *Christianity and the Religions: A Biblical Theology of World Religions*, Evangelical Missiological Society Series 2 (Pasadena: William Carey Library, 1995), pp. 92–112 (106).

12. We shall explore the relationship between them in more detail in the next chapter.

13. For more detail on Paul's allusion to Deut. 32 in these passages see Guy Waters, *The End of Deuteronomy in the Epistles of Paul*, ed. Jorg Frey, WUNT (Tübingen: Mohr Siebeck, 2006), pp. 138–145.

provoking the Lord to jealousy?' (NRSV), with its allusion to Deuteronomy 32:21, 'They made me jealous by what is no god', Bauckham writes:

> His choice of the allusion shows that he takes very seriously the Jewish understanding of monolatry as required by God's jealous desire for the sole devotion of his covenant people. . . . In this sense, God's jealousy is closely connected with the Shema. This makes it more noteworthy that Paul attributes the divine jealousy of Deuteronomy to Jesus Christ . . . The implication for Jewish monotheism and Christology is remarkable: the exclusive devotion that YHWH's jealousy requires of his people is required of Christians by Jesus Christ. Effectively he assumes the unique identity of YHWH.[14]

### b. 'False faith' in the Son

Secondly, and concerning Christ and our universal human predicament, we return to Turretin's description of sin as being ethically unjustifiable 'false faith'. Using this term and commenting on the asymmetry of John 3:36, 'Whoever *believes* in the Son has eternal life; whoever *disobeys* [*not* disbelieves] the Son will not see life, but must endure God's wrath' (NRSV), Michael Ovey notes that 'this disobedience is not merely to the Son incarnate: it is disobedience to the Father who sent him, for it is the will of the Father that people believe in Jesus in this way (Jn 6:29), and that Jesus be honoured as the Son (Jn 5:22–3)'.[15] He goes on to show Johannine instances of 'false faith' and lies told about Jesus which mirror that of Genesis 3:

> For he is the creative Word (Jn 1:1–3), yet the world sees him as untruthful. For example, in John 5:18 his claims to be God's Son are treated as blasphemy, while in John 7:12 some say he is a false teacher. In Genesis 3 God's word is seen as ineffective: as Son he claims to have life within him (Jn 5:26) and to be the one who will rise from the dead (Jn 2:19). Yet the tone of the mockery at the crucifixion (e.g. Mt. 27:39–44) shows a dismissal of Jesus' words as ineffective. Further in Genesis 3, God's goodness is

---

14. Bauckham, *Jesus and the God of Israel: God Crucified and Other Studies on the New Testament's Christology of Divine Identity* (Cambridge: Eerdmans, 2008), p. 100. See also Brian Rosner, '"No Other God": The Jealousy of God and Religious Pluralism', in Andrew D. Clarke and Bruce W. Winter (eds.), *One God, One Lord: Christianity in a World of Religious Pluralism* (Cambridge: Baker, 1992), pp. 149–159.

15. Michael Ovey, 'The Cross, Creation and the Human Predicament', in David Peterson (ed.), *Where Wrath and Mercy Meet: Proclaiming the Atonement Today* (Carlisle: Paternoster, 2001), pp. 100–135 (110).

implicitly denied, while in the New Testament Jesus is seen as morally wrong. Finally, of course, in Genesis 3, God's rightful claims are defied, while in Jesus humanity crucifies its king ('Pilate asked them, "Shall I crucify your King?" The chief priests answered, "We have no king but the emperor"', Jn 19:15).[16]

In considering this 'false faith' in the Son the conclusion to which we are drawn is that not to recognize the risen and ascended Lord Jesus for who he truly is, is an act of idolatry and again provokes divine wrath, a wrath that will be most intensely revealed on that day when everyone will call on mountains and rocks: 'They called to the mountains and the rocks, "Fall on us and hide us from the face of him who sits on the throne and from the *wrath of the Lamb*! For the great day of their wrath has come, and who can withstand it?"' (Rev. 6:16–17). For all the many personal and societal, spiritual and physical implications of fallenness and idolatry, it is this theocentric perspective that is the hub from which we understand the human predicament.

### c. The character of Jesus' work
Thirdly, concerning Christ's saving work, we may say that if divine wrath lies at the heart of the human predicament, then the 'good news' of the gospel is that in Christ's life, death and resurrection this wrath has been dealt with for his people, that

> Jesus Christ our Lord, moved by a love that was determined to do everything to save us, endured and exhausted the destructive divine judgment for which we were inescapably destined, and so won us forgiveness, adoption and glory.[17]

It is to be remembered here that this 'propitiatory' substitutionary work is both theocentric and triune in nature, as the late John Stott so memorably summarized:

> It is God himself who in holy wrath needs to be propitiated, God himself who in holy love undertook to do the propitiating, and God himself who in the person of his Son died for the propitiation of our sins. Thus God took his own loving initiative to appease his own righteous anger by bearing it his own self in his own Son when he took our place and died for us.[18]

---

16. Ibid., pp. 110–111.
17. J. I. Packer, *What Did the Cross Achieve? The Logic of Penal Substitution* (Leicester: RTSF, 2002), p. 35.
18. John R. W. Stott, *The Cross of Christ* (Leicester: Inter-Varsity Press, 1986), p. 175.

As before, although there are multiple perspectives concerning the benefits of Christ's work, it is this Godward reference that must be considered both 'linchpin' and hermeneutical 'key'.[19] It is only *because* Christ's death is propitiatory that *Christus Victor* is possible, for in Christ there are no accusations against God's people (Rom. 8:33). No one, not even Satan the accuser and his demonic horde, can make the charge stick. The case is closed – Christ is our righteousness.[20]

### d. The necessity of faith in Christ for salvation

Fourthly, and because of the above, we return full circle to the necessity of God's verbal revelation to hear this good news. Although authoritative, God's revelation of himself through his 'works' lacks the specificity of his disclosure through his words, and the Word. God's words have always been needed to interpret, supplement and therefore complement God's works: these two modes of revelation were never meant to be separated from one another or to work independently of each other.

This objective epistemological insufficiency of natural revelation becomes more acute after the fall with the universal suppression and substitution of God's revelation. After the fall, what sinners need is spiritual illumination, the regenerating power of the Spirit through the gospel to know God as Creator and Redeemer; and general revelation is an inappropriate vehicle because knowledge of the gospel of our Lord Jesus Christ is not contained in it:

> Man the sinner, as Calvin puts it, through the testimony of the Spirit receives a new power of sight by which he can appreciate the new light given in Scripture. The new light and the new power of sight imply one another. The one is fruitless for salvation without the other.[21]

---

19. See Daniel Strange, 'The Many-Splendoured Cross: Atonement, Controversy and Victory', *Foundations* (autumn 2005), pp. 5–22.
20. For more on this see ibid.; Henri Blocher, 'Agnus Victor: The Atonement as Victory and Vicarious Punishment', in John Stackhouse (ed.), *What Does It Mean to Be Saved? Broadening Evangelical Horizons of Salvation* (Grand Rapids: Baker, 2002), pp. 67–91; Mark Thompson, 'No Charge Admitted: Justification and the Defeat of the Powers', in Peter G. Bolt (ed.), *Christ's Victory Over Evil* (Nottingham: Inter-Varsity Press, 2009), pp. 123–149.
21. Cornelius Van Til, 'Nature and Scripture', in Paul Woolley (ed.), *The Infallible Word: A Symposium* (Philadelphia: Presbyterian Guardian, 1946), pp. 255–293 (281).

Special revelation is necessary because with it comes the regenerating work of the Spirit in special grace.

Unlike special revelation, general revelation simply does not contain the truth content necessary for saving faith, and so is not an appropriate vehicle for the Spirit's saving work of regeneration. Faith cannot maintain its fully orbed character of *notitia, fiducia* and *assensus*[22] if the object changes from Christ to God (or even Reality), as it is a knowledge of who Christ is and what he has done that defines saving faith. Looking outside ourselves to the objective work of Christ tells us also something of the role of faith and its efficacy.[23]

Concerning the oft-made analogy between the chronologically pre-messianic (Israel and 'holy pagans') and those today who are 'informationally' pre-messianic (almost always within the context of soteriology), I refer the reader to my previous work on this topic.[24] In summary, I believe this analogy to be invalid, a better analogy being made between Israel (into which 'holy pagans' were engrafted and so not 'pagan' at all) and Christians. Concerning the relationship between believers before Christ and those after Christ, the relationship is one of historical discontinuity in redemptive continuity. From the *proto-evangelium* in Genesis onwards, despite widespread suppression and devolution of true knowledge of God, God by his illuminating and regenerating Spirit preserves authentic and genuine knowledge of himself and his salvation in his chosen people (who of course are meant to be a blessing to others), and while

---

22. The knowledge of our minds of Jesus Christ; the trust in our hearts in Jesus Christ; the assent of our wills to Jesus Christ.

23. As Murray states, 'It is to be remembered that the efficacy of faith does not reside in itself. Faith is not something that merits the favour of God. All the efficacy unto salvation resides in the Saviour . . . , it is not faith that saves but faith in Jesus Christ; strictly speaking, it is not even faith in Christ that saves but Christ that saves through faith. Faith unites us to Christ in the bonds of abiding attachment and entrustment and it is this union which ensures that the saving power, grace, and virtue of the Saviour become operative in the believer. The specific character of faith is that it looks away from itself and finds its whole interest and object in Christ. He is the absorbing preoccupation of faith' (John Murray, *Redemption – Accomplished and Applied* [Edinburgh: Banner of Truth Trust, 1955], p. 112).

24. Daniel Strange, *The Possibility of Salvation Among the Unevangelised: An Analysis of Inclusivism in Recent Evangelical Theology* (Carlisle: Paternoster, 2001), ch. 6. For a monograph on this 'fulfilment' analogy see Adam Sparks, *One of a Kind: The Relationship Between Old and New Covenants as the Hermeneutical Key for Christian Theology of Religions* (Eugene: Pickwick, 2009).

we may speak of the gradual progression in the specificity of revelation as redemptive history progresses, type and antitype, promise and fulfilment remain in continuity. As Kuyper notes, the revelation Old Testament believers received 'produced in their minds such a fixed and tangible form of the Messiah that fellowship with Him, which alone is essential to salvation, was made possible to them by anticipation as to us by memory'.[25] All this is to say, therefore, that it is illegitimate to compare those who, by the regenerating Spirit, responded to God faithfully according to the redemptive revelation given to them at their time in redemptive history (Israel and those engrafted into Israel) with those who respond to God idolatrously with the revelation they have been given in nature or history.

It is worth noting in all the above, and contra inclusivists such as Clark Pinnock and Amos Yong, the economy between Spirit and Son, whereby the special work of the Spirit in regeneration is tied to the crucified and risen Christ as proclaimed in the gospel. As Vanhoozer notes, we are to see the Spirit 'as the deputy of Christ rather than as an independent itinerant evangelist'.[26] Such a tie is not a denial of the Spirit's universal activity in providence, nor in his external non-salvific common-grace activities,[27] but it is a distinction between different aspects of the Spirit's presence in creation and in re-creation. What *is* being denied here is the conflation of these categories that appear to posit a deeply problematic uniformity of pneumatological presence. As before, I have addressed this point in some detail in my analysis of Clark Pinnock's pneumatological inclusivism.[28]

---

25. Abraham Kuyper, *The Work of the Holy Spirit*, tr. Henri De Vries (1900; Grand Rapids: Eerdmans, 1941), p. 166.

26. Kevin J. Vanhoozer, 'Does the Trinity Belong in a Theology of Religions? On Angling in the Rubicon and the "Identity" of God', in Kevin J. Vanhoozer (ed.), *The Trinity in a Pluralistic Age: Theological Essays on Culture and Religion* (Cambridge: Eerdmans, 1997), pp. 41–71 (246).

27. Already commented on in a previous chapter as an excitation to civic good among those not inwardly regenerated.

28. See Strange, *Possibility of Salvation*. See also Daniel Strange, 'Presence, Prevenience, or Providence? Deciphering the Conundrum of Pinnock's Pneumatological Inclusivism', in Tony Gray and Christopher Sinkinson (eds.), *Reconstructing Theology: A Critical Assessment of the Theology of Clark Pinnock* (Carlisle: Paternoster, 2000), pp. 220–258; 'A Little Dwelling on the Divine Presence: Towards a "Whereness" of the Triune God', in T. Desmond Alexander and Simon Gathercole (eds.), *Heaven on Earth: The Temple in Biblical Theology* (Carlisle: Paternoster, 2004), pp. 211–230.

*e. The Logos, and the 'times of ignorance'*
Finally, in this section it is appropriate here that I quickly mop up two other
Christologically related themes that have been used by evangelicals and others
in their support of a more positive attitude to the religious Other: Jesus as
the Logos who 'gives light to everyone' (John 1:9), and God's overlooking of
the times of 'ignorance' in Acts 14:16–17; 17:30–31. I believe them both to be
theological red herrings.

*i. John 1:9*
Much has been made of John 1:9, 'The true light that gives light to everyone
was coming into the world.' It is used by Justin Martyr in his concept of *logos
spermatikos*,[29] clearly alluded to in both of the most relevant Vatican II documents
(*Lumen Gentium*[30] and *Nostra Aetate*),[31] and is a key building block in 'fulfilment'
models within the theology of religions.[32] Within evangelicalism the verse is a
major building block used by Wesleyan theologians in their own defence of a
'prevenient grace',[33] and, in a more radical variation on this particular theme, it
is used by those such as Clark Pinnock to support a form of soteriological inclusivism.[34] As has been argued elsewhere, I am not sure that the verse in question
is able to bear the weight put upon it.[35]

However, there are still a number of evangelicals who, while rejecting a
soteriological reference to John 1:9, still tie the Logos to a universal internal
anthropological enlightening in terms of general revelation and the *imago
Dei*. Offering up Calvin in support of such a view, Sparks concludes the
following:

---

29. See Justin, *Apology* 2.13. For a sensible account of Justin's use of *logos spermatikos* see
    Gerald Bray, 'Explaining Christianity to Pagans: The Second Century Apologists', in
    Vanhoozer, *The Trinity in a Pluralistic Age,* pp. 9–25.

30. See Austin Flannery O.P. (ed.), *Vatican Council II: The Conciliar and Post Conciliar
    Documents* (New York: Costello, 1998), pp. 367–369.

31. Ibid., pp. 738–742.

32. See Sparks, *One of a Kind*, pp. 229–257.

33. For a helpful exposition of this doctrine see Randy L. Maddox, *Responsible Grace:
    John Wesley's Practical Theology* (Nashville: Kingswood, 1994).

34. Clark Pinnock, *A Wideness in God's Mercy: The Finality of Jesus Christ in a World of
    Religions* (Grand Rapids: Zondervan, 1992), pp. 103–104; *Flame of Love: A Theology
    of the Holy Spirit* (Downers Grove: InterVarsity Press, 1996), p. 61.

35. Sparks, *One of a Kind*, pp. 229–235.

I maintain therefore that John is writing here about the enlightening of people –
as people, *not* about the possibility of light within non-Christian religions. Thus, the
suggestion that the light has shone through other religious leaders or founders is not
supported by the text. 'It is not talking about the special light of a religious nature
to be found in special people, but about universal light that every human being
everywhere shares simply by being human.'[36]

I wonder, though, whether even this connection might be something of an
exegetical stretch. While I continue to defend both general revelation and the
*imago Dei*, is this what John is referring to in his prologue? In his comments on
this verse Don Carson refers to the work of Ed Miller, whose study on this verse
is one of the most detailed both historically and lexically.[37] After surveying the
possible options, Miller argues exegetically that

> the light . . . was coming into the world (not [into] every person) and that the verse
> thus bears a clear incarnational teaching. It seems to me, further that the most natural
> interpretation, in view of many other Johannine passages, would construe the shining
> of the light with the *advent* of the light.[38]

Moreover, intratextually 'the idea of a universal revelation by which people in
general are illuminated with respect to some basic knowledge of God or spiritual
truths is otherwise utterly inimical to the Johannine literature'.[39] Miller's conclusion, with which Carson appears to concur, is that rather than relating this
Logos to an inward concept (e.g. the *imago Dei*), a restrictive and 'external'
interpretation is in view, and one that is fully consistent with the Johannine
literature: 'The "light" of John 1:9 is to be conceived as a *special* revelation,
radiating specifically from the incarnate Logos and holding consequences and

---

36. Ibid., p. 235 (his italics; quote from C. J. H. Wright, *Thinking Clearly About the
Uniqueness of Christ* [Crowborough: Monarch, 1997], p. 128). I note here that even
my great hero J. H. Bavinck makes this connection. See e.g. J. H. Bavinck, *The
Church Between Temple and Mosque* (Grand Rapids: Eerdmans, 1966), p. 127.
37. D. A. Carson, *The Gagging of God: Christianity Confronts Pluralism* (Leicester:
Apollos, 1996), p. 303. The work to which he refers is Ed L. Miller, 'The True Light
Which Illumines Every Person', in Ed L. Miller (ed.), *Good News in History* (Atlanta:
Scholars Press, 1993), pp. 63–83.
38. Miller, 'True Light', p. 79 (his italics).
39. Ibid.

benefits only for those whose lives are touched by it'.[40] In other words, 'the illumination in John 1:9 is tied to the incarnation, not to some inner or mystical light, that may, perhaps, be tied to the *imago Dei*'.[41]

*ii. The 'times of ignorance'*
Paul's statement in Acts 17:30, 'In the past God overlooked such ignorance, but now he commands all people everywhere to repent,' and the similar statement in Acts 14:16, 'In the past, he let all nations go their own way,' have been argued by some as demonstrating occasions when false worship has not been culpable. A 'weak' version of this is put forward by Goldingay and Wright. In the context of Joshua 24:15, a verse I discussed in the previous chapter, they understand the Acts 17 verse to be 'Paul's affirmation of God's apparently differential attitude to human religion at different stages of either history or awareness . . . The knowledge of Christ requires repentance even from things God had previously overlooked.'[42] A 'strong' version is put forward by Clark Pinnock, who goes further by seemingly applying these verses in Acts contemporaneously:

> Some would question whether God would put up with a religion that was grossly deficient. Would God accept people whose beliefs fall far short of the complete truth? Yes, I think he would. For Scripture often hints at how merciful he is, even in the realm of religion.[43]

Such readings, however, in both weaker and stronger versions, would appear to go against the grain, not only of the apostles' teaching elsewhere (e.g. Rom. 1:18–32), but against Scripture as a whole, which, as we have seen, never appears to portray God as taking anything other than a proscriptive stance on idolatry. While it can certainly be affirmed that there are degrees of responsibility according to revelation received,[44] all are responsible and none are ignorant, for God has not left himself without a witness (Acts 14:17).

---

40. Ibid., p. 81.
41. Carson, *Gagging of God*, p. 303.
42. John E. Goldingay and Christopher J. H. Wright, '"Yahweh Our God Yahweh One": The Oneness of God in the Old Testament', in Clarke and Winter, *One God, One Lord*, pp. 43–62 (51). Cf. Christopher J. H. Wright, *Deuteronomy*, NIBCOT (Peabody: Hendrickson, 1996), pp. 51–52.
43. Pinnock, *Wideness in God's Mercy*, p. 101.
44. And therefore degrees of punishment for revelation received. Those who have suppressed both general and special revelation will be judged more harshly than

What, then, is Paul speaking of in these verses? I believe his point to be redemptive historical in nature. As Sparks notes:

> What Paul is arguing in these passages is that until the full revelation of God came to the Gentiles, God 'overlooked' the errors which arose through ignorance of his will. However, this overlooking 'betokened not indifference but patience'. Therefore, although God did allow the nations to 'go their own way', this should *not* be taken as an indication that he condoned their guilt, but rather an acknowledgement that his redemptive plan was targeted in the former times at Israel.[45]

Carson gives Pinnock's interpretation especially short shrift:

> This is an astonishing inference. It would mean that the Athenians were better off before they heard Paul's preaching about Jesus: they were nicely spared any blame because they were ignorant, but now, poor chaps, for the first time they are held accountable. What Paul means, rather, is that God graciously overlooked their ignorance in the past, however culpable their ignorance was, for he did not punish them instantly, but in his forbearance 'left the sins committed beforehand unpunished' (Rom. 3:35). Now, however, as salvation has been brought near, so also has judgement drawn close. That is characteristic of realized eschatology in the New Testament: the blessings of the age to come have dawned, but concomitantly the dangers have increased proportionately. . . . If, in the past, culpable ignorance was graciously overlooked by God – not in the sense that he assigned no guilt, but in the sense that he bore with it – now it is inexcusable: 'now he commands all people everywhere to repent' (17:30), and has backed up this demand with the threat of judgment threatening from the impending last day (17:31).[46]

---

those who have received only general revelation. This appears to be the meaning behind texts such as Luke 12:47–48 with its 'few blows' and 'many blows', and also Jesus' words in sending out the seventy-two in Luke 10:12, 'I tell you, it will be more bearable on that day for Sodom than for that town.'

45. Adam Sparks, 'Salvation History, Chronology, and Crisis: A Problem with Inclusivist Theology of Religions, Part 2 of 2', *Them* 33 (2008), pp. 48–62 (49; his italics).

46. Carson, *Gagging of God*, p. 310. For a similar conclusion with much greater detail and justification see Flavien Olivier Cedric Pardigon, 'Paul Against the Idols: The Areopagus Speech and Religious Inclusivism', PhD diss., Westminster Theological Seminary, 2008, pp. 314–321.

J. H. Bavinck offers a missiological exhortation, noting that 'we are the bearers of the "now" in this text':[47]

> We stand in that momentous divine 'now,' the 'now' of a new chapter in God's involvement with this world. All missionary proclamation only stands on solid ground when it is done in this conviction: 'God has been busy with you for a very long time, but you have not understood this. Through my preaching, God is coming to you once again in order to call you to conversion.'[48]

## 2. The perilous exchange

> The wrath of God is being revealed from heaven against all the godlessness and wickedness of people, who suppress the truth by their wickedness, since what may be known about God is plain to them, because God has made it plain to them. For since the creation of the world God's invisible qualities – his eternal power and divine nature – have been clearly seen, being understood from what has been made, so that people are without excuse.
>
> For although they knew God, they neither glorified him as God nor gave thanks to him, but their thinking became futile and their foolish hearts were darkened. Although they claimed to be wise, they became fools and exchanged the glory of the immortal God for images made to look like a mortal human being and birds and animals and reptiles.
>
> Therefore God gave them over in the sinful desires of their hearts to sexual impurity for the degrading of their bodies with one another. They exchanged the truth about God for a lie, and worshipped and served created things rather than the Creator – who is for ever praised. Amen.
> (Rom. 1:18–25)

And so, after a lengthy journey, we finally reach our destination: Rome, and the apostle's description of the human religious predicament. Of course, while Romans 1:18–25 is the summit of our journey, in the context of the book of Romans it forms only the foothills of Paul's detailed argument in demonstrating that the gospel is 'the power of God that brings salvation to everyone who

---

47. J. H. Bavinck, 'Religious Consciousness and Christian Faith', in James D. Bratt, John Bolt and Paul J. Visser (eds.), *The J. H. Bavinck Reader* (Cambridge: Eerdmans, 2013), pp. 145–299 (278).

48. Ibid.

believes: first to the Jew, then to the Gentile' (Rom. 1:16). I have decided to stay and explore this pericope because of its universal scope, which includes all people, together with its complementary distillation of many of the themes we have explored from Genesis onwards. The pericope therefore offers a fitting conclusion to this chapter and prepares us for a more systematic exposition in the next chapter.

There are many qualified to lead us in a tour around these verses, but I have decided that our guide will be the Dutch Reformed missiologist J. H. Bavinck, a scholar we have already encountered in this study. Bavinck evocatively exegetes this passage within the larger context of his expertise within the theology of religions and a life spent studying and interacting with the religious Other on the mission field. Bavinck's thoughts on these verses are scattered throughout various writings, and at this point I shall merely attempt to offer some highlights, recognizing that we shall return in the next chapter to further extrapolations Bavinck makes.

Bavinck's exposition can be split into two parts: the reality and nature of God's objective revelation, and humanity's subjective response to this revelation.

### a. A clear and present revelation

First, J. H. Bavinck notes that in the created order there is true and objective knowledge of God, but that the nature of this knowledge is not static and found through philosophical reflection but 'occurs in the living connection between people and the world around them, in what one would call the symbiotic relationship of people and the world'.[49] This revelation is dynamic, personal and relational in character: 'The meeting point of general revelation and the human being is not isolated . . . It lies first of all simply in the problems inherent in being human, that is, in being a fallen human being.'[50] Elsewhere he comments further on the existential nature of this revelation:

> The Greek *nooumena*, literally 'being intelligently observed', emphasises that seeing with the eye is not intended in this verse; but at the same time it does not mean that seeing God's everlasting power and Godhead is attained by a process of reasoning. It is reached not as a logical conclusion, but in a moment of vision. It suddenly comes upon a person; it overwhelms him.[51]

---

49. Ibid.
50. Ibid., p. 279.
51. J. H. Bavinck, *The Church Between Temple and Mosque* (Grand Rapids: Eerdmans, 1966), p. 120.

If we wish to use the expression 'general revelation' we must not do so in the sense that one can logically conclude God's existence from it. This *may* be possible, but it only leads to a philosophical notion of God as the first cause. But that is not the biblical idea of 'general revelation.' When the Bible speaks of general revelation it means something quite different. There it has a much more personal nature. It is divine concern for men collectively and individually. God's deity and eternal power are evident; they overwhelm man; they strike him suddenly, in moments when he thought they were far away. They creep up on him; they do not let go of him, even though man does his best to escape them.[52]

Concerning the content of this revelation, Bavinck notes that God's 'eternal power' and 'divine nature' pertain to the dependence and accountability of human beings to God. 'Eternal power' 'conveys the sense that in all things God is the only initiator; he completes everything by virtue of his own capability'.[53] The issue of power has always been associated with religion: 'the amazing, mysterious potentials inherent in things on the strength of which those things become threats and dangers or produce anticipation and hope'.[54] God's 'divine nature' 'conveys the "wholly otherness" of God; God belongs to a completely different order than we human beings'.[55] The term also notes personality; it 'designates a *Someone*, a mysterious *Someone*, who meets us in our interaction with the world around us':[56]

> And there is something deep within people – despite all their stubborn attempts to reduce that *Someone* to a force, to *mana*, or to *Brahman* – that persuades them with unmistakable emphasis that it still really is a Someone. . . . All of this is presented to people with overwhelming evidence, and they know that they are accountable to this *Someone*.[57]

He remarks that both terms ('eternal power' and 'divine nature') can be seen in the world's religions, with one more accentuated than the other:

> Various human religions always vacillate between eternal power and divinity. Either they dissolve God into an impersonal, vague force and thus lose sight of his divinity, or

---

52. Ibid., p. 124 (his italics).

53. J. H. Bavinck, 'Religious Consciousness', p. 243.

54. Ibid., p. 280.

55. Ibid., p. 243.

56. Ibid., p. 281 (his italics).

57. Ibid. (his italics).

they push God far away and in the practice of daily life rely on other powers that are more concrete and more understandable. In all of this we see the uncertainty of religious consciousness.[58]

Finally, here Bavinck recognizes that while there must be in human beings some *principium internum* (inner principle), or organ, to receive this revelation, the Bible does not speak about it, but rather focuses on the divine initiative of God's objective revelation and the I–Thou dialogue that ensues. He notes that this is maybe what Calvin refers to as the *semen religionis* (seed of religion).

### b. The 'perilous exchange'

Secondly, Bavinck moves on to humankind's subjective reaction to this revelation. The first thing to note is that there is a reaction: general revelation 'does not simply slide past people like a drop of rain does off the waxy leaf of a tree'.[59] God's eternal power and divinity are clearly seen. Bavinck is emphatic here: 'Thus, people know. Yes, they know. They are addressed as "knowers". "For although they knew God . . ." are words that Barthian theology will never give full due. People know.'[60] However, Bavinck immediately admits a paradoxical situation between a de jure (juridical) knowledge but a de facto (actual) not knowing:

> This puts us right in the middle of an incredible problem, since it cannot be denied that Scripture clearly states that people do not know. 'You sacrifice to one you do not know.' 'You worship that which you do not know.' The heathen 'that did not know God.' An overwhelming flood of places in the Bible emphasize this not knowing. This forces the conclusion that the position of human beings is paradoxical. They know, and they do not know. Their legal position is that of knowing but their actual position is that of not knowing. They proceed as unknowing knowers, as though they 'might possibly find him.'[61]

Elucidating this paradox further, Bavinck focuses on Paul's use of the word 'suppression' (*katechein*) and 'exchange' (*allassō/met'allassō*), and employs terminology more associated with psychology.[62] The dynamic nature of what is occurring is reiterated.

---

58. Ibid., pp. 243–244.
59. Ibid., p. 283.
60. Ibid.
61. Ibid., p. 284.
62. Ibid., pp. 284–290.

*i. Suppression*

Suppression carries with it the sense of violently holding down.[63] The sinner constantly suppresses general revelation and is therefore without excuse. Bavinck notes that

> the idea might well be that this suppression occurs so directly, so spontaneously, so simultaneously with the 'understanding' and 'seeing clearly' that at the precise moment that people see, they already no longer see; at the very moment they know, they no longer know.[64]

This suppression occurs 'in unrighteousness'; 'it occurs with the mysterious, always unstated, often also entirely unconscious motive of moral opposition to God'.[65]

Bavinck adds three supplementary points here. First, he notes 'a definite unsettledness deep within . . . As a rule, the engine of this supressing process runs noiselessly, but not so noiselessly that they never feel it running now and then and thereby realise that something is amiss in their lives.'[66] They 'play hide-and-seek with God. They are honest neither with themselves nor with life.'[67] However, 'when a person begins to be illumined by the light of the gospel, they sometimes suddenly become aware of the horror of this suppressing process and realize that they have always known but have never wanted to know'.[68]

Secondly, the variegated nature of this suppression in human beings. In some the impact of revelation hardly makes a ripple, while others are overwhelmed by it: 'The history of religion as well as missionary experience teaches us that it makes no sense to paint all pagans with the same brush.'[69] The reason for such variation is not the 'goodness' of humans

---

63. An illustration might be that of a child's playing with an inflatable ball in the water. She tries to push the ball under the water with all her might and thinks she has succeeded, but the ball always pops up to the surface again for the child to try again, and so on. Here is the 'game' between revelation and suppression.

64. J. H. Bavinck, 'Religious Consciousness', p. 284.

65. Ibid., p. 285.

66. Ibid.

67. Ibid.

68. Ibid.

69. Ibid., p. 286.

but rather the restraining grace of God through the operation of the Holy Spirit:

> We always encounter the powers of repression and exchange, but that does not mean they are always of the same nature and strength. We meet figures in the history of the non-Christian religions of whom we feel that God wrestled with them in a particular way. We still notice traces of that process of suppression and substitution in the way they responded, but occasionally we observe a far greater influence of God there than in many other human religions. The history of religion is not always and everywhere the same; it does not present a monotonous picture of only folly and degeneration. There are culminating points in it, not because human beings are much better than others, but because every now and then divine compassion interferes, compassion which keeps man from suppressing and substituting the truth completely.[70]

Bavinck gives a little more substance to this point by noting that the Buddha in the night of the *bhodi* (enlightenment) and Muhammad in the 'night of power' are examples of a divine–human struggle and subsequent repression: 'The great moments in the history of religion are the moments when God wrestled with man in a very particular way'.[71]

Finally, we must remember that suppression is not obliteration. Here, as before, he takes Barth to task:

> At one point, Karl Barth says about missionary preaching that it is not a repeating but a beginning. 'It proceeds as teaching. It occurs as hope against hope. It can only connect with those points that it has to establish itself, not ones that were already present beforehand.' I think this is just plain wrong. I am prepared to acknowledge everything else that Barth says about the fallen condition of humanity, but on this one point I stand in clear opposition to him. Barth does not see that human beings, even fallen and sinful human beings, can and may never be thought to exist beyond God's revelation. People are always more than as people they actually are. They are people with a wound that cannot be closed – they suppress. But in the most critical moments of their existence, they feel assailed by what they have with such determined certainty attempted to push away. They are people who have assaulted God, who do so every day anew, and who have some sense of what they are doing – however vague that sense may be. They can never entirely rid themselves of the truth about God that

---

70. J. H. Bavinck, *Church Between Temple and Mosque*, p. 126.
71. Ibid., p. 125.

they have suppressed, held back, pushed away, sublimated, or crucified. This is what they fear; it is their tragedy.[72]

## ii. Substitution

As well as suppression comes substitution. General revelation is not obliterated: 'The cavity or empty space that occurs as a result of supressing needs to be filled. It has to be the case that what replaces truth and sweeps across the entire terrain must manifest in something resembling eternal power and divinity.'[73] In a memorable statement he declares:

> Man has repressed the truth of the everlasting power of the divinity of God.
> It has been exiled to the unconscious, to the crypts of his existence. That does
> not mean, however, that it has vanished forever. Still active, it reveals itself again
> and again. But it cannot become openly conscious; it appears in disguise, and it is
> exchanged for something different. Thus, all kinds of ideas of God are formed;
> the human mind as the *fabrica idolorum* (Calvin) makes its own ideas of God and
> its own myths. This is not intentional deceit – it happens without man knowing it.
> He cannot get rid of these ideas and myths. So he has religion; he is busy with a god;
> he serves his god – but he does not see that the god he serves is not God himself. An
> exchange has taken place, a perilous exchange. An essential quality of God has been
> blurred because it did not fit in with the human pattern of life, and the image man
> has of God is no longer true. Divine revelation indeed lies at the root of this image,
> but man's thoughts and aspirations cannot receive it and adapt themselves to it. In
> the image man has of God we can recognize the image of
> man himself.[74]

To illustrate the nature of this substitution Bavinck, using the metaphor of dreaming, once again employs psychoanalytic language. Again, it is worth quoting him at length here:

> This mysterious process of repressing and replacing is difficult, in a certain sense
> even impossible, to explain clearly. If I would have to do so, I would prefer to use

---

72. J. H. Bavinck, 'Religious Consciousness', p. 287. The quotation from Barth is Karl
      Barth, 'Die Theologie und die Mission in der Gegenwart: Vortrag, gehalten an der
      Brandenburgischen Missionskonferenz in Berlin am 11. April 1932', *Zwischen den
      Zeiten* 10 (1932), pp. 189–215 (197).

73. J. H. Bavinck, 'Religious Consciousness', p. 288.

74. J. H. Bavinck, *Church Between Temple and Mosque*, p. 122.

the metaphor of the dream. In a dream, this remarkable phenomenon sometimes emerges, namely that objective and completely real things play a part in it. The ticking of an alarm clock, water flowing through a gutter, the light flashing from the headlights of a passing car, the rumbling of a moving train in the distance – in short, all kinds of outside impressions can enter into the consciousness of the dream. Often they assume gigantic proportions in the dream. The monotonous ticking of the alarm clock then becomes the rhythmic marching of passing soldiers. The flowing gutter water then becomes a mighty waterfall in the middle of a forest. The lights of the car become sharp flashes of lightning. In short, each impression that flows in from the outside world is appropriated, but at the same time it is torn from its real context, hugely distorted, and made the heart of an entirely different chain of ideas. This being the case, we find here the two processes of repressing and replacing in their inner connection. Here the reality is in fact repressed, and yet that repressed reality functions creatively. But what is born out of it is a sheer fantasy, a colorful collection of chaotic images from which the objective elements can only be distinguished with great effort.

With the help of this metaphor, then, I would like to clarify what people do with God's general revelation. That revelation impinges on them and compels them to listen, but it is at the same time pushed down and repressed. And the only aspects of it that remain connected to human consciousness, even while torn from their original context, become the seeds of an entirely different sequence of ideas around which they crystallize. Definite connections exist between general revelation and human religious consciousness, but those connections are extremely complicated because the repressing and replacing actions are inescapably involved in the process.

Simply because the power of repressing and replacing is illustrated so compellingly in the dream, the dream is such an excellent metaphor of all human religion. Calvin talks about 'dreamed up gods' with a great deal of emphasis. We are automatically reminded of the words of the prophet Jeremiah here, when he says, 'They think the dreams they tell one another will make my people forget my name, just as their fathers forgot my name through Baal worship' (Jer. 23:27). Truly, paganism is a dream, a fearful and unending dream. 'Wake up, O sleeper, rise from the dead, and Christ will shine on you' (Eph. 5:14).[75]

For Bavinck, the 'long, disastrous dream'[76] is ended only in surrender to the Christ whom the non-Christian now meets in the preaching of the gospel.

---

75. J. H. Bavinck, 'Religious Consciousness', pp. 289–290.
76. J. H. Bavinck, *Church Between Temple and Mosque*, p. 127.

## Conclusion

This, then, is Bavinck's analysis or, better, 'anatomy' of human religion and religiosity as expounded by the apostle in Romans 1, the central tenet being that of an idolatrous human response to divine revelation. What I have attempted to do in this and the previous chapter is to demonstrate how both the Old and New Testament are testimony to the condensed picture sketched out in these seminal verses at the beginning of Romans. To repeat what I said at the beginning of chapter 5, what is first seen in embryonic form in Eden, developed at Babel and then later summarized by Paul to those in Rome has been shown to be instantiated, illustrated and 'incarnated' in the history of Israel and now in the church of Jesus Christ, as the people of God, living under the revelation of God, engage with the religious Other. What I have done diachronically in terms of biblical theology I now attempt to do synchronically from the perspective of systematic theology. This is the subject of the next chapter.

# 7. 'FOR THEIR ROCK IS NOT AS OUR ROCK': THE GOSPEL AS THE 'SUBVERSIVE FULFILMENT' OF THE RELIGIOUS OTHER

'For their rock is not as our Rock.'

(Deuteronomy 32:31 ESV)

## Introduction

From the perspective of a *fides quaerens intellectum* (faith seeking understanding), what are non-Christian religions? Why are there non-Christian religions? These seemingly crude and almost childlike inquisitions of nature and purpose are in reality deeply profound questions, for without pretension they encapsulate much of the essence of the discipline known as the theology of religions. How one decides to answer these questions sets a theological trajectory with far-reaching implications for contemporary Christian missiological engagement with other religions. My attempted answers will form the remainder of this work, as I seek to pull together into a systematic and coherent whole the material surveyed in previous chapters. Such synthesizing is a daunting task, not because God's revelation presents multiple conflicting theologies of religion, but because within a unified revelation there is a sophistication and nuance in understanding non-Christian religion and religions that defies simplistic and reductionist explanations. As we have seen, even if we survey just the biblical revelation, the canonically limited polyphony of Scripture is complex as we take into account such features as literary genre and the contours of redemptive history. To this complexity we add further extra-biblical revelation in terms of historical and phenomenological evidence.

Before such explanation begins, and lest anyone be disappointed, it is worth once again reiterating what I am and am not attempting to describe and justify in this chapter. First, what I want to set out here is a general theological and dogmatic framework of religion that can act as both a fence and a foundation for particular religious tradition-specific instantiations that further 'flesh out' this skeleton. While I shall give some illustrative examples, it is the dogmatic outline that is the focus. Similarly, for those who, perhaps rightly, wish me to head straight to missiological application in terms of apologetics, context-ualization, dialogue, and so on, a degree of patience will be required as, while this theological analysis provides a necessary and firm springboard for such missiological application, the actual detailed discussion and treatment of these issues will not be included here but will be sketched out briefly in the next chapter.[1]

Secondly, I recognize that as I break down my theology of religions and summarize its component parts, each one of these parts merits much more expansive treatment than can be given here. I hope my brief description will whet the appetite for others to undertake further research in these areas that all contribute to a Reformed evangelical theology of religions, and a Reformed evangelical 'theological religious studies'. For while it was confessional Christianity that pioneered the detailed study of other religions,[2] apart from a few exceptions,[3] we have lagged well behind in these areas of academic studies, with the result that agendas have been set and presuppositions assumed that rule out historic orthodox Christian faith.

Thirdly, and once again, I am not embarrassed to admit the somewhat deriva-tive and synthesized nature of my theology of religions given one of my initial goals: that in writing this monograph I wish to bring out of the shadows and back into the limelight a few seminal Reformed missiological scholars, scholars who for me come asymptotically closest to articulating biblical teaching con-cerning the nature of the religious Other. Here the spotlight falls on Hendrik

---

1. I hope to cover in much more detail in a later volume the missiological implications for my theology of religions.

2. See Gavin D'Costa, *Christianity and World Religions: Disputed Questions in the Theology of Religions* (Chichester: Wiley-Blackwell, 2009), pp. 69–71.

3. E.g. the work of Winfried Corduan. See Winfried Corduan, *The Tapestry of Faiths: The Common Threads Between Christianity and World Religions* (Downers Grove: InterVarsity Press, 2002).

Kraemer and J. H. Bavinck. My own prescription of the nature of the religious Other is largely a description and re-articulation of their articulations.[4]

At the beginning of this study I gave a definition of religion and the religions I now seek to explain and defend: *From the presupposition of an epistemologically authoritative biblical revelation, non-Christian religions are sovereignly directed, variegated and dynamic, collective human idolatrous responses to divine revelation behind which stand deceiving demonic forces. Being antithetically against yet parasitically dependent upon the truth of the Christian worldview, non-Christian religions are 'subversively fulfilled' in the gospel of Jesus Christ.*

Throughout this study I have been attempting to both describe and justify this definition from Scripture, alluding to each of its component parts in varying degrees of detail. Such a definition, while verging on the dialectical and contradictory, is believed to be no more than the particular instantiation of the complex anthropological mix that is *Homo adorans*, which historically Reformed theology has attempted to articulate, and which I summarized in chapter 1 both systematically and redemptive historically. As was seen in that chapter and subsequent chapters, this pre-prepared tradition-specific 'ingredient' is perhaps best contained, explained and resolved by recognizing humanity's 'religious' response to and reinterpretation of God's revelation of himself. The Bible describes this conceptually in the language of 'idolatry'. This Reformed dynamic of a subjective idolatrous response to an objective divine revelation is summarized in passages such as Romans 1:18–32 but is, as I hope I have demonstrated, evidenced throughout the entire biblical plotline. It is this dynamic that serves as the 'grammar' of this articulation. However, one more ingredient must be mentioned, for shadowing this major theme of idolatry, and 'behind' it, is the presence of the demonic. This is a minor theme but deserves some mention and analysis.

---

4. Given my reliance on and extensive use of both Kraemer and J. H. Bavinck, it is worth noting that while I believe their theology of religions is remarkably similar at key points (remembering that Kraemer was Bavinck's teacher), their respective broader theological frameworks admit to some important differences (see Paul Visser, *Heart for the Gospel, Heart for the World: The Life and Thought of a Reformed Pioneer Missiologist, Johan Herman Bavinck (1895–1964)* [Eugene: Wipf & Stock, 2003], pp. 30–32). I noted in a previous chapter Bavinck's criticism of Kraemer with regard to the latter's critique of 'historical' religion that is called 'Christianity', and where Kraemer takes a somewhat neo-orthodox turn. Similarly, in chapter 1 I noted a word of caution regarding Kraemer's doctrine of revelation as it impinges upon his doctrine of Scripture. As always, a degree of critical distance is required at this point.

It is now possible to elucidate further this definition, breaking it down into four constituent parts. First, I shall describe the antithetical nature of the religious Other; secondly, I shall note the pseudo-similarity of the religious Other compared to true revelation; thirdly, I shall summarize what can be said regarding the role of the demonic behind the religious Other; finally, I shall attempt to show how this description paves the way for a relational dynamic between non-Christian religions and the gospel of Jesus Christ, which, and borrowing Kraemer's term, I have called 'subversive fulfilment'.

## 1. Defining other religions as idolatrous interprets them as antithetical distortions of divine revelation

As we saw in chapter 1, the perpetuity of the *imago Dei* means the perpetuity of relationship with the living, self-revealing God of Scripture. Scripture often attests to an extreme opposition or 'antithesis' within humanity, a conflictual relationship between those who have 'truth faith' in this God, and those who have 'false faith'. This false faith amounts to believing 'lies' about this God. Consequently, and again mentioned previously, despite the plethora of world-views and religions that exists in the world, in reality there are only two: those rooted and built up in Christ, and those founded on 'hollow and deceptive philosophy, which depends on human tradition and the elemental spiritual forces of this world rather than on Christ' (Col. 2:6–10).

Calvin summarizes this well at the beginning of the *Institutes*:

> They do not therefore apprehend God as he offers himself, but imagine him as they have fashioned him in their own presumption. When this gulf opens, in whatever direction they move their feet, they cannot but plunge headlong into ruin. Indeed, whatever they afterward attempt by way of worship or service of God, they cannot bring as tribute to him, for they are worshipping not God but a figment and a dream of their own heart.[5]

In chapters 2 and 3 we saw the historical outworking of this antithetical principle, in the self-revelation and description of God as Yahweh, the transcendentally unique Creator.

The worship of the created rather than this revealed Creator is a definition of human sin and fallenness, and can be seen not only in *displacements* of the

---

5. John Calvin, *Institutes of the Christian Religion*, ed. John T. McNeill, tr. Ford Lewis Battles, 2 vols., LCC (Philadelphia: Westminster, 1960), 1.4.1.

true God but also in *distortions* and even *denials* of him.[6] As a result of this de-creational reversal we simultaneously pull God down to our level and raise ourselves up to his level, thus obliterating a fundamental building block of the Christian worldview: the Creator–creature distinction. The reason for such a reversal is our desire to hide from the living God:

> Sin predisposes us to want to be independent of God, to be laws unto ourselves or autonomous, so that we can do what we want without bowing to His authority. At the most basic level, idols are what we make out of evidence for God within ourselves and in the world – if we do not want to face the face of God Himself in His majesty and holiness. Rather than look to the Creator and have to deal with His Lordship, we orient our lives toward the creation, where we can be more free to control and shape our lives in our desired directions . . . An idol is something within creation that is inflated to function as a substitute for God.[7]

As we saw in Bavinck's exposition of Romans 1:18–23, this 'perilous exchange' of substitution fills the vacuum caused by our suppression of the true knowledge of God. Again, it is important to reiterate that such suppressions and exchanges are our futile attempts to flee from the living God of the Bible. For example, John Frame argues that in Yahweh's revealing himself as covenant head of his people, he demonstrates himself to be both transcendent and immanent, these concepts beautifully fitting together when understood biblically. However, idolatrous worship disrupts and distorts this delicate balance: transcendence is stressed to the point of denying immanence and vice versa: 'Those false concepts of transcendence and immanence fit together in a peculiar way: both satisfy sinful man's desire to escape God's revelation, to avoid our responsibilities, to excuse our disobedience'.[8]

The epistemological and ethical consequences of such idolatrous worship are described in great detail throughout Scripture. As we have seen, Yahweh is jealous

---

6. Remembering that I have noted in previous chapters the evolution of idolatry before Babel and after. Atheism is a form of idolatry, for to deny God's existence is a work of fiction and is therefore 'false faith'.

7. Richard Keyes, 'The Idol Factory', in Os Guinness and John Seel (eds.), *No God but God* (Chicago: Moody, 1992), pp. 29–48 (31).

8. John M. Frame, *The Doctrine of the Knowledge of God* (Phillipsburg: P & R, 1987), p. 14. Frame's point here is that if God is either *so* other to us, or *so* near to us, his personality is lost, and we can act as if he did not exist and take the role of God ourselves.

for his own name and will not share his glory with another. By our worshipping idols God is deprived of his glory and we are deprived of our God:

> Such idolatrous lies falsify a person, obscuring and distorting who the person is. The lie destroys true relationship as humans stop relating to God as he knows himself to be, instead treating him as they have fashioned him. Idolatry strongly expresses human sovereignty, but sovereignty at the expense of true relationship. God is treated not as a person we encounter (a 'Thou' in Martin Buber's terms), but as an object (an 'It'), indeed a plastic, malleable one. Buber writes 'The *Thou* meets me.' Imposing identities on other persons risks not 'meeting' them – preventing them being a 'Thou'. The biblical God reveals he is not infinitely plastic and malleable. To treat him as that involves counterfeit, not true, relationship, with him. The price for being makers of God, albeit attractive, is that the God we make is not real. The true God is hidden, because we attempt to reduce him to an 'It' of our choosing. Buber notes: 'This selfhood . . . steps in between and shuts off from us the light of heaven.'[9]

It is because of these 'lies' being told about him that God's holy and righteous wrath is kindled and is 'being revealed' from heaven,[10] a foretaste and warning of God's unrestrained wrath to come. Idols and the religious traditions built on them do not save, but lead only to divine judgment and condemnation. Idolatry also brings about human disintegration. Idols deceive, and no one stops to consider this deception.[11] As counterfeits, they promise much and mimic divine attributes and actions, but ultimately bring only disappointment, disillusionment and destruction.

The above analysis means that we must be cautious of speaking about 'truth' and 'goodness' in other religions. With Kraemer I affirm the 'radical difference' between Christianity and other religions. Religions are hermetically sealed interpretations of reality (worldviews) and as such are incommensurable, defying superficial comparison:

> Every religion is a living indivisible . . . [u]nity of existential apprehension. It is not a series of tenets, dogmas, prescriptions, institutions, practices, that can be taken one by one as independent items of religious life, conception or organization, and then can

---

9. Michael Ovey, 'Idolatry and Spiritual Parody: Counterfeit Faith', *Cambridge Papers* 11.1 (Mar. 2002), p. 3 (his italics).
10. The 'being revealed' of Rom. 1:8 here is a present passive.
11. This is Isaiah's complaint in his cutting satire of idol worship in Isa. 44:19.

arbitrarily be compared with, and somehow related to, and grafted upon the similar item of another religion. Every part of it – a dogma, a rite, a myth, an institution, a cult – is so vitally related to the whole that it can never be understood in its real function, significance and tendency, as these occur in the reality of life without keeping constantly in mind that vast and living unity of existential apprehension in which this part moves and has its being.[12]

J. H. Bavinck is helpful here:

Everything depends on what we mean by an element of 'truth'. If taken in a vague and general sense, it must be admitted that such elements are found in the non-Christian religions. If taken in a more special and defined meaning, then it will be hardly tenable. All central ideas involved in Christian belief . . . are found in most religions, but they are all understood in a fundamentally different sense, and applied in a quite different connection. The deeper one enters into them, the more one grows aware that all is different in non-Christian religions.[13]

The dynamic nature of a religious refashioning of revelation can once more be affirmed:

The residues of revelation never lie hidden as petrified fossils in the soil of pseudo religion. False religion always presents itself as, and in actual fact invariably constitutes, a monolithic aggregate. Consequently, all ideas it absorbs become amalgamated with and deformed by the whole. In other words, it is not possible for isolated elements of verity, sparks of divine truth to exist in the midst of falsehood and error – in fact, if such sparks were present, they would lead to friction in and destruction of the very essence of pseudo religions.[14]

This 'radical difference' between the Christian worldview and all other worldviews can be broken down into the component parts of metaphysics, epistemology, ethics and gospel.

In metaphysics we are able to delineate the *sui generic character* of the Christian faith in a number of ways. First, Christianity offers a unique metaphysics. In

---

12. Hendrik Kraemer, *The Christian Message in a Non-Christian World* (London: Edinburgh House, 1938), p. 135.

13. J. H. Bavinck, 'General Revelation and the Non-Christian Religions', *FUQ* 4 (1955), pp. 43–55 (54).

14. Visser, *Heart for the Gospel*, p. 172.

contrast to other religions, the Christian God reveals himself to be absolutely independent (*a se*) and self-contained, and yet absolutely personal, both transcendent and immanent, both 'other to humanity' (we are not like him) and like humanity (we are made in his 'image').[15] God reveals himself to be triune, both one and many,[16] neither unitarian, henotheistic, polytheistic but trinitarian: one God, Father, Son and Spirit:

> Christianity offers the triune God, the absolute personality . . . as the God in whom we believe. This conception of the God is the foundation of everything else that we hold dear. Unless we can believe in this sort of God, it does us no good to be told that we may believe in some other sort of God, or in anything else. For us everything depends for its meaning upon this sort of God. Accordingly we are not interested to have anyone prove to us the existence of any other sort of God but this God. Any other sort of God is no God at all.[17]

Such a metaphysic has implications for epistemology. Christians claim that the triune God, who is both transcendent and immanent, originally created us to know things truly (because God has revealed himself) but not exhaustively (because we are not God). There is a difference between *archetypal* knowledge (God's exhaustive knowledge of himself) and *ectypal* knowledge (knowledge God gives us of himself). God has revealed himself through both his works and his words. The triune God is able to speak because he is a personal, rather than impersonal, Being. This same God is able to speak authoritatively because he is a personal absolute.

In ethics again we see a radical difference between Christianity and other systems. Frame classifies (and internally critiques) the ethical approaches of other religions into three broad types: those based on fate, those as self-realization and those as law without gospel.[18] For Frame the first two options presuppose an impersonal deity, and commit the genetic fallacy that 'is' equals 'ought': 'The

---

15. John M. Frame, 'Divine Aseity and Apologetics', in K. Scott Oliphint and Lane G. Tipton (eds.), *Reason and Revelation: New Essays in Reformed Apologetics* (Phillipsburg: P & R, 2007), pp. 115–130.

16. And is the only solution to that perennial philosophical conundrum of universals and particulars that has haunted philosophy since the Greeks.

17. Cornelius Van Til, *The Defense of the Faith*, ed. K. Scott Oliphint, 4th ed. (Phillipsburg: P & R, 2008), p. 29.

18. John M. Frame, *The Doctrine of the Christian Life* (Phillipsburg: P & R, 2008), pp. 54–71.

absolute moral standard must be an absolute person'.[19] The third category is soteriologically founded upon works-righteousness as opposed to Christianity's personal God, who reveals himself to be the supreme standard of right and wrong, and where, for the Christian, 'good works' are not understood to be a cause of salvation but rather a willing and faithful response to God's free gift of grace and salvation in the propitiatory death of Christ and his vindicating resurrection from the dead.

Distinguishing Christian uniqueness by isolating metaphysics, epistemology and ethics is somewhat artificial and atomistic. All these separate elements are necessary interconnected strands of a unique and unified system of thought or, more correctly, a unique historical and eschatological story or meta-narrative that places all humanity within an epic cosmic drama of creation–fall–redemption–consummation with a particular focal point. This history of redemption and redemptive history is thoroughly Christocentric – it is the good news of Jesus Christ, which is both the message of Christianity and the heart of the Christian worldview and philosophy. It is the person and work of Christ that distinguishes Christianity from all other 'faiths' and gives Christianity its exclusive or particular claims.

In summary, what is being argued for is the 'all or nothing' systemic and *solus Christus* character of Christianity in matters of both salvation and truth. Although living in different centuries, both Calvin and Van Til recognized this:

> For even if many men once boasted that they worshiped the Supreme majesty, the Maker of Heaven and Earth, yet because they had no Mediator it was not possible for them truly to taste God's mercy, and thus be persuaded that he was their Father. Accordingly, because they did not hold Christ as their Head, they possessed only a fleeting knowledge of God. From this also came about that they at last lapsed into crass and foul superstition and betrayed their own ignorance. So today the Turks, although they proclaim at the top of their lungs that the Creator of heaven and earth is God, still while repudiating Christ, substitute an idol in the place of the true God.[20]

> It is accordingly no easier for sinners to accept God's revelation in nature than to accept God's revelation in Scripture. They are no more ready of themselves

---

19. Ibid., p. 63. I try to make the case that Paul Knitter commits this fallacy in his defence of pluralism. See Gavin D'Costa, Paul Knitter and Daniel Strange, *Only One Way? Three Christian Responses to the Uniqueness of Christ in a Religiously Pluralist World* (London: SCM, 2011), pp. 173–174.

20. Calvin, *Institutes* 2.6.4.

to do the one than to do the other. From the point of view of the sinner, theism is as objectionable as Christianity. Theism that is worthy of the name is Christian theism. Christ said that no man can come to the Father but by him. No one can become a theist unless he becomes a Christian. Any God that is not the Father of our Lord Jesus Christ is not God but an idol. It is therefore the Holy Spirit bearing witness by and with the Word in our hearts that alone effects the required Copernican revolution and makes us both Christians and theists.[21]

## 2. Defining other religions as idolatrous acknowledges their pseudo-similarity to, and false counterfeiting of, true divine revelation

The picture I have sketched so far is both stark and bleak, as the antithesis must be. It is also extremely counter-intuitive, for a posteriori within our own religiously plural context we do experience similarity and commonality between various religious traditions. Adherents of other religions often appear to do 'good' works, can have a belief system like those of the Christian, and aspire to common human goals and values. How are we theologically to explain these things, while still upholding the principle of the antithesis? That is to say, within an overarching pattern of discontinuity between Christianity and other faiths, can there be elements of continuity also?

First, we remember the complex anthropological mix that makes up *Homo adorans*. Although at the principial or 'root' level of religious presuppositions, the antithesis between Christian and non-Christian is stark: the practical and 'lived' worldviews built upon these fundamental commitments are often inconsistent at the level of 'fruit'. Within the unbeliever the theological explanation for this inconsistency is the non-salvific work of the Holy Spirit who, in his common grace, restrains sin and excites to a civic righteousness. Non-Christians live off the 'borrowed capital' or, better, steal the 'fruit' of the Christian worldview and claim it for their own.

Secondly, we return to the analytical tool of idols and idolatry. Ironically, understanding other religions in terms of idolatry *supports* a structural or formal 'commonality' between Christianity and other religions. Idols are not created *ex nihilo*, for they are created things made to replace the Creator: 'To speak of an idol in the biblical sense assumes that there is a true God of whom the idol

---

21. Cornelius Van Til, 'Nature and Scripture', in Paul Woolley (ed.), *The Infallible Word: A Symposium* (Philadelphia: Presbyterian Guardian, 1946), pp. 255–293 (280).

is a counterfeit.'[22] Idols and their worshippers are parasitic and mimic true divine revelation. Therefore, as I stated in an earlier chapter, the nature of idolatry means that there is a legitimate sense in which one can speak of religion as a *genus*.

I wish to break down this structural similarity into four categories, all of which to a greater or lesser degree are the 'revelatory' raw material from which non-Christian religions are idolatrously fashioned: *imaginal* 'revelation', *remnantal* 'revelation', *influental* 'revelation' and *demonic* 'revelation'.

### a. 'Imaginal' revelation

In this first category the revelatory source on which non-Christian religions idolatrously draw is metaphysical, being the *imago Dei* itself. I have called this 'imaginal' revelation, but equally it could be labelled as 'intuitional' or even 'vestigial'. Being a metaphysical reality, this imaginal revelation is not the prerogative of the so-called 'great religious traditions', but is found in all human experience. That said, more 'established' religious traditions and communities often evidence a more explicit institutional awareness of this response to revelation.

In chapter 1 I unpacked the doctrine of the *imago Dei*, stating that all human beings are ontologically created 'religious' beings, revealing God, representing God, built for relationship with God, with each other and with the rest of creation. At the fall, while the living God is replaced by idols these metaphysical or 'structural' categories remain intact and give a certain universal creaturely limitation to religious expression.

First, we saw that these categories can be articulated in the language of 'worldview'. Let me restate Sire's definition:

> A worldview is a commitment, a fundamental orientation of the heart, that can be expressed as a story or in a set of presuppositions (assumptions which may be true, partially true or entirely false) which we hold (consciously or subconsciously, consistently or inconsistently) about the basic constitution of reality, and that provides the foundation on which we live and move and have our being.[23]

On this definition of worldview I am not simply saying that 'religion' and 'religions' can be understood in terms of 'worldview' (which they can), but rather that even the definition of worldview (which includes non-Christian religions) is dependent upon the Christian worldview. If this is the case, then all worldviews

---

22. Keyes, 'Idol Factory', p. 31.

23. James Sire, *Naming the Elephant* (Downers Grove: InterVarsity Press, 2004), p. 122.

will bear some structural relationship and similarity to the Christian religion. Let me unpack this idea a little more.

### i. The object of idolatrous religion

First, we can speak of the object of worship. As worshipping beings, *Homo adorans* is created to worship someone or something, but what we choose to worship will always be 'related' in some way to the living God, albeit in a self-refuting relationship of distortion and perversion. The Christian worldview describes a unique triune God (a personal absolute and absolute personality) with unique attributes (a God who is *both* transcendent and immanent), and whose actions are unique (in providing salvation not on the basis of works but by grace). Non-Christian religions worship counterfeit gods and parodies. So, for example, all religions and worldviews will have their own *a se* ultimate explanation of everything,[24] but this will often be impersonal rather than personal. In a similar observation to the one made earlier regarding the idolatrous distortions of divine transcendence and immanence, A. A. Hodge makes a point in grouping false religion into three categories: deism, pantheism and polytheism, which 'have grades of merit, yet they all alike embrace some elements of important truth, and yet are all, upon the whole false and injurious'.[25] Deism preserves transcendence but stresses divine distance: 'The world is a machine which is wholly inexorable in all its movements, shutting in the struggling souls of men, separating them from their absent Father, and holding them fast in the toils of fate'.[26] Pantheism preserves omnipresence but presents an impersonal 'current of force': 'He is not a Person who knows and loves us, for he has no existence except as he exists in the thinking, coming and going which constitute the phenomenal world.'[27] Finally, for Hodge:

> Even the gross fictions of polytheism have a tincture of truth to give them power over the human mind. If God is moral, there must be a personal distinction and a social basis in his essential nature. If the infinite and the absolute One is to exert a moral and educating influence on human life, he will appear to us self-limited under the conditions of time and space: 'all the fullness of the Godhead' must appear to us 'bodily.'[28]

---

24. Remembering that this is how I have defined 'religion' in a previous chapter.
25. A. A. Hodge, *Evangelical Theology: A Course of Popular Lectures* (Edinburgh: Banner of Truth Trust, 1976), p. 107.
26. Ibid., p. 108.
27. Ibid.
28. Ibid.

## ii. The structure of idolatrous religion

The parodying nature of non-Christian religion can be seen not merely with natural revelation but with special revelation as well. In classical Reformed systematic theology the modes of God's communication with humanity in 'special' revelation have been classified into three categories: theophany, prophecy and miracle. In their respective descriptions of the modes of special revelation both Van Til and Berkhof compare 'true' manifestations of these modes with their 'false' counterparts. In counterfeit theophanies we see our human need for God to be near and at hand; hence in other religious traditions we often see the appearance or visitation of the gods. In counterfeit prophecy we see our need for the divine communication; hence we often see practices such as divination, and of course scriptures. In counterfeit miracles we see our human need for the gods to intervene in times of need.[29]

## iii. The content of idolatrous religion

Finally, we can speak of the content of religious worship. In chapter 1 I noted Peter Leithart's observation on the history of literature that human imagination and creativity are never absolutely free but limited to that of a creature. This can be pushed further here in service of my thesis. For Leithart human creativity means more than simply that humans are general 'storytellers'. Rather, human beings are constrained to telling the same story, albeit in distorted forms:

> Now, we need to add that the God imaged in our speaking and making is not some abstract and unknown character, some God-in-general, but the God revealed in the story revealed in creation, history and Scripture. If we cannot help but manifest God's character in our creations (including our story-telling), and if the character of God manifested in our creations is known through a story, it follows that we cannot help but retell His stories in our own. God's story tells of a good creation, marred by a rebellion and a curse, which is overcome by the coming of a Redeemer to restore the world. All other stories are contained in that basic story. This does not at all mean that every writer is self-consciously and deliberately writing Christian allegory. It means that every writer tells stories that reflect in some way God's story . . . Because of the way God created and governs the world, and because knowledge of the Creator and Governor of the world is inescapable, the rebellion of the imaginative writer is

---

29. See Cornelius Van Til, *An Introduction to Systematic Theology*, ed. William Edgar, 2nd ed. (Phillipsburg: P & R, 2007), pp. 204–205; Louis Berkhof, *Systematic Theology: New Combined Edition* (Grand Rapids: Eerdmans, 1996), pp. 134–139.

constrained. Somewhere, even in the stories of the most self-consciously rebellious story-teller, God's story shines through.[30]

In a brief analysis of primitive religions, ancient India and Greek tragedians Kraemer notes a similar 'likeness': 'There are to be found deep *Ahnungen* (intuitions) of sin, of guilt, of surrender to the divine will, expectations of a Saviour, of Grace, of Divine Love, of sacrifice of self, etc.'[31]

Largely based on his extensive acquaintance with living religious traditions, J. H. Bavinck goes into much more detail here, putting forward a morphology of religious consciousness: what might be called a theological comparative religion. Following Witte, Bavinck distinguishes between the 'thatness' and 'whatness' of humanity's religious quest.[32] The *thatness* refers to a universal 'basal consciousness',[33] and provides a form and structure. These are the perennial questions humans ask. The *whatness* consists of the answers given to these questions, 'the manner in which people interpret and give substantive form to this consciousness'.[34] While in non-Christian religions the *whatness* is always the radical difference of idolatrous response, the *thatness* remains constant in both true religion and false religion.

---

30. Peter Leithart, *Heroes of the City of Man* (Moscow, Idaho: Canon, 1999), p. 35.

31. Hendrik Kraemer, *Religion and the Christian Faith* (London: Lutterworth, 1956), p. 333. Although I am more circumspect, less optimistic (especially soteriologically) and obviously more Reformed in terms of theological presuppositions, there are similarities between what I am postulating here and C. S. Lewis's doctrine of Christological prefigurement, which he discerned in many of the world's great myths and other religious traditions, particularly Hinduism. For an exhaustive description and fascinating analysis of Lewis's doctrine see P. H. Brazier, *C. S. Lewis – The Work of Christ Revealed* (Eugene: Pickwick, 2012), pp. 191–264; *C. S. Lewis – On the Christ of a Religious Economy II: Knowing Salvation* (Eugene: Pickwick, 2014), ch. 6. Despite the different theological frameworks in operation here, I think there is material in Lewis's work that can be appropriated to enrich the Reformed theology of religions. Ironically, though, it is perhaps Lewis's assessment of myths just before he became a Christian (and which Tolkein subsequently countered in his poem 'Mythopoeia') that is nearer to my own theology of religions than Lewis's later thinking: 'lies and therefore worthless, even though breathed through silver . . .' (Brazier, *C. S. Lewis – The Work*, p. 192).

32. J. Witte, *Die Christus-Botschaft und die Religionen* (Göttingen: Vandenhoeck & Ruprecht, 1936), pp. 37–39, quoted in Visser, *Heart for the Gospel*, p. 171.

33. Visser, *Heart for the Gospel*, p. 171.

34. Ibid.

Concerning this *thatness*, Bavinck discerns

a sort of framework within which the religious thought of humankind must move. . . .
There appear to be certain intersections around which all sorts of ideas crystallize . . .
[or] magnetic points [in the form of primal questions] to which the religious thinking
of mankind is irresistibly attracted.[35]

'We see that the history of religion depicts a great variety of divine forms and
myths. That is why it is such a remarkable history. Again and again the same
ideas crop up. Also, this history repeats itself many times.'[36] Humans are 'always
restricted by their anthropological structure',[37] man can never 'outgrow his own
qualities and dispositions':[38]

If only people could shed their self-awareness, their individuality, their sense of royalty;
if only they could simply dissolve into the world around them like plants and animals
do, without norms or morals! But they cannot. They are human. They exist with the
indescribable greatness as well as the pathetic woefulness that that term covers.[39]

In several of his writings Bavinck delineates five such interconnected 'magnetic
points' and takes time to describe in detail each point and how it manifests itself
in religious traditions:

It appears that humanity always and everywhere has fallen back on definite ideas and
presumptions, and that these ideas and presumptions always resurface in surprising
ways whenever they may have been temporarily repressed for various reasons. . . .
This is a universal religious consciousness that remains indestructible in the midst
of all disturbing and confusing developments.[40]

---

35. Ibid., p. 157.
36. J. H. Bavinck, *The Church Between Temple and Mosque* (Grand Rapids: Eerdmans,
    1966), p. 111.
37. Ibid., p. 31. As Visser comments nicely in his own exposition of J. H. Bavinck on
    this identical point, 'Humans are limited by their human beingness' (Visser, *Heart
    for the Gospel*, p. 147).
38. J. H. Bavinck, *Church Between Temple and Mosque*, p. 31.
39. J. H. Bavinck, 'Religious Consciousness and Christian Faith', in James D. Bratt,
    John Bolt and Paul J. Visser (eds.), *The J. H. Bavinck Reader* (Cambridge: Eerdmans,
    2013), pp. 145–299 (279).
40. Ibid., pp. 150–151.

I can offer only brief definitions of each point here.

In 'I and the cosmos' we are confronted with human responses to 'a sense of belonging to the whole', and questions that concern 'the place of man in the totality of the universe'.[41] Here human beings oscillate between experiences of great insignificance in the face of the cosmos, and significance in recognizing they are part of this divine world.

In 'I and the norm' we are confronted with a 'sense of transcendent norms' to which we are subjected and under which we struggle for freedom:

A standard exists that overarches everything, and illuminates everything. A person is in conversation with himself. Or to put it more precisely, a person is constantly in dialogue with the norm within him and yet does not originate from him. He attempts to justify himself and plead his innocence, but there comes a time when he simply has to bow his head to that norm that is obviously more powerful than he is. This dialogue is what, above all, makes him human. It is the nobility and at the same time the deep tragedy of his existence. He can flee nowhere to escape the majesty of that norm, for it follows him wherever he goes.[42]

In 'I and the riddle of my existence' there is experienced 'a sense of the governance of existence by a providential or destining power'.[43] Visser puts this well as being 'the tension experienced between deed and destiny: they lead but they also undergo their lives'.[44] Humans are active doers and passive victims.

In 'I and salvation' there is 'a recognition of the need for redemption', that something somewhere has gone wrong and that deliverance is needed: 'Man has that remarkable tendency not to accept reality as it presents itself to him, but he always dreams of the better world in which life will be healthy and safe'.[45]

Finally, in 'I and the Supreme Power' we have 'the reality behind the reality',[46] 'a sense of relatedness to a Superior or Supreme Power'. Bavinck intentionally keeps this category vague:

We find a universal development in human history of the awareness that this world and all that happens in it is intimately connected to the mysterious, supernatural world

41. J. H. Bavinck, *Church Between Temple and Mosque*, p. 38.

42. J. H. Bavinck, 'Religious Consciousness', pp. 172–173.

43. Visser, *Heart for the Gospel*, p. 159.

44. Ibid.

45. J. H. Bavinck, *Church Between Temple and Mosque*, p. 33.

46. Ibid.

of the gods. Something of that mystery, of that divine force, is found in everything that exists. People know in every moment of their existence that they are connected to higher powers that they can never fully understand, before which they tremble with fear and that nevertheless draw them to themselves with magnetic power.[47]

As to why we ask these questions, Bavinck answers that 'these questions concern man's existential relationships':[48]

As long as he is occupied with himself only and looks no further, he can fancy himself to be self-sufficient. But as soon as he becomes aware of his relationships, he becomes stupefied, and asks: What am I in this great cosmos? What am I over and against the norm, that strange phenomenon in my life that has authority over me? What am I in my life that speeds on and on – a doer or a victim? What am I in the face of that remarkable feeling that overwhelms me sometimes, that feeling that everything must change and that things are not right as they are? What am I over against that very mysterious background of existence, the divine powers? It is in this area of existential relations that man is confronted with the crucial matters of life – and one of these is religion. Religion convinces man that there are relations. It reveals the 'seams' of creation where one thing is connected with another. We can now give the following definition of religion: Religion is the way in which man experiences the deepest existential relations and gives expression to this experience.[49]

Finally, although Bavinck notes that each of the magnetic points implies the other, in 'Religious Consciousness' he offers a particular construal with two dimensions, 'I and the cosmos' and 'I and the riddle of my existence', presenting

---

47. J. H. Bavinck, 'Religious Consciousness', p. 183. Interestingly, it is under this magnetic point that J. H. Bavinck mentions the recognition of the demonic: 'What definitely can be acknowledged is that wherever the names of gods are mentioned, the figures of demons also immediately appear. Clearly and from earliest times, people have been moved by the phenomenon that our capricious world could not be adequately explained or understood only in terms of the god, but that other horrible forces exist and are revealed. The world in which we live is a double-sided world. Something of the divine smile is present over the world, but at the same time the demonic work of mysterious forces aimed at our destruction is also palpable' (ibid., p. 182).

48. J. H. Bavinck, *Church Between Temple and Mosque*, p. 112.

49. Ibid.

an axis of totality and fate (what Visser calls 'an overpowering *du bist*'[50]), and 'I and the norm' and 'I and salvation' presenting an axis of norm and deliverance (what Visser calls 'a compelling *du sollst*'[51]). At the borderline of these axes lies 'I and the Supreme Power':

> For on the one hand, that higher power is on the side of totality, of which it is the heart and core. Thus, it is also the all-determinative power that possesses unlimited control of our lives. On the other hand, however, that higher power presents itself as our norm, as the mighty 'though shalt,' or as the ominous law that is at the same time our only hope for deliverance.[52]

### b. 'Remnantal' revelation

This second category of revelation is described in detail in chapter 2, and so there is little more to be said here. Although some theologians place it under the category of 'general' revelation, and others 'special' revelation, as well as the ever-present dynamic revelation of God in nature and the *imago Dei*, there is a historical 'remnantal' revelation within religious traditions. Though entropically distorted over time, through for example the mechanisms of etymology or euhemerism, remnantal revelation gives us a comparative theological explanation of 'commonalities' and 'continuities' between religious traditions, for example certain events, themes and archetypes. In chapter 2 I explored the biblical and theological basis for this revelation as well as its extra-biblical support in the historical traditions of the *prisca theologia* and comparative mythology, together with certain anthropologists in the history of religions, especially Wilhelm Schmidt and his espousal of 'original monotheism'. J. H. Bavinck sums up this category well:

> All peoples have kept some recognisable memory of what happened in Paradise, be it ever so distorted. In particular, those people that we usually call primitive have numerous myths telling of a glorious primeval age in which god and men had free intercourse. And according to the myths this blessed period was finished by some blunder or accident. It is plain that human guilt is reasoned away, or at least smothered over in all these myths. But it is equally plain that something of the common memory of the things that are related to these first few chapters of Genesis is kept alive by all peoples. So, considering non-Christian religions, we are not only confronted with

---

50. Visser, *Heart for the Gospel*, p. 161.

51. Ibid.

52. J. H. Bavinck, 'Religious Consciousness', p. 202.

general revelation, but also with memories of God's revelation in the remotest history of man.[53]

## c. 'Influental' revelation

Closely related to the concept of *remnantal* revelation is that of *influental* revelation, by which I am referring to the impact or 'influent' of the Judeo-Christian worldview on living religious traditions, both historically and presently. The idea that pagans plagiarized earlier Israelite sources was a foundational apologetic building block in many of the early Christian fathers, for example Tatian and Justin,[54] but more recent scholars have posited a similar position.

---

53. J. H. Bavinck, 'General Revelation', p. 51. There are others who support this thesis, e.g. Corduan: 'The picture, then, is this: Religious belief began with the first humans and religious cultus soon thereafter with Enosh, the son of Seth, as mentioned in Genesis 4:26. As the human race expanded, contracted drastically at the flood, and then expanded again, the beliefs and practices did not slip from the collective memory but retained a presence within the tribes least affected by cultural development. There it was (rightly) attributed to some form of divine self-disclosure, but also (rightly) reinforced by the question, Who made it? Finally, one sees evidence of this pattern even in the more highly developed religious cultures insofar as one can find a monotheism at many of their roots. The continuity of monotheism is based on an original special revelation and reinforced by general revelation' (Corduan, *Tapestry of Faiths*, p. 42). Interestingly, W. G. T. Shedd in his classic systematic theology proposes a similar thesis: 'The relics of monotheism found outside the pale of revelation, in various countries and civilizations, are traceable to two sources: 1) to the monotheistic structure of the human mind, . . . this is the subjective and fundamental requisite; and 2) to the influence of the primitive revelation from God made in the line of Seth, fragments of which have floated down among the races of mankind. Both of these sources and causes of monotheism should be recognized. If only the first is acknowledged, justice is not done to the traditional records and data. If only the second is acknowledged and all monotheism in human history is referred to a special revelation in early times, justice is not done to the constitution of the human mind. It conflicts moreover, with St Paul's representation in Romans 1' (William G. T. Shedd and Alan W. Gomes, *Dogmatic Theology*, 3rd ed. [Phillipsburg: P & R, 2003], p. 197).

54. See Gerald Bray, 'Explaining Christianity to Pagans: The Second Century Apologists', in Kevin J. Vanhoozer (ed.), *The Trinity in a Pluralistic Age: Theological Essays on Culture and Religion* (Cambridge: Eerdmans, 1997), pp. 9–25. Bray himself questions the validity of this pursuit.

J. H. Bavinck speaks of the gospel penetrating India and notes the influence this may have had on grace and bhakti traditions within Hinduism. Similarly, he refers to the work of the Norwegian Lutheran missionary Karl Ludvig Reichelt, whose studies on Chinese Buddhism posited the influence of Nestorianism at an early stage. Bavinck concludes:

> Even if we think all this to be very uncertain, we should still make the allowance for the possibility that such influence actually occurred. All this would mean the interesting datum that non-Christian religions are not truly religions that bloomed fully outside the sphere of special revelation, but that a certain measure of influx has to be regarded as a probability in several cases.[55]

> If we were asked whether the rise of the idea of grace as the way of salvation, which is traceable in Hinduism and Buddhism, may be considered as a result of the permeating power of the Christian message, we could not give an answer. But one thing seems to be sure: here and there, now and then, Christian ideas penetrated other religions, melted into them, and became one with them. These ideas could not preserve their original purity. They were frequently adjusted to the main current of the other religions. Often they were mutilated, stained, and polluted. But the question rises if it was possible to deprive them absolutely of their original strength. God's way with the Gentile nations is a very mysterious one.[56]

A similar argument is put forward by Peter Leithart in his paper *Did Plato Read Moses?*[57] Concerning the existence of a universal moral consensus, Leithart's thesis is not to deny its existence but rather its source:

> I hope to make a plausible case that much of what has been identified as a moral consensus based on natural revelation is more accurately seen as a product of general and special revelation. Pagans hold to certain moral principles that are compatible with Christian morality not only because they are inescapably confronted with God's revelation in creation, but also because they have been directly or indirectly exposed to an influence by the Spirit operating through special revelation and the other means of grace. Whatever moral consensus exists is thus not a product of pure 'common grace'

---

55. J. H. Bavinck, 'General Revelation', p. 52.

56. J. H. Bavinck, *The Impact of Christianity on the Non-Christian World* (Grand Rapids: Eerdmans, 1949), p. 106.

57. Peter Leithart, *Did Plato Read Moses? Middle Grace and Moral Consensus*, Biblical Horizons Occasional Paper 23 (Niceville, Fla.: Biblical Horizons, 1995).

(devoid of all contact with revelation), nor of 'special grace' (saving knowledge of God through Christ and his word), but what I call . . . 'middle grace' (non-saving knowledge of God and his will derived from both general and special revelation).[58]

After noting the church fathers' deployment of such a thesis, and concentrating primarily on Greek paganism, Leithart looks first at modern archaeological, mythological and literary evidence that suggests the influence of elements of a Judeo-Christian worldview. He then turns to the biblical evidence and gives several examples in both Old and New Testament where God's covenant people came into contact with pagan nations. He concludes:

[T]he Bible indicates that special revelation was transmitted throughout the ancient world in written form, and no doubt in oral tradition as well. Extra-biblical evidence supports this conclusion. I would thus generalize Augustine's final conclusion concerning Plato: It is impossible to determine whether whatever moral or theological consensus existed in the ancient world was the product of general or special revelation. The evidence shows that ancient cultures were exposed to both.[59]

Concerning both remnantal and influental revelation, it is worth expanding on a brief remark I made earlier in my description of the *prisca theologia* and comparative mythology in the sixteenth and seventeenth centuries. Given the cataclysmic intellectual and ideological changes from these centuries until now, and more specifically how such changes have affected a discipline such as the history of religions (from vibrant discipline to virtual extinction), it is easy to be carried along by the implausibility structures of the academic establishment and to dismiss not only the early phenomenological attempts to prove a single-source theory of religion, but also any contemporary attempt to make a connection between biblical religion and human religion. Certainly, in the sixteenth and seventeenth century many of the links made between biblical revelation and religious traditions appear speculative and tenuous and reflect the rudimentary first steps of the discipline. However, for those whose doctrine of Scripture leads them to have a theological a priori commitment to a single-source theory and a monogenetic theory of human origins, we are in *exactly* the same theological position as those scholars of a previous century. As indicated in an earlier chapter, what is called for here is serious scholarly evangelical investment in a properly *theological* religious studies, which could produce

---

58. Ibid., pp. 4–5.
59. Ibid., p. 19.

*evangelical* Mircea Eliades and Joseph Campbells. Such research should be seen as worthwhile and should be encouraged. While each example must be examined on its merits, given the solid theological base of remnantal and influental revelation, it should come as no surprise that revelatory evidence is found in non-Christian religious traditions. Indeed, we would expect to see it.[60]

### d. 'Demonic' revelation

In his recent study *Ancient Near Eastern Themes in Biblical Theology,* Jeffrey Niehaus explores the close parallels between the Old Testament and ancient Near Eastern religion. His conclusion is not only that 'the pagan cultures of the ancient Near East had certain fundamentally important concepts in common with the biblical authors', but that 'those pagan cultures shared a theological structure of thought with that of the biblical writers'.[61] Echoing the theological and methodological presuppositions outlined within this current study, Niehaus accounts for these parallels in terms of derivation of 'revealed truth in the Old Testament and the Bible, and distorted truth in the ancient Near East'.[62] Accounting for these parallels he does not eschew the possibility of what I have called *remnantal revelation*, and also the idea that the 'Old Testament uses literary and legal forms long current in the ancient Near East as vehicles of God's special revelation'.[63] However, he decides to major on a third source for the accounting of these parallels.

Comparing and contrasting occasions where ancient Near Eastern kings received direct revelation and insight,[64] he asks the following:

> When a pagan king makes the same claim that a biblical king does, and when that claim is a spiritual one and involves divine guidance, an evaluation that says the biblical king is just understanding these things the way any ancient Near Eastern monarch would understand them does not do justice to the data. David either got guidance from

---

60. One recent example of such a study, albeit at a more popular level, is Chan Kei Thong, *Finding God in Ancient China: How the Ancient Chinese Worshipped the God of the Bible* (Grand Rapids: Zondervan, 2009). For a cautious appreciation of Thong's work see Winfried Corduan, *In the Beginning God: A Fresh Look at the Case for Original Monotheism* (Nashville: Broadman & Holman, 2013), pp. 333–335.

61. Jeffrey J. Niehaus, *Ancient Near Eastern Themes in Biblical Theology* (Grand Rapids: Kregel, 2008), p. 177.

62. Ibid., p. 178.

63. Ibid., p. 29.

64. His examples are those of King David and King Thutmose III.

God, or he did not . . . If it was true, then David's experience of inspiration, or divine guidance, was a genuine experience that produced the results God wanted. But how are we to understand the similar claims of divine guidance made by Thutmose III? It would be most bizarre if an Egyptian who pre-dated David by centuries made an almost identical claim to divine guidance for making temple furnishings for his god and made that claim by coincidence. Or, to put it another way, the true God just happened to do to David what Thutmose claimed his god did for him a few centuries earlier.[65]

Niehaus's explanation for such parallels is that of *demonic counterfeiting*, a characteristic I have noted in chapter 6:

Passages such as Deut 32:16–19; 1 Cor 10:20; 1 Tim 4:1 tell us clearly enough that demonic powers and intelligences are behind false religion, . . . Demonic inspiration of false religion (which produces the sort of parallels we have considered, including the major paradigm in its pagan articulations) is one of the things the Bible teaches clearly.[66]

Niehaus, noting the parallels 'between pagan divine assemblies and the biblical assembly of angels, or "sons of God," '[67] schematizes counterfeit pagan pantheons:

Holy angels refuse worship, but fallen angels clearly do not. It seems reasonable to agree with these biblical writers, and such agreement leads us to understand that the common pagan theological structure above is a theological counterfeit not only endorsed by all ancient pagan thought, but imposed upon the ancients by the misleading inspiration of fallen angels (or, to use Paul's words to Timothy, 'doctrines of demons,' 1 Tim. 4:1 RSV).[68]

## Summary

To summarize this section, my contention is that the raw revelatory material out of which idolatrous religion is fashioned comes from four sources: the *imaginal*, the *remnantal*, the *influental* and the *demonic*. They are mixed together in a myriad of combinations and variations over time, meaning that untangling them will be very difficult, although this is where a properly theological religious

---

65. Niehaus, *Ancient Near Eastern Themes*, pp. 178–179.

66. Ibid., p. 179.

67. Ibid., p. 180.

68. Ibid., pp. 180–181.

studies could help us in our understanding, thus providing important detail and texture to aid the church in its missiological tasks.

### 3. Defining other religions as idolatrous recognizes the reality of demonic deception behind them

From the beginning of this study I have indicated in various places some connection between the religious Other and the satanic and demonic. In chapter 2 I wrote of Satan's presence and influence in the fall of Adam and Eve. In chapter 4 I speculated on the relationship between the religio-genesis of Babel, its possible connection to the unnatural activities of Genesis 6:1–4 and the 'commentary' on these events noted in Deuteronomy 4:19, and especially in Deuteronomy 32 with its mentions of the *běnê hā'ělōhîm* and the worship of demons. In chapter 5 I noted that though references are scarce, the Old Testament does posit a link between idols and demons. This link was reiterated in chapter 6, where Paul affirms a Christological Shema and Jesus' transcendent uniqueness within Paul's discourse on the nature of idolatry in 1 Corinthians 8 and 10, where he too posits a relationship between idols and demons. It is appropriate at this point that I attempt to collect these strands and weave them into my theology of religions.

Here, however, we must tread carefully. I have already noted on more than one occasion the speculative nature of my discussions in this area in terms of exegesis and theological construction. Moreover, before I can make any substantive points I recognize that since the 1980s there has been a heated methodological debate within evangelical theology and missiology regarding the legitimacy and place of a 'theology of the evil powers'.[69] I hope it is not too much of a generalization to note that the lines of battle drawn here are often a priori ones regarding charismatic or non-charismatic allegiances. It is beyond the scope of this study to plunge into the details of this debate, but it may not be necessary given my theological rather than missiological focus here. Peter Bolt, for example, notes the paucity of biblical evidence on this subject and describes (and critiques) various extra-biblical evidences used to

---

69. See James K. Beilby and Paul Rhodes Eddy (eds.), *Understanding Spiritual Warfare: Four Views* (Grand Rapids: Baker Academic, 2012). As the subject has been discussed within missiology, see Edward Rommen (ed.), *Spiritual Power and Missions: Raising the Issues*, Evangelical Missiological Society Series 3 (Pasadena: William Carey Library, 1995).

'supplement' the biblical material.[70] He is critical of those who he believes become unbiblical in their 'expansive' overmapping of evil powers, thus inducing fear by exaggerating a gap between God and humanity that should remain closed. However, concerning the 'mudslinging'[71] where both sides accuse the other of being wedded to unbiblical cultural presuppositions, he notes:

> In my opinion the debate is not about their existence [of Satan and demons] or influence (about both of which I, for one, have no doubt); it is about what we are supposed to do with them once we acknowledge their existence. It is a question not of metaphysics, but of *practice*.[72]

It is concerning this metaphysical focus that I wish to make a number of points.

### a. The 'dark margin'

In sympathy with Bolt I recognize the paucity of biblical material not only concerning demons in general but concerning the relationship between idols and demons in particular. That references to the demonic are scarce is surely theologically significant. As I mentioned in chapter 5, C. J. H. Wright notes that too much focus on the demonic element of idolatry may distract us from recognizing the 'balance of responsibility for the sin of idolatry where it truly belongs – with us human beings'.[73] Bolt believes this scriptural gap should stay open because rather than our view being filled with an elaborate demonology, our focus should be on Jesus Christ and his gospel, 'what God has done about the disorder in the world'.[74] Indeed, Bolt is unhappy with even speaking of a 'biblical theology of evil powers', for this grants 'the devil a significance which he no doubt appreciates, but which is far more than he deserves'.[75] Rather, 'when we address the evil powers in relation to the central messages of the Scriptures, it becomes clear that we must only ever deal with them from the perspective of

---

70. Peter G. Bolt, 'Towards a Biblical Theology of the Defeat of the Evil Powers', in Peter G. Bolt (ed.), *Christ's Victory over Evil: Biblical Theology and Pastoral Ministry* (Nottingham: Apollos, 2009), pp. 35–81.

71. Ibid., p. 43.

72. Ibid., n. 16 (his italics).

73. Christopher J. H. Wright, *The Mission of God: Unlocking the Bible's Grand Narrative* (Nottingham: Inter-Varsity Press, 2006), p. 162.

74. Bolt, 'Towards a Biblical Theology', p. 48.

75. Ibid., p. 37.

their defeat'.[76] Hence his preferred title 'towards a biblical theology of Christ's victory (over the evil powers)'.

However, and without wishing immediately to contradict myself, while biblical references to idols and demons are scarce, they *are* present, and moreover, thinking particularly of Deuteronomy 32:17 and 1 Corinthians 10:20, are presented in explicit fashion. Given my own tradition-specific background, which would not locate itself in the more 'charismatic' end of the evangelical spectrum, I do not want to commit what Hiebert famously called the 'flaw of the excluded middle', which acknowledges humanity and God but forgets the existence and presence of other beings in the supernatural realm.[77] I hope that in my exegesis of certain key passages, for example the assertion of the existence of a divine council and the supernatural nature of the *bĕnê hā'ĕlōhîm*, I have not committed this fallacy. In constructing a theology of religions, therefore, it would be remiss *not* to include some reference to the role of the demonic, especially in an academic environment when an antithetical approach to the religious Other is extremely countercultural. Kraemer notes the relative importance of this theme by referring to it ominously as a 'dark margin':[78]

> We often have said that one should not forget the demonic side of the religious, Christianity included, and of the expressions of spiritual life in man. Many scholars are always so exclusively concentrated on building bridges, pointing to continuities and fulfilments, that they become wholly blind to the realism of the Bible, which calls Peter by the name of Satan, when he expresses his loving concern for his Master; which sees in the most interesting religious phenomena the demonic perversion of God's will; which repeatedly speaks about the Devil appearing in the figure of an angel of light. All this simply means that not only patently degraded types of religion, but also highly efficient saviours and leaders, and very attractive and magnificent expressions of insight and spiritual counsel, may be the *demonic* perversion of genuine truth; the more dangerous, because it commends itself so strongly to sensitive high-minded persons.[79]

J. H. Bavinck makes the same point in speaking of 'the dark shadow that lies over all the religions of the peoples':[80]

---

76. Ibid., p. 39.
77. Paul G. Hiebert, 'The Flaw of the Excluded Middle', *Missiology: An International Review* 10.1 (1982), pp. 35–47.
78. Kraemer, *Religion and the Christian Faith*, p. 379.
79. Ibid. (his italics).
80. Quoted in Visser, *Heart for the Gospel*, p. 154.

Paul, referring to the Ephesians, could truly say that they were 'having no hope and without God in the world' at the time when they were still heathen, and were so notwithstanding they yet had a religion of their own (Eph. 2:12). The frightening power of Satan, 'the prince of the power of the air, of the spirit that now worketh in the sons of disobedience' (Eph. 2:2), is revealed in heathendom. Something like a horrible void is in all these beautifully drawn religious systems of the peoples, in all their profound liturgy, in all their rich philosophical speculation, in all their devotions. It is not God himself who is searched for and served, not the living God who stooped himself over this sorry world in Jesus Christ.[81]

Finally here, and I trust it should go without saying, in recognizing the existence and role of the demonic in our definition of the religious Other, our Christian attitude and behaviour to those in the grip of such influence should never to be to demonize but requires the meeting-in-love I spoke of right at the beginning of this study.[82]

### b. Demonic identity and co-option

We now turn to the nature of the relationship between demons and idols in passages such as Deuteronomy 32:17 and 1 Corinthians 10:20. Here some of the most detailed recent work has been done by Mody, whose doctoral thesis explores this relationship in 1 Corinthians 8:4–5 and 10:18–32 in the context of the Pauline corpus and early Judaism. I have already drawn on Mody's research in chapter 4 when I speculated on the possible identity of the *běnê hā'ělōhîm* in Deuteronomy 32. For this section I shall continue with Mody's analysis, offering it up as one plausible way through what continues to be rather murky terrain.

Before coming to Mody's argument on the nature of the relationship between idols and demons, let us return to the issue of the personal identity of these demons. Mody tentatively offers three possibilities, which do not have to be exclusive categories but may rather overlap. First, he includes demons as the more personal side in the make-up of the structural principalities and powers mentioned in Ephesians 6:12. Secondly, he returns to the notion that the demons are the *běnê hā'ělōhîm* of Deuteronomy 32. These are the many 'gods' and 'lords' of 1 Corinthians 8:5. Although Mody shies away from speaking of 'territorial spirits' and certainly from certain practices used to 'defeat' these spirits (i.e.

---

81. J. H. Bavinck, 'General Revelation', p. 54.
82. Cf. Eph. 6:12: 'For our struggle is not against flesh and blood, but against the rulers, against the authorities, against the powers of this dark world and against the spiritual forces of evil in the heavenly realms.'

SLSW, Strategic Level Spiritual Warfare),[83] he does posit a version of territoriality, not in terms of geography but rather nationality or people group:

> Thus today in, say, London, there would be a demon in charge over, say Punjabi Hindu religions, one over Iranian Muslims, one of Thai Buddhists, etc. The demons may be under the authority of Satan, given references to Satan in 1 Cor. 5:5 and 7:5. The demons who rule over a nationality's cults may extend Satan's power and influence over the different nationalities and cults of Corinth and, indeed in the world today.[84]

Thirdly, and building on the work of Archie Wright, the identification of demons with the spirits of the dead giants, again a connection already noted in a previous chapter. Mody recognizes that such a postulation may offend modern evangelical sensibilities, but that theologically there are sound reasons to make such a connection. The unholy union between angelic and human nature is the epitome of sin's de-creational nature and also makes a link to the nature of idolatry:

> Idols represent an unholy rebellion against God's creation order and are an exchange of the Creator for created things and the truth of God for a lie (Rom. 1:21–25) . . . It is therefore fitting that deceiving demons should use deceptive idols, created things as weapons in their war against God's creation order by enslaving humanity into the worship of spiritually *dead* things. Pagans start to resemble the character of the gods they worship and reflect the opposition to the purposes of God which is inherent in the character of demons. On judgement day, God's fitting verdict on those who have worshipped spiritually *dead* things under the influence of demons / the spirits of the *dead*, will be eternal spiritual *death* in hell.[85]

This brings us to the relationship between idols and demons. After surveying a number of theories put forward, Mody proffers what he calls a 'co-optative' view that identifies demons and idols as distinct entities, the personal former standing behind and manipulating the lifeless latter. In describing this co-option, Mody notes three interconnected features.

---

83. Rohintan Mody, *Evil and Empty: The Worship of Other Faiths in 1 Corinthians 10:18–22 and Today* (London: Latimer Trust, 2010), p. 40. See also Chuck Lowe, *Territorial Spirits and World Evangelization?* (Fearn: Christian Focus, 1998).
84. Mody, *Evil and Empty*, p. 18.
85. Ibid., p. 42 (his italics). Bolt also thinks this connection is often missed but is theologically important, Bolt; 'Towards a Biblical Theology', pp. 65–67.

First, 'the demons are powerful and may enslave humanity into idolatry'.[86] This recognizes a dangerous combination that brings together a certain spiritual power and authority demons have with the inherent human propensity to worship idols. Although cult images are lifeless and nothing, worshipping them puts the worshipper in the sphere of influence of demons; hence Paul's insistence for Christians to disassociate themselves from such practices.

Secondly, 'the demons deceive humanity into sacrifices to idols'.[87] For Mody, this deception can occur in various ways: the demons' counterfeiting can deceive idolaters into believing in the spiritual reality of idols and therefore lead them away from God; the idols themselves are deceptive and illusory; and paralleling Paul's remarks in 2 Corinthians 11:13–15a, 'the demons may disguise themselves and appear to be real gods, worthy of worship':[88]

> These disguises seem to be plausible but in fact are cloaks of the evil demons. Thus under this suggestion, Krishna, for example, seems to be a spiritually real and living god who will bring blessing if worshipped but it may be a fictitious role played by a demon in order to deceive the worshippers of Krishna. The cult image of Krishna may be the image of the disguise of a demon, and to worship Krishna's cult image would be to worship the cult image of a demon in disguise. Under this possibility, the *daimonia*/demons can be equated with the many 'gods' and lords' in 1 Cor. 8:5b, not in terms of their nature and essence, but in terms of the roles the demons play.[89]

Although he is less detailed and sophisticated than Mody, Poston proposes a similar thesis:

> The Bible indicates that Satan and his angelic hordes *initiated* the beliefs and practices of the non-Christian religions. In the case of some faith systems, demonic angels assume the roles of various so-called deities for the purpose of receiving worship for themselves and keeping people from knowledge of the One True God. In exchange for this adoration, they dispense certain kinds of 'power' and provide so-called 'revelations.' The Bible indicates that these foundational deceptions are received

---

86. Mody, *Evil and Empty*, p. 25.

87. Rohintan Mody, 'The Relationship Between Powers of Evil and Idols in 1 Corinthians 8:4–5 and 10:18–22 in the Context of the Pauline Corpus and Early Judaism', PhD diss., Aberdeen University, 2008, p. 277.

88. Mody, *Evil and Empty*, p. 28.

89. Ibid., p. 29.

by human beings and expanded further because of the sinful, rebellious nature of humankind.[90]

What is interesting here is that Poston, again using 2 Corinthians 11:14, is not afraid to posit a genealogy that traces these demonic elements in various world religions, including Islam: 'If we begin with the premise that the Bible is the true Word of God, it must be concluded that, based upon a comparison of the teachings of Islam with those of the Christian faith, the angel seen and heard by Muhammad was a demonic angel.'[91]

Finally, the third aspect of Mody's thesis is that 'the demons "stand behind" the idols and co-opt the worship consciously intended for the idols'.[92] Mody's argument here is that through their deception, demons co-opt the worship and sacrifices intended for the idols, and thereby bring the idolater under a demonic sphere of influence. The triggers for this are the sacrifice to, and invocation of, the idol, which Paul explicitly says are in fact sacrifices to demons (1 Cor. 10:20): 'The "co-optative" view . . . does not assume that the demons hover as unseen presences at pagan sacrifices, or that the pagan consciously worships demons. Rather the sacrifices mean that the worshippers come under the sphere of power or influence of demons.'[93]

## 4. Defining the other religions as idolatrous interprets the gospel of Jesus Christ as being their 'subversive fulfilment'

After much preparation, I am now finally in a position to describe the overall relationship between the revelation of the Christian gospel of Jesus Christ and the idolatrous response that is the religious Other. Given what I have already said concerning elements of discontinuity and continuity between counterfeits and the reality upon which they are based, the relationship will be complex and sophisticated, teetering on the brink of the dialectical and paradoxical, but not, I believe, falling into either of these categories. The term I believe most accurately and succinctly describes this particular relationship is that of 'subversive fulfilment', a felicitous phrase used by Hendrik Kraemer,

---

90. Larry Poston, 'The Bible and the Religions', in *The Narrow Gate* (unpublished manuscript, n.d.), pp. 68–82 (78; his italics).

91. Ibid., p. 75.

92. Mody, *Evil and Empty*, p. 30.

93. Ibid., p. 32.

seemingly only once, in an essay he wrote in 1939, an essay that served as a further explanation and elaboration of his book *The Christian Message in a Non-Christian World*:

> This apprehension of the essential 'otherness' of the world of divine realities revealed in Jesus Christ from the atmosphere of religion as we know it in the history of the race cannot be grasped merely by way of investigation and reasoning. Only an attentive study of the Bible can open the eyes to the fact that Christ, 'the power of God' and 'the wisdom of God', stands in contradiction to the power and wisdom of man. Perhaps in some respects it is proper to speak of contradictive or *subversive fulfilment*.[94]

Although Kraemer may have been the one to put these two words together to form one term, both ideas appear in close proximity in other thinkers whom I have referenced constantly throughout this work. So Herman Bavinck, writing a few decades before Kraemer writes:

> All the elements and forms that are essential to religion . . , though corrupted, nevertheless do occur in pagan religions. Here and there even unconscious predictions and striking expectations of a better and purer religion are voiced. Hence Christianity is not only positioned antithetically toward paganism; it is also paganism's fulfilment. Christianity is the true religion, therefore also the highest and purest; it is the truth of all religions. What in paganism is the caricature, the living original is here. What is appearance there is essence here. What is sought there can be found here. Christianity is the explanation of 'ethnicism'. Christ is the Promised One to Israel and the desire of

---

94. Hendrik Kraemer, 'Continuity or Discontinuity', in G. Paton (ed.), *The Authority of Faith: International Missionary Council Meeting at Tambaram, Madras* (London: Oxford University Press, 1939), pp. 1–21 (5; my italics). I am not the first to make use of this concept. Willem Visser't Hooft refers to it in Willem A. Visser't Hooft, 'Accommodation: True or False', *SEAJT* 8.3 (1967), pp. 5–18 (13–14); Lesslie Newbigin picked up the term via Visser't Hooft and mentions it in Lesslie Newbigin, *A Word in Season: Perspectives on Christian World Missions* (Grand Rapids: Eerdmans, 1994), p. 163. To complete this line of succession, Newbigin scholar Mike Goheen uses the term in his own work on Newbigin. See Michael Goheen, *'As the Father Has Sent Me, I Am Sending You': J. E. Lesslie Newbigin's Missionary Ecclesiology* (Zoetermeer: Boekencentrum, 2000), pp. 423–424, 436; 'Gospel, Culture, and Cultures: Lesslie Newbigin's Missionary Contribution', paper presented at Cultures and Christianity A.D. 2000, Hoeven, Netherlands, 2000.

all the Gentiles. Israel and the church are elect for the benefit of humankind. In Abraham's seed, all the nations of the earth will be blessed.[95]

Similarly, Cornelius Van Til, writing a few decades after Kraemer, notes:

In false theophanies, prophecies and miracles, we have an indication of man's deepest needs. Christianity stands, to be sure in antithetical relation to the religions of the world, but it also offers itself as the fulfilment of that of which the nations have unwittingly had some faint desire.[96]

Finally, Chris Wright:

The fallen duplicity of man is that he simultaneously seeks after God his Maker and flees from God his Judge. Man's religions, therefore, simultaneously manifest both these human tendencies. This is what makes a simplistic verdict on other religions – whether blandly positive or wholly negative – so unsatisfactory and, indeed, unbiblical.[97]

What does the term 'subversive fulfilment' convey? Let me spend a few moments focusing on both parts of this phrase.

### a. The gospel as subversion

On the one hand, the gospel of Jesus Christ stands as the subversion, antithetical contradiction, confrontation, condemnation and crisis of all manifestations of the religious Other. The universal sinful suppression and substitution of our knowledge of God, the *whatness* of religion, means that even the most con-textualized communication of the gospel must issue in an appeal and a call for repentance: a turning from idols to the living and true God.[98] J. H. Bavinck and

---

95. Herman Bavinck, *Reformed Dogmatics*, ed. John Bolt, tr. John Vriend, 4 vols. (Grand Rapids: Baker, 2004), vol. 1, pp. 319–320.

96. Van Til, *Introduction to Systematic Theology*, pp. 204–205.

97. Christopher J. H. Wright, 'The Christian and Other Religions: The Biblical Evidence', *Them* 9.2 (1984), pp. 4–15 (2).

98. See 1 Thess. 1:9. Referring to Paul's command in Acts 17:30 for the Athenians to repent, Pardigon gets it exactly right: 'The command from God is to repent, not to complement or supplement one's preexisting knowledge. It requires from mankind to recognize and confess the sinfulness and guilt of their former ways, and therefore to make a radical break with them. It is abandoning wholeheartedly

Kraemer both capture this perspective well, and it is worth quoting them at length here. First, J. H. Bavinck:

> The gods of heathen worship are not God, but the product of human imagination. The concept of grace which is to be found here and there is not the grace of god, but it is as a blade of straw that is grasped in desperation and misery. The redeemers and saviours about whom heathendom dreams are not types of what Christ is and would be but they are saviours conjured by the fancy of men. Such evidence the need of the man who has lost God.
>
> Such altars, dedicated to the 'unknown god' are the cries of distress of a heart torn loose from God, a heart with no inner resting. Such manifestations are not to be understood as in any way pointing to the real Christ. The real Christ differs radically from the so-called saviours conjured up by the religions of man. His gospel is not the answer to man's inquiry, but in a deep and profound sense the gospel of Christ is rather a condemnation of all such human fancy and speculation. Consequently, if we begin with the ideas of those we would convert, a point will be reached when the breach between our view and theirs is clearly evident. There is no direct uninterrupted path from the darkness of paganism to the light of the gospel. Pagan systems of thought can be examined and, humanly speaking, their beauty, inner consistency, scope, and systematic character can even be admired to a degree, but somewhere along the line, we must pause to point out our tremendous differences. Without that, our argument is not finished and it may even be dangerous and misleading. There is no detour that can bridge the gap; the transition from paganism to Christianity is not continuous and smooth, and it would be dishonest and unfaithful to Christ if we were to try to camouflage the gulf separating the two.[99]

---

the entirety of their pagan beliefs and practices, and replacing them by the Christian gospel and church (both as community and "place" of worship). There is no "nuanced judgment" that would see both positive and negative aspects to paganism, praising their religiosity but making "a few negative comments" pointing to some "dark sides." No, it is man qua idolater who is under God's wrath and judgment, and therefore it is idolatry and paganism as such and as a whole that is man's sin. Worshiping anything or anyone else than Yahweh the Maker-Lord-Judge who raised Jesus the Christ is turning away from him and mutiny' (Flavien Olivier Cedric Pardigon, 'Paul Against the Idols: The Areopagus Speech and Religious Inclusivism', PhD diss., Westminster Theological Seminary, 2008, pp. 319–320).

99. J. H. Bavinck, *An Introduction to the Science of Mission*, tr. David H. Freeman (Phillipsburg: P & R, 1960), pp. 136–137.

And Kraemer:

> It is, when we take the biblical revelation seriously, illegitimate to speak of a rectilinear transition from the world of the religion . . . to the world of revelation. Therefore as we have said above, over every achievement remains written *metanoia*, 'repent ye and believe the gospel' (Mark 1:15). Becoming a disciple of Christ means always a radical break with the past. Christ is, as we have repeatedly said, the *crisis* of all Religion (and philosophy good and bad); that is to say, as well the Judge as the great Transformer of all religion. It never means a gradual transformation.[100]

> Even when we recognise that Christ may in a certain sense be called the fulfilment of some deep and persistent longings and apprehensions that everywhere in history manifest themselves in the race, this fulfilment, when we subject the facts to a close scrutiny, never represents the perfecting of what has been before. In this fulfilment is contained a radical recasting of values, because these longings and apprehensions, when exposed to the searching and revolutionary light of Christ, appear blind and misdirected. That does not detract in the least from the fact that these longings and apprehensions, humanly speaking, are heart-stirring and noble, but if we want to be loyal to the divine reality that has come to us in Jesus Christ, this appreciation, which is simply a matter of justice and honesty in the human plane, must not obscure our eyes to the truth that in Christ all things become new, because He is the crisis of all religions. In this we recognise that God as He is revealed in Jesus Christ is contrary to the sublimest picture we made of Him before we knew of Him in Jesus Christ.[101]

### b. The gospel as fulfilment

However, while the gospel is an appeal, it is also appealing – subversion, yes, but also fulfilment: 'No continuity exists between the gospel and human religious consciousness, although definite continuity does exist between the gospel and what lies behind human religious consciousness, namely God's general revelation.'[102] There is a relationship between the disastrous dream and glorious reality. Because we are metaphysically all made in God's image, because of God's variegated common grace, which restrains the depth of our suppression and substitution, because idols are parasites and counterfeits of *the* God, Yahweh, there is a *thatness* to our humanity. Perennial metaphysical, epistemological ethical

---

100. Kraemer, *Religion and the Christian Faith*, p. 338 (italics my transliteration or translation of the Greek).

101. Kraemer, 'Continuity or Discontinuity', p. 4.

102. J. H. Bavinck, 'Religious Consciousness', p. 297.

questions that other religions all ask but cannot ultimately answer, *are* answered by the self-contained ontological triune Creator and Saviour. Philosophically speaking, Christianity is true because of the impossibility of the contrary. Biblically speaking, the cracked cisterns of idolatry that bring only disillusionment, despair and unfulfilled desires are wonderfully fulfilled and surpassed in the fount of living water, Jesus Christ the Lord. There is always a point of contact: 'This is the only chink in the Goliath armour of pseudo-religion, where the shepherd boy with his stone – if God guides his hand – can hit people'.[103] Positively, we are able to show that, compared to all other religions, the gospel of Jesus Christ is worthy of our hope and desire. We are able to persuade adherents of other religions that the gospel of Jesus Christ, while confrontational, costly and sacrificial, is wonderful enough, trustworthy enough to exchange old desires and hopes for new ones because these new ones are the originals from which all others are but smudged and ripped copies.

To illustrate, let us return to two expositions already mentioned in this chapter. First, A. A. Hodge notes how God's triunity both subverts and fulfils the errors of deism, pantheism and polytheism:

> It is easily seen how wonderfully the revealed doctrine of the Trinity comprehends in a harmonious and pure form all of the straggling and apparently conflicting rays of light preserved in these human systems of false religion. The Father sits apart as the distant and incommunicable God, the origin and end of all things, the ultimate source of all authority and power, but beyond all human thought and touch, separate on his eternal throne in the highest of heavens. The truth in pantheism is realized in the Holy Ghost, who, while of the same substance as the Father, is revealed to us as immanent in all things, the basis of all existence, the tide of all life, springing up like a well of water from within us, giving form to chaos and inspiration to reason, the ever-present Executive of God, the author of all beauty in the physical world, of all true philosophy, science, and theology in the world of thought, and of all holiness in the world of the Spirit. The eternal Son has stooped to a real and permanent incarnation, and has done sublimely what the incarnations of the heathen mythology have only caricatured. We have what the polytheists merely dreamed of, and never really saw – the unfolding of the ethical constitution of the Godhead, revealing his existence in a plurality of persons, the actual and permanent dwelling of the absolute God in the form of human flesh.[104]

---

103. J. H. Bavinck, *Het probleem van de pseudo-religie en de algemene openbaring* (*The Problem of Pseudo-Religion and General Revelation*), n.d., n.p., quoted in Visser, *Heart for the Gospel*, p. 266.

104. Hodge, *Evangelical Theology*, p. 108.

Secondly, having described his five 'magnetic points', which provide the structure and *thatness* of religious consciousness, J. H. Bavinck is able to describe how the gospel of Jesus Christ answers these perennial questions by showing that the kingdom of God 'is a Totality, embracing everything; and is the meaningful coherence that those people [whose souls are overflowing with the results of their suppression and exchange] have been dreaming about for centuries. But it is different from what they expected.'[105]

'I and Cosmos' emphasized universal being as god, the goal being a self-deifying denial of egos and delusions 'in order to be able to enter the divine state of the All'.[106] Jesus' kingdom comes as something completely different with its realized eschatology of now and not-yet, of a world perishing and under vanity:

> People delude others when they say that to stand within the totality of all things is to be swallowed up and to lose all sense of self as one is overwhelmed by the swelling sea of all-that-is. 'Not at all,' says Jesus Christ. Taking one's stand within the new kingdom definitely does mean dying. But it also means finding oneself anew in the resurrection of the Lord Jesus Christ. This is the ultimate dying and the ultimate rising to a new life.[107]

In 'I and the norm' human life is associated with law, but a law often impersonalized and wrestled with. As Bavinck says, 'In Jesus this is different':[108]

> Transgression of the law is not an assault on good order or agreement, but it is very definitely rebellion against God and an attempt to pry oneself loose from God's grip and to attack his image of God. That law is Jesus Christ, in whom the entire law is fulfilled and who kept every commandment in our place out of the depths of his divine love. The living reality of that Someone, that God, always stands behind the law. Our lives find fullness and meaning in fellowship with that God, and outside of him safety is nowhere and never found.[109]

In 'I and the riddle of my existence' we see 'a wonderful interplay of fate and activity' in karma and *takdir* (destiny). In the gospel both these aspects are personalized and understood as human accountability and a divine plan:

---

105. J. H. Bavinck, 'Religious Consciousness', p. 291.
106. Ibid., p. 292.
107. Ibid., p. 293.
108. Ibid., p. 294.
109. Ibid.

The lot that is assigned a person is not some dark fate nor is it a cosmic determinism. But in its deepest sense it is the unfolding plan of God. The dialogue that a person experiences between his or her activity and his or her destiny increasingly takes on the character of a dialogue between a child and its father.[110]

In 'I and salvation' we see the perennial cry for deliverance and liberation from all manner of threats both natural and supernatural. Again, salvation in Christ is radically different:

> There is but one thing from which people must be saved, and that is their guilt before him whom they attempt to push away all the time in their pursuit of unrighteousness. It is salvation from enmity and from being lost. That salvation included all other forms of being made free, like kernels on the ear. It is only imaginable as a whole, with all its dimensions growing from one root.[111]

Finally, in 'I and the Supreme Power', humanity recognizes its relatedness to a higher power, but in the process of suppression and exchange this higher power has been fashioned in man's image. In the gospel this higher power is revealed as a Father and a King, and comes to us: 'That Higher power is the one that came into the world in the form of Jesus Christ and removed the veil over his face so that we might know the Son and Father'.[112]

## Conclusion

In conclusion, it is my contention that subversive fulfilment, or alternatively 'fulfilling subversion', captures better than any model I have come across the relationship between the gospel of Jesus Christ and the religious Other. Such a model demonstrates both continuity and discontinuity and coheres well with both the complex theological anthropology of human beings and the fundamental analysis and anatomy of idolatry, that pervasive biblical concept that has been offered as the hermeneutical lens through which we are to view the religious Other. This then is my theology of religions. In the next chapter I turn to the implications such a theology of religions has for missiological theory and praxis.

---

110. Ibid., p. 296.
111. Ibid., p. 295.
112. Ibid., p. 294.

## 8. 'A LIGHT FOR THE GENTILES': MISSIOLOGICAL IMPLICATIONS OF 'SUBVERSIVE FULFILMENT'

For the work of missions is the work of God; it is not lawful for us to improvise. At each step we must ask what it is that God demands. Although it will not always be easy to find the right course, our search must surely be led by what God has said in his word.

(J. H. Bavinck)[1]

### Introduction

I stated at the beginning of the previous chapter that my focus was to be theological rather than missiological. However, having now described in some detail both the nature of the religious Other and its relationship to the gospel of Jesus Christ, it is perhaps appropriate to offer some thoughts, which really can be no more than a postscript, on missiological application, remembering that those whom I have referenced most in the previous chapter were first and foremost missiological practitioners. What is the 'cash value' of the theology of religions I have described in previous chapters? While the following is only in sketch form, I hope the outline is clear enough to show the shape of praxis informed by this construal of the religious Other. The chapter will consist of four parts.

---

1. J. H. Bavinck, *An Introduction to the Science of Missions*, tr. David H. Freeman (Phillipsburg: P & R, 1960), p. 5.

First, I shall make a number of quick missiological definitions and observations. Secondly, I shall pause for a little longer on the perennial issue of contextualization. Thirdly, I shall return once again to the Areopagus in order to demonstrate how the apostle Paul's approach is an (and possibly *the*) instantiation par excellence of a missiological approach built upon a subversive fulfilment theology of religions. Fourthly, and focusing on Islam, I shall present a worked example of how a subversive fulfilment approach might take shape in a particular religious tradition. Finally, I shall conclude by reminding us of the importance of the gathered church's embodying subversive fulfilment.

## 1. A brief mission statement

The following points can be no more than a rushed tour around some foundational missiological sites. Each one could be, and indeed has been, dwelt upon at length. Each one continues to be the source of discussion and disagreement within the evangelical community. For the sake of context I simply offer my own definitional notes here, before we spend a little longer reflecting on the theme of contextualization, where I think a 'subversive fulfilment' theology of religions can make a significant contribution.

### a. The motivation for mission

First, the motivation and 'vision' of Christian mission. Commenting on Romans 1:5 the late John Stott gets straight to the point in typically inspirational manner:

> The highest of missionary motives is neither obedience to the Great Commission (important as that is), nor love for sinners who are alienated and perishing (strong as that incentive is, especially when we contemplate the wrath of God . . .), but rather zeal – burning and passionate zeal – for the glory of Jesus Christ . . . Only one imperialism is Christian . . . and that is concern for His Imperial Majesty Jesus Christ, and for the glory of his empire.[2]

This empire is eschatologically inaugurated, that is to say, our present situation in redemptive history is that between the 'already' of Christ's life, death, resurrection and ascension, and the 'not yet' of the consummation of the kingdom and final judgment. This entails both continuity and discontinuity between the

---

2. John R. W. Stott, *The Message of Romans: God's Good News for the World* (Leicester: Inter-Varsity Press, 1994), p. 53.

earth now and the new heaven and the new earth to come. Even though we recognize the pattern of discipleship given to us by Christ of suffering followed by glory, we still note the inexorable growth of the kingdom:

> The Calvinist and Reformed concept of the commonwealth is linked to the doctrine of the kingdom of God by being the kingdom's slowly realised, still imperfect, but proleptic expression. In the end at the last judgment, Jesus Christ the Lord completely 'restores' and 'renews' the whole world. He restores a completely 'just order'. The kingdom of God or Christ is cosmic in scope and utterly invincible. All things *will* be made new. With a Marxist-like paradox of zeal for the inevitable, the church serves as a witness to the new order, as agent for it, and as first model or exemplar of it. For the decisive turn has already been taken in the work of Christ.[3]

### b. The comprehensiveness of mission

Secondly, concerning the Christian content of mission, I advocate a holistic, transformative or integral approach to mission, which recognizes, on the one hand, the spiritual and social dimensions of sin and idolatry, and, on the other, the scope of the gospel and its entailments to transform individuals, communities and cultures, spiritually, socially, economically, politically, and so on.[4] As Christians we are to take every thought captive for Christ (2 Cor. 10:5).

In order to further this mission, and in terms of interreligious sociopolitical involvement, it is possible that there may be times when a strategic 'co-belligerence' between Christians and those from non-Christian religions might be appropriate. For although there is a principal antithetical relationship between the two, because of the inconsistency of non-Christian worldviews (due to God's common grace and the *imago Dei*), other faiths may agree with a Christian stance on a certain ethical or political issue, because they are using the 'borrowed capital' of the Christian worldview.[5] However, such co-belligerence must be conducted with discernment and can only be temporary:

---

3. Cornelius Plantinga Jr., 'The Concern of the Church in a Socio-Political World: A Calvinist and Reformed Perspective', *CTJ* 28.2 (1983), pp. 190–205 (203; his italics).
4. On this see e.g. Udo Middlemann, *Christianity Versus Fatalistic Religions in the War Against Poverty* (Colorado Springs: Paternoster, 2008).
5. The important apologetic point here, and the heart of what is known as 'presuppositional apologetics', is not *whether* those in non-Christian religions argue for a similar position as Christians (they can and do), but whether they can give a *justification* for their position based on their own religious presuppositions. This 'common' ground is not 'neutral' ground but 'Christian' ground.

Christians must realise that there is a difference between being a co-belligerent and being an ally. At times we will seem to be saying exactly the same things as those without a Christian base are saying . . . We must say what the Bible says when it causes us *to seem to be saying* what others are saying, such as Justice or Stop the meaningless bombings. But we must never forget that this is only a passing co-belligerency and not an alliance.[6]

We must be careful that in our co-belligerence we do not communicate the possibility of religious neutrality or the dilution of the exclusivity of Christ and the gospel.

### c. The ultimacy of evangelism in mission

Thirdly, although in terms of God's sovereignty there is a sense in which the whole universe is God's 'kingdom',

in the New Testament the word more commonly refers to that invasive aspect of his sovereignty under which there is eternal life. Everyone is under the kingdom in the first sense, whether they like it or not; only those who have passed from the kingdom of darkness to the kingdom of God's dear Son (Col. 1:13), those who have been born from above (John 3:3, 5), are under or in the kingdom in the second sense.[7]

Given that eternal life is only to be found in the gospel of Christ, and that normatively this comes through the human messenger in this life, in terms of missionary activity we must speak about the ultimacy[8] and radicalness[9] of evangelism, that is, the verbal proclamation of the gospel message with the call for faith and repentance in Christ.

---

6. Francis Schaeffer, *The Complete Works of Francis A. Schaeffer*, vol. 4: *The Church at the End of the Twentieth Century* (Wheaton: Crossway, 1982), p. 30 (his italics). See also Daniel Strange, 'Co-belligerence and Common Grace: Can the Enemy of My Enemy Be My Friend?', *Cambridge Papers* 14.3 (Sept. 2005).

7. D. A. Carson, *The Gagging of God: Christianity Confronts Pluralism* (Leicester: Apollos, 1996), p. 410.

8. Chris Wright's term in Christopher J. H. Wright, *The Mission of God: Unlocking the Bible's Grand Narrative* (Nottingham: Inter-Varsity Press, 2006), p. 319.

9. Tim Keller's term in Timothy J. Keller, *Ministries of Mercy* (Grand Rapids: Zondervan, 1989), p. 114.

### d. The elenctic task of mission

Fourthly, given my a priori approach, which sees all non-Christian religions in an antithetical relationship with Christianity, some people might be surprised to see a desire to engage in both interreligious dialogue and the phenomenological study of religions. Both these activities are necessary, providing they are understood within the discipline of missionary apologetics, historically known as 'elenctics'.[10] Elenctics is the convicting work of the Holy Spirit as described in John 16:8:

> The Holy Spirit will convince the world of sin. The Holy Spirit is actually the only conceivable actor of the verb, for the conviction of sin exceeds all human ability. Only the Holy Spirit can do this, even though he can and will use us as instruments in his hand. Taken in this sense, elenctics is the science which is concerned with the conviction of sin. In a special sense then it is the science which unmasks all false religion as sin against God and calls people to the knowledge of the one, true God.[11]

Elenctics is a trialogue in which the Christian enters into the already existing relationship between the non-Christian and the Holy Spirit, the dynamic relationship between divine revelation and human suppression and substitution: 'We do not open the discussion, but we need only to make it clear that the God who has revealed his eternal power and Godhead to them, now addresses them in a new way, through our words'.[12] In such a trialogue it is essential that the Christian takes time to listen compassionately and understand the religious Other to discover what they have done with God. To achieve this goal, one needs to be familiar with both a general 'scientific awareness' of other religions (historically, psychologically, philosophically and phenomenologically) and a more particular 'living approach', which appreciates the individualistic nature of religious consciousness. In all our missionary endeavours there must always be gentleness and respect, and there can be no self-righteous superiority, 'for at each moment the person knows the weapons which he turns against another have wounded himself'.[13]

---

10. 'Elenctics' means 'to convict' or 'to rebuke'. Cornelius J. Haak, 'The Missional Approach: Reconsidering Elenctics (Part 1)', *CTJ* 44.1 (2009), pp. 37–48.

11. J. H. Bavinck, *Introduction*, p. 222. See also Brian A. De Vries, 'The Evangelistic Trialogue: Gospel Communication and the Holy Spirit', *CTJ* 44.1 (2009), pp. 49–73.

12. J. H. Bavinck, *The Impact of Christianity on the Non-Christian World* (Grand Rapids: Eerdmans, 1949), p. 109.

13. J. H. Bavinck, *Introduction*, p. 272. Haak is similar here: 'The practice of elenctics is evidence of God's love for unbelievers. Why does the evangelist proclaim this love?

## 2. The nature of contextualization in mission

And so after the quick march past the above themes, we stop now for a little while. How does our theological description of the religious Other affect our understanding of the perennial missiological question of 'contextualization'?[14] With regard to my understanding and use of this notoriously slippery term, four points should immediately be noted. First, by 'contextualization' I mean 'the goal of a process whereby the universal good news of Jesus Christ is authentically experienced in the particularities of a local context'.[15] Secondly, contextualization is presumed to be an inevitable task:

> Each time the gospel is preached in a different language, to a different people, it has to transmute a variety of words, as it were and give them new content. The Gospel does not find anywhere in the world a ready language that fits completely and absolutely like a garment.[16]

Thirdly, contextualization does not weaken claims to universal truth: 'No truth which human beings may articulate can ever be articulated in a culture-transcending way – but that does not mean that the truth thus articulated does

---

Because he or she knows all too well his or her own sinful condition apart from Christ, standing condemned before God's throne *if he himself does not take shelter with Jesus Christ.* Knowing this, he reaches out to the unbeliever, aiming to protect him from God's wrath. Indeed elenctics is combat. However, it is not combat to kill but to rescue. Satan attacks to 'kill'. The divine struggle is driven by God's love and is inspired by the wonderful sacrifice of Christ; a sacrifice that was made out of love for all humanity. The coming judgment at the end of times is real. Let, then, the messengers of the gospel, the soldiers of peace, go into the world to rescue and heal' (Haak, 'Missional Approach', p. 48 [his italics]).

14. For a helpful and short delineation of different approaches to contextualization from a more anthropological perspective, see Paul G. Hiebert, *The Gospel in Human Contexts: Anthropological Explorations for Contemporary Missions* (Grand Rapids: Baker, 2009), pp. 19–35.

15. Timothy C. Tennent, *Theology in the Context of World Christianity* (Grand Rapids: Zondervan, 2007), p. 198.

16. J. H. Bavinck, *Christus en de mystiek van het Oosten* (Kampen: J. H. Kok, 1934), p. 109. Quoted in Paul Visser, *Heart for the Gospel, Heart for the World: The Life and Thought of a Reformed Pioneer Missiologist, Johan Herman Bavinck (1895–1964)* (Eugene: Wipf & Stock, 2003), p. 286.

not transcend culture'.[17] Finally, the goal of biblically faithful contextualization should be one that steers a course between extractionism and syncretism.

I would like to break down this question into two related but distinct areas: that of *missional* theologizing and that of *ecclesial* theologizing.[18] It should come as no surprise that (for the last time in this study) I shall once again lean heavily on J. H. Bavinck.

### a. Missional theologizing

By missional theologizing I mean the task of gospel communication from one culture to another. My theology of religions has given me the necessary conceptual framework to be able to comment on the thorny issue concerning the 'point of contact' between those proclaiming the gospel and those hearing the gospel.

Given all I have said about the hermetically sealed and totalitarian nature of religious worldviews, finding a point of contact would appear somewhat futile. As both J. H. Bavinck and Kraemer note, the coming together of the gospel and religious Other is within the context of incommensurability and antithesis.[19] The religious Other's understandings of 'god' and 'salvation' are radically different from our own. Here we are faced with an inevitable dilemma because 'no-one can be reached in a vacuum. A person can be reached only within a certain conceptual world. There is no other way.'[20] Therefore in our desire to communicate within 'the native conceptuality of given culture',[21] we 'inadvertently swallow a number of pagan conceptions every moment . . . Infected terms are used simply because it is impossible not to use them.'[22] For

---

17. D. A. Carson, 'Maintaining Scientific and Christian Truths in a Postmodern World', *SCB* 14.2 (2002), pp. 107–122 (120).

18. I owe this distinction to Brian DeVries.

19. J. H. Bavinck, *Introduction*, p. 137. Kraemer writes that 'points of contact in the real, deep sense of the word can only be found by antithesis. This means by discovering in the revealing light of Christ the fundamental misdirection that dominates all religious life and at the same time the groping for God which throbs in this misdirection, and which finds an unsuspected divine solution in Christ' (Hendrik Kraemer, *The Christian Message in a Non-Christian World* [London: Edinburgh House, 1938], p. 139).

20. J. H. Bavinck, *Introduction*, p. 139.

21. Richard Lints, *The Fabric of Theology: A Prolegomenon to Evangelical Theology* (Grand Rapids: Eerdmans, 1993), p. 101, n. 19.

22. J. H. Bavinck, *Introduction*, p. 138.

Bavinck this is a perilous activity: 'The missionary exhales many pagan ideas with every word that he speaks. He cannot do otherwise, since he has no other vocabulary at his disposal, but he will shudder at times when he is conscious of what he is doing.'[23]

However, there remain a number of factors that make communication not only possible but powerful. The gospel is both subversion and fulfilment. First, even though the *thatness* of a universal religious consciousness is almost immediately 'filled' by the *whatness* of the sinful suppression and substitution of this knowledge of God, *thatness* is still missiologically essential:

> Sometimes people cannot resist God's approach and are overwhelmed by it: 'We may say that by the grace of God repression and substitution does not always succeed. Time and again we notice things in the history of religion which show that God has really concerned Himself with' people of other faiths, and 'we may thankfully state *that* they believe in God.' Why this matter of gratitude? Because without this 'thatness', this objective fact of religious consciousness . . . missionary communication would be 'utterly impossible'.[24]

Secondly, Bavinck notes that as the Christian patiently defines and redefines the terms he is using,

> They become gradually and slowly detached from their old intellectual milieu and receive, at least when used by the missionary, a special significance which becomes more sharply differentiated to an ever increasing degree. The means of words is in general pliable and plastic. Words receive their precise sense from the context in which they occur. So it is not at all strange that within the framework of the preaching of the gospel certain words acquire an increasingly new meaning for those who hear them, and such words are thus gradually purified to a certain extent.[25]

Finally, Bavinck notes we should never forget the regenerating and illuminating work of the Holy Spirit who mysteriously enables blind eyes to open: 'men now understand that the old words now receive their proper meaning for the first time and that they had formerly always misunderstood and misused them'.[26]

---

23. Ibid.
24. Visser, *Heart for the Gospel*, pp. 171–172 (his italics).
25. J. H. Bavinck, *Introduction*, pp. 138–139.
26. Ibid., p. 139.

Thus, concerning a 'point of contact', we are left with principial discontinuity and yet a practical continuity. As Bavinck concludes:

> We are now in a position to reach a conclusion concerning the problem of 'a point of contact'. From a strictly theological point of view there is no point of contact within pagan thought which offers an unripe truth that can simply be taken over and utilized as a basis for our Christian witness. If this is what is meant by a point of contact, then there just is none. But, practically speaking, in actual missionary experience, we cannot avoid making frequent 'contact'; no other way is open. But, we must never lose sight of the dangers involved, and we must endeavor to purify terms we have borrowed from their pagan connotations. This is what the apostles did with concepts such as salvation, redemption, 'logos', and many others, which undoubtedly could easily have led to a world of misunderstanding.
>
> We would like to distinguish, therefore, a 'point of attack' from a 'point of contact'. The point of attack signifies for us the awareness of need, poverty, and inability, which we frequently encounter in non-Christian nations, as well as in our own surroundings.[27]

### b. Ecclesial theologizing

By ecclesial theologizing I mean the task of gospel living once the gospel has taken root within a particular culture. As with *missional* theologizing, the question is one of how much indigenous culture can be adopted and/ or adapted in the Christian community of faith. Once again a 'subversive fulfilment' model is able to answer such a question. Bavinck notes that in contradistinction to Catholic models of contextualization, a Reformational worldview finds it difficult to separate cultural fruit, however external, from religious roots. Principial discontinuity is once again highlighted. But, so is practical continuity, for Bavinck goes on to note two factors that must be remembered. First, there is God's common grace: 'The cultures met on mission fields are, in other words indivisible structures in a certain sense, but here and there loopholes are in evidence . . . Our judgement of heathendom is not thereby changed in principle, but in practice our course of action is

---

27. Ibid., p. 140. Howell echoes the same idea, noting how he himself has attempted to do this within a Japanese context: Don N. Howell, 'The Apostle Paul and First Century Religious Pluralism', in Edward Rommen and Harold A. Netland (eds.), *Christianity and the Religions: A Biblical Theology of World Religions*, Evangelical Missiological Society Series 2 (Pasadena: William Carey Library, 1995), pp. 92–112 (97–98).

changed.'[28] Secondly, Bavinck notes that over time 'religions display signs of wear and tear'.[29] Cultural practices that once had great religious significance gradually can become 'detached from this coherence and lose their original character'.[30] Bavinck goes on to delineate certain considerations that enable Christians to discern 'the proximity that customs and practices sustain to the essence of paganism'.[31] His conclusion is as follows:

> The term 'accommodation' is really not appropriate as a description of what actually ought to take place. It points to an adaptation to customs and practices essentially foreign to the gospel. Such an adaptation can scarcely lead to anything other than syncretistic entity, a conglomeration of customs that can never form an essential unity. 'Accommodation' connotes something of a denial, of a mutilation. We would, therefore prefer to use the term *possessio*, to take in possession. The Christian life does not accommodate or adapt itself to heathen forms of life, but it takes the latter in possession and thereby makes them new. Whoever is in Christ is a new creature. Within the framework of the non-Christian life, customs and practices serve idolatrous tendencies and drive a person away from God. The Christian life takes them in hand and turns them in an entirely different direction; they acquire an entirely different content. Even though in external form there is much that resembles past practices, in reality everything has become new, the old in essence has passed away and the new has come. Christ takes the life of a people in his hands, he renews and re-establishes the distorted and deteriorated; he fills each thing, each word, and each practice with a new meaning and gives it a new direction. Such is neither 'adaptation' nor 'accommodation'; it is in essence the legitimate taking possession of something by him to whom all power is given in heaven and on earth.[32]

---

28. J. H. Bavinck, *Introduction*, p. 174.
29. Ibid.
30. Ibid.
31. Ibid.
32. Ibid., p. 179. In typically stimulating fashion, Peter Leithart helpfully describes something akin to the subversive fulfilment approach to contextualization I am advocating. In *Against Christianity* he notes aphoristically, 'Contextualization be damned. We have our own story, and if it clashes with other stories we find around us, so much the worse for the other stories. Our story, after all, is big enough to encompass every other' (Peter Leithart, *Against Christianity* [Moscow, Idaho: Canon, 2003], p. 58). A few years later, and commenting favourably on Don Richardson's classic books *Peace Child* and *Eternity in Their Hearts*, he writes the following: 'As one who has written "Contextualization be damned," it might seem a tad inconsistent for me to be enthusiastic about Richardson's work. He is one of the granddaddies of

Bavinck's concept of *possessio* is an understanding of missiological contextualization that I believe is built upon the theology of religions I have outlined in this study and a guide that is indeed able to steer us safely between the dangers of extractionism and syncretism. Jesus Christ is Lord of all and the fulfilment of every desire sinfully parodied and perverted in idolatry. Therefore concepts that are not true within the framework of other religions can still be seen to represent suppressed truth. These concepts can be taken and redefined with great pastoral care and sensitivity, so that they might be purified and thus 'owned' once again by Christ. We might call this a kind of 'subversive entropy' of the 'purity' of a false religion.

J. H. Bavinck's *An Introduction to the Science of Missions* and Kraemer's *Religion and the Christian Faith* are now more than half a century old. In the intervening years the world has changed beyond recognition, as has, it could be argued, the discipline of missiology. Both J. H. Bavinck and Kraemer are largely forgotten figures, relegated to historical surveys, if mentioned at all.[33]

---

contextualization. But I don't think it's inconsistent. What I have condemned elsewhere was a kind of contextualization that shies away from radical transformation or a kind that acts as if the gospel does not come with a cultural form of its own. If contextualization becomes a matter of adjusting the particular and exclusive claims of the gospel to an existing cultural system, or if contextualization operates on the assumption that the gospel can slip into the cracks of any culture because it is a-cultural, then I need not damn it; it's damned already. But if contextualization means proclaiming the gospel as the fulfillment (and therefore radical transfiguration) of an existing culture's best hopes and intentions, then this is precisely what the apostles did. The gospel was fundamentally the fulfillment of Israel's hopes and culture, but that fulfillment meant fundamental changes in the way Israel looked and lived. The gospel was also the fulfillment of Roman hopes and culture, its hope for peace and security, for a universal KURIOS, for an *imperium sine fine*, but in fulfilling Roman hopes, the gospel radically transformed both Roman culture and the very hopes it fulfilled. So: On the one hand, "contextualization be damned." On the other hand, "three cheers for contextualization"' (available at http://www.leithart.com/archives/000727.php [accessed 17 Sept. 2013]).

33. I should mention the recent establishing of The Bavinck Institute at Calvin Theological Seminary under the leadership of John Bolt, which exists to promote scholarship related to both Herman Bavinck and J. H. Bavinck. As well as its regular journal *The Bavinck Review*, it is The Bavinck Institute that has been responsible for the publication of John Bolt, James D. Bratt and Paul J. Visser (eds.), *The J. H. Bavinck Reader* (Cambridge: Eerdmans, 2013).

And yet, when it comes to issues of contextualization at the time of writing this book, in 2013, time and again I find myself returning to their analyses, for they offer a firm, nuanced and biblically faithful theology of religions with which to underpin their missiological constructions. It is my contention that the model I have called 'subversive fulfilment' best encapsulates not only the relationship between the gospel and formal religion and religions, but more generally the gospel and every human culture. It is a rich seam that demands further mining.[34]

### 3. Paul at the Areopagus: 'subversive fulfilment' par excellence

And so we return to or, maybe better, are drawn back to Athens and Paul's Areopagus speech in Acts 17:16–34. Knowing the amount of ink shed on this

---

34. Encouragingly, while not calling it 'subversive fulfilment', or mentioning Bavinck and Kraemer by name, some contemporary Reformed thinkers have been employing such a model in their teaching and preaching, *and are being listened to*. In chapter 1 I mentioned the important teaching and preaching ministry of Tim Keller, noting his theological lineage from Bavinck via Harvie Conn. Keller's approach to contextualization is very much a 'subversive fulfilment' approach. For example, take what I think is a typical Keller statement: 'Contextualising is not telling people what they want to hear but entering in and in some ways affirming their world (because there will be aspects of it that are God glorifying) while at the same time challenging their presuppositions . . . bringing the Gospel to bear on their inconsistencies. Paul did this in 1 Cor. 1 recognising how the Gospel affects different people ( Jews and Greeks) in different ways. Jews and Greeks have different baseline narratives ( Jews = power, Greeks = philosophy) and he engaged with them in different ways, contextualising his message to suit. The cross offends differently according to different cultures/worldviews . . . we need to be aware of this and we need to address those different contexts appropriately. This is where the affirmation and challenge must be held together – we take and challenge cultural idols but in Jesus Christ we point them to the true answer to their true longing. Affirm what they believe where it is consistent with a Christ-centred worldview but GO FOR their idols as well. If we over-adapt we join them in idolatry, if we under-adapt (or not at all) we buy into our own idols (because we prioritise forms/attitudes over lost people' (transcription of talk given at Oak Hill College, London, 2009).

passage by commentators and missiologists over the years,[35] sometimes coming to diametrically opposed conclusions as to what Paul in the speech, Luke in his recording of the speech, and God in Scripture are saying and doing, it is with a little fear and trembling that I offer to make further comment on it. However, it is my contention that, without being guilty of eisegesis, a faithful exegesis of this passage becomes a, and perhaps *the*, microcosm and instantiation of not only the theology of religions I have outlined in this study but also the missiological approach built upon such a theology of religions. Not only is it the example of subversive fulfilment par excellence, but its purpose is to serve as an exemplar of the apostolic preaching to pagans. As such it becomes a satisfying final destination, indeed homecoming, that brings together not only the theological and missiological themes discussed in this study, but also a number of biblical passages and events I have covered.

In order to justify such a claim, I acknowledge that my reading of the speech does not come *ex nihilo*, but is within an interpretative tradition concerning the content and context of the speech in Luke-Acts. The most recent contribution that fits into this interpretative stream is that of Pardigon.[36] Drawing on the work of David Pao and others,[37] Pardigon argues that the determinant hermeneutical key for the whole of Luke-Acts is that of the Isaianic New Exodus. It is through this lens that the Areopagitica is to be read, and is indeed its climax.[38] Thus,

---

35. F. F. Bruce notes that 'probably no ten verses in the Acts of the Apostles have formed the text for such an abundance of commentary as has gathered around Paul's Areopagitica' (F. F. Bruce, *The Book of Acts*, NICNT [Grand Rapids: Eerdmans, 1954], p. 353).

36. Flavien Olivier Cedric Pardigon, 'Paul Against the Idols: The Areopagus Speech and Religious Inclusivism', PhD diss., Westminster Theological Seminary, 2008. See also John Span, 'The Areopagus: A Study in Continuity and Discontinuity', *SFM* 6.3 (2010), pp. 517–582, who also draws on Pardigon's work.

37. David W. Pao, *Acts and the Isaianic New Exodus*, Biblical Studies Library (Grand Rapids: Baker Academic, 2000).

38. 'In this context, Paul's address to the Areopagus takes on a role and value which go beyond that of a mere exemplary. Did Luke include this speech in order to give a model or type of apostolic proclamation to pagans? Without doubt. Yet Luke finds in this event much more than that: Paul's speech has an eschatological and universal value. With Paul, the word of God and the "way" of salvation of the eschatological New Exodus have reached the cultural and religious heart of the entire inhabited world. The "light" of Acts 13:47 (Isa 49:6) has shone in the darkest place' (Pardigon, 'Paul Against the Idols', pp. 199–200).

contrary to some treatments of this encounter that purport its 'foreignness' in Luke-Acts, Paul's speech at the Areopagus shows an intra-coherence and unity: narratively, literarily and theologically.

More pointedly, and supporting my own hermeneutical key throughout this study, a subtheme of the Isaianic New Exodus that looms large in Acts is an anti-idol polemic. Pardigon's summary of this polemic shows considerable overlap with material I have already covered: the transcendent uniqueness of Yahweh, the importance of his glory, the ability and power he has to save his people, the exposure and 'trial' of idols, and the summons to turn from idols, and their deleterious consequences, to the risen Christ.[39] Moreover, though, if, as I have argued, idolatry is the analytical tool that, first, helps us explain the anthropological complexity of human religiosity and, secondly, allows for both radical discontinuity and structural continuity between the gospel and non-Christian religion, then it is now idolatry with the accompanying hermeneutic of 'subversive fulfilment' that is able to make best sense of the Areopagitica, thus offering a more nuanced and faithful reading and transcending the interpretative impasse of what I would call 'reductionist' readings, which stress continuity at the expense of discontinuity and vice versa.

As we begin to look at the account itself, it is this anti-idol polemic that forms the 'discursive framing'[40] of Paul's speech. Paul's revulsion and paroxysm (*paroxysmos*) ('not a sudden loss of temper but rather a continuous settled reaction to what Paul saw'[41]) to a city submerged in idolatry bear remarkable similarity to God's reaction to idolatry in Deuteronomy 32, a passage already encountered in this study and one that has been argued is a template for Acts 17:

They provoked me (LXX *paroxynan me*) with foreign gods;
with their abominations they infuriated me.
They sacrificed to demons (LXX *daimonia*) not to God;
to gods whom they did not know.
New (LXX *kainoi*) and fresh ones came in, whom their fathers did not know.

---

39. Ibid., pp. 204–213.

40. A term used by Kenneth D. Litwak, 'Israel's Prophets Meet Athens' Philosophers: Scriptural Echoes in Acts 17:22–31', *Bib* 2 (2004), pp. 199–216 (211), quoted in Span, 'Areopagus', p. 527.

41. John R. W. Stott, *The Message of Acts: The Spirit, the Church, and the World*, BST (Leicester: Inter-Varsity Press, 1990), p. 278.

You have abandoned the God who begot you
and forgotten the God who feeds you. (vss. 16–19)[42]

It is this violent reaction to idolatry that sets both the scene and the mood for
Paul's speech and is able to explain an address that *at the same time* displays
elements of continuity in 'contact' within a context of discontinuity and 'attack'
– of the appealing nature of the gospel together with an appeal for repentance
in the face of universal judgment.

Moving on to Paul's speech itself, and with the anti-idol polemic always in
mind, I wish to demonstrate the Areopagitica's support and confirmation of
subversive fulfilment by offering it up as the solution to three puzzling features
within Paul's speech.

First, Paul's meaning in verses 22–24, consisting of the hapax legomenon
*deisidaimonesterous*, translated in the NIV as 'very religious', and the subsequent
reference to the inscription 'to an unknown God'. Interpretations here seem to
range on a spectrum from Paul's positively commending Athenian religion and
noting a definite point of contact between God and the unknown God, to that
of a simple negative ironic derision.[43] Once again within the context of idolatry
we are able to affirm both point of contact and point of attack.[44] Paul recognizes
at the same time both the Athenians' awareness of God and their ignorance of
him. It is a profound example of antithesis complemented by imaginal
revelation and common grace, of *thatness* (the awareness) and *whatness* (the
ignorance), of the innate itch to worship but only irritated by religious
scratching.[45]

Pardigon's conclusion here is that 'very religious' is essentially descriptive in
nature but

[a]t the same time, this religion is depicted as idolatrous, polytheistic to the extreme,
and as one of self-confessed utter ignorance concerning the identity and nature of

---

42. Quoted in Span, 'Areopagus', p. 526.

43. David Peterson, *The Acts of the Apostles* (Nottingham: Apollos, 2009), p. 494.

44. If we insist on using the term 'point of contact', perhaps the best way to understand
    it theologically is not the contact of a handshake but rather the contact of a rugby
    football scrum.

45. This is a helpful euphemism, as scratching the itch may seem immediately not only
    to identify the problem but to feign to solve it, bringing relief. However, rather than
    being healed, the itch is further incited. We might say here that what can only bring
    healing is not human scratching but the balm of Gilead, the Lord Jesus Christ.

the divine. This is not a religion in need of adjustment, complement or supplement (whether large or small), but one that needs to be replaced altogether by the gospel of Jesus Christ proclaimed by the apostle Paul. The Athenians are therefore the apex of idolatrous mankind.[46]

Missiologically here, Paul's reference is a good example of what Bavinck means regarding the 'point of attack':

This universal feeling of need or of anxiety is not in itself a thirsting for Christ, but we can use it in our preaching to bring to light the deeper need of man, the need for God. It appears to me that Paul chose such a point in his speech on the Areopagus when he began by referring to the altar of the unknown God. In this altar heathendom experienced its impotence and helplessness, its endless multiplication of gods and goddesses, and it was upon this confession that Paul laid hold in his sermon. Paul knew very well that his altar had nothing to do with the worship of the God who appeared to us in Jesus Christ, but Paul here heard the cry of misery, and this made it possible for him to sketch boldly the sole way of escape.[47]

---

46. Pardigon, 'Paul Against the Idols', p. 248. See also Bahnsen here: 'It is not beyond possibility that Paul cleverly chose this term precisely for the sake of its ambiguity. His readers would wonder whether the good or bad sense was being stressed by Paul, and Paul would be striking a double blow: men cannot eradicate a religious impulse within themselves (as the Athenians also demonstrate), and yet this good impulse has been degraded by rebellion against the living and true God (as the Athenians also demonstrate). Although men do not acknowledge it, they are aware of their relation and accountability to the living and true God who created them. But rather than come to terms with Him and His wrath against their sin (cf. Rom. 1:18), they pervert the truth. And in this they become ignorant and foolish (Rom. 1:21–22)' (Greg Bahnsen, *Always Ready: Directions for Defending the Faith* [Nacogdoches, Tex.: Covenant Media, 1996], p. 254).

47. J. H. Bavinck, *Introduction*, p. 140. Similar here is Francis Watson: 'The altar "to an unknown God" serves as a point of contact between Paul and his audience, but not in such a way as to establish a common ground on which both parties can agree. On the contrary, this small fragment of Athenian religious life is identified as the weak point which makes it possible to destroy the entire edifice . . . An obscure altar is the point at which the deconstruction of the Athenian sacred canopy can begin and that is the only sense in which this constitutes a "point of contact" between Paul and his audience' (Francis Watson, *Text and Truth: Redefining Biblical Theology* [Grand Rapids: Eerdmans, 1997], pp. 277–278).

The gulf separating paganism and Christianity is clear even in Paul's Areopagus address. Paul appears extremely polite and appreciative in his references to Greek philosophy, but toward the end of his discourse he makes a reference to 'repentance' and 'judgement,' and these two words place what he first said in a new light. Paul issued to the proud and to the wise a call to repentance (*metanoia*). Their profound notions of the deity stand condemned, and their paths lead to destruction, for the deity about whom they spoke such exalted things is not the true God who has shown mercy in Jesus Christ, but is what Calvin referred to as the *umbratile numen*, the nebulous all-pervading being, fabricated by us to fill the emptiness caused by our unwillingness to recognize the true God. Our argument may begin with the ideas of our audience, it may be modest, friendly, polite, and cautious, but it may never omit the call to repentance. This is the truth in the expression that our point of contact exists within an antithesis.[48]

Secondly, we have Paul's actual proclamation in contradistinction to this idolatrous ignorance. Here I note first the strong allusion of verses 24–25 to the anti-idol polemic of Isaiah 42:5, which, as Beale notes, has strong allusions back to the creational accounts of Genesis 1 and 2 and Exodus 20:11.[49] Verses 26–27 are notoriously complex and difficult to interpret and merit a detailed analysis that cannot be undertaken here.[50] However, with Witherington, Pardigon and Stonehouse, I wish to note the crucial distinction[51] between God's original positive creational design pre-fall (the parallel purpose infinitives 'to dwell' and 'to seek'[52]) and the current post-fall and more specifically post-Babel polytheistic idolatrous state, which describes in much more negative and pessimistic terms the result of this seeking ('perhaps reach out for him and find him'). What is most interesting here is the possible allusion to one of the 'set texts' of our study,

---

48. J. H. Bavinck, *Introduction*, p. 137.

49. G. K. Beale, 'Other Religions in New Testament Theology', in David W. Baker (ed.), *Biblical Faith and Other Religions: An Evangelical Assessment* (Grand Rapids: Kregel, 2004), pp. 79–105 (83–89).

50. For a clear summary of the issues see Ben Witherington, *The Acts of the Apostles: A Socio-Rhetorical Commentary* (Grand Rapids: Eerdmans, 1998), pp. 526–529. For a more detailed investigation see Pardigon, 'Paul Against the Idols', pp. 266–297.

51. 'Verse 27 ("seeking") does not explain the reason for the "dwelling" of v. 26 or the populating of the earth. Reciprocally, v. 26 does *not* describe "arrangements" designed to nudge man into "seeking" God, and even less ways that would allow man to find him' (Pardigon, 'Paul Against the Idols', p. 272 [his italics]).

52. In the sense of trusting and obeying.

Deuteronomy 32:8, and further evidence of the religious significance of Babel. As Pardigon notes:

> The result of Babel is the failure by the [*sic*] mankind as a whole to fulfil its most fundamental purposes as God's creatures: the unity of the race is broken into pieces (implying competition and enmity), the 'filling' of the earth becomes 'scattering,' and the 'seeking' of the one God and Lord becomes turning away to all sorts of gods and idols. Hence the perspective provided by the first clause of v. 26 involves at the same time the primordial design for all of mankind and man's failure to fulfill it because of his sinful and perverted pursuit of it. Eden is seen through, and colored by, the lens of Babel.[53]

Witherington, among others, notes the uncertainty of the results of this seeking, possibly countering a Stoic belief in natural theology. Moreover, the phrase 'reaching out' (*psēlaphēseian*) 'refers to the groping of a blind person or the fumbling of a person in the darkness of night':[54]

> The image is not an encouraging one . . . The overall effect of this verse is to highlight the dilemma and irony of the human situation. Though God is omnipresent, and so not far from any person, ironically human beings are stumbling around in the dark trying to find God. When one is blind, even an object right in front of one's face can be missed. The sentence does not encourage us to think the speaker believes that the finding of the true God is actually going on, apart from divine revelation. To the contrary the true God remains unknown apart from such revelation.[55]

However, it is in this despair and darkness that the message of the New Exodus can be proclaimed, a continuation of Isaiah 42 that Paul alluded to at the

---

53. Pardigon, 'Paul Against the Idols', p. 277. He continues in a footnote, 'We note with Witherington, *Acts*, 527, that Deut 32:8–9 (and its reference to Babel) correlates the multiplicity of nations with the multiplicity of gods. This means that God's plan to unite all nations under one God and one Lord in Jesus Christ is at the same time the fulfilling of the creational purposes and the undoing of Babel's curse, since the "new Jerusalem" is at the same time God's kingdom, God's temple, God's people, and the "new heaven and new earth." Acts 1:8 seems to fit very well this perspective: the spread of the church "to the end of the earth" leads to the turning of all peoples to the one God and one Lord. The gospel of Jesus Christ is therefore by nature a polemic against all forms of polytheism and idolatry' (p. 277, n. 178).

54. Witherington, *Acts of the Apostles*, p. 528.

55. Ibid., p. 529.

beginning of his address, 'a light for the Gentiles, to open eyes that are blind, to free captives from prison and to release from the dungeon those who sit in darkness' (vv. 6–7).[56]

Thirdly, and possibly most puzzling,[57] is Paul's decision to quote from the pagan poets Epimenides, 'For in him we live and move and have our being' (v. 28a), and Aratus, 'we are his offspring' (v. 28b). Given our context of the anti-idol polemic, and everything Paul has said up to now, Paul cannot be endorsing elements within the Stoic pantheistic worldview to support his case: 'Luke's point is thoroughly biblical and therefore antithetical to the "authorial meaning"'.[58] However, a simplistic Christianizing is also unfounded:

> Paul distances himself from a *carte blanche* acceptance of the quote by saying 'one of *your* poets.' He does not give it the meaning they do. Here Cornelius Van Til remarked, 'By this time the men that heard him knew that Paul did not mean the same thing as their poets had meant when they too said that men live and move and have their being and that they are the offspring of God.' To atomistically take a phrase from a poet who demonstrated his paganism in the rest of his writings, and then to 'sprinkle holy water on it' is to wrench it out of its larger context.[59]

A better, but admittedly more sophisticated, answer matches the sophistication of idolatry and the complexity of a religious anthropology that affirms simultaneously antithesis (ignorance) and restraint (knowledge). Unsurprisingly, those who hold to such a religious anthropology have, to my mind, come closest to what I believe Paul is doing here. Given the difficulty of articulation, it is worth giving a few representative statements. Bahnsen argues these statements are evidence of what Paul has established in verse 27: that despite God's

---

56. Beale, 'Other Religions', p. 85; Pardigon, 'Paul Against the Idols', p. 297.

57. Or, as Stonehouse admits, 'formidable': Ned B. Stonehouse, *Paul Before the Areopagus and Other New Testament Studies* (Grand Rapids: Eerdmans, 1957), p. 34.

58. Pardigon, 'Paul Against the Idols', p. 311.

59. Span, 'Areopagus', p. 566 (his italics). On v. 28, 'one of your poets', Stonehouse notes, 'In arguing from the quotations to his Christian conclusions Paul appears unmistakably to be attaching validity to them even while he is taking serious account of their presence within the structure of pagan thought. The formula confirms indeed an observation made previously: it intimates that the quotations are not offered as foundation features of the Pauline proclamation, but only quite subordinately and even incidentally to the main thrust of the address, which stands on strong biblical ground' (Stonehouse, *Paul Before the Areopagus*, p. 36).

not being far from humanity, human beings 'grope' for the truth as if blind. These statements by Epimenides and Aratus are therefore the gropings of unbelief that show true knowledge of God, but suppressed as in Romans 1:18–32:

> Within the ideological context of Stoicism and pantheism, of course, the declarations of the pagan philosophers about God were not true. And Paul was surely not committing the logical fallacy of equivocation by using pantheistically conceived premises to support a Biblically theistic conclusion. Rather, Paul appealed to the distorted teachings of the pagan authors as evidence that the process of theological distortion cannot fully rid men of their natural knowledge of God. Certain expressions of the pagans manifest this knowledge *as suppressed*. Within the philosophical context espoused by the ungodly writer, the expressions were put to false use. Within the framework of God's revelation – a revelation clearly received by all men but hindered in unrighteousness, a revelation renewed in writing in the Scriptures possessed by Paul – these expressions properly expressed a truth of God. Paul did not utilize pagan ideas in his Areopagus address. He used pagan expressions to demonstrate that ungodly thinkers have not eradicated all ideas, albeit suppressed and distorted, of the living and true God.[60]

I have just noted above how Stonehouse in his own exposition regards the quotations as incidental to the thrust of the address. However, he still admits that Paul 'appears to occupy common ground with his pagan hearers to the extent of admitting a measure of validity to their observations concerning religion'.[61] His answer is to remind us of the broader anthropological picture post-fall of those who suppress the truth:

---

60. Bahnsen, *Always Ready*, p. 261 (his italics). In support of this reading he draws on Berkouwer, who states regarding these verses, 'This is to be explained only in connection with the fact that the heathen poets have distorted the truth of God . . . Without this truth there would be no false religiousness. This should not be confused with the idea that false religion contains elements of truth and gets its strength from those elements. This kind of quantitative analysis neglects the nature of the distortion carried on by false religion. Pseudo-religion witnesses to the truth of God in its apostasy' (G. C. Berkouwer, *General Revelation* [Grand Rapids: Eerdmans, 1955], p. 145). See also Stonehouse, *Paul Before the Areopagus*, p. 30; Cornelius Van Til, *Paul at Athens* (Phillipsburg: L. J. Grotenhuis, n.d.), p. 12.

61. Stonehouse, *Paul Before the Areopagus*, p. 37.

As creatures of God, retaining a sensus divinitatis in spite of their sin, their ignorance of God and their suppression of the truth, they were not without a certain awareness of God and of their creaturehood. Their ignorance of, and hostility to, the truth was such that their awareness of God and of creaturehood could not come into its own to give direction to their thought and life or to serve as a principle of interpretation of the world of which they were a part. But the apostle Paul, reflecting upon their creaturehood, and upon their religious faith and practice, could discover within their pagan religiosity evidences that the pagan poets in the very act of suppressing and perverting the truth presupposed a measure of awareness of it. Thus while conceiving of his task as basically a proclamation of One of whom they were in ignorance, he could appeal even to the reflections of pagans as pointing to the true relation between the sovereign Creator and His creatures.[62]

Finally Pardigon says:

[The quotation's] very meaning is defined by what precedes, and therefore their function is rather that of an illustration which a skillful orator uses to help bring his point across to his audience, connecting his message to their thought world. The speaker is here appealing to the Athenians' *sensus divinitatis* in exactly the same way (in both its positive and negative dimensions) as when he mentioned their altar 'to an unknown god' in v. 23. Paul/Luke recognizes a true insight is hidden behind its erroneous interpretation found in the pagan doctrine proclaimed by Aratus, one that can be made to shine again when embedded in a biblical framework that gives it its proper meaning. By doing this 'translation,' the apologist turns the Athenians' own weapons against themselves, using their own confession of 'unknowing' (v. 23) and of being God's 'offspring' (v. 28) as incriminating evidence demonstrating their failure and guilt. This is very similar to the self-condemning silence of the idols and their 'witnesses' in Isaiah's anti-idol polemic trial scenes. It is therefore perfectly natural for the theme of God's universal judgment of idolaters to follow immediately thereafter.[63]

## 4. A contemporary example of subversive fulfilment (Sunni Islam)

In concluding this short chapter I would like to draw together a number of strands by offering a worked example of what a 'subversive fulfilment' theology of religions might look like in practice. To do this I draw on the recent work of

---

62. Ibid.
63. Pardigon, 'Paul Against the Idols', p. 313.

Christopher Flint, who has explicitly applied my approach to that of Sunni Islam.[64] Flint's methodology roughly follows my sequence in this chapter.

First, Flint notes the principial discontinuity between the personal and relational triune God of Christianity and the non-relational and undifferentiated monad of Sunni Islam. Salvation-narratively, the Christian gospel is dependent upon the nature of the Christian God. In the Qur'an, which denounces the Trinity, such a gospel narrative is denied — indeed, it is an impossibility. Consequently, and theological-propositionally,

> [u]nder pressure from a metanarrative hostile to the gospel, basic Christian propositions, when placed in an orthodox Sunni Islamic context, are radically distorted and denied. Are Christians,[65] or Muslims,[66] the true heirs of Abraham?[67] Are we condemned for rejecting,[68] or accepting,[69] Jesus in His divinity? Is Jesus the Son of God,[70] or only a prophet?[71] Was Jesus crucified,[72] or not?[73] Did Jesus bear the sins of His people,[74] or not?[75] Are the Scriptures unchanged,[76] or corrupted?[77] Who is

---

64. Christopher Robert Flint, 'How Does Christianity "Subversively Fulfil" Islam?', *SFM* 8 (2012), pp. 776–822. Flint is a former postgraduate student of mine now working with WEC in Indonesia. In the following quotations from Flint I replicate his own footnotes as my own.

65. Rom. 4:18–25; Gal. 3:29.

66. *Al-Baqarah* 2.135–140; *Á'lay Imrān* 3.65–68.

67. Cf. Chris Flint, 'God's Blessing to Ishmael with Special Reference of Islam', *SFM* 7.4 (2011), pp. 1–53.

68. John 3:36; 1 John 2:22–23; 5:12; 2 John 9.

69. *An-Nisā'* 4.48, 116. Of course, the doctrine of inseparable operation means that the Christian is not affirming in Christ a *rival* to God.

70. Matt. 3:17; Mark 9:7; Luke 1:35; John 3:16; Acts 9:20; Rom. 1:4; Heb. 4:14; 1 John 5:12.

71. *Al-Baqarah* 2.252–253; *Á'lay Imrān* 3.59–60, 84; *An-Nisā'* 4.163; *Bani Isrâîl* 17.111; *Az-Zukhruf* 43.81.

72. Matt. 27:35; Mark 15:27; Luke 23:33; John 19:18; Acts 2:23.

73. *An-Nisā'* 4.157.

74. Isa. 53:4–6; Gal. 3:13; Heb. 9:28; 1 Peter 2:24.

75. *Bani Isrâîl* 17.13–15; *Az-Zumar* 39.7; *An-Najm* 53.38–40.

76. Ps. 119:89, 152; Isa. 40:8; Matt. 5:18; 24:35; Mark 13:31; Luke 16:17; 21:33; 1 Peter 1:25.

77. *An-Nisā'* 4.46; *Al-Mā'idah* 5.18. This is the common Muslim interpretation of these verses today; apparently, however, Muslims initially accepted the Bible as authentic. See *Al-Baqarah* 2.41; *Á'lay Imrān* 3.3; *An-Nisā'* 4.136; *Al-Mā'idah* 5.46–47; *Yûnus* 10.94; *An Nahl* 16.43.

the eschatological mediator: Jesus,[78] or Muhammad?[79] For Christians, such doctrines are matters 'of first importance.'[80] The Qur'anic inconsistency with these, and other,[81] biblical teachings, then, renders Christianity and Islam irreconcilably discontinuous.[82]

Secondly, Flint notes the practical continuity between Christianity and orthodox Sunni Islam. *General revelation* can account for the distorted truth of Islamic doctrines, particularly concerning the nature and characteristics of Allah. *Imaginal revelation* is evident in an ethical code that overlaps the Decalogue. Although *remnantal revelation* might be seen in the Qur'anic narratives of Adam and Eve, Cain and Abel, and Noah, Flint himself argues that a stronger case for the origination of these 'biblical' stories (as well as the five pillars of Islam) is more likely due to *influental revelation*, whereby the author(s) had come into contact with heterodox Jewish and Christian sources.[83]

Thirdly, and having noted both discontinuity and continuity, Flint now looks at Sunni Islam through the prism of idolatry. Here he notes the distortions, displacements and denial of Yahweh in the doctrine of god compared to Yahweh, and the Qur'anic Isa compared to the biblical Jesus.

Fourthly, Flint comes to 'subversive fulfilment':

> Having identified several instances of 'suppression and exchange' in orthodox Sunni Islam, we may now run the process of idolatry in reverse, and so reveal Christianity as the 'subversive fulfilment' of these parasitically corrupted truths. Our analysis will in each instance involve three steps: *affirm* the deeper truth which has been perverted; *expose* the distortion; and *evangelise* by demonstrating that the gospel alone offers true satisfaction. Examples of this process are tabulated below:

---

78. 1 Tim. 2:5.

79. *Sahih Al-Bukhâri* 60.3.3340 (Khan 4.333–335); 97.19.7410 (Khan 9.304–306); 97.24.7440 (Khan 9.325–328).

80. 1 Cor. 15:3.

81. These include numerous historical contradictions. E.g. *Maryam* 19.27–28 and *At-Tahrîm* 66.12 conflate Miriam, the sister of Moses and Aaron, and daughter of Amram, with Mary, the mother of Jesus; *Al-Qasas* 28.38 identifies Haman as a servant of Pharaoh; *Al-Baqarah* 2.249 confuses King Saul with Gideon; and *Al-Qasas* 28.9 states Moses was adopted by Pharaoh's wife, not Pharaoh's daughter.

82. Cf. Gal. 1:6–9.

83. Flint does note the category of *demonic revelation* but believes *influental revelation* to be a much likelier source.

| Affirm | Expose | Evangelise |
|---|---|---|
| God will reward human obedience. | The rewards Allah offers in the Qur'an cannot satisfy,[84] and are themselves illicit.[85] | Mankind can ultimately only be satisfied by knowing and loving God. The barrier to this is not ontological necessity, but relational hostility. Thus those 'in Christ,' credited with Jesus' perfect obedience, can eternally delight in God as His adopted children. |
| God will punish human disobedience. | If human disobedience is simply the weakness inherent to our created nature,[86] then Allah is unjust to punish us for it; yet if human obedience is truly blameworthy, then Allah is unjust to overlook any of it.[87] | We are justly rendered guilty, ashamed, and worthy of condemnation, for disobeying God, because doing so betrays our personal hostility towards Him. While fear of damnation may be a proper inducement to initial repentance,[88] on-going fear of God is motivated on the basis of His forgiveness in Christ.[89] |

84. Prov. 27:20.

85. 1 John 2:16. Cf. *Al-Baqarah* 2.187 and *Al-Mā'idah* 5.90–91, which characterize wine as sinful and satanic, versus *Muhammad* 47.15 and *Al-Mutaffifīn* 83.25, which promise rivers of wine in heaven!

86. See Sam Schlorff, *Missiological Models in Ministry to Muslims* (Upper Darby, Pa.: Middle East Resources, 2006), p. 148.

87. *Al-Anbiyâ'* 21.47 describes Judgment Day as Allah's weighing on the scales each life *as a whole*. Jesus, however, warns that God's standard is actually required of each life *in every part* (Matt. 12:36). Thus, for any to be forgiven, the cross is all the more necessary to vindicate God's justice (Rom. 3:25).

88. Matt. 3:10; Luke 13:1–9.

89. Ps. 130:4; Matt. 18:21–35; Rom. 12:1; 1 Cor. 6:9–11, 18–20.

| Affirm | Expose | Evangelise |
|---|---|---|
| We need revelation and an intercessor. | The Qur'an and Muhammad cannot meet these needs: the Qur'an contradicts God's revelation through His prophets,[90] apostles,[91] and Son;[92] and Muhammad himself needs intercession.[93] | Only God's Son is close enough to God to fully reveal Him to us,[94] and to intercede for sinners:[95] thus His incarnation,[96] and His atoning death and resurrection, ever to intercede for us.[97] |
| We need divine forgiveness, and God requires a sufficient basis for granting it. | From those rebelling against God,[98] 'righteous deeds' and 'sincere worship' can never be an acceptable basis for forgiveness,[99] for even these works must be repented of.[100] | The only worthy basis for perfect forgiveness is perfect submission. Only Jesus thus fasted,[101] prayed,[102] and went on pilgrimage,[103] doing so even for His enemies' sake. |

---

90. Luke 24:25–27, 44–49; John 5:45–47.

91. Acts 3:17–26.

92. Heb. 1:1–4.

93. Al-Ahzâb 33.56; hence, whenever Muhammad's name is mentioned, Muslims immediately follow it with the prayer 'sallallahu alayhi wa-salam' (the prayers of Allah be upon him and peace). Yûnus 10.15 and Az-Zumar 39.13 portray Muhammad as being unsure of his own salvation.

94. Matt. 11:27; Luke 10:22.

95. Rom. 8:34.

96. John 1:18; 3:13.

97. Heb. 7:23–28. Note that only a *sinless priest* can perfectly intercede for sinners, and only an *immortal priest* can intercede for us perpetually. Muhammad is neither.

98. Titus 1:15.

99. Isa. 64:6.

100. Phil. 3:7–11.

101. John 19:28.

102. Heb. 5:7.

103. Luke 9:51.

| Affirm | Expose | Evangelise |
|---|---|---|
| God is One. | Being monadic, the 'oneness' of Allah can only be correlative to, and thus is necessarily dependent upon, the creation. Allah's 'oneness' therefore comes at the expense of his aseity. Allah's monadic impersonality also makes his communication to us inexplicable. | YHWH is both personal and absolute: qualities which arise from His nature alone, independently of creation.[104] Moreover, being triune, eternal, other-person-centred love,[105] is God's very essence;[106] a love which motivates,[107] and is supremely expressed to us in,[108] the gospel.[109] |

Finally, Flint notes the presuppositional apologetic and elenctic implications in adopting this subversive-fulfilment approach to Sunni Islam. It is worth quoting him at length here:

First, the evangelist seeks elements of truth which, by virtue of the *imago dei* and common grace, their conversation partner already accepts, in (often unconscious) opposition to their traditional Islamic worldview. This truth need not be anything overtly 'religious.' Second, the evangelist, building rapport, enthusiastically affirms that, as a Christian, s/he also holds this truth dear. Third, the evangelist proclaims how this truth is fulfilled in the gospel; thus, implicitly, if not explicitly, the incongruity between the particular truth the Muslim here recognises, and the wider Islamic worldview s/he confesses, is exposed. Finally, the evangelist calls for repentance and faith. Since truth and unbelief are incompatible, ultimately, the choice the Muslim faces is inevitable: either submit to Christ, in Whom alone

---

104. See John Frame, *Cornelius Van Til: An Analysis of His Thought* (Phillipsburg: P & R, 1995), p. 65.
105. The self-centred love of a monad is not genuine love as the Bible describes it, but narcissism.
106. 1 John 4:8, 16. Cf. D. A. Carson, *The Difficult Doctrine of the Love of God* (Wheaton: Crossway, 2000), p. 45.
107. John 3:16.
108. Rom. 5:8.
109. Flint, 'How Does Christianity "Subversively Fulfil" Islam?', p. 807.

their glimpse of truth may legitimately be held;[110] or else, in hatred of Christ, snuff out that glimmer of light also, and retreat yet further into the darkness.[111]

Consider the following personal example. During the 'fasting month' a couple of years ago, I asked some of my Muslim friends the reason why Muslims fast in Ramadhan. 'There is much wisdom in it,' they told me, 'but one reason is that it helps us show compassion for all the poor and starving people in the world.' 'Why is that?' I asked. 'Well,' they replied, 'you can't have true compassion for a starving person just by hearing about them: to be truly compassionate, you need to experience what they experience.' 'Really?' I asked. 'So you believe that true love and compassion doesn't just mean hearing about someone from a distance, but actually suffering what they suffer?' 'Yes,' they replied. 'Wow, as a Christian, that's what I believe, too! Let me ask you, who do you believe is the most loving and compassionate being of all?' They responded, in line with the opening verse of almost every *surah* in the Qur'an, 'God is the most merciful and compassionate.' 'Really?' I asked, 'That's what I believe too! But as you've said, true compassion means not staying at a distance, but suffering what they suffer, and experiencing what they experience. So, if God really is the most compassionate to us, what does that mean? Well, it means that He also needs to suffer what we suffer, and experience what we experience.' They sat for a moment in silence, not knowing how to respond to this. Then I continued, 'And that's Who Jesus is! Because God really is the most merciful and compassionate, He didn't just stay at a distance, He came down to earth as a man, Jesus Christ, to suffer what we suffer and experience what we experience. That's why He died on the cross – because He is really the most merciful and the most compassionate, just as we said earlier.'[112]

In this short summary of Flint's theological analysis and missiological application, I hope one can see the potential the subversive-fulfilment model offers in providing a biblically orthodox theology of religions. Like Flint, it is my hope and prayer that many other Christians will take up this model and apply it with increasing sophistication and nuance in their encounters with the religious Other.

## Conclusion: the church as a subversive-fulfilment community

At the beginning of this chapter I quoted affirmatively Cornelius Plantinga, who stated that 'the church serves as a witness to the new order, as agent for it, and

---

110. 2 Cor. 10:5; Col. 2:2–3.

111. John 3:19–21.

112. Flint, 'How Does Christianity "Subversively Fulfil" Islam?', p. 812.

as first model or exemplar of it'.[113] Subsequent to making this statement, I am conscious that much of the rest of this chapter on missiology has been ecclesiologically rather 'light'. To put it another way, much of my talk on the gospel being the subversive fulfilment of the religious Other has been precisely that – talk: what one might call a verbal missiological methodology. Vital and fundamental as this methodology is for our understanding of gospel communication, contextualization and apologetics, I wish to recognize, albeit briefly, that subversive fulfilment has, indeed *must have*, an embodied, ecclesial perspective that recognizes the centrality of witness of the Christian community, and can be an antidote to those Enlightenment idols Christians can often unwittingly bow down to: rationalism and individualism.[114]

Here I am not talking about the ecclesial practice of *possessio*, but the necessity of the church's living in the eye of the world (cf. Col. 4:5; 1 Thess. 4:12; 5:15; 1 Tim. 3:7) in order to arouse envy (cf. Phil. 2) by reflecting the glory and greatness of Christ (Eph. 5:16; Phil. 1:27; Col. 4:5–6). The missiological application of subversive fulfilment should therefore always have an ecclesiological angle, with the church embodying the sort of life the religious Other longs for.[115] Although not writing about other religions specifically, Francis Schaeffer's words are still applicable if we see the religious Other as being a subset of the 'world': 'Our relationship with each other is the criterion the world uses to judge whether our message is truthful. Christian community is the ultimate apologetic.'[116]

One of the more extended and influential explorations of this perspective can be found in the work of Lesslie Newbigin.[117] For Newbigin, the church is the community chosen by God to advertise God's saving work in its life and verbal witness; it is the preview and anticipation of the future kingdom. The church is therefore the hermeneutic of the gospel,[118] wrought in Jesus' image, providing

---

113. See n. 3 above.

114. I am indebted to Jon Putt for highlighting this to me.

115. J. H. Bavinck recognized this element himself: 'Time after time in the New Testament it appears that this witness can bear fruit only if the church which utters the witness itself lives as "glorified" body. Christ spoke of the city set on a hill, the light of the world. "By this shall men know that ye are my disciples, if ye have love one to another" (John 13:35)' (J. H. Bavinck, *Introduction*, p. 46).

116. Francis Schaeffer, *The Mark of the Christian* (Downers Grove: InterVarsity Press, 1970), pp. 14–15.

117. Recalling that Newbigin was aware of J. H. Bavinck's concept of *possessio* and Kraemer's term 'subversive fulfilment'.

118. Lesslie Newbigin, *The Gospel in a Pluralistic Society* (London: SPCK, 1989), pp. 222–231.

the lenses by which its members understand the world. To put it in my terms, the Christian community therefore subverts the religious culture around it, offering fulfilment at the same time.[119] Indeed, with more development, I wonder whether understanding the church as embodying subversive fulfilment to the religious Other might offer some clarifying light to what can be quite heated intra-evangelical debates on both the mission of the church and our understanding of the church as 'missional'.[120]

---

119. Newbigin offers six characteristics of the church that accomplish this: (1) a
    community of praise subverts a culture of scepticism by its reverence and trust, (2)
    a community of truth provides a plausibility structure to rival others, (3) a community
    of local service acts as God's embassy to a neighbourhood, (4) a community active
    in discipleship equips its people to act as priests in the world (cf. 1 Peter 2:5, 9; John
    20:19–23), (5) a community of mutual responsibility subverts individualism and
    acknowledges multiplicity, and finally, (6) a community of hope subverts a culture
    marked by despair and offers future security (ibid., pp. 227–232).

120. For a helpful description of the recent history of these discussions see Timothy J.
    Keller, *Center Church: Doing Balanced, Gospel-Centered Ministry in Your City*
    (Grand Rapids: Zondervan, 2012), pp. 251–263. Keller's own prescription of the
    marks of a mission church is to my mind biblically balanced and resonates well with
    the theology of religions and missiological implications as outlined in this study: (1)
    the church must confront society's idols, (2) the church must contextualize skilfully
    and communicate in the vernacular, (3) the church must equip people in mission in
    every area of their lives, (4) the church must be a counterculture for the common
    good, (5) the church must itself be contextualized and should expect non-believers,
    enquirers and seekers to be involved in most aspects of the church's life and ministry,
    and (6) the church must practice unity. For two recent influential and different
    'takes' on this mission/missional question see Christopher J. H. Wright,
    *The Mission of God's People*, ed. Jonathan Lunde, Biblical Theology for Life (Grand
    Rapids: Zondervan, 2010); Kevin DeYoung and Gregory D. Gilbert, *What Is the
    Mission of the Church? Making Sense of Social Justice, Shalom and the Great
    Commission* (Wheaton: Crossway, 2011).

# 9. 'BUT I HAVE RAISED YOU UP FOR THIS VERY PURPOSE . . .': PASTORAL PERSPECTIVES ON THE PURPOSE OF THE RELIGIOUS OTHER

The material that is presented from all sides about the various religions has increased and broadened so incredibly that there is urgent need for more scholarly work. We can no longer be satisfied with the old formulas and ideas. It is no longer possible to declare that Buddha, Zoroaster, and Muhammad are simply deceivers and instruments of Satan . . . Christians especially, who stand on the foundation of faith, have a difficult and serious task in this study of different religions. They must penetrate more deeply than they have thus far into the importance of all people for the history of God's kingdom. They must search for the relationship and the difference that exists between pagan religions and the Christian religion, and they must discover God's plan, insofar as Scripture and history reveal it.

(Herman Bavinck)[1]

## Introduction

I concluded the previous chapter with a clarion call consisting of two blasts. The first, for evangelicals to take up my definition of the religious Other, together with its gospel corollary of 'subversive fulfilment'. The second, to apply this

---

1. Herman Bavinck, *Essays on Religion, Science, and Society*, ed. John Bolt (Grand Rapids: Baker, 2008), p. 55.

model missiologically into a variety of contexts where the gospel encounters specific instantiations of the religious Other. I am satisfied that I have completed the foundational theological leg of this relay and that the baton can now safely be passed on to others who can take up the running.

However, regarding the religious Other, there remains at least one outstanding question that demands our attention, the answer to which might bring us some theological closure as well as offering much-needed succour to that bewitched, bothered and bewildered believer I identified at the start of this study. Christians proclaim that Jesus is Lord and that there is indeed 'no other name'. And yet throughout history many 'lords' and 'names' have abounded, and, if global sacralization is true, will continue to abound. The great world religions of Islam, Judaism, Hinduism and Buddhism, together with the myriad of smaller religious traditions, have millions, even billions, of followers and are having influence over all facets of human existence and experience: individual, familial, social, cultural, public and political. Therefore, from the perspective of Reformed theology, *Why has God ordained the rise and flourishing of other religions, and what purposes do they serve in the divine economy?* In other words, can we articulate a teleology of the religious Other that might give us some much-needed orientation in the universe of faiths?

Before offering some constructive suggestions to the above questions, my analysis up to this point should enable us to eliminate immediately not only a number of erroneous 'purposes' in particular, but also a number of erroneous ways of both conceptualizing and investigating 'purposes' in general. Concerning the latter, I must say two things. First, given the Reformed presuppositions affirmed throughout this work, any reflection on cause and purpose must be conducted within the constraints of a doctrine of divine providence that affirms both God's complete foreordination and sovereignty of all events, together with an affirmation of human, angelic and demonic free agency, and, crucially, responsibility that deems those parties accountable for their actions.[2] However contrary idolatry may be to God's revealed will, given this 'compatibilist' or 'divine deterministic' view of God's providence, we cannot entertain that the cause and purpose of non-Christian religions are due to libertarian acts of free will outside God's decretive will and control.[3] For whatever reasons, God has positively permitted the rise and flourishing of non-Christian religions.[4]

---

2. This is to affirm 'liberty of spontaneity' over and against 'liberty of indifference'.

3. For more on this see John M. Frame, *The Doctrine of God: A Theology of Lordship* (Phillipsburg: P & R, 2002), pp. 119–159.

4. We note with Calvin that there is 'no mere permission in God' (John Calvin, *Concerning the Eternal Predestination of God*, tr. J. K. S. Reid [Cambridge: J. Clarke, 1982], p. 176).

Secondly, while I believe and shall hopefully demonstrate that God's revelation allows us to enquire profitably into divine purposes, and particularly the divine purposes behind non-Christian religions, any such enquiry must carry with it an epistemological health warning which soberly reminds us that our human knowledge is always ectypal and never archetypal, true but limited. Given my characterizing of the religious Other as idolatrous, such limitations are particularly acute, for the 'why' of non-Christian religions can be categorized as a subset of the broader question as to why God has been pleased to permit sin, which necessarily entails permitting false religion. In answering this question, perhaps more than any other, it is worth remembering Deuteronomy 29:29: 'The secret things belong to the LORD our God, but the things revealed belong to us and to our children forever, that we may follow all the words of this law.' There will always be real mystery here, not in the sense of irrationality, but in the sense that we have no access to the truth here apart from special revelation, and even then there remain 'hidden things'. Therefore, while revelation allows us to say some things, even many things, about God's purposes in non-Christian religions, there are purposes in God's providence into which we cannot and should not want to pry.

Moving to purposes deemed 'off limits' to us, recall once again my definition of non-Christian religions as 'sovereignly directed, variegated and dynamic, collective human idolatrous responses to divine revelation behind which stand deceiving demonic forces'. We also remember how the gospel of Jesus Christ is both their 'subversion' and their 'fulfilment'. This definition and relationship to the gospel provides us with a fence and foundation with which to explore the teleological question.

Let me start with the affirmation of the 'subversive' side. First, and contrary to pluralism and some forms of inclusivism, non-Christian religions qua collective and systematized worldviews cannot be instrumentally salvific, being principially antithetical to the gospel.[5] Secondly, neither can they act as a *preparatio evangelica*, *if* by *preparatio* we mean a 'stepping stones' approach that sees them in a smooth and continuous trajectory with the gospel of Jesus Christ, where this gospel 'fulfils' them in the sense of lack or ignorance. Thirdly, given

---

5. Regarding the question of soteriology, I refer readers once more to my previous work in this area: Daniel Strange, *The Possibility of Salvation Among the Unevangelised: An Analysis of Inclusivism in Recent Evangelical Theology* (Carlisle: Paternoster, 2001); 'General Revelation: Sufficient or Insufficient', in Christopher W. Morgan and Robert A. Peterson (eds.), *Faith Comes by Hearing: A Response to Inclusivism* (Downers Grove: InterVarsity Press; Nottingham: Apollos, 2008), pp. 40–77.

the comprehensive nature of idolatry and its truth-supressing characteristics, and given that 'every religion is an indivisible, and not to be divided, unity of existential apprehension',[6] it is false to say that non-Christian religions are *simpliciter* 'truthful' or even that they contain isolated sparks of verity mixed with error. Difficult as it is, we can talk only in terms of 'supressed truth'. Fourthly, and as a result of the previous point, contrary to Gerald McDermott's significant work in this area,[7] Christians cannot learn from other religions, *if* by 'learning' we mean the reception of new or even neglected truth in the answers or *whatness*[8] the other religions might give to the perennial questions of existence, the 'magnetic points' concerning God, humanity and the world. Not only might such a view call into question the necessity and comprehensiveness of Scripture, but if non-Christian religions are fundamentally idolatrous, and idols by nature are parasitic and counterfeit, then no matter how good the counterfeit is, it can never simply enhance the original except through contrast.

Coming now to the 'fulfilment' side, while I affirm the antithesis and principal discontinuity between the gospel and non-Christian religions, simultaneously we must always recognize that practical continuity accounted for in the perpetuity of the *imago Dei*, together with the doctrine of common grace: that general and variegated operation of the Holy Spirit whereby he restrains sin and its consequences and excites to civic goodness. Recognizing this divine work means it is not possible to give a blanket or simplistic singular negative purpose to non-Christian religions. As long as we are able to talk about divine purposes behind God's common grace, we are able to talk about the divine purposes behind non-Christian religions, remembering John Murray's statement in his own work on common grace: 'A divine act may have diverse grounds according to the aspect from which it is viewed'.[9] In God's providence a divine act can be an instantiation both of divine curse and of divine blessing.

With the above limits in mind I shall shortly discuss the purpose of other religions. In what follows I shall argue that in God's sovereignty other religions serve, in a perspectival and polyvalent way, the purposes of God himself, God's

---

6. Hendrik Kraemer, *The Christian Message in a Non-Christian World* (London: Edinburgh House, 1938), p. 115.

7. See Gerald R. McDermott, *Can Evangelicals Learn from World Religions? Jesus, Revelation and Religious Traditions* (Downers Grove: InterVarsity Press, 2000).

8. To use J. H. Bavinck's term once again.

9. John Murray, *Collected Writings of John Murray*, 4 vols. (Edinburgh: Banner of Truth Trust, 1977), vol. 2, p. 99.

world and God's people. For God they are able to display his glory in judgment and mercy. For God's world they evidence divine restraint, the ultimate purpose of which is to serve God's glory. Finally, for God's people not only might they act as gospel *preparatio*[10] and gospel *possessio*,[11] but they can be used by God didactically and disciplinarily in the sanctification of his church, which exists for his glory.

Or, to put all this a little more poetically, we might say that non-Christian religions are not glorious, and yet God can be glorified through them, are not truthful, and yet God can teach us truth through them, are not good, and yet God can bring good through them, and are not salvific, and yet serve God's purposes in salvation.[12]

Before embarking on our task proper, there is one final introductory remark I must make. As has been emphasized throughout this study, rather than focusing on one non-Christian religion I have primarily been concerned with providing a dogmatic sketch of non-Christian religions in general. The same *modus operandi* continues into this final chapter in that all the divine purposes I am about to outline can be applied in variegated form to all non-Christian religions. However, while space precludes a detailed discussion, it would be remiss of me not to mention now that *in addition to* (but I do not believe contradicting) everything I shall go on to say, specific divine purposes are attached to both Judaism and Islam.[13]

Even within the narrow constraints of Reformed covenantal theology (as opposed to a biblical-theological framework like that of dispensationalism) there is still diversity regarding the continuing role and purposes of ethnic Israel, with much of the biblical focus revolving around exegeses of Romans 9 – 11, and Romans 11:26a in particular. There are those who do not hold to the permanent

---

10. In a restricted sense that I shall outline below.

11. To use J. H. Bavinck's term and outlined in the previous chapter.

12. Although I am responsible for the work in this final chapter, I wish to note a collaborative element in that I have integrated (with their permission) some fine insights by a number of my graduate students: Timothy Edwards, Paul Gibson, Luke Foster, Steffen Jenkins and Alex Richardson. I am profoundly indebted and grateful for our discussions both in and out of class on these issues and for their keen insights that have enhanced my own work.

13. With regard to Judaism and the place of Israel in Christian theology, one of the best recent surveys can be found in Adam Sparks, *One of a Kind: The Relationship Between Old and New Covenants as the Hermeneutical Key for Christian Theology of Religions* (Eugene: Pickwick, 2009), pp. 73–117.

replacement of Israel by the church,[14] and who argue, like Moo for example, that before Christ's return a great majority of ethnic Jews will be converted.[15] If so, a *sui generis* purpose for God's permitting Judaism is to keep this religion alive until this mass conversion.[16]

Concerning Islam, it has often been argued that Muslims are in some sense descended from Ishmael and therefore recipients of God's blessing in Genesis 17 to Ishmael. However, Flint has recently offered a detailed exegetical, theological and historical critique of such positions, which I find to be persuasive on this issue and rules this direct connection invalid.[17]

## 1. For God: glory in power, judgment and mercy

Anyone who either has read the introduction to this chapter or is vaguely acquainted with Reformed theology should already know *the* answer to the question asked earlier, 'Why has God ordained the rise and flourishing of other religions, and what purposes do they serve in the divine economy?' The triune God causes and permits anything and everything ultimately for his own glory: *soli Deo gloria*. Perhaps more than any other Reformed theologian, it is Jonathan Edwards[18] who has shown that God works all things for his glory; in particular, for 'the manifestation of God's *perfections*, his *greatness*, and *excellency*'.[19] In his

---

14. A position that might be called 'strict supercessionsim'.

15. Douglas J. Moo, *The Epistle to the Romans*, NICNT (Grand Rapids: Eerdmans, 1996), pp. 719–725.

16. Sparks himself opts for a 'modified supersessionism': 'This position maintains the Old Covenant has been fulfilled in Christ but does not maintain that the Church is the "new Israel" and does not consider God to have rejected the Jewish people. It insists the Jews are still in covenant relationship with God, and have a continuing and future place in God's plans for the world. However, this does not in any way remove the need for Jewish people to accept Christ as their Messiah for their salvation. A separate way of salvation for Jewish people does not exist' (Sparks, *One of a Kind*, p. 116).

17. Christopher Robert Flint, 'God's Blessing to Ishmael with Special Reference of Islam', *SFM* 7.4 (2011), pp. 1–53.

18. And I should also add the more contemporary popularizer of his work, John Piper.

19. Jonathan Edwards, 'Concerning the End for Which God Created the World', in John Piper (ed.), *God's Passion for His Glory: Living the Vision of Jonathan Edwards* (Wheaton: Crossway, 1998), p. 214 (his italics). 'All that is ever spoken of in the

sovereignty the triune God is not only the efficient cause of everything but also the final cause of everything. While there may be a number of subordinate ends, all flow into the one ultimate end of his glorification. More recently, James Hamilton Jr. has argued that the centre of biblical theology is God's glory in salvation through judgment, a centre, he contends, that best encompasses all other proposed 'centres' of biblical theology, and one 'that all the bible's themes flow from, exposit and feed back into'.[20] We are within standard Reformed territory to say that all things were created by Christ and for Christ (Col. 1:16), including thrones, dominions, rulers and authorities, which (given Col. 2:15 and Eph. 6:12) includes evil supernatural powers such as demons.[21] Unpacking this a little further, John Piper notes 'the apex of the glory of Christ is the glory of his grace . . . and the apex of this grace is the murder of the God-man outside Jerusalem around A.D. 33. The death of Jesus Christ was murder. It was the most spectacular sin ever committed.'[22] By his death, Christ defeated the 'powers' at the cross (Col. 2:15). Piper, linking Colossians 1:16 and 2:15, argues that Christ will be 'more highly honoured' because he allowed Satan (and implicitly the demons) to do evil for millennia before defeating them at the cross, than had he eliminated Satan immediately.[23] Given the constraints of this study, such axiomatic truth can be but asserted here with little further justification.

Given this assertion, however, what *does* require further reflection and justification is precisely how the sovereignly ordained, 'spectacularly sinful' and essentially God-denying worship of the religious Other can glorify the living God. Furthermore, if we are to answer such a question in terms of God's glory in judgment, we need to recognize that it is not simply whether we can account for his acts of judgment of individuals, but whether we can account for his judgment of the hugely successful organization of religious structures that seem to tower over our world and eclipse Christianity. Once again, it is fairly standard Reformed grammar to state that while it is God's desire for every individual considered in isolation to be saved (1 Tim. 2:4; 2 Peter 3:9; Ezek. 33:11), at the

---

Scripture as an ultimate end of God's works, is included in that one phrase, the glory of God; which is the name by which the ultimate end of God's works is most commonly called in Scripture; and seems most aptly to signify the thing' (ibid., p. 242).

20. James M. Hamilton Jr., *God's Glory in Salvation Through Judgement* (Wheaton: Crossway, 2010), p. 53.

21. John Piper, *Spectacular Sins: and Their Global Purpose in the Glory of Christ* (Wheaton: Crossway, 2008), p. 33.

22. Ibid., p. 12.

23. Ibid., p. 49.

same time, each individual is not in isolation, and it more greatly furthers the display of God's glory to his elect if *some* individuals are not saved. The question, then, is why are not *as few as possible* lost in order to display that glory? What is it about God's excellencies that requires not only the loss of many, but also the growth of vastly successful idolatrous systems of false worship?

As it relates directly to displaying God's glory, the macro-purpose I wish to unpack is that the Bible's presentation of the nature of non-Christian religions indicates that they must be understood as the impulse of opposition in fallen humanity towards the Creator God, who has made himself known in Christ Jesus. Idols and false gods feature in the narrative of Scripture as God's rivals. They are those things that, falsely credited with divine presence, vie for the affections of God's people, those things that contend with God. By virtue of Scripture's portrayal of this rivalry, idols are constantly set up in comparison with the one true God, a contest in which they always emerge as ultimately powerless and defeated. By their very deficiency, therefore, idols are constantly pointing to God's excellencies, his holiness, his power, his faithfulness and his mercy. Inasmuch as the narrative of Scripture provides us with a portrait of God, a meditation on his attributes and actions, idols function as a foil, a device to throw that portrait of God into sharper relief. They fulfil, so to speak, a hermeneutic function. God allows the religious Other to flourish because then its final defeat will glorify him all the more. It is only when this impulse of opposition is recognized that its purpose in God's economy may be understood properly.[24]

### a. The paradigm of the exodus

Exegetical support for such an argument takes us directly to Paul's vindication of the glory of God in Romans 9 – 11. In the face of opposition the apostle provides an essential framework for a discussion of the purposes of God in allowing the rise of idolatrous false religion, with God's dealing with Pharaoh serving as a paradigm of how he deals with the reprobate.[25] The opposition of

---

24. The idea here is very similar to the section in chapter 5 entitled 'Divine exploitation without divine assent', where I describe the excellent chapter by Daniel I. Block, his 'Other Religions in Old Testament Theology', in David W. Baker (ed.), *Biblical Faith and Other Religions: An Evangelical Assessment* (Grand Rapids: Kregel, 2004), pp. 43–78.

25. In a similar way that Abraham was paradigmatic of God's dealings with the faithful. In this sense paradigmatic does not necessarily mean typical: both of these were in many ways special cases; but that very specialness enables us to see the pattern that is then replayed elsewhere.

Pharaoh is certainly a religious phenomenon connected to his commitment to the false gods of Egypt, as seen for example in the audience that Moses and Aaron have with Pharaoh in Exodus 7.[26] Both Romans 9 – 11 and the exodus indicate that false religion has been ordained by God to display his glory – a glory displayed in judgment but primarily made known in salvation.

### i. Glory in judgment

In Romans 9:17 Paul notes Scripture's speaking to Pharaoh. The apostle has already begun with God's proclamation in Exodus 33:19 that God will have mercy on whom he will, and uses Pharaoh to add the corollary that 'he hardens whom he wants to harden' (v. 18). In Romans 9:17, Exodus 9:16 is quoted: 'I raised you up for this very purpose, that I might display my power in you and that my name might be proclaimed in all the earth.' The link between this proclamation through the *raising up* of Pharaoh and God's glory is made explicit in verse 23: it is specifically to make known to the elect 'the riches of his glory' that God *judges* Pharaoh. Already it can be demonstrated that the display of glory through judgment required first an exaltation of Pharaoh.

Moreover, Paul's exegesis of Exodus 33:19 speaks directly to our theme: a display of God's glory is exactly what Moses had just asked for in Exodus 33:18. God's choice in displaying mercy is at the heart of his name and is required for God to display his glory. Therefore, it is fitting for Paul to show how God's work in history displays his glory *by* displaying his freely chosen acts of mercy. If the exodus had already said to Pharaoh that his rise and fall would proclaim God's name, then Paul is not introducing anything alien by saying that God's mercy is better perceived by the elect in view of God's visible judgment.

The exodus had involved a dramatic and extravagant display of God's power, which in turn required God to *keep* hardening Pharaoh's heart so that subsequent plagues and judgments would be seen. Exodus mentions Pharaoh's heart hardening no fewer than seventeen times. God promises to harden his heart to bring about the plagues, to cause his chase in the desert, and to cause the army to follow into the Red Sea,[27] and God indeed does so.[28]

---

26. Exodus states that 'Pharaoh then summoned wise men and sorcerers, and the Egyptian magicians also did the same things by their secret arts' (Exod. 7:11). As Mackay notes, 'Throughout the ancient world magic was inseparable from religion, and in every court there would be priests who practised such black arts' (John L. Mackay, *Exodus: A Mentor Commentary* [Fearn: Mentor, 2001], p. 138).

27. Exod. 4:21; 7:3; 14:4, 17.

28. Exod. 7:13, 22; 8:15, 19, 32; 9:12, 34–35; 10:1, 20, 27; 11:10; 14:8.

This hardening is explained on three occasions. Each time it is for the sake of miraculous signs, judgment on Egypt and the salvation of his people, so that 'the Egyptians will know that I am the LORD' (Exod. 7:3–5) and 'that you may tell your children and grandchildren . . . and that you may know that I am the LORD' (Exod. 10:1–2) and 'I will gain glory for myself through Pharaoh and all his army, and the Egyptians will know that I am the LORD' (Exod. 14:3–4). The rescue of the Israelites is insufficient to achieve God's purpose of showing forth his glory: *simultaneous judgment on Egypt is needed.*

Having established this, we may go further and now analyse precisely how God has operated to display his glory. As already seen in this study, Paul in Romans 1:18–32 has identified God's visible attributes as *creator* as precisely what is seen, and that is suppressed instead of glorified. One might speculate that God could have redeemed Israel from Egypt by making Egypt propitious to them and letting them go (as with Cyrus), or by wiping out Egypt at a stroke (as with the firstborn in the Passover), or simply by miraculously transporting his people.[29] The question remains then as to why God chooses such a prolonged hardening and series of judgments. One answer is that the very features of Egyptian false religion are shaped in such a way as to allow Yahweh to reveal his identity as the sovereign creator through the judgments he exacts in the plagues.[30]

First, we are presented with a contest in which Yahweh triumphs over his rivals through the cycle of the plagues, where a number seem to be focused specifically to challenge particular Egyptian gods.[31] While I recognize that this is not a point the text explicitly highlights,[32] the idea of Yahweh's triumphing

---

29. See Philip in Acts 8:39.

30. J. A. Motyer, *The Message of Exodus: The Days of Our Pilgrimage* (Leicester: Inter-Varsity Press, 2005), p. 118, n. 7.

31. This e.g. could explain the positioning of the ninth plague, darkness, at the head of the third cycle of three plagues as challenging Ra, the sun god. In popular culture this reading of the plagues as being targeted against particular deities is expressed in Cecil B. de Mille's film *The Ten Commandments*, where, after the tenth plague, Pharaoh is shown presenting his firtborn's corpse to an idol of Osiris, who is found to be impotent in the face of Yahweh's judgment.

32. In conceding this point, Mackay offers the explanation that the text was written for later generations, for whom the details of Egyptian religiosity were of little relevance. However, given that Egyptian religion did exert an attraction for later generations, as seems to be reflected e.g. in Ezek. 8:10, we might be better off to see this as rooted in the generations immediately following the exodus, for whom

over the gods of Egypt is implicit in the narrative of the plagues and becomes explicit in the way later generations look back at these events. This note comes first in the announcement of the final plague, where Yahweh declares that he will perform judgment on all the gods of Egypt as he slays the firstborn (Exod. 12:12). Precisely the same language is repeated in the summary of the exodus events in Numbers 33:4. As Yahweh executes judgment on the gods of Egypt, he shows them to be powerless to defend their worshippers and impotent to enslave his elect. Hence it is that Exodus 12:12 concludes with the assertion 'I am the LORD' – as the Israelites behold the death of the firstborn, so they see Yahweh's judgment on the gods of Egypt, which makes him known as Yahweh.

Moreover, and secondly, we return to a theme encountered throughout this study: creation, conflict resulting in de-creation, and re-creation. As part of creation, God has set a series of boundaries: for example, between land and sea, and light and darkness. He prepares the land for crops and the multiplication of man and animals. Now in a fitting divine judgment of de-creation, the plagues break these boundaries within Egypt: water creatures (frogs) are no longer contained in rivers, darkness is no longer contained in night, and so on. Fruitful plants are destroyed and animals are killed and cannot multiply. Human fruitfulness is reversed with the death of each firstborn. The climax of this creative de-creation is when God newly creates dry ground in the Red Sea for the Israelites and then removes that water/land boundary to kill the Egyptians. The Israelites have to go to a land fit for creation purposes, because Egypt has become a land of de-creation. All this proclaims that Yahweh is the sovereign Creator God, but for it to be revealed required Pharaoh's heart to be hardened and for him to be raised up, which includes his entire empire (the greatest in the world at the time) with therefore the greatest religion of the world. It was a victory over the *gods* of Egypt.

In summary we must note that this account of God's purposes highlights the inadequacy of Gerald McDermott's suggestion that God's purposes are governed by the principle that 'God respects the freedom of his creatures'.[33] While he argues that God is reacting to a cosmic rebellion and preserving man's free will, I say that it is God who takes the initiative in raising up, hardening and judging Pharaoh. In considering the flourishing of religions at a time when God's

the Egyptian gods would not have been relevant precisely because of their comprehensive defeat in the exodus (Mackay, *Exodus*, p. 142).

33. Gerald R. McDermott, *God's Rivals: Why Has God Allowed Different Religions?* (Downers Grove: InterVarsity Press, 2007), p. 160.

people are heavily outnumbered, we should notice that the manifestation of God's glory in the exodus required the *apparent* helplessness of his people.

Thus God permits sinners to continue in false religions so that he might show his wrath against them, with the larger purpose of displaying his glory to his elect. God's end in permitting and finally judging religions is 'the magnification of God's great glory for the eternal enjoyment of his chosen people'.[34] As Edwards explains, the elect's 'happiness' will rise as they wonder at 'God's free grace in bestowing . . . their own enjoyments' in contrast to the fate of the vessels of wrath.[35] The plight of the damned may thus be understood to serve the happiness of the saved in their Saviour. The act of 'beholding the sight of the great miseries of those of their species that are damned will double the ardour of their love, and the fullness of the elect angels and men' as they witness the justice of God and are made to feel more acutely the grace they enjoy.[36] Paul's argument in Romans 9 – 11 is centred on the sovereign freedom of God – his vindication of the purposes of God is dependent on his characterization of saving grace as an opposition to the sinful will of fallen humanity. The freedom that governs Paul's argument is not the freedom of humanity, but the freedom of God.

## ii. Glory in salvation

While God's glory is displayed in his judgment on the false religion he has ordained, it is right to observe that 'it will by no means follow from thence that he delights in the creature's misery for its own sake'.[37] Instead, the glory that is revealed in judgment serves the glory that is revealed and enjoyed through salvation. Commenting on these sections in Romans, Schreiner notes:

> The mercy of God is set forth in clarity against the backdrop of his wrath . . . Thereby God displays the full range of his attributes: both his powerful wrath and the sunshine of his mercy. The mercy of God would not be impressed on the consciousness of human beings apart from the exercise of God's wrath, just as one delights more richly in the warmth, beauty and tenderness of spring after one has experienced the cold blast of winter. . . . God's ultimate purpose is to display his glory to all people. His glory is exhibited through both wrath and mercy, but especially through mercy.[38]

---

34. John Piper, *The Justification of God: An Exegetical and Critical Study of Romans 9:1–23* (Grand Rapids: Baker, 1993), p. 189.

35. Edwards, 'Concerning the End', p. 226.

36. Ibid., p. 226, n. 85.

37. Ibid., p. 221, n. 80.

38. Thomas R. Schreiner, *Romans*, BECNT (Grand Rapids: Baker, 2008), p. 519.

As the argument of Romans 9 – 11 builds, it becomes clear that God's glory is most acutely expressed in his work of salvation. In response to the opposition of false religion, this glory is God's 'sovereign freedom in having mercy on whomever he wills'.[39] Paul shows that it is primarily in the free act of mercy that God displays himself to be the sovereign creator who establishes his glory in creation. It is in mercy that God is glorified, as it is in mercy that the creative sovereignty of God is most acutely displayed. This logic continues in Paul's reference to Hosea in Romans 9:24–26. God's act of election is characterized as a work of creation, as it 'calls into being the opposite state of affairs that preceded the election'.[40] In addition to this, the reference to 'the living God' in Romans 9:26 'resonates nicely with Paul's claim in 4:17 that God is the one who "calls the things that do not exist into life"' so that His work of election serves 'as a prime example of God's life giving power'.[41]

This creative power is most acutely displayed in God's opposition to – and ability to overcome – the apparent realities of fallen creation. If creation displays God's glory as a sovereign work *ex nihilo*, then salvation all the more vividly displays the glory of God in a sovereign work *ex oppositione*.[42] Consequently, it is in God's mercy that there is the most vivid display of God's glory. In Paul's argument the historical movement from fall to restoration is ordained by God to display his glory. God's creative power is displayed as he establishes salvation history (*Heilsgeschichte*) for his people through 'fallen' history (*Unheilsgeschichte*). The fall of Adam, the hardening of Pharaoh and the apostasy of Israel are all made to serve the purposes of God's glory, as all provide the context for the display of his mercy.[43] God's dealings with Israel in Romans 9 – 11 exemplify his dealings with humankind as a whole. The false religion of apostate Israel – with

---

39. Piper, *Justification of God*, p. 103.

40. Sigurd Grindheim, *The Crux of Election: Paul's Critique of the Jewish Confidence in the Election of Israel* (Tübingen: Mohr Siebeck, 2005), p. 149.

41. Robert Jewett, *Romans: A Commentary* (Minneapolis: Fortress, 2007), p. 601.

42. I am indebted to Luke Foster for this idea.

43. This language is drawn from Beale, who observes in Rom. 9:17, 'The whole purpose of the *Heilsgeschichte* program: it is for Yahweh's glory. . . . The overarching theme of Ex 1–14 may now be stated: Yahweh hardens Pharaoh's heart primarily to create an Israelite *Heilsgeschichte* necessarily involving an Egyptian *Unheilsgeschichte* – all of which culminates in Yahweh's glory' (G. K. Beale, 'An Exegetical and Theological Consideration of the Hardening of Pharaoh's Heart in Exodus 4–14 and Romans 9', *TrinJ* NS 5.2 [1984], pp. 129–155 [149]).

its roots in the idolatry of Adam – provides a context in which the creative mercy of God may be the more dramatically displayed.

## b. The pattern of redemptive history

The paradigm established in Exodus and used by Paul in Romans 9 – 11 is one recapitulated throughout redemptive history. The purpose of idols is to act as a foil for Yahweh's glory: as empty, idols cannot save, and Yahweh is therefore glorified as the sole saviour; as evil, they must be defeated as enemies of Yahweh and his people, and Yahweh is therefore glorified by defeating other gods. Examples are legion but a few will suffice, some of which I have already mentioned in this study.

### i. Old Testament

In 1 Samuel 5 the ark is brought to the temple of Dagon in Ashdod. The Philistines' intention here is one of triumphal gesture: their people and their god have triumphed over Israel and their god. The ark will be displayed in Dagon's house like a trophy. But the reader of 1 Samuel knows that in truth the Philistines have defeated Israel because God is punishing their sin (in particular the sin of Eli and his sons) in line with the word he sent to his prophet back in 1 Samuel 3:11–14. In this context Yahweh makes clear his superiority over Dagon by leaving his idol battered and bruised after one night, and mutilated after the second.[44] Moreover, we clearly hear an echo of God's dealings with Egypt in the exodus, for the narrator in 1 Samuel 4:8 and 6:6 shows the Philistines themselves making this connection.

I mentioned the story of Joseph in a previous chapter, to which we can now add the story of Daniel. In both cases the religious magicians and sorcerers prove unable to interpret the king's dream, but Joseph and Daniel are shown the interpretation. In both passages there is a note of Yahweh's getting glory for being the only one who can reveal what is to come.[45]

In 1 Kings 18:20–40 the contest between God and idols is literal and didactic, the whole encounter being set up for the people of Israel as a revelation of the

---

44. Indeed, it is difficult to escape the sense that we are meant to see Dagon as bowing down before Yahweh, so that even the Philistines' false god is shown to worship Yahweh.

45. In Genesis, Joseph repeatedly attributes his insight not to himself but to God (e.g. Gen. 41:16, 25, 28), his attestation that God not only knows but controls the future (Gen. 41:32), and especially the response from Pharaoh in Gen. 41:38. In Daniel these themes are repeated throughout the book.

true God (v. 24). Generally, the story teaches that the name of the true God is Yahweh and not Baal. However, the particulars of the narrative tell us more: Baal is exposed as absent, powerless, unconcerned for his own name and, ultimately, to all intents and purposes dead; Yahweh, by contrast, is present, powerful, jealous for his name and, above all, living. This is not new information for the Israelites; rather, truths already known about the covenant God are brought home by a devastating contrast with his rival. Baal involuntarily helps a recalcitrant Israel to see Yahweh more clearly.

The striking 'idol' passages in Isaiah function in a similar way. Yahweh's power to predict the future is presented by contrast with idols' inability to do the same in Isaiah 41:21–29 and 48:3–5, as is his power to save in 43:10–12 and 45:20, and to guard from fear in 41:5–10; and the comparison with idols also establishes his incomparability in 40:18–20; 44:6–20; and 46:5–7.[46]

Idols are thus forcibly co-opted for and integrated into Scripture's revelation of the true God, where their distortions of deity serve as a foil for Yahweh.

*ii. New Testament*

When we move to the New Testament, we encounter similar themes: the God and Father of our Lord Jesus Christ is glorified by delivering out of the darkness of idolatry. Not only does God save those who trust in him, whereas idols cannot save, but he is shown even to save those who formerly trusted in idols. Supremely, God is glorified by triumphing over the powers in the cross. Not only does he defeat these idols, but he does so at the moment of their apparent triumph by using their power against them. As before, space allows only edited highlights.

Paul's missions in Lystra, Athens and Ephesus offer us a nice triptych of idolatry's being confronted with the gospel. In Lystra we have the first occasion that Luke has related of gospel preaching to pagans. First, God has not left himself without witness and, given the importance of witness language elsewhere in Luke-Acts, this would seem to function to leave people without excuse, so that they should have sought God rightly. Secondly, Paul describes the pagan religiosity of the Lystrans as 'vain', that is, they are pointless. So we have a contrast set up between the gospel of the only true and living God and pointless idolatry.

In Athens, by now a very familiar narrative to us, Paul does include a purpose clause when speaking of how God has providentially ordered history up to this point: 'so that they would seek him and perhaps reach out for him and find

---

46. See Block, 'Other Religions', pp. 71–74.

him' (Acts 17:27). However, this cannot be understood as meaning that God's purpose was that people should find him by their own exploring, much less by man-made religiosity. While this is hinted at grammatically,[47] the context is crucial, for Paul begins by speaking of the Creator as a God 'unknown' (v. 23), and by the end will have referred to the whole of history up to this point as 'times of ignorance' (v. 30 ESV), so that the fumbling after God of verse 27 is shown to be fruitless. As with Lystra, this is not because God has withheld himself – he is not far off. The function of this, then, is to shift the focus to the new age of salvation history that has been inaugurated by the resurrection of Jesus (vv. 30–31), which sets up a contrast between the former times (that were fruitless) and the gospel era.

Finally, in Ephesus, idolatry is more directly considered. The striking thing about the narrative here is that Demetrius and his fellow rioters are concerned that Artemis (whom they proclaim 'great') will be dethroned (Acts 19:23–41). What we have here is a replaying of the same theme we saw with Yahweh's judgment on the gods of Egypt, his forcing Dagon to bow before him, and Isaiah's merciless taunting of Babylonian idolatry. The false gods are powerless and need to be saved; this then serves to show the glory of the gospel through its contrast with other religions.

Moving to the New Testament epistles: having already noted the seminal passage of Romans 9, we note the complementary passage of 1 Thessalonians 1:8–10:

> The Lord's message rang out from you not only in Macedonia and Achaia – your faith
> in God has become known everywhere. Therefore we do not need to say anything
> about it, for they themselves report what kind of reception you gave us. They tell
> how you turned to God from idols to serve the living and true God, and to wait for his
> Son from heaven, whom he raised from the dead – Jesus, who rescues us from
> the coming wrath.

Whereas Romans 9 is concerned with those who remain in unbelief, this passage shows that the same purpose is also served in those who turn from idols to the living and true God. Because of their response, the word of God, accompanied by the report of their faith, has gone forth 'everywhere' (1 Thess. 1:8). Thus God is glorified, both in those whom he is pleased justly to harden in unbelief, and in those whom he is pleased graciously to turn to himself.

---

47. Within this verse, after the initial infinitive, the verbs are all in the optative mood – indicating that they describe a condition contrary to fact (finding God).

Finally, in the book of Revelation we see the repeated note of praise that surrounds the throne of God, a praise rooted in two realities: the Lamb's redemption of people from every tribe, tongue and nation to be a kingdom of priests (Rev. 5:9–10; 7:15–17; 11:17–18a; 15:3–4; 19:6–8) and his judgments upon those who would oppose his reign and oppress his people (Rev. 11:18b; 16:5–7; 18:1 – 19:4), so that when the Lamb wraps up history, he will have used other religions to display his glory, by judging them but by chiefly redeeming a countless multitude from their number. Eschatologically, these other religions' ultimate defeat will magnify God's victory, as God wins glory for himself by showing himself more powerful than all his rivals.

## 2. For God's world: divine restraint through religious cohesion and confusion

We move now from the direct, ultimate and theocentrically focused end of God's glory to more proximate and specific ends by focusing first on the purpose of non-Christian religions for God's world, and then for God's people.

As already noted, non-Christian religions are by nature antithetically de-creational. Left completely unrestrained and to their own (de)vices, humankind would unravel and self-destruct, the effects of which we noted in my exposition of idolatry – effects listed starkly in the societal sins outlined by Paul in Romans 1:19–32. The language of negation the Bible uses in its description of idolatry indicates this essential opposition to the preservation of created order. The idolatry described in Deuteronomy 32 is associated with 'not-gods' that belong to 'not-people', which thus expresses a negation of the Creator's work. Idolatrous religion itself is opposed to creation and order – an opposition that remains even as it is, appropriated by God for his purposes.

However, as noted in chapter 2, the antithesis between true and false religion is principial rather than practical, with the *imago Dei* serving as a metaphysical 'check' to the reality of the antithesis, and the restraint of sin by the Holy Spirit in common grace serving as an ethical 'check'. Because of the common grace order worked by the Holy Spirit, a work that is external and in opposition to the essential nature of idolatrous religion and fallen humanity, non-Christian religions are instrumental in accomplishing the purposes given to common grace in restraining sin and exciting to civic righteousness. It is through the prism of the *imago Dei* and common grace that we are able to speak further of God's purposes in the religious Other.

First, the *imago Dei* variously described and unpacked throughout this study in terms of Calvin's *sensus divinitatis*, *semen religionis* or J. H. Bavinck's *thatness* (together with his 'magnetic points') can function as a divine restraint on sin and its effects, thus preserving the order of creation. Just as God graciously preserves in animals a fear of humankind (Gen. 9:2), he uses false religion to preserve among humankind a fear of God.[48] As Calvin notes, God uses false religion to serve as a 'bridle' to sustain 'the thought that God is to be feared' and so places a restraint on the 'depraved affections of the flesh'.[49] Calvin's imagery of the bridle is able to preserve the notion of the coercive nature of God's action and the rebellious nature of false religion.

Secondly, given the relational aspect of the *imago Dei* together with the social aspects of idolatry, social and societal precepts that flow from idolatrous worship will have some restraining effect on sin. One can argue that God has caused the rise of organized religions, rather than allowing each person to worship their own idol, as a means of graciously providing agreed social norms within religious societies that save those societies from unrestrained evil and that provide an element of social cohesion.[50]

Thirdly, while we see restraining grace in God's allowing large religious cultures to benefit from the shared norms that produce civic righteousness, it is also true that allowing idolatrous religion to take too strong a hold might be a worse cure than the disease itself. To prevent a unified homogenous idolatrous religion, God has ordained a diversity of idolatrous religions. This ordination of diversity corresponds to the twin commands he has forced rebellious humankind to obey: 'Fill the earth and subdue it' (Gen. 1:28). As we saw in chapter 4, the scattering presented in the Babel narrative and the subsequent diversity of human culture and religion begin to affect the first part of this command. God acts to ensure that there is neither a 'self-securing homogeneity' as humankind is forced to scatter, 'nor a scattering of autonomous parts' as all of humankind is forced to share in the obedience to God's will.[51] As a

---

48. John Calvin, *A Commentary on Genesis*, tr. John King (London: Banner of Truth Trust, 1965), p. 290.

49. Ibid., p. 343.

50. E.g. Islam's prohibition on alcohol should protect from drunkenness (Eph. 5:18); prohibition of outright murder is a common religious tenet; marital arrangements often give at least some measure of security to women; the common proscription of witchcraft limits some of the demonic influence on society. Of course, each of these can be held up against the law of Christ and be found wanting, just as any counterfeit will be. Nevertheless, they do provide some level of civic righteousness.

51. Walter Brueggemann, *Genesis* (Atlanta: John Knox, 1982), p. 99.

consequence, humanity is forced to image a 'plural-unity' that reflects the character of its triune creator.[52]

In addition, the diversity of religion serves to ensure that humanity works to 'subdue the earth'. We have already seen that religion as a whole is used by God to express divine power and restrain the effects of sin. The presence of diverse religions itself exemplifies the restraint of sin that God has purposed false religion to achieve. Ethnic diversity 'compartmentalizes and decentralizes humanity' and so 'checks the flow of evil and power from one group to the next'.[53] By imposing diversity on false religion God restrains the consistent expression of its opposition to his purposes and his people. In God's restraining grace, on the one hand, multiple strong religions with incommensurable and therefore insurmountable doctrinal, ethical and cultural differences will not readily amalgamate, or even cooperate. And yet, on the other hand, even *within* these strong religions we often witness internal diversity, division and dissolution that too can have a restraining effect on the power and influence of any religion.[54]

In summary, the diversity of false religion is imposed on humanity by God. The Babel narrative interprets the scattering and diversity of humanity as an act of both grace and judgment as God forces rebellious humanity to fulfil his creational purposes. As God fulfils these creational purposes it is to be expected that even false religion will display the marks of God's creative work in the world: truth, beauty and order will all be evident in other religions and cultures. Just as diversity itself has been imposed on false religion, it is necessary to recognize that these creative works of the Spirit are themselves in opposition to the essentially de-creative character of the religions in which they take place. False religion, like the apostate from true religion, can offer evidences of the Spirit's work – but without true religion this is a work that results ultimately only in condemnation.

Before moving on, it is worth noting how both these functions of restraint and excitation serve the ultimate end of God's glory. In his seminal essay on common grace John Murray indicates that the most immediately apparent purpose of common grace is 'to serve the purpose of special or serving grace, and saving grace has as its specific end the glorification of the whole body of God's elect, which in turn has its ultimate end in the glory of God's name'.[55]

---

52. Mark Kreitzer, *The Concept of Ethnicity in the Bible: A Theological Analysis* (London: Edwin Mellen, 2008), p. 126.

53. Ibid., p. 19.

54. E.g. Sunni and Shi'ite groups within Islam.

55. Murray, *Collected Writings*, p. 113.

He continues:

> Common grace then receives at least one explanation from the fact of special grace, and
> special grace has its precondition and sphere of operation in common grace. Without
> common grace special grace would not be possible because special grace would have
> no material out of which to erect its structure. It is common grace that provides not only
> the sphere in which, but also the material out of which, the building fitly framed
> together may grow up into a holy temple of the Lord.[56]

As we saw in chapter 2, common grace provides the necessary scaffold of historical continuity in the world out of which particular redemptive history can flow.
In terms of the argument I have just outlined, we can say that the *diversity* of
false religion affords a protection for God's people as they seek to fulfil the
Creator's purposes in the true plural-unity of the church that seeks to restore his
image over the face of the whole earth. On the other hand, were *unifying* religions
absent, God's missionary people would be unable to perform general cultural
analytical and contextualization tasks prior to evangelism, as each individual
would require what now each religious group requires.

However, having noted that special grace is a precondition of the operation
of common grace, Murray notes that other divine purposes may be at work:

> What the other ends promoted by common grace may be it is precarious to conclude.
> Of one thing we are sure that the glory of God is displayed in all his works and the
> glory of his wisdom, goodness, longsuffering, kindness and mercy is made known in
> the operations of his common grace. In subservience to that ultimate end it may well
> be that a group of proximate reasons is comprised within that goal of glorifying him,
> of whom and through whom and to whom are all things.[57]

How, and in whatever degree, non-Christian religions display God's common
grace, they glorify him.


### 3. For God's people: *preparatio* and *possessio*, didactic and disciplinary

We move finally to look at a number of ways in which non-Christian religions
serve God's people – in their salvation and in their discipleship, remembering

---

56. Ibid.
57. Ibid., p. 117.

that for John Murray this is the most immediately apparent purpose of common grace: 'Common grace provides the sphere of operation of special grace and special grace therefore provides the rationale for common grace.'[58] We start with the two concepts discussed in the previous chapter, *preparatio* and *possessio*.

### a. Preparatio *and* possessio

Having seemingly rejected the notion of other religions being a *preparatio evangelica*, it might seem strange to return to the term now. However, I believe non-Christian religions can act as a *preparatio* providing that term is understood carefully within the context of subversive fulfilment. We have recognized the antithetical difference and oppositional nature between the gospel and the religious Other, which rules out any theory of *preparatio* in terms of humanity's being 'gradually led'[59] from false faith to true faith, implying that idolatrous religions and the gospel are but alternative ends of a 'continuum'.[60] However, we have also recognized the need for a 'point of attack'[61] for the elenctic enterprise, and therefore the necessity of the *thatness* of the religious other, 'because without this "thatness", this objective fact of religious consciousness . . . missionary communication would be utterly impossible'.[62] Just as the language of the Bible was drawn from sociocultural contexts shaped by false religion, the concepts and forms expressed by that language are intelligible only within those contexts. In the same way that today 'the missionary exhales pagan ideas with every word', revealed religion must work within the language and frameworks of idolatrous religion.[63] This appropriation, as noted previously, is neither 'accommodation' nor 'compromise', but *possessio*.

In the light of this *possessio* we are able to say yet again that God's power is expressed as non-Christian religions are forced to provide a framework within

---

58. Ibid., p. 116.

59. McDermott, *God's Rivals*, p. 160.

60. Gerald R. McDermott, *Jonathan Edwards Confronts the Gods: Christian Theology, Enlightenment Religion, and the Non-Christian Faiths* (Oxford: Oxford University Press, 2000), p. 128.

61. A more accurate term than a 'point of contact'.

62. Paul Visser, *Heart for the Gospel, Heart for the World: The Life and Thought of a Reformed Pioneer Missiologist, Johan Herman Bavinck (1895–1964)* (Eugene: Wipf & Stock, 2003), p. 172.

63. J. H. Bavinck, *An Introduction to the Science of Missions*, tr. David H. Freeman (Phillipsburg: P & R, 1960), p. 242.

which God's saving revelation might be expressed, while the saving work itself remains external to the false religion against which it works. The *possessio* of idolatrous religion in the purposes of God serves not to mitigate its offence; rather, it intensifies its judgment. The providential works of God are 'represented as works of goodness or mercy to his people',[64] but serve merely to render the falsely religious 'without excuse'.[65]

I am able to elaborate on this a little more by speaking into the two related but distinguishable categories demarcated in the previous chapter: missional theologizing (gospel communication) and ecclesial theologizing (gospel discipleship).

### i. Missional theologizing

Concerning missional theologizing, note that the pseudo-similarity and false counterfeiting of idolatrous religion expounded in the previous chapter in terms of *imaginal, remnantal, influental* and *demonic* revelation can all serve providentially as a form of *preparatio*. While I disagree with his own overly positive construal of *preparatio*, Gerald McDermott's analysis of a number of Jonathan Edwards's *Miscellanies* supports the notion of the *prisca theologia* not simply in the realm of knowledge of God the Creator but also of knowledge of God the Redeemer. The interaction between God's revelation to Israel and the knowledge of this revelation within the surrounding cultural context suggests that God has 'planted types of true religion in the religious systems that were finally false'.[66] God in his wise irony causes something of the true religion, for example animal sacrifice as a type of propitiation, to be taken over and corrupted by pagan religions in the form of human sacrifice. That human sacrifice becomes a fuller type of Christ's oblation on the cross than the animal sacrifice types. Thus what Satan intends as a cruel and evil perversion is used by God towards the redemption of a people when the gospel reaches them.

In a similar vein, but within the category of 'demonic revelation', Niehaus comments on the purpose of God's common grace, of demonic parallels between ancient Near Eastern religions and the Old Testament:

> The purpose was to make such ideas somewhat familiar to God's people so that when he actually broke into the historical plane and acted, his acts would be recognisable against their cultural background. God's revelation was so dynamic and (in his holiness) so

---

64. Edwards, 'Concerning the End', p. 227.
65. Rom. 1:20.
66. McDermott, *Jonathan Edwards*, p. 124.

challenging (cf. Ex. 20:18–19) that a background preparation for at least some aspects of that revelation was necessary for his people.[67]

And again, having commented that these parallels evidence truth even in idolatrous religions, he concludes thus:

> Truth in such forms could have no saving power. But it did prepare a matrix of thought, a background of theological understanding, so that when God did truly appear and did such things as the pagans claimed for their gods – instituting covenant, giving laws, commanding conquest and extending his kingdom, even by signs and wonders – his revelation would come to a people who had some theological preparation for it. In this way God was glorified even by the distortions of pagan religion, for even in their darkness the pagans retained or obtained common grace reflection of his truth. It is the fuller revelation of that truth that now makes true life possible, and also makes possible all the works of Christian theology.[68]

It bears repeating that while there is a correspondence between Christianity and the religious Other that makes such gospel communication possible, there remains an essential distinction. The correspondence must not be structured as a 'continuum' but rather as an opposition.[69] At this point it might be helpful to observe that the truth and validity of any form lies not in the form itself but in the revelation by which it has been appropriated. In his *Institutes* Calvin makes the distinction between 'matter and sign' that provides a framework in which this relationship may be understood.[70] He notes that the difference between 'crude and coined sliver' is that 'the one is merely in the natural state', while the other, 'stamped with an official mark . . . receives a new valuation'.[71] In a similar way it is only the revelation of true religion that raises the forms and language of human culture from their 'natural state'. The claim to express a truth apart from the 'official mark' of revealed truth is to engage in a counterfeit – however close the correspondence might be. Therefore, despite such external correspondence, an essential – and internal – opposition remains.

---

67. Jeffrey J. Niehaus, *Ancient Near Eastern Themes in Biblical Theology* (Grand Rapids: Kregel, 2008), p. 29.

68. Ibid., p. 181.

69. McDermott, *Jonathan Edwards*, p. 128.

70. John Calvin, *Institutes of the Christian Religion*, ed. John T. McNeill, tr. Ford Lewis Battles, 2 vols., LCC (Philadelphia: Westminster, 1960), vol. 2, p. 1290.

71. Ibid., p. 1295.

With these elements of correspondence and continuity, therefore, and *from the perspective of faith* of one rescued out of a non-Christian religion by Christ and regenerated by the Spirit in this life, it is legitimate to look back and recognize the Holy Spirit's common grace *preparatio* here. Even the truth that is distorted within other religions can be used by God pedagogically. So while non-Christian religions can never be constituted as a 'lawful'[72] conduit of saving grace, the pervasive legalism often encountered within them *can* be used pedagogically by God to teach respect for his law, which providentially becomes fortuitous preparation for seeing Christ as the fulfilment of the law and realizing that law cannot give the perfection needed to live in God's presence.[73]

However, without such a saving work of subversive fulfilment, and for those who die as non-Christians, this *preparatio* takes on another meaning, becoming the basis for God's just judgment, for we remain accountable for the good gifts from God that are spurned, for in spurning the gifts we are spurning the Giver. For those lawbreakers without Christ, this is a preparation not for eternal life but rather eternal death.[74]

---

72. To use Karl Rahner's term.

73. The despair often reached in our inability to keep God's holy law is one of Satan's main weapons against fallen humanity (he is 'The Accuser'). What I am suggesting here is that in his sovereignty God providentially uses these 'satanic' elements in non-Christian religions to drive his elect to Christ.

74. Here seems an appropriate place to mention briefly the phenomenon of dreams and visions of Isa, recorded particularly within Islam and believed by many Christians to be a legitimate modality of revelation in the conversion of Muslim-background believers. For a spectrum of views (both academic and popular) regarding this phenomenon see the following: John K., 'Dream Encounters in Christian and Islamic Societies and Its Implications for Christian Ministry and Mission', *Global Missiology* 1.3 (2005), available online at http://ojs. globalmissiology.org/index.php/english/article/view/425/1086 (accessed 4 Oct. 2013); Scott Breslin and Mike Jones, *Understanding Dreams from God* (Pasadena: William Carey Library, 2004); Dennis McBride, *An Evaluation of Muslim Dreams and Visions of Isa (Jesus)* (2010), available online at http://www.yoyomaster.com/ ministry.file/IsaDreams.pdf (accessed 22 Aug. 2012); Rick Kronk, *Dreams and Visions: Muslims' Miraculous Journey to Jesus* (Pescara: Destiny Image Europe, 2010). When discussing soteriological matters in previous work, I have argued that the whole tenor of the book of Acts and the sending of the church into the world seems to suggest the normativity and maybe even necessity of the human messenger in conversion: 'In all the biblical accounts of conversion, it appears that

## ii. Ecclesial theologizing

Concerning ecclesial theologizing, we start by once again returning to Murray's seminal study on common grace. Concerning salvation, while recognizing the radical spiritual and moral change in regeneration, Murray still notes elements of continuity between a person pre- and post-conversion:

> His personality is not changed, and the various endowments and qualities, gifts and possessions, with which he has been blessed by God are not destroyed . . .
> He enters the kingdom of God and exercises his membership and place in it as a person formed and moulded as to his distinct individuality by the antecedents and processes that fall outside the sphere of special grace. We need but remind ourselves of Paul as a student who sat at the feet of Gamaliel or of Moses learned in all the wisdom of the Egyptians. Long lines of preparation in the realm of common grace, designed in the plan of God's all comprehending providence, have fitted the most blessed of God's servants for the particular role they were to play in the kingdom of God.[75]

If this is true, then are we able to extrapolate from the individual to a non-Christian religion and culture? As I have argued previously, culture is the outworking of a people's religion, and because of the *imago Dei* and common grace that religion will produce many good cultural artefacts, a flourishing religion will produce many treasures that further the creation mandate to fill and subdue the earth. Moreover, when the church flourishes in that culture, it will encounter new situations that will cause previously unanswered

---

all people come into contact with a human messenger. Commenting on the Cornelius incident in Acts 10, Helm notes that it is "unacceptedly abstract and hypothetical to say . . . if Cornelius had not met Peter he would not be saved. Scripture does not invite us to break up the causal nexus of events as revealed and to speculate about each link in the chain"' (Strange, 'General Revelation', p. 76). However, what I also suggest is that if God uses other modalities, of which dreams would be one, 'then they can be seen as providentially pre-evangelistic and part of God's wonderful sovereignty in calling his people to himself' (ibid., pp. 76–77). While we may argue as to what category of revelation dreams fall into, if such phenomena fall more properly into the realm of common grace, then they can be called *preparation*, as outlined in the main text. Concerning the theological and missiological implications of this phenomenon, more work needs to be done.

75. Murray, *Collected Writings*, p. 114.

questions to be asked, and will thus enrich the theology of the church universal.[76]

We can go even further by arguing that when genuine *possessio* takes place in a new religio-cultural context, then the theology of the universal church is enriched. John Frame in his distinctively perspectival way defines the discipline of theology as 'the application of the Word of God by persons to all areas of life'.[77] Therefore, for him ethics encompasses the whole of theology because no

---

76. One of my graduate students, Steffen Jenkins, a native of Spain, gave me an example of this from his own country's history: 'One outworking of the cultural mandate is fine art. There is virtually no limit to the different objects, methods and effects available. Within the culture of Christendom, a great deal of visual art depicts living things, which is forbidden in Islamic art. This has given rise to an art form based on the beauty of geometric shapes and the interplay of colours and surfaces. That means that an art form that has not been exploited within Christendom has flourished in the Islamic world. The architecture of southern Spain post 1491 (the fall of Granada) has been greatly influenced, in particular, by tiling mosaics that use precisely this feature of Islamic art, which were introduced during the conquest and discovered as the border receded towards Morocco. Islamic art has in this way enriched Spanish culture. This is not to say that a Christian culture would necessarily be incapable of producing such art; however, God has chosen to provide the restrictions which allow such art to flourish through the rise of Islam, and, through common grace, the world has benefited from the result. When the church grows and flourishes in this culture, seeking to put everything under the Lordship of Christ, the same people now find on their hands an artistic tradition which they produced under Islam but who now wish to serve the Lord. The Christian world would not benefit by accommodating to a rule that proscribes the depiction of living things. On the contrary, here we have a trivial example of *possessio*, whereby the fruit of that rule can be claimed by Christ's wider body while the rule itself is not. Christian artists anywhere may adhere to the rule for the sake of producing particular art, just as a poet will adhere to certain conventions of rhyme and metre. Local churches in the former Islamic nation may well for missionary reasons or for the sake of weaker brethren continue to adhere to the rule. From early on in the process, the world and especially the church would benefit from art that was originally nurtured by another religion. One might say that it is a picture of the victory of God's anointed King being celebrated by other governments in Ps. 68:28–31, and of the riches which had adorned their idolatry being made part of Yahweh's temple (Isa. 60:4–13, Rev. 21:24).'

77. John M. Frame, *The Doctrine of the Knowledge of God* (Phillipsburg: P & R, 1987), p. 81.

theology is legitimate that does not answer the question of what we ought to do and think.[78] If we further consider that 'ethical judgment involves the application of a *norm* to a *situation* by a *person*',[79] we shall approach the theology of evangelized indigenous missionary fields with an expectant optimism. Different persons in unfamiliar situations will apply the same norm differently; but this application is theology as defined above. As Tennent observes, the global church is presenting Western theology with a host of new useful matters for consideration, and this is what we should rightly expect.[80] Once again, often these new matters for consideration arise not as a result of geography or culture, but specifically because of the history of another world religion among the new believers.

### b. Didactic and disciplinary

Faithful *possessio* implies Christ's both subverting and fulfilling a religious culture. But what about an 'un-possessed' non-Christian religion? To quote the title of McDermott's book and a question that will have been buzzing around the head of the attentive reader, *Can evangelicals learn from other religions?* As I said in the introduction to this chapter, given the idolatrous nature of the religious Other, surely the answer must be negative, if we mean untarnished truth not available previously. As already stated, not only would this have implications for our doctrine of Scripture in terms of the closure of the canon, but given the nature of the religious Other, how can it be that we could learn truth from a counterfeit? But is a straight 'no' too simplistic? I would like to suggest a number of ways in which we might better articulate God's providentially teaching his people through the religious Other, rather than his people learning from the religious Other. There are two areas to focus on: the didactic and the disciplinary.

### i. Didactic

First, we may highlight the 'subversive' and discontinuous nature of Christianity's relationship to the religious Other by speaking of a *learning through contrast*. In God's providence other religions may act as a foil, highlighting the truth, goodness and beauty of the Christian gospel. As the great early twentieth-century Reformed missiologist Samuel Zwemer notes:

---

78. John M. Frame, *The Doctrine of the Christian Life* (Phillipsburg: P & R, 2008), pp. 9–10.

79. Ibid., p. 33 (his italics). See J. H. Bavinck, *Introduction*, pp. 203–204.

80. Timothy C. Tennent, *Theology in the Context of World Christianity* (Grand Rapids: Zondervan, 2007), p. 250.

Contact with non-Christian thought and life often sheds light on various elements
of Christianity, deepens our conception of its truths and brings out forgotten or
underestimated doctrines. Against the darkness and twilight shadows of heathenism
and Islam, Christian beliefs and ideas are thrown into bold relief, like a sunlit face in
one of Rembrandt's paintings.[81]

J. H. Bavinck is similar:

The dogma of the incarnation of the Word again sparkles, if we compare it to the
doctrine of the numerous avatars (incarnation of the gods) which India knows. The
dogma of justification by God shines all the brighter, if we compare it to the doctrine
of the Karma, the automatic and magically operating justification of Buddhism. By
looking outside of itself, theology learns anew to look within.[82]

Secondly, if Christians are unable to learn from the *whatness* of other religions,
what about the *thatness*, their humanity being made in God's image and their
restraint through common grace? Is there a sense in which Christians can be
reminded and even corrected of their own continuing idolatry as the Spirit
continues that demolition work of tearing down the old man and building the
new man in Christ? Where there are errors in the theology of the church, these
may be brought to light and corrected in the missionary setting as a result of
seeing the world and God's Word with a different set of assumptions. For
example, our current Western materialistic and still late-modern culture could
make us guilty of Hiebert's 'flaw of the excluded middle'. A sense of the divine
presence and interaction may well be recovered through a reminder that results
from a missionary encounter with a religion with such a sense, however distorted,
of the transcendent. Andrew Walls points to the African context to show what
our Enlightenment has blinded us to: the activity of demons and witchcraft,
and the possibility of spiritual beings subordinate to God with territorial
mandates.[83]

---

81. Samuel M. Zwemer, *The Origin of Religion* (London: Marshall, Morgan & Scott,
    1935), p. 45.

82. J. H. Bavinck, *Introduction*, p. 246.

83. Andrew Walls, 'The Expansion of Christianity: An Interview with Andrew Walls',
    *ChrCent* 117.22 (Aug. 2000), pp. 792–795. Would my treatments of Gen. 6:1 and
    Deut. 32:8 appear less fantastical and more credible if Walls's points were taken on
    board?

*ii. Disciplinary*

One further way that God works for the good of his people is through purifying discipline (Heb. 12:7). This brings together a number of themes we have already explored. Calvin argued that God uses demons 'in exercising believers by warring against them'.[84] This may apply more widely to non-Christian religions, behind which lie demons. In Judges 3:1–4 God permits idol-worshipping Canaanites to remain in the land to test Israel. As Block rightly emphasizes, the test is not for God's benefit (he knows everything) but to show Israel 'the depths of their infidelity'.[85] As such, it is a test mixed with judgment. While we may not agree with the specific application given to Israel here (that of holy war), Judges 3:1–4 could point to a possible purpose for God's allowing other religions to coexist alongside the church, perhaps especially in a multicultural society: to test the church's faithfulness or expose its syncretism.

For Calvin, Islam was a 'rod of correction' for the church.[86] Similarly, Luther regarded Islam as God's tool to punish the church for its sin.[87] More recently, in what amounts to a Christian theology of Islam, Peter Leithart notes the disciplinary role Islam plays.[88] His argument comes in three parts.

First, Leithart begins by arguing for Islam's being an instantiation of what I have called *influental* revelation: that, and in agreement with the medieval church, Islam is to be viewed as Christian heresy. The Hadith reports Muhammad's contact with a Syrian monk, and the Middle East was predominantly (Nestorian) Christian at the time; furthermore, themes in the Qur'an such as the denial of the Trinity establish that Muhammad had contact with, and was influenced by, Christianity.[89]

Secondly, Leithart offers two biblical insights that illuminate the nature of Islam. First, occasions in the Old Testament where God raised up 'parodic versions of Israel . . . to call Israel to repentance' (e.g. Solomon's adversaries in 1 Kgs. 11).[90] Similarly, 'The Lord has raised up Islam as a parody or mirror of

---

84. Calvin, *Institutes*, vol. 1, p. 153.

85. Daniel I. Block, *Judges, Ruth*, NAC 6 (Nashville: Broadman & Holman, 1999), p. 139.

86. Stuart Bonnington, 'Calvin and Islam', *RTR* 68.2 (2009), pp. 77–87 (80). He cites Calvin's commentary on Jer. 5:15.

87. Robert O. Smith, 'Luther, the Turks, and Islam', *CurTM* 34.5 (2007), pp. 351–364.

88. P. J. Leithart, *Mirror of Christendom* (Mars Hill audio resource essay, 2005), available online at https://marshillaudio.org/downloads/Mirror-of-Christendom.pdf (accessed 4 Oct. 2013).

89. Ibid., p. 2.

90. Ibid., p. 3.

Christianity, which is designed to expose our failing and to call us to faithfulness.'[91] Secondly, the idea that Islam is a 'global and systematic form of Judaizing',[92] not simply at the level of historical contact between Muhammad and Judaism but rather ritually in that 'Islam has a number of affinities with the ancient Israelite religions and with later Judaism'.[93] Combining these insights, Leithart argues that 'Islam is a parody of Christianity, and more particularly, Islam is a Judaizing parody of Christianity'.[94]

Finally, and armed with the above theology of Islam, Leithart provocatively argues that Islam's parodic persistence exposes the failure of the Christian church:

> In general, this failure is in two directions: On the one hand, we are faced with a
> Judaizing parody of the Church because we have become a Judaizing parody of
> the Church; on the other hand and somewhat paradoxically, we are faced with a
> Judaizing parody of the Church because we are not nearly Jewish enough.[95]

Leithart goes on to to justify this claim in four areas, the Christological, ecclesiological, sacramental and political, before offering a four-point 'to do' list for the church as a response to this discipline.

## Conclusion

Whether one agrees or not with his solutions, Leithart's attempt to give a theology of Islam and then to embed this theology within a teleological framework is a helpful and much-needed piece of orientation that I hope will both inspire and provoke others to follow suit. The stakes are high, and we are already playing catch-up here. I repeat Leithart's challenge quoted in the opening pages of this study:

> Islam's account of history has a place for Jesus and Christianity. To be sure, the Jesus
> of Islam is not the Jesus of the New Testament: He is not the divine Son incarnate,
> He is not crucified and raised (cf. Sura 4.157), and He is not reigning at the Father's

---

91. Ibid., p. 4.
92. Ibid., p. 5.
93. Ibid.
94. Ibid., p. 7.
95. Ibid., p. 8.

right hand. Still, the prophet Jesus has a place in Muslim 'redemptive history,' and this poses the challenge to Christians: Has Christian theology been able to locate Islam within *its* history . . . ? Can Christians make theological sense of the persistence of Islam? Can we fit them [i.e. Muslims] into our story?[96]

This chapter has been an attempt to fit not simply Islam, but all non-Christian religions, into the Christian story. It is my hope that we can take this framework, contextualize it in our own situations and apply it as we exhort, encourage and rebuke one another, and as we proclaim the glories of Christ to the religious Other. *Soli Deo gloria.*

---

96. Ibid., p. 3.

# CONCLUSION

We seethe with religions. Christianity, I am pleased to note, is one of them . . .
Everything that can go on is going on all round us. Religions buzz about us like bees.

(C. S. Lewis)[1]

## 1. Looking backwards

We live in a strange world, a religious world, a world full of religions. To that bewitched, bothered and bewildered Christian I first identified in my Introduction, a Christian not just madly hand-flapping but actually stung by the swarm of theological questions posed by the existence of the religious Other, I hope and pray that my theology of religions has brought some welcome relief and protection. What I have attempted to articulate is a definition of the religious Other that is a distillation of the canonically limited polyphony of Scripture on the matter. To achieve this I have drawn on the perspectivally related and mutually enriching disciplines of biblical exegesis, biblical theology, systematics, missiology and religious studies. My articulation claims to be neither novel nor original. Precisely the opposite in fact, for I have been eager to demonstrate consonance

---

1. Quoted in P. H. Brazier, *C. S. Lewis – The Work of Christ Revealed II: Knowing Salvation*, C. S. Lewis: Revelation and the Christ (Eugene: Pickwick, 2014), n.p. The original quotation is from Lewis's essay 'Revival or Decay', which appeared in *God in the Dock* (Grand Rapids: Eerdmans, 1970), pp. 250–253.

with both Reformed orthodox confessionalism and a number of pan-evangelical statements on the theology of religions. Furthermore, one of the main purposes of this study has been to point the spotlight firmly towards those forgotten figures such as J. H. Bavinck, on whose shoulders I happily and securely rest.

I have summarized my thesis throughout the study as follows: *From the presupposition of an epistemologically authoritative biblical revelation, non-Christian religions are sovereignly directed, variegated and dynamic, collective human idolatrous responses to divine revelation behind which stand deceiving demonic forces. Being antithetically against yet parasitically dependent upon the truth of the Christian worldview, non-Christian religions are 'subversively fulfilled' in the gospel of Jesus Christ.*

Over nine chapters I have attempted to justify and fill out this definition. In chapter 2 I argued that we do not have to panic when reflecting on the religious Other with a knee-jerk decision to create a whole new theological anthropology. Rather, we need to keep calm and carry on, trusting in the already well-dug Reformed foundations from which we can build our theology of religions. Doctrines such as the Creator–creature distinction, the *imago Dei*, the antithesis and common grace are crucial in our portrayal of the complex make-up of *Homo adorans*. In essence, what the religious Other consists of is the dynamic of a subjective idolatrous response to an objective divine revelation, summarized in passages such as Romans 1:18–32 but evidenced throughout the entire biblical plotline. Chapters 3–4 sought to sketch both a theological and historical 'religio-genesis'. Chapters 5–6 traced, in a more biblico-theological manner, attitudes to the religious Other, with particular focus on the category of idolatry. Chapter 7 gave a more synthesized and systematic statement of my findings by introducing the key idea of the gospel of Jesus Christ being the *subversive fulfilment* of the religious Other. Chapter 8 looked at some of the missiological implications of my theology of religions, by returning to Acts 17 as a microcosm of my theology of religions and its missiological application. Finally, in chapter 9, and once again within a Reformed theological framework, we investigated the purpose of the religious Other by suggesting that in God's sovereignty other religions serve, in a perspectival and polyvalent way, the purposes of God himself, God's world and God's people.

## 2. Looking forwards

Having spent nine long chapters outlining my theology of religions, it might now seem a little odd to call what I have done a piece of theological scaffolding and furthermore to call upon Christian brothers and sisters to strengthen and nuance my thesis further. However, this was always my intention with this study: not only to give some theological answers and offer some pastoral comfort in our world of the religions, but also to propose, speculate and even provoke us into further theological reflection and missiological action. As I bemoaned at the beginning of this study, although there are signs that we are getting our act together, compared to other Christian traditions, and even other evangelical traditions, since the 1960s Reformed evangelicals have lagged well behind in providing a rich and detailed theology of religions. I hope this study will prompt us to engage further in a number of areas.

First, a call to evangelicals to have both a living knowledge of other religious traditions and a loving attitude towards those who are part of them. If Christians are convinced of my approach, then they will take this dogmatic outline and apply it to their own ministries and contexts. What we need to see emerging are detailed and sophisticated attempts, more scalpel than machete, that seek to demonstrate how the gospel of Jesus Christ is the subversive fulfilment of the myriad instantiations of the religious Other. While it may be anecdotal, having taught this material in a British seminary for a few years now to those about to enter Christian ministry, it is not unfair to say that in general my students have often grasped the theological framework of subversive fulfilment better than the actual application of the framework in a particular religious tradition. I have no doubt that in some part this reflects my primary vocation and calling as a theological educator and systematician, but I am concerned that, even in as multicultural a place as Britain, our working knowledge of other religious traditions is either too academic or just too shallow. For the sake of the gospel we need to be engaging and immersing ourselves in the lives of the religious Other. On the other hand, a number of missiological practitioners I have met over the years have spent their lives engaging with a particular religious tradition and have both this knowledge and love. However, and again I hope I am not being unfair, sometimes the theology of religions that guides their praxis can be unreflective, shallow and sometimes questionable in terms of both exegesis and systematic reflection. If my own contribution is weighted to the theological side, then what I have wanted to achieve in this study is to provide a solid but subtle theological basis for missiological engagement.

Secondly, just as the global church is enriched as a whole when Christians from different cultures come into contact with each other, so there needs to be a breaking down of the high walls (erected by Enlightenment builders) between different theological disciplines, so all can be enriched. In a rather inelegant way I have attempted to model this by recognizing my own strengths and weaknesses. To reiterate what I said in the Introduction, I am fully aware that this has been an ambitious, maybe overambitious, undertaking, but I am ideologically convinced that as evangelical scholars we need to break out of our specialized ghettoes and interact with each other, for our own sake as well as the health of the church for whom we write. Again, I hope those evangelical scholars who come from different disciplinary backgrounds will be charitable in recognizing the integration I have tried to achieve, but will now offer more rigorous contributions in the future, all with the aim of edifying God's church worldwide.

Thirdly, as evangelicals we need to rehabilitate and reclaim the discipline of religious studies. As I argued at the end of chapter 3, scholars such as Gavin D'Costa have done us a great service in both questioning and then deconstructing the alleged 'neutrality' and 'objectivity' of much academic religious studies, by arguing for a legitimate 'comparative theological' reading of religion, or alternatively a 'theological religious studies', which is able (and in the best place) to incorporate both 'insider' and 'outsider' interpretations.[2] D'Costa's own Roman Catholic construction will not be suitable for us, so what we need to develop is a distinctively Reformed religious studies. It is interesting to note that in his *Introduction to the Science of Missions* J. H. Bavinck in his chapter on elenctics notes, 'The peculiar object of elenctics is responsible for the fact that it not only cannot be thought of apart from dogmatics, but it is also closely connected with sciences which in part do not belong to the theological faculty'.[3] He goes on to talk about the history of religion, the science of religion, the psychology of religion, phenomenology and finally the philosophy of religion. Once again, I think this is an undernourished area of evangelical study and research.[4] To do this, though, we shall have to recognize the importance and legitimacy of the social sciences and how they can support theology in general and the theology of religions in particular. Moving back one stage further, we shall need to go back to basics by establishing methodological issues concerning interdisciplinarity and how this coheres with our commitment to *sola Scriptura*.[5]

The above 'to do' list forms an ambitious agenda for the whole body of Christ and especially those called to be leaders and teachers. However, I believe it is a necessary agenda both for the church's witness to the world and for the church's discipleship of her people. Under God's sovereignty, surrounded in prayer and

---

2. See Gavin D'Costa, *Theology in the Public Square: Church, Academy and Nation* (Oxford: Blackwell, 2005); *Christianity and World Religions: Disputed Questions in the Theology of Religions* (Chichester: Wiley-Blackwell, 2009).

3. J. H. Bavinck, *An Introduction to the Science of Missions*, tr. David H. Freeman (Phillipsburg: P & R, 1960), p. 233.

4. I should mention evangelical scholars such as Winfried Corduan and the late Paul Hiebert, who have been working in these areas.

5. One attempt to do this that I have drawn on already is Mark Kreitzer, *The Concept of Ethnicity in the Bible: A Theological Analysis* (London: Edwin Mellen, 2008), pp. 39–72.

in a bold humility we can have confidence in the power of the gospel to repossess and transform lives, cultures and, yes, religions. While there will always be challenges and costs in doing this, let us never forget the privilege of taking the wonderful, subversively fulfilling gospel of Jesus Christ to the end of the earth:

Facing a task unfinished
That drives us to our knees
A need that, undiminished
Rebukes our slothful ease
We who rejoice to know Thee
Renew before Thy throne
The solemn pledge we owe Thee
To go and make Thee known

Where other lords beside Thee
Hold their unhindered sway
Where forces that defied Thee
Defy Thee still today
With none to heed their crying
For life, and love, and light
Unnumbered souls are dying
And pass into the night

We bear the torch that flaming
Fell from the hands of those
Who gave their lives proclaiming
That Jesus died and rose
Ours is the same commission
The same glad message ours
Fired by the same ambition
To Thee we yield our powers

O Father who sustained them
O Spirit who inspired
Saviour, whose love constrained them
To toil with zeal untired
From cowardice defend us
From lethargy awake!
Forth on Thine errands send us
To labour for Thy sake.[6]

---

6. Frank Houghton, 'Facing a Task Unfinished' (1930).

# BIBLIOGRAPHY

Aguilar, Mario I., 'Changing Models and the "Death" of Culture: A Diachronic and
Positive Critique of Socio-scientific Assumptions', in M. I. Aguilar and L. J. Lawrence
(eds.), *Anthropology and Biblical Studies: Avenues of Approach* (Leiden: Deo, 2004),
pp. 299–313.

Alexander, Denis, *Creation or Evolution: Do We Have to Choose?* (Oxford: Monarch, 2008).

Anderson, Norman, *Christianity and the World Religions* (Leicester: Inter-Varsity Press, 1984).

Arnold, Bill T., 'Religion in Ancient Israel', in David W. Baker and Bill T. Arnold (eds.), *The
Face of Old Testament Studies: A Survey of Contemporary Approaches* (Leicester: Apollos,
1999), pp. 391–420.

Auberlen, C. A., *The Divine Revelation: An Essay in Defence of the Faith*, CFTL 16
(Edinburgh: T. & T. Clark, 1867).

Augustine, *Concerning the City of God Against Pagans*, tr. Henry Bettenson, Penguin Classics
(London: Penguin, 2003).

Badcock, Gary, 'Karl Rahner, the Trinity and Religious Pluralism', in Kevin J. Vanhoozer (ed.),
*The Trinity in a Pluralistic Age: Theological Essays on Culture and Religion* (Cambridge:
Eerdmans, 1997), pp. 143–155.

Bahnsen, Greg, *Always Ready: Directions for Defending the Faith* (Nacogdoches, Tex.:
Covenant Media, 1996).

——, 'At War with the World: The Necessity of the Antithesis', *Antithesis* (1990), available
online at http://www.cmfnow.com/articles/pa083.htm (accessed 25 Sept. 2013).

——, 'The Theonomic Position', in Gary Scott Smith (ed.), *God and Politics* (Phillipsburg:
P & R, 1989), pp. 21–53.

——, *Van Til's Apologetic: Readings and Analysis* (Phillipsburg: P & R, 1998).

Barrett, John K., 'Does Inclusivist Theology Undermine Evangelism?', *EvQ* 30.3 (1998), pp. 219–245.

Barth, Karl, 'Die Theologie und die Mission in der Gegenwart: Vortrag, gehalten an der Brandenburgischen Missionskonferenz in Berlin am 11. April 1932', *Zwischen den Zeiten* 10 (1932), pp. 189–215.

Barton, Stephen C. (ed.), *Idolatry: False Worship in the Bible, Early Judaism and Christianity* (London: T. & T. Clark, 2007).

Bauckham, Richard, *The Bible and Mission* (Carlisle: Paternoster, 2003).

——, 'Biblical Theology and the Problems of Monotheism', in Craig Bartholomew (ed.), *Out of Egypt: Biblical Theology and Biblical Interpretation* (Milton Keynes: Paternoster, 2004), pp. 187–232.

——, *Jesus and the God of Israel: God Crucified and Other Studies on the New Testament's Christology of Divine Identity* (Cambridge: Eerdmans, 2008).

Baugh, Steven M., '"Savior of All People": 1 Tim. 4:10 in Context', *WTJ* 54 (1992), pp. 331–340.

Bavinck, Herman, *Essays on Religion, Science, and Society*, ed. John Bolt (Grand Rapids: Baker, 2008).

——, *Our Reasonable Faith* (Grand Rapids: Baker Book House, 1956).

——, *Reformed Dogmatics*, ed. John Bolt, tr. John Vriend, 4 vols. (Grand Rapids: Baker, 2004).

Bavinck, J. H., *Christus en de mystiek van het Oosten* (Kampen: Kok, 1934).

——, *The Church Between Temple and Mosque* (Grand Rapids: Eerdmans, 1966).

——, 'General Revelation and the Non-Christian Religions', *FUQ* 4 (1955), pp. 43–55.

——, *The Impact of Christianity on the Non-Christian World* (Grand Rapids: Eerdmans, 1949).

——, *An Introduction to the Science of Missions*, tr. David H. Freeman (Phillipsburg: P & R, 1960).

——, 'The Problem of Adaptation and Communication', *IRM* 45 (1956), pp. 307–313.

——, *Religieus besef en christelijk geloof* (Kampen: Kok, 1948).

——, 'Religious Consciousness and Christian Faith', in John Bolt, James D. Bratt and Paul J. Visser (eds.), *The J. H. Bavinck Reader* (Cambridge: Eerdmans, 2013), pp. 145–299.

Beale, G. K., 'An Exegetical and Theological Consideration of the Hardening of Pharaoh's Heart in Exodus 4–14 and Romans 9', *TrinJ* NS 5.2 (1984), pp. 129–155.

——, 'Other Religions in New Testament Theology', in David W. Baker (ed.), *Biblical Faith and Other Religions: An Evangelical Assessment* (Grand Rapids: Kregel, 2004), pp. 79–105.

——, *We Become What We Worship: A Biblical Theology of Idolatry* (Nottingham: Apollos, 2008).

Beilby, James K., and Paul Rhodes Eddy (eds.), *Understanding Spiritual Warfare: Four Views* (Grand Rapids: Baker Academic, 2012).

Berger, Peter (ed.), *The Desecularization of the World: Resurgent Religion and World Politics* (Grand Rapids: Eerdmans, 1999).

Berkhof, Louis, *Systematic Theology: New Combined Edition* (Grand Rapids: Eerdmans, 1996).

Berkouwer, G. C., *General Revelation* (Grand Rapids: Eerdmans, 1955).

——, *Man: The Image of God* (Grand Rapids: Eerdmans, 1962).

Blauw, Johannes, 'The Biblical View of Man in His Religion', in Gerald H. Anderson (ed.), *The Theology of the Christian Mission* (London: SCM, 1961), pp. 31–41.

Blocher, Henri, 'Agnus Victor: The Atonement as Victory and Vicarious Punishment', in John Stackhouse (ed.), *What Does It Mean to Be Saved? Broadening Evangelical Horizons of Salvation* (Grand Rapids: Baker, 2002), pp. 67–91.

——, 'Immanence and Transcendence in Trinitarian Theology', in Kevin J. Vanhoozer (ed.), *The Trinity in a Pluralistic Age: Essays on Culture and Religion* (Cambridge: Eerdmans, 1997), pp. 104–124.

Block, Daniel I., *The Gods of the Nations: Studies in Ancient Near Eastern National Theology*, 2nd ed. (Leicester: Apollos, 2000).

——, *Judges, Ruth*, NAC 6 (Nashville: Broadman & Holman, 1999).

——, 'Other Religions in Old Testament Theology', in David W. Baker (ed.), *Biblical Faith and Other Religions: An Evangelical Assessment* (Grand Rapids: Kregel, 2004), pp. 43–78.

Bock, Darrell L., 'Athenians Who Have Never Heard', in W. V. Crockett and J. G. Sigountos (eds.), *Through No Fault of Their Own? The Fate of Those Who Have Never Heard* (Grand Rapids: Baker, 1991), pp. 117–123.

Boice, James Montgomery, *Genesis: An Expositional Commentary* (Grand Rapids: Zondervan, 1982), vol. 1.

Bolt, John, James D. Bratt and Paul J. Visser (eds.), *The J. H. Bavinck Reader* (Cambridge: Eerdmans, 2013).

Bolt, Peter G., 'Towards a Biblical Theology of the Defeat of the Evil Powers', in Peter G. Bolt (ed.), *Christ's Victory over Evil: Biblical Theology and Pastoral Ministry* (Nottingham: Apollos, 2009), pp. 35–81.

Bolt, Peter, and Mark Thompson (eds.), *The Gospel to the Nations* (Leicester: Apollos, 2000).

Bonnington, Stuart, 'Calvin and Islam', *RTR* 68.2 (2009), pp. 77–87.

Borland, James, 'A Theologian Looks at the Gospel and the World Religions', *JETS* 26.1 (1990), pp. 3–11.

Bradley, James E., '*Logos* Christology and Religious Pluralism: A New Evangelical Proposal', in David K. Clark et al. (eds.), *Proceedings of the Wheaton Theological Conference. The Challenge of Religious Pluralism: An Evangelical Analysis and Response* (Wheaton: Wheaton Theology Conference, 1992), pp. 190–208.

Brandewie, Ernest, 'The Exile of Wilhelm Schmidt, S. V. D. from Austria', *Academici* (2008), available online at http://www.academici.net/blog.aspx?bid=4559 (accessed 25 Sept. 2013).

——, *When Giants Walked the Earth: The Life and Times of Wilhelm Schmidt SVD*, SIA 44 (Fribourg: Fribourg University Press, 1990).

——, *Wilhelm Schmidt and the Origin of the Idea of God* (Lanham: University Press of America, 1983).

Bray, Gerald, 'Explaining Christianity to Pagans: The Second Century Apologists', in Kevin J. Vanhoozer (ed.), *The Trinity in a Pluralistic Age: Theological Essays on Culture and Religion* (Cambridge: Eerdmans, 1997), pp. 9–25.

Brazier, P. H., *C. S. Lewis – The Work of Christ Revealed*, C. S. Lewis: Revelation and the Christ (Eugene: Pickwick, 2012).

——, *C. S. Lewis – The Work of Christ Revealed II: Knowing Salvation*, C. S. Lewis: Revelation and the Christ (Eugene: Pickwick, 2014).

Breslin, Scott, and Mike Jones, *Understanding Dreams from God* (Pasadena: William Carey Library, 2004).

Brow, Robert, *Religion: Origins and Ideas* (London: Tyndale, 1966).

Bruce, F. F., *The Book of Acts*, NICNT (Grand Rapids: Eerdmans, 1954).

Brueggemann, Walter, *Genesis* (Atlanta: John Knox, 1982).

——, *Theology of the Old Testament* (Minneapolis: Fortress, 1997).

Bullinger, E. W., *Witness of the Stars* (Grand Rapids: Kregel, 1967).

Burnside, Jonathan, *God, Justice, and Society: Aspects of Law and Legality in the Bible* (Oxford: Oxford University Press, 2011).

——, *The Status and Welfare of Immigrants* (Cambridge: Jubilee Centre, 2001).

Calvin, John, *A Commentary on Genesis*, tr. John King (London: Banner of Truth Trust, 1965).

——, *Concerning the Eternal Predestination of God*, tr. J. K. S. Reid (Cambridge: J. Clarke, 1982).

——, *Genesis*, ed. Alister McGrath and J. I. Packer, CCC (Nottingham: Crossway, 2001).

——, *Institutes of the Christian Religion*, ed. John T. McNeill, tr. Ford Lewis Battles, 2 vols., LCC (Philadelphia: Westminster, 1960).

Cameron, Nigel M. de S. (ed.), *Universalism and the Doctrine of Hell* (Carlisle: Paternoster, 1992).

Candlish, Robert S., *The Book of Genesis: Expounded in a Series of Discourses* (Edinburgh: A. & C. Black, 1868).

Carson, D. A., 'Adam in the Epistles of Paul', in N. M. de S. Cameron (ed.), *In the Beginning . . . : A Symposium on the Bible and Creation* (Glasgow: Biblical Creation Society, 1980), pp. 28–43.

——, 'Athens Revisited', in D. A. Carson (ed.), *Telling the Truth: Evangelizing Postmoderns* (Grand Rapids: Zondervan, 2000), pp. 384–398.

——, *The Difficult Doctrine of the Love of God* (Wheaton: Crossway, 2000).

——, *Evangelicalism: What Is It and Is It Worth Keeping?* (Wheaton: Crossway, 2009).

——, *The Gagging of God: Christianity Confronts Pluralism* (Leicester: Apollos, 1996).

——, *How Long, O Lord? Reflections on Evil and Suffering*, 2nd ed. (Grand Rapids: Baker; Leicester: Inter-Varsity Press, 2006).

——, *The Intolerance of Tolerance* (Nottingham: Inter-Varsity Press, 2012).

——, 'Maintaining Scientific and Christian Truths in a Postmodern World', *SCB* 14.2 (2002), pp. 107–122.

Carson, D. A., and John Woodbridge (eds.), *Hermeneutics, Authority and Canon* (Leicester: Inter-Varsity Press, 1986).

——, *Scripture and Truth* (Leicester: Inter-Varsity Press, 1983).

Chapman, Colin, *Cross and Crescent* (Leicester: Inter-Varsity Press, 1995).

Chung, Sung Wook (ed.), *Christ the One and Only: A Global Affirmation of the Uniqueness of Jesus Christ* (Milton Keynes: Paternoster, 2005).

Clarke, Andrew D., and Bruce W. Winter (eds.), *One God, One Lord: Christianity in a World of Religious Pluralism* (Grand Rapids: Baker, 1992).

Clarke, David K., 'Is Special Revelation Necessary for Salvation?', in W. V. Crockett and J. G. Sigountos (eds.), *Through No Fault of Their Own? The Fate of Those Who Have Never Heard* (Grand Rapids: Baker, 1991), pp. 35–45.

Clouser, Roy, *The Myth of Religious Neutrality* (Notre Dame: University of Notre Dame Press, 1991).

Conn, Harvie M., *Eternal Word and Changing Worlds: Theology, Anthropology, and Mission in Trialogue* (Grand Rapids: Zondervan, 1984).

Cooper, Bill, *After the Flood* (Chichester: New Wine, 1995).

Corduan, Winfried, *In the Beginning God: A Fresh Look at the Case for Original Monotheism* (Nashville: Broadman & Holman, 2013).

——, 'In the Beginning, God: Ethnology and Original Montheism', plenary paper, International Society of Christian Apologetics, Kansas City, Mo., 2–3 June 2007.

——, *The Tapestry of Faiths: The Common Threads Between Christianity and World Religions* (Downers Grove: InterVarsity Press, 2002).

Corrie, John (ed.), *Dictionary of Mission Theology: Evangelical Foundations* (Nottingham: Inter-Varsity Press, 2007).

Cross, Frank Moore, *Canaanite Myth and Hebrew Epic* (Cambridge, Mass.: Harvard University Press, 1973).

Currid, John D., *Deuteronomy*, EPSC (Darlington: Evangelical Press, 2006).

Davis, John J., 'The Patriarch's Knowledge of Jehovah', *GTJ* 4.1 (1963), pp. 29–43.

D'Costa, Gavin, *Christianity and World Religions: Disputed Questions in the Theology of Religions* (Chichester: Wiley-Blackwell, 2009).

——, *The Meeting of Religions and the Trinity* (Maryknoll: Orbis, 2000).

——, *Theology in the Public Square: Church, Academy and Nation* (Oxford: Blackwell, 2005).

——, 'Theology of Religions', in David Ford (ed.), *The Modern Theologians* (Oxford: Blackwell, 1989), pp. 274–290.

D'Costa, Gavin, Paul Knitter and Daniel Strange, *Only One Way? Three Christian Responses to the Uniqueness of Christ in a Religiously Pluralist World* (London: SCM, 2011).

Delitzsch, Franz, *A New Commentary on Genesis* (Edinburgh: T. & T. Clark, 1888).

——, *Old Testament History of Redemption* (Peabody: Hendrickson, 1998).

Demarest, Bruce, *General Revelation: Historical Views and Contemporary Issues* (Grand Rapids: Zondervan, 1982).

De Vries, Brian A., 'The Evangelistic Trialogue: Gospel Communication and the Holy Spirit', *CTJ* 44.1 (2009), pp. 49–73.

——, 'The Evangelistic Trialogue: Gospel Communication with the Holy Spirit', *CTJ* 44.1 (2009), pp. 37–48.

DeYoung, Kevin, and Gregory D. Gilbert, *What Is the Mission of the Church? Making Sense of Social Justice, Shalom and the Great Commission* (Wheaton: Crossway, 2011).

Dooyeweerd, Herman, *A New Critique of Theoretical Thought*, tr. David H. Freeman and William S. Young (Phillipsburg: P & R, 1969).

Driver, S. J., *A Critical and Exegetical Commentary on Deuteronomy*, ICC (Edinburgh: T. & T. Clark, 1895).

Drummond, Richard Henry, *Toward a New Age in Christian Theology* (Maryknoll: Orbis, 1985).

Dupuis, Jacques, *Toward a Christian Theology of Religious Pluralism* (Maryknoll: Orbis, 1997).

Edgar, William, *Truth in All Its Glory: Commending the Reformed Faith* (Phillipsburg: P & R, 2004).

Edwards, Jonathan, 'Concerning the End for Which God Created the World', in John Piper (ed.), *God's Passion for His Glory: Living the Vision of Jonathan Edwards* (Wheaton: Crossway, 1998), pp. 117–252.

Eliade, Mircea, *A History of Religious Ideas*, 3 vols. (Chicago: University of Chicago Press, 1978–85).

Fane, Violet, *From Dawn to Noon: Poems* (London: Longmans, Green, 1872), pp. 83–85.

Fernando, Ajith, *Sharing the Truth in Love: How to Relate to People of Other Faiths* (Grand Rapids: Discovery House, 2001).

Fitzgerald, F. Scott, *The Curious Case of Benjamin Button: And Six Other Stories*, Penguin Modern Classics (London: Penguin, 2008).

Flannery, Austin, O.P. (ed.), *Vatican Council II: The Conciliar and Post Conciliar Documents* (New York: Costello, 1998).

Flett, John G., 'In the Name of the Father, the Son and the Holy Spirit: A Critical Reflection on the Trinitarian Theologies of Religion of S. Mark Heim and Gavin D'Costa', *IJST* 10.1 (2008), pp. 73–90.

Flint, Christopher Robert, 'God's Blessing to Ishmael with Special Reference of Islam', *SFM* 7.4 (2011), pp. 1–53.

——, 'How Does Christianity "Subversively Fulfil" Islam?', *SFM* 8 (2012), pp. 776–822.

Frame, John M., *Apologetics to the Glory of God: An Introduction* (Phillipsburg: P & R, 1994).

——, *Cornelius Van Til: An Analysis of His Thought* (Phillipsburg: P & R, 1995).

——, 'Divine Aseity and Apologetics', in K. Scott Oliphint and Lane G. Tipton (eds.), *Reason and Revelation: New Essays in Reformed Apologetics* (Phillipsburg: P & R, 2007), pp. 115–130.

——, *The Doctrine of the Christian Life* (Phillipsburg: P & R, 2008).

——, *The Doctrine of God: A Theology of Lordship* (Phillipsburg: P & R, 2002).

——, *The Doctrine of the Knowledge of God* (Phillipsburg: P & R, 1987).

——, 'Machen's Warrior Children', in Sung Wook Chung (ed.), *Alister McGrath and Evangelical Theology: A Dynamic Engagement* (Grand Rapids: Baker, 2003), pp. 113–146.

——, 'Men and Women in the Image of God', in John Piper and Wayne Grudem (eds.), *Biblical Manhood and Womanhood: A Response to Evangelical Feminism* (Wheaton: Crossway, 1991), pp. 228–236.

——, 'A Primer on Perspectivalism' (2008), available online at http://www.frame-poythress. org/a=primer-on=perspectivalism/ (accessed 9 Oct. 2012).

——, *Salvation Belongs to the Lord: An Introduction to Systematic Theology* (Phillipsburg: P & R, 2006).

Freytag, Walter, *The Gospel and the Religions* (London: SCM, 1957).

Gaffin, Richard B., Jr., 'Systematic Theology and Biblical Theology', *WTJ* 38 (1975–76), pp. 284–299.

Garrett, Duane A., *Angels and the New Spirituality* (Nashville: Broadman & Holman, 1995).

——, *Rethinking Genesis: The Sources and Authorship of the First Book of the Pentateuch* (Fearn: Christian Focus, 2000).

Glaser, Ida, *The Bible and Other Faiths: What Does the Lord Require of Us?* (Leicester: Inter-Varsity Press, 2005).

Gnuse, Robert Karl, *No Other Gods: Emergent Monotheism in Israel*, JSOTSup 241 (Sheffield: Sheffield Academic Press, 1997).

Godawa, Brian, 'Storytelling as Subversive Apologetics: A New View from the Hill in Acts 17', *Christian Research Journal* 30.2 (2007), n.p.

Goheen, Michael, 'As the Father Has Sent Me, I Am Sending You': J. E. Lesslie Newbigin's Missionary Ecclesiology* (Zoetermeer: Boekencentrum, 2000).

——, 'Gospel, Culture, and Cultures: Lesslie Newbigin's Missionary Contribution', paper presented at Cultures and Christianity A.D. 2000, Hoeven, Netherlands, 2000.

Goheen, Michael W., and Craig G. Bartholomew, *Living at the Crossroads: An Introduction to Christian Worldview* (Grand Rapids: Baker Academic, 2008).

Goldenberg, Robert, *The Nations That Know Thee Not: Ancient Jewish Attitudes Toward Other Religions* (New York: New York University Press, 1998).

Goldingay, John E., *Genesis for Everyone, Part 1: Chapters 1–16* (London: SPCK, 2010).

——, 'How Does the First Testament Look at Other Religions', in John Goldingay, *Key Questions About Christian Faith: Old Testament Answers* (Grand Rapids: Baker, 2010), pp. 248–265.

Goldingay, John E., and Christopher J. H. Wright, '"Yahweh Our God Yahweh One": The
    Oneness of God in the Old Testament', in Andrew D. Clarke and Bruce W. Winter (eds.),
    *One God, One Lord: Christianity in a World of Religious Pluralism* (Grand Rapids: Baker,
    1992), pp. 43–62.

Grindheim, Sigurd, *The Crux of Election: Paul's Critique of the Jewish Confidence in the
    Election of Israel*, WUNT 202 (Tübingen: Mohr Siebeck, 2005).

Gunkel, Hermann, *Genesis* (Macon: Mercer University Press, 1997).

Haak, Cornelius J., 'The Missional Approach: Reconsidering Elenctics (Part 1)', *CTJ* 44.1
    (2009), pp. 37–48.

Halbertal, Moshe, and Avishai Margalit, *Idolatry* (London: Harvard University Press,
    1992).

Hamilton, James M., Jr., *God's Glory in Salvation Through Judgement* (Wheaton: Crossway,
    2010).

Hamilton, Victor P., *The Book of Genesis: Chapters 1–17*, NICOT (Grand Rapids: Eerdmans,
    1990).

Harrison, Peter, *'Religion' and the Religions in the English Enlightenment* (Cambridge:
    Cambridge University Press, 1990).

Hays, Richard, *Echoes of Scripture in the Letters of Paul* (London: Yale University Press, 1989).

Heiser, Michael S., 'Deuteronomy 32:8 and the Sons of God', *BSac* 158 (2001), pp. 52–74.

——, 'The Divine Council in Late Canonical and Non-Canonical Second Temple Jewish
    Literature', PhD diss., University of Wisconsin – Madison, 2004, available online at http://
    digitalcommons.liberty.edu/cgi/viewcontent.cgi?article=1092&context=fac_dis. (accessed 4
    Oct. 2013).

——, 'Monotheism, Polytheism, Monolatry, or Henotheism? Toward an Assessment
    of Divine Plurality in the Hebrew Bible', *BBR* 18.1 (2008), pp. 1–30.

Hess, Richard S., 'Yahweh and His Asherah? Religious Pluralism in the Old Testament
    World', in Andrew D. Clarke and Bruce W. Winter (eds.), *One God, One Lord:
    Christianity in a World of Religious Pluralism* (Cambridge: Tyndale House, 1991),
    pp. 5–33.

Hesselgrave, David J., *Paradigms in Conflict: 10 Key Questions in Christian Missions Today*
    (Grand Rapids: Kregel, 2005).

Hick, John, *God and the Universe of Faiths* (Oxford: Oneworld, 1973).

Hick, John, and Brian Hebblethwaite, *Christianity and Other Religions: Selected Readings*
    (Oxford: Oneworld, 2001).

Hiebert, Paul G., 'The Flaw of the Excluded Middle', *Missiology: An International Review* 10.1
    (1982), pp. 35–47.

——, *The Gospel in Human Contexts: Anthropological Explorations for Contemporary Missions*
    (Grand Rapids: Baker, 2009).

——, *Transforming Worldviews: An Anthropological Understanding of How People Change*
    (Grand Rapids: Baker, 2008).

Hodge, A. A., *Evangelical Theology: A Course of Popular Lectures* (Edinburgh: Banner of Truth Trust, 1976).

Hoekema, Anthony A., *Created in God's Image* (Grand Rapids: Eerdmans, 1986).

Horton, Michael S., *The Christian Faith: A Systematic Theology for Pilgrims on the Way* (Grand Rapids: Zondervan, 2011).

——, 'Consistently Reformed: The Inheritance and Legacy of Van Til's Apologetic', in K. Scott Oliphint and Lane G. Tipton (eds.), *Revelation and Reason: New Essays in Reformed Theology* (Phillipsburg: P & R, 2007), pp. 131–148.

——, 'Image and Office: Human Personhood and the Covenant', in Richard Lints, Michael S. Horton and Mark R. Talbot (eds.), *Personal Identity in Theological Perspective* (Grand Rapids: Eerdmans, 2006), pp. 178–203.

House, Paul R., and Gregory A. Thornbury, *Who Will Be Saved? Defending the Biblical Understanding of God, Salvation and Evangelism* (Wheaton: Crossway, 2000).

Howell, Don N., 'The Apostle Paul and First Century Religious Pluralism', in Edward Rommen and Harold A. Netland (eds.), *Christianity and the Religions: A Biblical Theology of World Religions*, Evangelical Missiological Society Series 2 (Pasadena: William Carey Library, 1995), pp. 92–112.

Hughes, Dewi, *Has God Many Names?* (Leicester: Apollos, 1996).

Jensen, Peter, *The Revelation of God* (Leicester: Inter-Varsity Press, 2002).

Jewett, Robert, *Romans: A Commentary* (Minneapolis: Fortress, 2007).

Johnson, Gregory, 'The Inadequacy of General Revelation for the Salvation of the Nations' (Covenant Theological Seminary, 1996), available online at http://gregscouch.homestead. com/files/Generalrev.html (accessed 4 Oct. 2013).

Jordan, James B., *The Bible and Nations: A Syllabus* (Niceville, Fla.: Biblical Horizons, 1988).

——, *The Handwriting on the Wall: A Commentary on the Book of Daniel* (Powder Springs, Ga.: American Vision, 2007).

——, *Primeval Saints* (Moscow, Idaho: Canon, 2001).

——, *Through New Eyes: Developing a Biblical Worldview* (Brentwood, Tenn.: Wolgemuth & Hyatt, 1988).

K., John, 'Dream Encounters in Christian and Islamic Societies and Its Implications for Christian Ministry and Mission', *Global Missiology* 1.3 (2005), available online at http://ojs.globalmissiology.org/index.php/english/article/view/425/1086 (accessed 4 Oct. 2013).

Kaiser, Walter C., *Mission in the Old Testament: Israel as a Light to the Nations* (Grand Rapids: Baker, 2000).

Kärkkäinen, Veli-Matti, 'Evangelical Theology and the Relgions', in Timothy Larsen and Daniel J. Treier (eds.), *The Cambridge Companion to Evangelical Theology* (Cambridge: Cambridge University Press, 2007), pp. 199–212.

——, *An Introduction to the Theology of Religions: Biblical, Historical and Contemporary Perspectives* (Downers Grove: InterVarsity Press, 2003).

Keller, Timothy J., *Center Church: Doing Balanced, Gospel-Centered Ministry in Your City* (Grand Rapids: Zondervan, 2012).

——, *Counterfeit Gods: When the Empty Promises of Love, Money and Power Let You Down* (London: Hodder & Stoughton, 2010).

——, *Deconstructing Defeater Beliefs* (2000), available online at http://www.thegospelcoalition.org/resources/a/Deconstructing-Defeater-Beliefs-Leading-the-Secular-to-Christ (accessed 9 Oct. 2012).

——, *Exclusivity: How Can There Be Just One Religion?* (audio talk, 2006), available online at http://www.bethinking.org/other-religions/intermediate/exclusivity-how-can-there-be-just-one-true-religion.htm (accessed 9 Oct. 2012).

——, *Ministries of Mercy* (Grand Rapids: Zondervan, 1989).

——, *The Reason for God: Belief in an Age of Scepticism* (London: Hodder & Stoughton, 1998).

Kennedy, D. James, *The Real Meaning of the Zodiac* (Fort Lauderdale, Fla.: Coral Ridge Ministries, 1989).

Keyes, Richard, 'The Idol Factory', in Os Guinness and John Seel (eds.), *No God but God* (Chicago: Moody, 1992), pp. 29–48.

Kline, Meredith, *Kingdom Prologue: Genesis Foundation for a Covenantal Worldview* (Eugene: Wipf & Stock, 2006).

Knitter, Paul F., *No Other Name? A Critical Survey of Christian Attitudes Towards the World Religions* (Maryknoll: Orbis, 1985).

——, *Theologies of Religions* (Maryknoll: Orbis, 2003).

Köstenberger, Andreas, 'The Contribution of the General Epistles and Revelation to a Biblical Theology of Religions', in Edward Rommen and Harold Netland (eds.), *Christianity and the Religions: A Biblical Theology of World Religions*, Evangelical Missiological Society Series 2 (Pasadena: William Carey Library, 1995), pp. 113–140.

Kraemer, Hendrik, *The Christian Message in a Non-Christian World* (London: Edinburgh House, 1938).

——, 'Continuity or Discontinuity', in G. Paton (ed.), *The Authority of Faith: International Missionary Council Meeting at Tambaram, Madras* (London: Oxford University Press, 1939), pp. 1–21.

——, *Religion and the Christian Faith* (London: Lutterworth, 1956).

Kreitzer, Mark, *The Concept of Ethnicity in the Bible: A Theological Analysis* (London: Edwin Mellen, 2008).

Kronk, Rick, *Dreams and Visions: Muslims' Miraculous Journey to Jesus* (Pescara: Destiny Image Europe, 2010).

Kuyper, Abraham, *The Work of the Holy Spirit*, tr. Henri De Vries (1900; Grand Rapids: Eerdmans, 1941).

Leithart, Peter J., *1 and 2 Kings*, ed. R. R. Reno, SCM Theological Commentary on the Bible (London: SCM, 2006).

——, *Against Christianity* (Moscow, Idaho: Canon, 2003).

——, *Did Plato Read Moses? Middle Grace and Moral Consensus*, Biblical Horizons Occasional Paper 23 (Niceville, Fla.: Biblical Horizons, 1995).

——, 'Don Richardson and Contextualization' (2004), blog post, available online at http://www.firstthings.com/blogs/leithart/2004/06/22/don–richardson–and–contextualization (accessed 10 Oct. 2013).

——, *Heroes of the City of Man* (Moscow, Idaho: Canon, 1999).

——, *Mirror of Christendom* (Mars Hill audio resource essay, 2005), available online at https://marshillaudio.org/downloads/Mirror-of-Christendom.pdf (accessed 4 Oct. 2013).

Lints, Richard, *The Fabric of Theology: A Prolegomenon to Evangelical Theology* (Grand Rapids: Eerdmans, 1993).

——, 'Imaging and Idolatry: The Sociality of Personhood in the Canon', in Richard Lints, Michael S. Horton and Mark R. Talbot (eds.), *Personal Identity in Theological Perspective* (Grand Rapids: Eerdmans, 2006), pp. 204–225.

Little, Christopher R., *The Revelation of God Among the Unevangelized: An Evangelical Appraisal and Missiological Contribution to the Debate* (Pasadena: William Carey Library, 2000).

Litwak, Kenneth D., 'Israel's Prophets Meet Athens' Philosophers: Scriptural Echoes in Acts 17:22–31', *Bib* 2 (2004), pp. 199–216.

Lloyd, Stephen, 'Christian Theology and Neo-Darwinism Are Incompatible: An Argument from the Resurrection', in Graeme Finlay, Stephen Lloyd, Stephen Pattermore and David Swift (eds.), *Debating Darwin* (Carlisle: Paternoster, 2009), pp. 1–29.

Long, V. Philips, 'The Art of Biblical History', in Moises Silva (ed.), *Foundations of Contemporary Interpretation: Six Volumes in One* (Leicester: Apollos, 1997), pp. 287–434.

——, 'Historiography of the Old Testament', in David W. Baker and Bill T. Arnold (eds.), *The Face of Old Testament Studies: A Survey of Contemporary Approaches* (Leicester: Apollos, 1999), pp. 145–175.

Lowe, Chuck, *Territorial Spirits and World Evangelization?* (Fearn: Christian Focus, 1998).

MacDonald, Nathan, *Deuteronomy and the Meaning of 'Monotheism'*, FAT 2.1 (Tübingen: Mohr Siebeck, 2003).

Mackay, John L., *Exodus: A Mentor Commentary* (Fearn: Mentor, 2001).

Macleod, Donald, *Behold Your God* (Fearn: Christian Focus, 1995).

Maddox, Randy L., *Responsible Grace: John Wesley's Practical Theology* (Nashville: Kingswood, 1994).

Masuzawa, Tomoko, *In Search of Dreamtime: The Question for the Origin of Religion* (Chicago: University of Chicago Press, 1993).

Mathews, Kenneth A., *Genesis 1–11:26*, ed. E. Ray Clendenen, NAC 1A (Nashville: Broadman & Holman, 1996).

Mathison, Keith A., *The Shape of Sola Scriptura* (Moscow, Idaho: Canon, 2001).

Mavrodes, George, *Belief in God* (New York: Random House, 1970).

May, Gordon, 'Some Aspects of Solar Worship at Jerusalem', *ZAW* 55.14 (1937),
     pp. 269–281.

McBride, Dennis, *An Evaluation of Muslim Dreams and Visions of Isa (Jesus)* (2010),
     available online at http://www.yoyomaster.com/ministry.file/IsaDreams.pdf (accessed
     22 Aug. 2012).

McConville, J. G., *Deuteronomy*, ed. David W. Baker and Gordon J. Wenham, AOTC
     (Leicester: Apollos, 2002).

McDermott, Gerald R., *Can Evangelicals Learn from World Religions? Jesus, Revelation and
     Religious Traditions* (Downers Grove: InterVarsity Press, 2000).

——, *God's Rivals: Why Has God Allowed Different Religions?* (Downers Grove: InterVarsity
     Press, 2007).

——, *Jonathan Edwards Confronts the Gods: Christian Theology, Enlightenment Religion, and
     the Non-Christian Faiths* (Oxford: Oxford University Press, 2000).

——, 'What If Paul Had Been from China? Reflections on the Possibility of Revelation
     in Non-Christian Religions', in John Stackhouse (ed.), *No Other Gods Before Me?
     Evangelicals and the Challenge of World Religions* (Grand Rapids: Baker, 2001), pp. 17–36.

McKitterick, Alistair, 'The Language of Genesis', in Norman C. Nevin (ed.), *Should Christians
     Embrace Evolution? Biblical and Scientific Responses* (Nottingham: Inter-Varsity Press,
     2009), pp. 27–42.

Meeter, H. H., *The Heavenly High Priesthood of Christ: An Exegetico-Dogmatic Study*
     (Eerdmans: Grand Rapids, 1915).

Merrick, James R. A., 'The Spirit of Truth as Agent in False Religions? A Critique of Amos
     Yong's Pneumatological Theology of Religions with Reference to Current Trends', *TrinJ* 29,
     NS (2008), pp. 107–125.

Merrill, Eugene H., *Deuteronomy*, NAC (Nashville: Broadman & Holman, 1994).

Middlemann, Udo, *Christianity Versus Fatalistic Religions in the War Against Poverty*
     (Colorado Springs: Paternoster, 2008).

Milbank, John, 'The End of Dialogue', in Gavin D'Costa (ed.), *Christian Uniqueness
     Reconsidered* (New York: Orbis, 1990), pp. 174–191.

Miles, Todd L., *A God of Many Understandings? The Gospel and a Theology of Religions*
     (Nashville: B&H Academic, 2010).

Miller, Ed. L., '"The True Light Which Illumines Every Person"', in Ed. L. Miller (ed.), *Good
     News in History* (Atlanta: Scholars Press, 1993), pp. 63–83.

Moberly, R. W. L., *The Old Testament of the Old Testament: Patriarchal Narratives and Mosaic
     Yahwism*, OBT (Minneapolis: Fortress, 1992).

——, *The Theology of the Book of Genesis*, OTT (Cambridge: Cambridge University Press,
     2009).

Mody, Rohintan, *Evil and Empty: The Worship of Other Faiths in 1 Corinthians 10:18–22 and
     Today*, Latimer Studies 71 (London: Latimer Trust, 2010).

——, 'The Relationship Between Powers of Evil and Idols in 1 Corinthians 8:4–5 and 10:18–22 in the Context of the Pauline Corpus and Early Judaism', PhD diss., Aberdeen University, 2008.

Moo, Douglas J., *The Epistle to the Romans*, NICNT (Grand Rapids: Eerdmans, 1996).

Moreau, A. Scott (ed.), *Evangelical Dictionary of World Missions*, Baker Reference Library (Grand Rapids: Baker, 2000).

Morgan, Christopher W., and Robert A. Peterson (eds.), *Faith Comes by Hearing: A Response to Inclusivism* (Nottingham: Apollos, 2008).

Morris, Henry, *The Genesis Flood* (London: Evangelical Press, 1969).

——, *The Genesis Record: A Scientific and Devotional Commentary on the Book of Beginnings* (Grand Rapids: Baker, 1974).

——, *The Long War Against God: The History and Impact of the Creation/Evolution Debate* (Green Forest: Master, 2000).

Motyer, J. A., *The Message of Exodus: The Days of Our Pilgrimage* (Leicester: Inter-Varsity Press, 2005).

——, *The Revelation of the Divine Name* (London: Tyndale, 1959).

Moucarry, Chawkat, *Faith to Faith: Christianity and Islam in Dialogue* (Leicester: Inter-Varsity Press, 2001).

——, *The Search for Forgiveness: Pardon and Punishment in Islam and Christianity* (Leicester: Inter-Varsity Press, 2004).

Muck, Terry, and Frances S. Adeney, *Christianity Encountering World Religions: The Practice of Mission in the Twenty-First Century* (Grand Rapids: Baker, 2009).

Murray, John, *Collected Writings of John Murray*, 4 vols. (Edinburgh: Banner of Truth Trust, 1977).

——, *Redemption – Accomplished and Applied* (Edinburgh: Banner of Truth Trust, 1955).

Musk, Bill, *The Unseen Face of Islam* (London: Monarch, 1989).

Naugle, David K., *Worldview: The History of a Concept* (Grand Rapids: Eerdmans, 2002).

Netland, Harold A., 'Christian Mission Among Other Faiths: The Evangelical Tradition', in Lalsangkima Pachuau and Knud Jørgensen (eds.), *Witnessing to Christ in a Pluralistic Age: Christian Mission Among Other Faiths* (London: Regnum, 2011), pp. 45–56.

——, *Dissonant Voices: Religious Pluralism and the Question of Truth* (Leicester: Apollos, 1991).

——, *Encountering Religious Pluralism: The Challenge of Christian Faith and Mission* (Leicester: Apollos, 2001).

Netland, Harold A., and Keith E. Yandell, *Spirituality Without God: Buddhist Enlightenment and Christian Salvation* (Milton Keynes: Paternoster, 2009).

Nevin, Norman C. (ed.), *Should Christians Embrace Evolution? Biblical and Scientific Responses* (Nottingham: Inter-Varsity Press, 2009).

Newbigin, Lesslie, *The Gospel in a Pluralistic Society* (London: SPCK, 1989).

——, *A Word in Season: Perspectives on Christian World Missions* (Grand Rapids: Eerdmans, 1994).

Niehaus, Jeffrey J., *Ancient Near Eastern Themes in Biblical Theology* (Grand Rapids: Kregel, 2008).

——, 'An Argument Against Theologically Constructed Covenants', *JETS* 50.2 (2007), pp. 259–273.

——, 'Covenant: An Idea in the Mind of God', *JETS* 52.2 (2009), pp. 225–246.

——, *God at Sinai: Covenant and Theophany in the Bible and Ancient Near East* (Carlisle: Paternoster, 1995).

Nikides, Bill, 'A Response to Kevin Higgins' "Inside What?" Church, Culture, Religion and Insider Movements in Biblical Perspective', *SFM* 5.4 (2009), pp. 92–112.

Noss, David S., *A History of the World's Religions*, 12th ed. (New York: Pearson Prentice Hall, 2008).

Oberman, Heiko, *The Dawn of the Reformation* (Edinburgh: T. & T. Clark, 1986).

Okholm, Dennis L., and Timothy R. Phillips (eds.), *More Than One Way: Four Views on Salvation in a Pluralistic World* (Grand Rapids: Zondervan, 1995).

Ovey, Michael, 'The Cross, Creation and the Human Predicament', in David Peterson (ed.), *Where Wrath and Mercy Meet: Proclaiming the Atonement Today* (Carlisle: Paternoster, 2001), pp. 100–135.

——, 'Idolatry and Spiritual Parody: Counterfeit Faith', *Cambridge Papers* 11.1 (Mar. 2002).

Owen, John, *An Exposition of Hebrews* (Marshallton, Del.: National Foundation for Christian Education, 1969), vol. 3.

Packer, J. I., *What Did the Cross Achieve? The Logic of Penal Substitution* (Leicester: RTSF, 2002).

Pao, David W., *Acts and the Isaianic New Exodus*, Biblical Studies Library (Grand Rapids: Baker Academic, 2000).

Pardigon, Flavien Olivier Cedric, 'Paul Against the Idols: The Areopagus Speech and Religious Inclusivism', PhD diss., Westminster Theological Seminary, 2008.

Partridge, Christopher (ed.), *Dictionary of Contemporary Religion in the Western World*, IVP Reference Collection (Leicester: Inter-Varsity Press, 2002).

——, *The Re-Enchantment of the West: Alternative Spiritualities, Sacralization, Popular Culture and Occulture*, 2 vols. (London: T. & T. Clark, 2004).

Perry, Tim S., *Radical Difference: A Defence of Hendrik Kraemer's Theology of Religions* (Waterloo, Ont.: Wilfrid Laurier University Press, 2001).

Peters, Ted, 'Re-framing the Question: How Can We Construct a Theology of Religions?', *Dialog: A Journal of Theology* 46.4 (2007), pp. 322–334.

Petersen, D. L., 'Israel and Monotheism: The Unfinished Agenda', in G. M. Tucker, D. L. Petersen and R. R. Wilson (eds.), *Canon, Theology, and Old Testament Interpretation: Essays in Honour of Brevard S. Childs* (Philadelphia: Fortress, 1988), pp. 92–107.

Peterson, David, *The Acts of the Apostles* (Nottingham: Apollos, 2009).

Phillips, Richard (ed.), *Only One Way? Reaffirming the Exclusive Truth Claims of Christianity* (Wheaton: Crossway, 2006).

Pinnock, Clark, *Flame of Love: A Theology of the Holy Spirit* (Downers Grove: InterVarsity Press, 1996).

——, *A Wideness in God's Mercy: The Finality of Jesus Christ in a World of Religions* (Grand Rapids: Zondervan, 1992).

Piper, John, *The Justification of God: An Exegetical and Critical Study of Romans 9:1–23* (Grand Rapids: Baker, 1993).

——, *Spectacular Sins: And Their Global Purpose in the Glory of Christ* (Wheaton: Crossway, 2008).

Plantinga, Alvin, 'A Defense of Religious Exclusivism', in Thomas D. Senor (ed.), *The Rationality of Belief and the Plurality of Faith* (London: Cornell University Press, 1995), pp. 191–215.

Plantinga, Cornelius, Jr., 'The Concern of the Church in a Socio-Political World: A Calvinist and Reformed Perspective', *CTJ* 28.2 (1983), pp. 190–205.

Pongratz-Leisten, Beate, *Reconsidering the Concept of Revolutionary Monotheism* (Winona Lake: Eisenbrauns, 2011).

Powlison, David, *Power Encounters: Reclaiming Spiritual Warfare* (Grand Rapids: Baker, 1995).

Poythress, Vern S., *Symphonic Theology: The Validity of Multiple Perspectives in Theology* (Phillipsburg: P & R, 1987).

Pramuk, Christopher, ' "*They Know Him by His Voice*": Newman on the Imagination, Christology, and the Theology of Religions', *HeyJ* 48 (2007), pp. 61–85.

Pratt, Richard L., *He Gave Us Stories: The Bible Student's Guide to Interpreting Old Testament Narratives*, 2nd ed. (Phillipsburg: P & R, 1993).

Provan, Iain W., 'In the Stable with the Dwarves: Testimony, Interpretation, Faith, and the History of Israel', in V. Philips Long, David W. Baker and Gordon J. Wenham (eds.), *Windows into Old Testament History: Evidence, Argument, and the Crisis of 'Biblical Israel'* (Cambridge: Eerdmans, 2002), pp. 161–197.

Race, Alan, *Christians and Religious Pluralism: Patterns in the Christian Theology of Religions* (London: SCM, 1983).

Race, Alan, and Paul Hedges (eds.), *Christian Approaches to Other Faiths*, SCM Core Text (London: SCM, 2008).

Rad, Gerhard von, *Genesis: A Commentary* (London: SCM, 1961).

Rademaker, C. S. M., *Life and Work of Gerardus Joannes Vossius (1577–1649)* (Assen: Van Gorcum, 1981).

Reed, Annette Yoshiko, *Fallen Angels and the History of Judaism and Christianity: The Reception of the Enochic Literature* (Cambridge: Cambridge University Press, 2005).

Reeves, Michael, 'Adam and Eve', in Norman C. Nevin (ed.), *Should Christians Embrace Evolution? Biblical and Scientific Responses* (Nottingham: Inter-Varsity Press, 2009), pp. 43–56.

Reymond, Robert, *A New Systematic Theology of the Christian Faith* (Nashville: Thomas Nelson, 1998).

Richardson, Don, *Eternity in Their Hearts*, 2nd rev. ed. (Ventura: Regal, 1981).

Richie, Tony, 'Hints from Heaven: Can C. S. Lewis Help Evangelicals Hear God in Other Religions?', *ERT* 32.1 (2008), pp. 38–55.

Robertson, O. Palmer, *The Christ of the Covenants* (Phillipsburg: P & R, 1980).

Robinson, Mike A., *One Way to God: Christian Philosophy and Presuppositional Apologetics Examine World Religions* (Denver: Outskirts, 2008).

Romanowski, William, *Pop Culture Wars* (Downers Grove: InterVarsity Press, 1996).

Rommen, Edward (ed.), *Spiritual Power and Missions: Raising the Issues*, Evangelical Missiological Society Series 3 (Pasadena: William Carey Library, 1995).

Rommen, Edward, and Harold A. Netland (eds.), *Christianity and the Religions*, Evangelical Missiological Society Series 2 (Pasadena: William Carey Library, 1995).

Rosner, Brian, '"No Other God": The Jealousy of God and Religious Pluralism', in Andrew D. Clarke and Bruce W. Winter (eds.), *One God, One Lord: Christianity in a World of Religious Pluralism* (Cambridge: Baker, 1992), pp. 149–159.

Ross, Allen P., 'The Table of Nations in Genesis 10: Its Content', *BSac* 138 (1980), pp. 22–34.

Sailhamer, John H., *The Meaning of the Pentateuch: Revelation, Composition and Interpretation* (Downers Grove: InterVarsity Press, 2009).

Sarna, Nahum M., *Genesis*, JPSTC (New York: Jewish Publication Society, 1989).

Schaeffer, Francis, *The Complete Works of Francis A. Schaeffer*, vol. 4: *The Church at the End of the Twentieth Century* (Wheaton: Crossway, 1982).

——, *Genesis in Space and Time* (Downers Grove: InterVarsity Press, 1972).

——, *The Mark of the Christian* (Downers Grove: InterVarsity Press, 1970).

Schlorff, Sam, *Missiological Models in Ministry to Muslims* (Upper Darby, Pa.: Middle East Resources, 2006).

Schmemann, Alexander, *For the Life of the World: Sacrament and Orthodoxy* (New York: St. Vladimir's Seminary Press, 1973).

Schmidt, Wilhelm, *The Origin and Growth of Religion: Facts and Theories* (London: Methuen, 1931).

Schreiner, Thomas R., *Romans*, BECNT (Grand Rapids: Baker, 2008).

Scrivener, Steve R., 'Principles for Apologetics from Paul at Athens' (2009), available online at http://www.vantil.info/articles/Principles%20for%20apologetics%20from%20Paul%20 at%20Athens.pdf (accessed 4 Oct. 2013).

Seely, Paul H., 'The Date of the Tower of Babel and Some Theological Implications', *WTJ* 63 (2001), pp. 15–38.

Seiss, Joseph A., *The Gospel in the Stars* (Grand Rapids: Kregel, 1979).

Seznec, Jean, *The Survival of the Pagan Gods: The Mythological Tradition and Its Place in Renaissance Humanism and Art*, tr. Barbara F. Sessions (New York: Harper, 1961).

Shedd, William G. T., and Alan W. Gomes, *Dogmatic Theology*, 3rd ed. (Phillipsburg: P & R, 2003).

Sinkinson, Christopher, 'John Hick: Religion for the Modern World?', in Philip Duce and
    Daniel Strange (eds.), *Getting Your Bearings: Engaging with Contemporary Theologians*
    (Leicester: Apollos, 2003), pp. 17–74.
——, *The Universe of Faiths: A Critical Study of John Hick's Religious Pluralism* (Carlisle:
    Paternoster, 2001).
Sire, James, *Naming the Elephant* (Downers Grove: InterVarsity Press, 2004).
Smith, James K. A., *Desiring the Kingdom: Worship, Worldview and Cultural Formation*
    (Grand Rapids: Baker Academic, 2009).
Smith, Robert O., 'Luther, the Turks, and Islam', *CurTM* 34.5 (2007), pp. 351–364.
Span, John, 'The Areopagus: A Study in Continuity and Discontinuity', *SFM* 6.3 (2010),
    pp. 517–582.
Sparks, Adam, *One of a Kind: The Relationship Between Old and New Covenants as the
    Hermeneutical Key for Christian Theology of Religions* (Eugene: Pickwick, 2009).
——, 'Salvation History, Chronology, and Crisis: A Problem with Inclusivist Theology
    of Religions, Part 2 of 2', *Them* 33 (2008), pp. 48–62.
Spencer, Nick, *Asylum and Immigration* (Carlisle: Paternoster, 2004).
Spenser, Duane E., *Mazzaroth* (San Antonio: Word of Grace, 1972).
Stackhouse, John (ed.), *No Other Gods Before Me? Evangelicals and the Challenge of World
    Religions* (Grand Rapids: Baker, 2001).
Stob, Henry, 'Observations on the Concept of the Antithesis', in Peter De Klerk and Richard
    R. De Ridder (eds.), *Perspectives on the Christian Reformed Church* (Grand Rapids: Baker,
    1983), pp. 241–258.
Stonehouse, Ned B., *Paul Before the Areopagus and Other New Testament Studies* (Grand
    Rapids: Eerdmans, 1957).
Stott, John R. W., *Christian Mission in the Modern World* (London: Falcon, 1975).
——, *The Cross of Christ* (Leicester: Inter-Varsity Press, 1986).
——, *The Message of Acts: The Spirit, the Church, and the World*, BST (Leicester: Inter-Varsity
    Press, 1990).
——, *The Message of Romans*, BST (Leicester: Inter-Varsity Press, 1994).
—— (ed.), *Making Christ Known: Historic Mission Documents from the Lausanne Movement
    1974–1989* (Carlisle: Paternoster, 1996).
Strange, Daniel, 'Co-belligerence and Common Grace: Can the Enemy of My Enemy Be My
    Friend?', *Cambridge Papers* 14.3 (Sept. 2005).
——, 'Defending the Indefensible: The Exclusivity of Christ in an Intolerable World',
    *Tabletalk* 25 (summer 2009), n.p.
——, 'Exclusivisms: "Indeed Their Rock Is Not Like Our Rock"', in Alan Race and Paul
    Hedges (eds.), *Christian Approaches to Other Faiths* (London: SCM, 2008), pp. 36–62.
——, 'General Revelation: Sufficient or Insufficient', in Christopher W. Morgan and Robert
    A. Peterson (eds.), *Faith Comes by Hearing: A Response to Inclusivism* (Downers Grove:
    InterVarsity Press; Nottingham: Apollos, 2008), pp. 40–77.

——, 'A Little Dwelling on the Divine Presence: Towards a "Whereness" of the Triune God',
    in T. Desmond Alexander and Simon Gathercole (eds.), *Heaven on Earth: The Temple in
    Biblical Theology* (Carlisle: Paternoster, 2004), pp. 211–230.

——, 'The Many-Splendoured Cross: Atonement, Controversy and Victory', *Foundations*
    (autumn 2005), pp. 5–22.

——, *The Possibility of Salvation Among the Unevangelised: An Analysis of Inclusivism in Recent
    Evangelical Theology* (Carlisle: Paternoster, 2001).

——, 'Presence, Prevenience, or Providence? Deciphering the Conundrum of Pinnock's
    Pneumatological Inclusivism', in Tony Gray and Christopher Sinkinson (eds.),
    *Reconstructing Theology: A Critical Assessment of the Theology of Clark Pinnock* (Carlisle:
    Paternoster, 2000), pp. 220–258.

Stuckenbruck, L. T., 'Giant Mythology and Demonology', in A. Lange, H. Lichtenberger and
    K. F. D. Romheld (eds.), *Die Dämonen: Die Dämonologie der israelitisch-jüdischen und
    frühchristlichen Literatur im Kontext ihrer Umwelt* (Tübingen: Mohr Siebeck, 2003),
    pp. 318–338.

Tennent, Timothy C., *Christianity and the Religious Round Table: Evangelicalism in
    Conversation with Hinduism, Buddhism, and Islam* (Grand Rapids: Baker, 2002).

——, *Theology in the Context of World Christianity* (Grand Rapids: Zondervan, 2007).

Thompson, Mark, 'No Charge Admitted: Justification and the Defeat of the Powers', in Peter
    G. Bolt (ed.), *Christ's Victory over Evil* (Nottingham: Inter-Varsity Press, 2009),
    pp. 123–149.

Thong, Chan Kei, *Finding God in Ancient China: How the Ancient Chinese Worshipped the
    God of the Bible* (Grand Rapids: Zondervan, 2009).

Tiessen, Terrance L., *My Reflections on the Conversation Between Strange and D'Costa*
    (2012), available online at http://thoughtstheological.com/d-costas-critique-of-
    stranges-subversive-fulfilment-interpretation-of-other-religions (accessed 8 Oct.
    2012).

——, *Who Can Be Saved? Reassessing Salvation in Christ and World Religions* (Leicester:
    Inter-Varsity Press, 2004).

Tigay, Jeffrey H., *Deuteronomy*, ed. Nahum M. Sarna, JPSTC (Philadelphia: Jewish
    Publication Society, 1996).

Tsumura, David T., 'Genesis and Ancient Near East Stories of Creation and Flood', in Richard
    S. Hess and David T. Tsumura (eds.), *I Studied Inscriptions Before the Flood*, SBTS
    (Winona Lake: Eisenbrauns, 1994), pp. 27–57.

Turnau, Ted, *Popologetics: Popular Culture in Christian Perspective* (Phillipsburg: P & R,
    2012).

Turretin, Francis, *Institutes of Elenctic Theology*, ed. James T. Dennison Jr., tr. George
    Musgrave Giger, 3 vols. (Phillipsburg: P & R, 1992).

VanGemeren, Willem A., 'The Sons of God in Genesis 6:1–4: An Example of Evangelical
    Demythologization', *WTJ* 43 (1981), pp. 320–348.

Vanhoozer, Kevin J., 'Does the Trinity Belong in a Theology of Religions? On Angling
    in the Rubicon and the "Identity" of God', in Kevin J. Vanhoozer (ed.), *The Trinity in
    a Pluralistic Age: Theological Essays on Culture and Religion* (Cambridge: Eerdmans, 1997),
    pp. 41–71.
——, 'What Is Everyday Theology? How and Why Christians Should Read Culture', in
    Kevin J. Vanhoozer, Charles A. Anderson and Michael J. Sleasman (eds.), *Everyday
    Theology: How to Read Cultural Texts and Interpret Trends* (Grand Rapids: Baker, 2007),
    pp. 15–60.
Van Til, Cornelius, *Christian Apologetics*, ed. William Edgar, 2nd ed. (Phillipsburg: P & R,
    2003).
——, *A Christian Theory of Knowledge* (Philadelphia: P & R, 1969).
——, *The Defense of the Faith*, ed. K. Scott Oliphint, 4th ed. (Phillipsburg: P & R, 2008).
——, 'Introduction', in Samuel G. Craig (ed.), *B. B. Warfield, The Inspiration and Authority
    of the Bible* (London: Marshall, Morgan & Scott, 1951), pp. 3–68.
——, *An Introduction to Systematic Theology*, ed. William Edgar, 2nd ed. (Phillipsburg:
    P & R, 2007).
——, 'Nature and Scripture', in Paul Woolley (ed.), *The Infallible Word: A Symposium*
    (Philadelphia: Presbyterian Guardian, 1946), pp. 255–293.
——, *Paul at Athens* (Phillipsburg: L. J. Grotenhuis, n.d.).
Venning, Ralph, *Plague of Plagues* (Edinburgh: Banner of Truth Trust, 1965).
Visser, Paul, *Heart for the Gospel, Heart for the World: The Life and Thought of a Reformed
    Pioneer Missiologist, Johan Herman Bavinck (1895–1964)* (Eugene: Wipf & Stock, 2003).
——, 'Religion in Biblical and Reformed Perspective', *CTJ* 44.1 (2009), pp. 9–36.
Visser't Hooft, Willem A., 'Accommodation: True or False', *SEAJT* 8.3 (1967),
    pp. 5–18.
Vos, Geerhardus, *Biblical Theology: Old and New Testaments* (Grand Rapids: Eerdmans, 1948;
    Edinburgh: Banner of Truth Trust, 1975).
Walker, D. P., *The Ancient Theology: Studies in Christian Platonism from the 15th to the 18th
    Century* (Ithaca, N.Y.: Cornell University Press, 1972).
Walls, Andrew F., 'The Expansion of Christianity: An Interview with Andrew Walls', *ChrCent*
    117.22 (Aug. 2000), pp. 792–795.
——, 'The Gospel as Prisoner and Liberator of Culture', in Andrew F. Walls (ed.), *The
    Missionary Movement in Christian History: Studies in the Transmission of Faith* (Maryknoll:
    Orbis, 1996), pp. 3–15.
Walsh, Jerome T., 'Genesis 2:4b–3:24: A Synchronic Approach', *JBL* 96.2 (1977),
    pp. 161–177.
Waltke, Bruce K., *Genesis: A Commentary* (Grand Rapids: Zondervan, 2001).
Ward, Timothy, 'The Diversity and Sufficiency of Scripture', in Paul Helm and Carl Trueman
    (eds.), *The Trustworthiness of God: Perspectives on the Nature of Scripture*
    (Grand Rapids: Eerdmans; Leicester: Apollos, 2002), pp. 192–218.

——, *Words of Life: Scripture as the Living and Active Word of God* (Nottingham: Inter-Varsity Press, 2009).

Waters, Guy, *The End of Deuteronomy in the Epistles of Paul*, ed. Jorg Frey, WUNT (Tübingen: Mohr Siebeck, 2006).

Watson, Francis, *Text and Truth: Redefining Biblical Theology* (Grand Rapids: Eerdmans, 1997).

Webster, John, 'Karl Rahner's Theology of Grace', *Evangel* (1983), pp. 9–11.

Weinfeld, Moshe, *Deuteronomy 1–11: A New Translation and Commentary*, vol. 5, AB (London: Doubleday, 1991).

Wenham, Gordon J., *Genesis 1–15*, WBC (Waco: Word, 1987).

——, 'The Religion of the Patriarchs', in A. R. Millard and D. J. Wiseman (eds.), *Essays on the Patriarchal Narratives* (Leicester: Inter-Varsity Press, 1980), pp. 157–188.

——, *Story as Torah: Reading Old Testament Narrative Ethically* (Edinburgh: T. & T. Clark, 2000).

Williams, Paul, *The Unexpected Way: On Converting from Buddhism to Catholicism* (London: Continuum, 2002).

Winter, Bruce W., 'In Public and in Private: Early Christians and Religious Pluralism', in Andrew D. Clarke and Bruce W. Winter (eds.), *One God, One Lord: Christianity in a World of Religious Pluralism* (Cambridge: Tyndale House, 1991), pp. 125–148.

Witherington, Ben, *The Acts of the Apostles: A Socio-Rhetorical Commentary* (Grand Rapids: Eerdmans, 1998).

Witte, J., *Die Christus-Botschaft und die Religionen* (Göttingen: Vandenhoeck & Ruprecht, 1936).

Wright, A. T., *The Origin of Evil Spirits*, WUNT 2.198 (Tübingen: Mohr Siebeck, 2005).

Wright, Christopher J. H., 'The Christian and Other Religions: The Biblical Evidence', *Them* 9.2 (1984), pp. 4–15.

——, 'Deuteronomic Depression', *Them* 19.2 (1994), pp. 1–3.

——, *Deuteronomy*, NIBCOT (Peabody: Hendrickson, 1996).

——, 'Editorial: P for Pentateuch, Patriarchs and Pagans', *Them* 18.2 (1993), pp. 1–2.

——, *The Mission of God's People*, ed. Jonathan Lunde, Biblical Theology for Life (Grand Rapids: Zondervan, 2010).

——, *The Mission of God: Unlocking the Bible's Grand Narrative* (Nottingham: Inter-Varsity Press, 2006).

——, *Old Testament Ethics for the People of God* (Leicester: Inter-Varsity Press, 2004).

Yates, Frances A., *Giordano Bruno and the Hermetic Tradition* (London: Routledge & Kegan Paul, 1964).

Yong, Amos, *Hospitality and the Other: Pentecost, Christian Practices, and the Neighbor* (New York: Orbis, 2008).

——, 'Discerning the Spirit(s) in the World of Religions: Toward a Pneumatological Theology of Religions', in John Stackhouse (ed.), *No Other Gods Before Me? Evangelicals and the Challenge of World Religions* (Grand Rapids: Baker, 2001), pp. 37–61.

Zwemer, Samuel M., *The Origin of Religion* (London: Marshall, Morgan & Scott, 1935).

# INDEX OF SCRIPTURE REFERENCES

# INDEX OF AUTHORS

# INDEX OF SUBJECTS